MW01222164

# COUNTERBALANCE

## gendered perspectives for writing and language

# COUNTERBALANCE

gendered perspectives for writing and language

---

edited by

Carolyn Logan

---

**broadview press**

**Cataloguing in Publication Data**

Counterbalance : gendered perspectives for writing and language

Includes bibliographical references.
ISBN 1-55111-127-6

1. College readers.  2. English literature - Women authors.  3. English language - Rhetoric.  I. Logan, Carolyn.

PE1417.C68 1997     808'.0427     C97-930450-4

Broadview Press Ltd. is an independent, international publishing house, incorporated in 1985.

**North America:**

PO Box 1243, Peterborough Ontario, Canada K9J 7H5

3576 California Road, Orchard Park NY USA  14127

phone, fax and e-mail addresses for North America: (705) 743-8990 (phone); (705) 743-8353 (fax); 75322.44@COMPUSERVE.COM

**UK and Europe:**

BRAD (Book Representation and Distribution Ltd.)

244a London Rd., Hadleigh, Essex UK   SS7 2DE  (1702) 552912

**Australia:**

St. Clair Press, PO Box 287, Rozelle  NSW 2039  (02)818 1942

**elsewhere:**

Please order through local wholesalers or direct from North America.

PRINTED IN CANADA

# Preface

COUNTERBALANCE: GENDERED PERSPECTIVES FOR WRITING AND LAN-
GUAGE is for women and men who want to learn to improve their writing
through a better understanding of the language with which they work. *Counterbalance* differs from other language-focused textbooks because it anthologizes
more women than men writers and has feminist perspectives. It includes more
material by women than by men because most language-focused composition
texts under-represent women writers. Its deliberate feminist perspective means
that it does not automatically assume the male as the standard. Feminist perspectives question assumptions and take women's theories, needs, and contributions
into account.

*Counterbalance* does not ignore or attack men. Language shapes men and
women, and both women and men must take responsibility for their linguistic
choices. In addressing ways in which language shapes the thoughts of those who
use language, the text raises several questions about women's and men's use of
language, about sexist language perpetuating sexist ideology, and about power
and oppression. Both women and men may be embarrassed and angry to learn
that their language has oppressed other people, particularly when they did not
intend to oppress or disparage. Both women and men may be defensive when
they learn that words like "mankind," "he," and "girl" do not communicate to
others gender-free or value-free meanings. Women and men may feel both un-
settled and empowered to learn that they can change their linguistic habits.
Women and men may have different views as they examine questions of power,
awareness, assumptions, and habitual thinking.

I hope that students and teachers will discuss directly these controversial
issues and the feelings and thoughts they arouse. I hope that teachers will encourage students who are defensive or angry or resentful to discuss their responses and to examine the various ideologies that inform our language. Such
discussions can lead to clearer understanding of the ways language influences

thought and can build an atmosphere in which neither men nor women silence each other. Such discussions can also encourage students to see that learning is not always without risk or discomfort but usually leads to understanding and growth.

*Counterbalance* points out that even though people have no choice about the language into which they were born and are not responsible for the language as it was when they were born into it, each of us is responsible for what we do with language and, to some degree, for what the language becomes. The thesis of *Counterbalance* is that both women and men can think more clearly and can use language more effectively if we know how language influences us and if we pay attention to our linguistic choices; we can use language to question received wisdom and to challenge the built-in biases of language.

To the teacher: for introductory composition courses at the postsecondary level, I want an anthology that focuses on one subject, and I believe that language is the best subject for study in those classes. Although students usually have not articulated what they know about language, they do know a great deal about it, and students I have worked with during the past 20 years are interested in language as a subject. As they read and write about language, they learn to use it more effectively.

This book is about language. Unlike other anthologies that focus on language, this one provides feminist perspectives. It discusses language as an environment in which people learn how to conduct themselves, and it concentrates on what women have written about that environment. Its thesis is that we can make language work for us if we know our choices, and that language may work against us if we are not attentive and informed. Also, unlike other language anthologies that group essays according to theme (politics, sexism, advertising, for example), this one is a sequential study for one semester's work. It moves from simpler to more complex readings, concepts, and writing assignments in order to help students build an understanding of the connections among language and behavior, habit, and thought.

The first six chapters discuss some aspects of language, include essays selected to stimulate further thought and discussion, and suggest questions for discussion and topics for writing assignments. Chapter Seven provides several essays for further reading.

I have written the book for a student audience, but your students will need your help and expertise to discuss the content and to develop and practice their writing skills. I hope that you will enjoy the book with them.

# Table of Contents

**Preface**

**Chapter One: Check Your Baggage**

**Chapter Two: Take Your Choice**

**Chapter Three: Why Do You Think That?**

# Chapter Four: Is Anybody Out There?

# Chapter Five: It's a Maze

# Chapter Six: Keep Moving

# Chapter Seven: Pleasure and Power

# Chapter One:

# Check Your Baggage

# Check Your Baggage

## Introduction

EACH OF US IS BROUGHT UP in family and in language, and both shape us. From language and from family we inherit some characteristics and characteristic ways that we can change and some that we cannot change. In addition to giving us some of our characteristics and habitual ways, both language and family tell us who we are, how we are to behave, how we are to think and talk, and what we are to think and talk about. As adults we can examine all of that inheritance to see what we are stuck with and what we can change. We may decide to keep some of what is changeable because it works for us or because we like it. We may choose to change or to get rid of what we do not like or what is not useful to us as we grow and progress.

As you think about your inheritance, consider what parts of it you can change and what parts you cannot change. List the characteristics, qualities, and values that you inherited and learned from your parents or family. Include family traditions such as holiday and birthday celebrations. Include behaviors such as treatment of people older and younger than yourself, treatment of animals, coping with unfamiliar situations. Include habits and standards, such as how you value promptness, money, grades, trustworthiness, friendships, honesty. Are any of those characteristics, values, or qualities unchangeable? I cannot change the fact—nor would I want to—that I grew up in a working-class family and that I learned working-class values, any more than I can change the bone structure I inherited from my parents. But I can examine my values and behaviors and I can change those that I do not want to keep. And I can create different traditions for myself. Can you change any items in your list? Which qualities or traditional ways would you keep even though you might be able to change them? Perhaps, as I would, you would keep the high value you learned to place on well-maintained equipment and property. Perhaps you would continue to respect honesty. Perhaps you would celebrate your birthday as you learned to celebrate it as a child, even though that ritual may be time-consuming. How are any items on your list useful or comfortable for you? On the other hand, how might you benefit by changing any of them? In your list, you probably included some judgments or assessments that you learned from your family and your society—friends and other people around you, your neighborhood, your school, as well as the larger society that you know from television, movies, books, magazines, newspapers, and music. Those assessments may have included ways of thinking about people unlike you, ways of thinking about people like you, what is appropriate behavior and work and play, what is appropriate language. You may have learned, for example, that people like you are trustworthy, and that you should fear and maybe even hate people who are not like you. Or you may have learned that people unlike you can teach you interesting information and customs. You may have learned, as I did, that it was appropriate in elementary school for little girls to sit quietly in a corner of the schoolground playing jacks and dolls, and that it was appropriate for little boys to take up most of the schoolyard playing ball games or cowboys. I learned that it is appropriate for young women to work as clerks, secretaries, nurses, and elementary school-teachers, and that it is appropriate for men to work as mechanics, doctors, college teachers, carpenters, engineers, U.S. Presidents. Did you learn similar lessons? What we learned as children, the information we inherited from our societies, may or may not be useful to us as adults. As adults, we may decide that some of what we learned as children is outdated in the world we live in as adults. As adults we have the opportunity to challenge our knowledge and to change our minds and our habits.

To examine some of what you learned as a child, list the phrases you learned about how women and men are supposed to behave. You might start, for example, with the well-known rhyme, "Sugar and spice and everything nice," which indirectly states behaviors expected of girls and of boys. You might list words and phrases like "tomboy," "sissy," "hysterical," "effeminate," "woman driver," "boys don't cry," "act like a lady," and "smile pretty," all of which suggest behaviors appropriate or inappropriate for a particular society. Or you might list sayings like the following: "Man may work from sun to sun, but woman's work is never done"; "Every woman is infallibly to be gained by every sort of flattery, and every man by one sort or other"; "Man is the hunter; woman is his game"; "He should marry her and make an honest woman of her"; "It is a woman's business to get married as soon as possible, and a man's to keep unmarried as long as he can"; "Each man for himself"; "Women should be struck regularly, like gongs."

The phrases and sayings in your list are examples of attitudes conveyed by language, and they are part of our inheritance from our families and from our society. They are only words, but they embody and perpetuate notions of what a culture takes to be appropriate behavior for women and men. As adults, we know that words matter; "only words" hides the importance of language and the fact that words perpetuate attitudes. As adults, we may want to question those

attitudes and notions. Who created the sayings? How do they shape our behavior? Who benefits from those behaviors? Who is hurt by the sayings or the
behaviors? What assumptions do the sayings convey about women and about
men?

Now let's look more specifically at our language inheritance, especially, in
this chapter, at our language inheritance that tells us who we are and how we
are to behave. List the phrases you have learned that specifically teach us about
how women and men, girls and boys, are thought to use language. If you have
two or more languages, make the following lists for each language. You might
start with a list of verbs that describe "women's talk" and "men's talk":

| women/girls | men/boys |
|---|---|
| chatter | discuss |
| gossip | debate |
| nag | talk |
| become hysterical | become angry |
| fuss | |
| _____ | _____ |
| _____ | _____ |
| _____ | _____ |

Or you might list clichés and jokes about women/girls and men/boys as language
users:

| women/girls | men/boys |
|---|---|
| never shut up | can't get a word in |
| talk all the time | are strong and silent |
| talk but don't act | act |
| Q. "What are the three fastest ways to spread information?" | are sweet talkers |
| A. "Telegraph, telephone, and tell a woman." | _____ |
| don't know how to tell jokes | _____ |
| _____ | _____ |
| _____ | _____ |
| _____ | _____ |

To review your knowledge about how women and men are thought to use language, you might list the language restrictions you learned as a child:

| women/girls | men/boys |
|---|---|
| Ladies don't swear | Gentlemen don't swear in the company of women |
| Nice girls don't tell off-color jokes | Gentlemen don't tell off-color jokes in the company of women |
| Don't interrupt adults | Don't interrupt superiors |
| _____ | _____ |
| _____ | _____ |
| _____ | _____ |

Or, you might list famous sayings about linguistic use: "The Great Communicator" (as Ronald Reagan liked to be known); "The greatest glory of a woman is to be least talked about by men, whether they are praising you or criticizing you"; "Let the woman learn in silence...suffer not a woman to teach...but to be in silence"; "A talking girl and a clucking hen—both shall come to no good end"; "A woman's preaching is like a dog's walking on his hinder legs. It is not done well; but you are surprised to find it done at all"; "A man's word is his bond"; "Whenever a woman dies there is one quarrel less on earth."

In your lists, you have stated some items in the linguistic environment or environments in which you grew up, some of the ideas in your language inheritance. What do you discover about that language inheritance as you look over the lists you have made? Have you inherited a rich, active position in your language? Are you, according to the language, a functioning adult? Can you hold your own in any discussion and be heard seriously? Will you be left out of some discussions because of your sex? When you consider the language environment you were born into, do you think that it is going to give you fair treatment? How does your inheritance tell you to behave and to value yourself? If you have two or more languages, how do your lists compare? Do different languages provide different inheritances?

If it appears to you that you were born into a sexist language, one that automatically values one sex more than the other simply on the basis of sex, you are seeing what a number of scholars have seen about English and some other languages: in many ways, they devalue women. Each of us was born into a language that already had in place several clichés, sayings, and notions about female and male linguistic use. From those words, we learned how we were "supposed" to talk, and we learned what to expect of other people. Before we were old enough to question the validity of those ideas conveyed and perpetuated by language, we were influenced and affected by them. As children, many of us learned to protect our feelings by saying "sticks and stones may break my bones, but words will never hurt me." Perhaps even as children we had difficulty believing the saying, especially when words *did* hurt our feelings. As adults we can understand more fully the complex ways in which language can hurt and stunt us.

As adults, we can re-examine our language inheritance just as we can re-examine our physical and cultural inheritances. And we can change some aspects of our language use if they are not useful or helpful for us. We can ask, "Does my language inheritance tell truths? Do women talk all the time? Is women's language nothing more than chatter?" "Does the linguistic inheritance make me appear inadequate or silly?" "Does it make me appear more authoritative than I really am?" "Do I consider my own talk to be gossip, trivial?" "Do I consider women's talk to be trivial? Why do I? Is it because women talk about subjects that I don't know about, subjects that don't interest me?" "Have I made my language fit what I know is expected and accepted—even when I knew it didn't convey what I wanted to say?" And we can ask, "Is my language effective?" "How can I change my language to be more effective?"

These questions raise several other questions about how we use language, about how our language influences us, and about what we mean by "effective." In this book we will examine several of these questions. As we examine in detail our language inheritance and environment, remember that none of us is responsible for language as it was when we inherited it, but because language is a human product, we can change it in certain ways. When we know that we have choices with language, we can determine how we will use it, and we can determine that we will not allow language to use us.

Each essay in this chapter discusses our linguistic environment and includes some information about how we learn linguistic behaviors and how language tells us to conduct ourselves. As you read these essays, consider what you have inherited from the language or languages into which you were born and how language has influenced you.

# The Dilemma of the Unwanted Kiss

## Eileen Kalinowski

A MAN YOU DON'T KNOW VERY WELL sees you at the office. You smile and say "hello," and he, in an instant is in your space, in your face, kissing you hello. If you want to set a limit you might offer a cheek, but if you're not quick enough, he'll kiss you on the mouth. It will probably be just a peck, but if you don't want to be kissed at all, what do you do?

You are in a conversation with friends at a conference. A colleague you have met at other conferences and have talked to once or twice on the phone at work walks by. When he greets you, he shakes your hand and leans in to kiss you. Other people are watching, and you are clearly uncomfortable. In that moment, these questions come to mind: What are people thinking of this? Why is he kissing me? What can I do? Is there a way to stop this that wouldn't cause a scene? Why am I not stopping him?

You are meeting a friend and her husband for dinner at a restaurant. You don't like your friend's spouse, but you've known each other for years. Kissing someone you've known for years is expected, isn't it? Wouldn't your friend be offended if you refused to kiss him now, after all this time? How can you change this custom you haven't liked but never objected to before?

Why is it that nearly every woman I know has been in this situation and usually admits to "putting up with it"? Is it too much of a bother to take a stand? Is it really a "little thing"? Is it a token of affection or a nonverbal power play? Are men being demonstrative of their feelings (God, we don't want to put the brakes on that!) or is it an unconscious extension of ownership and something they've learned we'll put up with?

When someone wants to kiss my daughter—any adult, male or female—and she doesn't want them to, she either looks and moves away, or else, if the person is putting her on the spot, with "Oh, come on, you can give me a little kiss," she looks to me to handle the situation.

If adults can't accept a simple refusal from a nine-year-old girl, I feel fine saying, "She doesn't seem to want to be kissed right now." Then, I often hear some indictment of how kids are too afraid these days, there are too many stories on the news of strangers...In my heart, I know that it's my job as her mother to protect her from people who invade her boundaries until she's learned how to fend for herself. In observing these situations, I have come to realize that our culture often feels "entitled" to some contact with pretty little girls—as if children were community property—and this is unhealthy.

But why is it I hear a nagging voice inside me saying "Oh, what's the harm? Why can't she just go along with it? It would make things much easier. There she goes being difficult again." "Difficult" means she's bucking the social system; she's not doing the expected, easy thing. She's not greasing the wheel; she's making it squeak.

Time and again, I learn simple, valuable lessons by watching my daughter's natural reactions to the world around her and the people in it. Since her patterns are not yet "ingrained," she often goes "against the grain." That's what real interaction between people is, though, not always acting in predictable ways, but responding authentically from your insides to the information and stimulation from the outside.

My natural response patterns were tampered with in my childhood, first by my parents, then by church and school authorities, then by my peers. When the conflicts first appeared, I just knew that what people expected from me was different from what I was doing. Then I entered into a confused state, where I didn't know what to do, or what was expected, and spent a great deal of my energy trying to figure out the culture I was living in. Because of my own set of circumstances and the reinforcement of unhealthy and damaging lessons about boundaries, over time, I became so steeped in the information and authority of the outside world that I lost contact with my own inner voice and reality. I forgot that I am my own author and that I need not wait for a script in order to have something to say.

Researchers at Harvard's psychology of women project have eloquently and painfully described the loss of voice that is so common to girls and young women in our society, irrespective of class, color, and religion, due to, among other things, the "tyranny of nice and kind." Girls learn that if they can't say something nice, they shouldn't say anything at all. Since we all have a full range of experience, emotion, and response to any situation, making girls censor themselves by the age of eleven or twelve is, in effect, coercing them into a duplicitous life wherein they must keep to themselves anything that might upset or hurt the feelings of someone else, especially someone they love.

So, the message is, if you really love someone, you'll lie to them about your anger, you'll act as if unacceptable behavior is okay, you'll do whatever it takes to make someone you love feel better. That's what it means to care about someone, we teach them—to give up your own truth, your own experience, your very integrity, to make someone else more comfortable.

Far from being nit-picking or trivial, whether or not I want someone to kiss me is a substantive question. More important than the kiss itself is the rule that makes me keep silent about it, swallow it, let it pass without comment. These rules of silence are betraying us; we gain nothing from them but more of the same treatment, more of the same expectations, more of the same disconnection from ourselves.

The truth is, I don't want any man to kiss me but the one with whom I'm in love. There, I've said it. It's pretty simple—I can offer my hand when I'm greeting someone and practice leaning back when I'm used to freezing up. I can give myself all the permission I need to establish boundaries that are comfortable for me, knowing that it may take time to learn new behaviors.

The woman sitting next to me may have different ideas, and that's fine. I need to tell the truth about me. I would like it if men and women, in light of all of the attention to sexual harassment, would step back and ask themselves these questions: "Is kissing this person really mutual? Do I really know how we both feel about it? Have I ever asked him/her? Have I asked myself?"

So much of what we all need to do is question our assumptions about things we've taken for granted, things that "go without saying." I'm finding that less and less really does go without saying. We are a diverse lot, women and men, adults and children, New Englanders and Californians, North Americans and Asians, whites and people of color, wealthy and economically struggling. There is no one right code of behavior that governs all situations, that takes all of our differences into account. What is required is a willingness to speak our own truth, to respect each other's limits, and to practice in an atmosphere that is imperfect but constantly improving. Communication is a wonderful thing, as is respect, mutuality, and the freedom to be ourselves.

**For discussion**

*Content*

1. Do women/girls and men/boys generally learn the same linguistic restrictions?

2. Do both women/girls and men/boys learn the linguistic restriction "If you can't say something nice, don't say anything at all"? How does that particular restriction sometimes put in uncomfortable situations those of us who learned it?

3. Are the situations in the three opening examples of the essay familiar to you? In what way are they familiar to you? If you are a woman, are you uncomfortable in those situations? If you are a man, have you been in similar situations in which you were expected to respond with a kiss you did not want to give? Whether you are a woman or a man, have you ever created a situation in which you forced someone to respond to your touch or kiss?

4. In paragraph 12, Kalinowski writes: "These rules of silence are betraying us...." Discuss the implications of silence as a sign of submission and the implications of the cultural notion that women should be silent.

5. Discuss some of the "things we've taken for granted, things that 'go without saying'" (final paragraph). What ideas about women's and men's behavior do you think we ought to challenge and discuss?

*Style*

1. What do you think of Kalinowski's beginning her essay with three examples? Do you think the essay would be better if she had stated her point at the beginning?

2. What is the effect of Kalinowski's shifting the discussion (in paragraph five) from women to a nine-year-old girl?

3. Paragraph seven begins with "But." What signal does that word give you as a reader?

**For writing**

1. Write an expository paragraph about the linguistic restrictions you learned and the disadvantages or advantages those restrictions gave you.

2. Write an expository paragraph in which you state and illustrate a point about silence and submission or about language-learning and being taken advantage of.

3. Using a dictionary of quotations, find several quotations about women as language users, and write a paragraph about what you find. You might consider who wrote the quotations, and you might want to see if you can find an equal number of quotations written by women about men as language users.

# A White Man's Word

## Debra Swallow

THE SCREEN DOOR SLAMMED SHUT, and I just knew eighty flies came in. Then I heard wailing and gibberish and ran to see who it was. My nine-year-old son was running toward me with blood, tears and dirty sweat trickling off his chin, making my knees go weak.

"What happened? Who did this to you?" I asked, kneeling to wipe his round face with a cool, damp cloth.

"I got in a fight, Mom. Mom, what's a half-breed?"

I felt like my blood stopped running, and I closed my eyes to kill my tears, my mind opening up a day I'd almost forgotten.

I opened my eyes to see how under-water looked, and a sting like cactus tips closed them fast. Surfacing, I looked across the pool for my friend. The water shimmered turquoise blue, reflecting nothing but the painted concrete bottom and rectangles of green light from the roof. Forty or fifty pale faces and arms bobbed and floated above the water, but no sign of my friend's brown, familiar face.

"Maybe it's time to go," I thought and swam to the closest edge. Feeling the rough, slimy cement on the palms of my hands, I hauled myself out of the water. Unsure of my footing, I walked slowly toward the shower rooms.

Screams, giggles and little-girl conversation filled the room, along with spraying, splashing and draining water. Stooping to peek under the first shower stall, I saw two white feet and moved on to the second door. Also two white feet. Next door, four white feet. I could feel myself starting to shiver now and my breath felt trapped in my chest. "What if they left me? I don't know anybody here," I thought.

My friend and her mom took me with them to Rushville to swim. My first time alone away from my family, and here I was, scared among white people—the only Indian in sight.

I decided to just kind of stand around in the shower room. I knew she wasn't in the pool, so she had to come here, where our clothes were. Trying to be as unnoticeable as possible, I leaned against a cool, wet wall and watched the white girls in the room, curious because I'd never been around any before.

"My dad bought me a brand-new bike and it has a blue daisy basket on the handlebars," one girl whined to her friend. "Well, I already knew that, but did you know my dad bought me a new bed and it has a canopy on it!" she whined back in a sing-song voice. The two girls were probably eight years old like me, but both were chubby with blonde ringlets and painted toenails.

Spacing out their words, I was thinking about the bike Dad made my sister and me. He made it from all different parts he found at the trash pile, and it looked funny and rusty, but it worked real well. Daddy also made us a pair of stilts, a playhouse and a pogo stick, which all of our friends wanted to play with. I knew my dad was better than theirs, he BUILT stuff for us.

I noticed the first girl was dressed now, and while waiting for her friend to finish, she pulled out a whole handful of red licorice and chewed on one while her friend jabbered, every once in a while glancing at me, not knowing my tongue ached to taste just one mouthful of her licorice. Every time she looked at me, I wanted to evaporate. I had on a borrowed swimsuit a size too big, dull and old-fashioned compared to the bright-colored flower or print-covered two-pieces all the other girls wore. My hair hung down my back, straight and thick and dark.

The first girl said, "Look, this Indian is staring at us," and glared at me with icy blue eyes, her nose pointing to the ceiling. The second girl said, "Oh, she don't know what we're saying anyhow. Dirty Indians don't know anything." Her friend said, "I don't think she's really a real Indian. My dad says some of them are half-breeds. So she's not *all* dirty."

"Only half-dirty," her friend said, and they giggled together and laughed at me.

My face felt hot and my arms were heavy as I walked carefully across the wet, slippery floor towards them. I noticed from far away that the room's noises started to fade.

I grabbed one of them by her hair and threw her away, wrapped my arm around the other one's neck and wrestled her down, and sitting on her, I kept punching her till her friend grabbed me. I stood up, and jerking away, I tripped her, landing her by her friend. They were both still crying and screaming on the floor when I walked out, carrying my bundle of clothes under my arm.

Standing outside in the shade of the pool building, I was really scared. There was someone yelling, "Debi! Debi!" but I wouldn't look. Somehow I thought they found out my name and were going to do something to me. But it was my friend's mom; she and my friend went for popsicles and just got back. I ran to their car and told them what I did, so my friend's mom went in after the clothes my friend left in the shower room and we headed back for home.

Safe once again with my family, I told Mom and Dad I got in a fight.

"Daddy, what's a half-breed?" I asked him.

The house got quiet, the only sound was the wind. Daddy looked at me and his eyes were sad.

"My girl, you're an Indian. The way of living is Indian. Lakota."

I said, "Yes, but what is a half-breed?"

"A white man's word," is what he said. "It's just a white man's word."

Now, eighteen years later, I was wiping blood from my son's face, and his question made my body shake with anger, sadness, frustration and hatred. Opening my eyes, I answered, "You're Lakota, son. The way of living is Indian. You're Lakota."

He looked at me with black eyes shining with tears he now refused to shed, and asked me again what a half-breed was.

"A white man's word," is what I said. "It's just a white man's word."

**For discussion**

*Content*

1. We don't all grow up in a friendly language environment. Did you? Have you ever been angry enough to want to fight someone who called you a name? What was the name? Why did it anger you?

2. Does being called "half-breed," "spic," "nigger," or "honky" affect women and men of the named group in the same ways? Do the words have different meanings when they refer to women than they have when they refer to men?

3. Perhaps we have been part of making an unfriendly or even a hostile environment for others. Have you ever been conscious of doing that? Having read Swallow's essay, will you be more conscious of the effects your words might have on someone else? What will you do with your raised consciousness?

4. Swallow uses an extended narrative to illustrate her point about language. Do you think this method of development is as effective as Kalinowski's method? Why or why not?

*Style*

1. In the first four paragraphs, Swallow describes her son's experience, then she jumps in paragraph five to describing her own childhood experience. Is the jump too abrupt? Should Swallow have provided a transition there?

2. What do you think of Swallow's sentence fragments in paragraph seven? How can a sentence fragment be effective?

3. Although we will discuss "effectiveness" many times throughout this book, now is a good time to start thinking about what "effective language choice" means. As you discuss "effective language" with your classmates, you will raise several questions: Whose definition of "effective" do you accept? effective for whom? What effect is the writer trying to create? Do words and sentence structures have different effects on different people? Does situation influence effective language choice?

**For writing**

1. Write a paragraph in which you analyze the words that, to you, are "fighting words." You might consider whether "fighting words" are "fighting words" regardless of who uses them, and you might consider whether women and men would think of different words as "fighting words."

2. Write a paragraph in which you analyze differences in the ways a derisive term might affect a woman and a man in the same ethnic or race group.

3. Although we will discuss stereotype labels in some detail in Chapter Five, here you might begin thinking about those words by writing a paragraph about words or labels that you think are particularly hurtful to you or to another person.

# Talk Control: An Illustration from the Classroom of Problems in Analysing Male Dominance of Conversation

## Joan Swann

### Women and Men Talking

THE STEREOTYPE OF THE OVER-TALKATIVE WOMAN stands out in stark contrast to most research studies of interactions between women and men, which argue that, by and large, it is men who tend to dominate the talk. For instance, men have been found to use more interruptions (Zimmerman & West 1975; Eakins & Eakins 1976; West & Zimmerman 1983; West 1984) and simply to talk more than women (e.g. Soskin & John 1963; Bernard 1972; Swacker 1975; Eakins & Eakins 1976). In mixed-sex conversations it has been found that men's topics are more often pursued, while women play a 'support-ive' role (Fishman 1978, 1983; see also Hirschman 1974; and Leet-Pellegrini 1980). The picture is not universally one-sided: Beattie (1981), in a study of uni-versity tutorials, found that women students interrupted as often as men and Edelsky (1981), looking at university committee meetings, found that women could hold their own in informally organized, 'collaboratively developed', talk, though not in the more formal 'one-person-at-a-time' talk that tends to be prev-alent in meetings. In most contexts, however, the evidence remains that men tend to be the dominant parties in mixed-sex conversations and discussions.

Related to these findings is the suggestion that women tend, more often than men, to use a speech style that gives the impression of politeness, tact, hesitancy and uncertainty. One of the best known exponents of this view is Lakoff who suggested that the characteristics of 'women's language' include: 'empty' adjectives such as *divine, charming* and *cute*; question-intonation in statement contexts, e.g.: *'What's your name, dear?'*—*'Mary Smith?'*; tag questions (a question tagged on to a declarative, of the form *isn't it? wasn't she? don't you?*—e.g. 'It's so hot, isn't it?'); and the use of hedges that might normally indicate uncertainty—e.g. *sort of, kinda, I guess*; (see Lakoff 1975: 53ff). It's worth noting here that Lakoff's work was based on her intuitions as a member of a North American, educated, White, middle-class community rather than on any formal survey. Some of her claims at least have been contested by other researchers (for instance, tag-questions have been found as frequently in male as in female speech—Baumann (1976); Dubois and Crouch (1975)....

Some interpretations of the research mentioned above have focused on gender differences per se. Maltz and Borker (1982), like Lakoff, draw up a list of 'women's features' (such as a greater tendency to ask questions, and to make use of positive minimal responses such as *mhm* or *yeah*, p. 197) and 'men's features' (such as a tendency to interrupt women, p. 198). Maltz and Borker argue that these differences arise because women and men come from different 'sociolinguistic subcultures', have learnt different rules of friendly interaction and interpret the use of certain conversational features differently.

Gender differences in conversation are, however, more commonly interpreted in terms of differences in power between women and men. West and Zimmerman (1977), for instance, note that differential use of interruptions is related not simply to gender but can be found in other asymmetrical talk such as that between parents and children. West and Zimmerman see gender and power as inextricably linked: 'gestures of power [such as interruptions etc.]—minor in import viewed one by one—are an integral part of women's *placement* in the social scheme of things. These daily gestures are constant "reminders" which help constitute women's subordinate status' (1983: 110; authors' italics). In a later study of doctor-patient talk, West (1984) suggests gender may function as a superordinate status, taking primacy over other indicators of power such as professional status.

O'Barr and Atkins (1980) interpret differences in women's and men's speech in terms of power *rather than* of gender. In a study of courtroom discourse they found occurrences of Lakoff's 'women's' features in the speech of both men and women, and suggest that the use of such features is associated with status, and not directly with gender. They argue, therefore, that these features are characteristic of a speaking style that they term 'powerless language'. While they do not dispute that the features of their 'powerless language' may, in many contexts, occur more frequently in the speech of women than of men, they suggest this is due simply to the fact that women tend to occupy less powerful social positions than men.

................

## Classroom Talk: An Illustration

Classroom talk is an interesting area of study partly because many educationists argue that talk itself is an important vehicle for learning:

> The way into ideas, the way of making ideas truly one's own, is to be able to think them through, and the best way to do this for most people is to talk them through. Thus talking is not merely a way of conveying existing ideas to others; it is also a way by which we explore ideas, clarify them, and make them our own. Talking things over allows the sorting of ideas, and gives rapid and extensive practice towards the handling of ideas. (Marland 1977:129)

The classroom is also one place in which children learn social roles. An influential argument is that socially appropriate behaviour (including gender-appropriate behaviour) is learnt in part (though not by any means exclusively) through classroom talk.

Studies of classroom life have found many ways, linguistic and non-linguistic, in which girls and boys are treated differently. For instance, pupils are often segregated by gender as an aid to classroom administration, or told to do things as boys or as girls as a form of motivation (girls may be told to leave first very quietly, boys to sing as nicely as the girls); pupils are often told that certain topics are 'boys'' topics or will 'mainly appeal to the girls'; topics are often chosen specifically with a view to maintaining boys' interests; boys insist on, and are given, greater attention by the teacher; in practical subjects such as science boys tend to hog the resources; boys are more disruptive; and boys in various ways, dominate classroom talk. (See Byrne 1978; Deem 1978; and Delamont 1980, for a general discussion of these and other findings; Whyte 1986, for a report on science teaching; and Clarricoates 1983, for a discussion of classroom interaction.)

Talk may, therefore, be seen to play its part alongside much more general patterns of difference and discrimination. Studies that focus on characteristics of mixed-sex classroom talk produce results that are similar in many respects to the general studies of talk between women and men mentioned above. For instance, in an American study of over 100 classes Sadker and Sadker (1985) found that boys spoke on average three times as much as girls, that boys were eight times more likely than girls to call out answers, and that teachers accepted such answers from boys but reprimanded girls for calling out. French and French (1984) suggest that particular strategies may enable talkative boys to gain more than their fair share of classroom talk. In a study of (British) primary classrooms they found that simply making an unusual response to a teacher's question could gain a pupil extra speaking turns—and those who made such responses were more often boys.

Most studies of classroom talk focus on the role of the teacher as much as on different pupils. One characteristic of classroom talk (that distinguishes it from talk in many other contexts) is that this is often mediated (if not directly controlled) by the teacher. If boys are to dominate, therefore, they must do so with the teacher's assistance or at least tacit acceptance. The argument that teachers pay boys more attention and, in other ways, encourage them to talk more has led some people consciously to attempt to redress the balance. Such evidence as is available, however, suggests that old habits are hard to break. Spender (1982) claims that it is virtually impossible to divide one's attention equally between girls and boys. Whyte (1986) is less pessimistic. Observations of science lessons by researchers involved in the Manchester-based Girls Into Science and Technology project revealed that teachers were able to devote an equal amount of attention to girls and boys, and therefore to encourage more equal participation from pupils. This was only achieved with some effort, however. Whyte reports a head of science who, having managed to create an atmosphere in which girls and boys contributed more or less equally to discussion, remarked that he had felt as though he were devoting 90 per cent of his attention to the girls (1986: 196).

While the fact of male dominance of classroom talk makes this similar to mixed-sex talk in other contexts, it's worth noting that not all of the same indicators of conversational dominance are present. For instance, although the findings that boys act assertively in the classroom (by calling out, etc.) may seem to be in line with the results from some adult 'interruption' studies, I know of no systematic studies (similar to those of Beattie or Zimmerman and West) of the use of interruptions by pupils in classrooms. With regard to minimal responses, one would not expect to find them heavily used by pupils in certain types of classroom talk (such as teacher-led question-and-answer sessions). Question-usage itself is hardly restricted to girl pupils—and questions used by the teacher may function as a form of control rather than as a means of gaining attention or the right to a speaking turn (see for instance D. Edwards 1980). If boys are to attempt to dominate classroom talk (relative to girls), such dominance must fit with the context and with the behaviours of other participants—in this case chiefly the teacher, who is meant to be in control, overall, of what is going on.

. . . . . . . . . . . . . . . .

## Works Cited

Baumann, M. (1976) 'Two features of "women's speech"?' in B.L. Dubois & I. Crouch (eds), *The Sociology of the Languages of American Women,* Papers in Southwest English IV. Trinity University, San Antonio.

Byrne, E. M. (1978) *Women and Education.* Tavistock Publications, London.

Clarricoates, K. (1983) 'Classroom interaction' in J. Whyld (ed.), *Sexism in the Secondary Curriculum.* Harper and Row, New York.

Deem, R. (1978) *Women and Schooling*. Routledge & Kegan Paul, London.

Delamont, S. (1980) *Sex Roles and the School*. Methuen, London.

Dubois, B.L. & I. Crouch (1975) 'The question of tag questions in women's speech: they don't really use more of them, do they?', *Language in Society* 4, 289–94.

Eakins, B. & G. Eakins (1976) 'Verbal turn-taking and exchanges in faculty dialogue' in Dubois & Crouch (eds).

Edelsky, C. (1981) 'Who's got the floor?' *Language in Society* 10, 383–421.

Edwards, D. (1980) 'Patterns of power and authority in classroom talk' in P. Woods (ed.) *Teacher Strategies: exploration in the sociology of the school*. Croom Helm, London.

Fishman, P.M. (1978) 'What do couples talk about when they're alone?' in D. Butturf & E.L. Epstein (eds), *Women's Language and Style*. Department of English, University of Akron.

——. (1983) 'Interaction: the work women do' in B. Thorne, C. Kramarae & N. Henley (eds). *Language, Gender and Society*. Newbury House, Rowley, Massachusetts.

French, J. & P. French (1984) 'Gender imbalance in the primary classroom: an interactional account', *Educational Research* 26 (2), 127–36.

Hirschman, L. (1974) 'Analysis of supportive and assertive behaviour in conversations', paper presented to the Linguistic Society of America, July 1974. (see abstract in B. Thorne & N. Henley [eds], [1975] *Language and Sex: difference and dominance*. Rowley House, Newbury, Massachusetts.)

Lakoff, R. (1975) *Language and Woman's Place*. Harper & Row, New York.

Maltz, D.N. & R.A. Borker (1982) 'A cultural approach to male–female miscommunication', in J. Gumperz (ed.) *Language and Social Identity*. Cambridge University Press.

Marland, M. (1977) *Language across the Curriculum*. Heinemann, London.

O'Barr, W. & B. Atkins (1980) '"Women's language" or "powerless language"?' in S. McConnell-Ginet, R. Barker & N. Furman (eds) (1980) *Women and Language in Literature and Society*. Praeger, New York.

Soskin, W. F. & V. P. John (1963) 'The study of spontaneous talk' in R. Barker (ed.), *The Stream of Behaviour*. Appleton–Century–Crofts, New York.

Spender, D. (1982) *Invisible Women: The Schooling Scandal*. Writers and Readers Publishing Cooperative Society, London.

West, C. & D. Zimmerman (1977) 'Women's place in everyday talk: reflections on parent—child interaction', *Social Problems* 24, 521–29.

Whyte, J. (1986) *Girls into Science and Technology: the story of a project*. Routledge & Kegan Paul, London.

Zimmerman, D. & C. West (1975) 'Sex roles, interruptions and silences in conversation' in Thorne & Henley (eds), *Language and Sex: difference and dominance*. Rowley House, Newbury, Massachusetts.

**For discussion**

*Content*

1. Explain how differences in power would influence differences in speech styles.

2. Does the information in paragraph eight ("Talk may, therefore...") match your experiences in classrooms? If it does, what does that tell you about the language environment in which you grew up?

3. Do you think the information in paragraph eight describes the classroom experiences of children in white middle-class schools? Might children of different race and/or class have different classroom experiences? If so, might their language environment be somewhat different? Can you think of other examples in which class, race, and sex influence language use?

4. Does Swann provide enough evidence to make her essay convincing?

*Style*

1. Paragraph two in "Classroom Talk: An Illustration" is a good example of an expository paragraph. Examine its topic sentence (the sentence that states the paragraph's point) and its specific development to see what makes it a good expository paragraph.

2. In the first two paragraphs, Swann uses "tend to" or "tend" several times. Are these effective word choices?

**For writing**

1. Write a paper in which you discuss ways teachers might ensure equal talking time for women and men in college/university classes.

2. Write about your experiences in a class. Have you had your fair share of speaking time? What is a fair share?

# Men and Women Talking

## Gloria Steinem

ONCE UPON A TIME (that is, just a few years ago), psychologists believed that the way we chose to communicate was largely a function
of personality. If certain conversational styles turned out to be more common to
one sex than the other (more abstract and aggressive talk for men, for instance,
more personal and equivocal talk for women), then this was just another tribute
to the influence of biology on personality.

Consciously or otherwise, feminists have challenged this assumption from
the beginning. Many of us learned a big lesson in the sixties when our generation spoke out on the injustices of war, as well as of race and class; yet women
who used exactly the same words and style as our male counterparts were less
likely to be listened to or to be taken seriously. When we tried to talk about this
and other frustrations, the lack of listening got worse, with opposition and even
ridicule just around every corner. Only women's own meetings and truth telling
began to confirm what we had thought each of us was alone in experiencing. It
was also those early consciousness-raising groups that began to develop a more
cooperative, less combative way of talking, an alternative style that many wom-
en have maintained and been strengthened by ever since.

The problem is that this culturally different form has remained an almost
totally female event. True, it has helped many, many women arrive at understanding each other and working out strategies for action. But as an influence
on the culturally male style of public talking, it has remained almost as removed
as its more domestic versions of the past.

One reason for our decade or so of delay in challenging existing styles of talking makes good tactical sense. Our first task was to change the words themselves. We did not feel included (and usage studies showed that, factually, we were not) in hundreds of such supposedly generic terms as *mankind* and *he, the brotherhood of man* and *statesman*. Nor could we fail to see the racial parallels to being identified as "girls" at advanced ages, or with first names only, or by our personal connection (or lack of one) to a member of the dominant group.

Hard as it was (and still is), this radical act of seizing the power to name ourselves and our experience was easier than taking on the politics of conversation. Documenting society-wide patterns of talking required expensive research and surveys. Documenting the sexism in words, and even conjuring up alternatives, took only one courageous woman scholar and a dictionary (for instance, *Guidelines for Equal Treatment of the Sexes,* the pioneering work of Alma Graham for McGraw–Hill). That was one good economic reason why such works were among the first and best by feminist scholars.

In retrospect, the second cause for delay makes less feminist sense—the long popularity of assertiveness training. Though most women needed to be more assertive (or even more aggressive, though that word was considered too controversial), many of these courses taught women how to play the existing game, not how to change the rules. Unlike the feminist assault on sexist language, which demanded new behavior from men, too, assertiveness training was more reformist than revolutionary. It pushed one-way change for women only, thus seeming to confirm masculine-style communication as the only adult model or the most effective one. Certainly, many individual women were helped, and many men were confronted with the educational experience of an assertive woman, but the larger impact was usually to flatter the existing masculine game of talk-politics by imitating it.

Since then, however, a few feminist scholars have had the time and resources to document conversational patterns of mixed- and single-sex groups, both here and in Europe. Traditional scholarship, influenced by feminism, has also begun to look at conversational styles as functions of power and environ-ment. For instance, employees pursue topics raised by their employers more than the reverse, older people feel free to interrupt younger ones, and subord-inates are more polite than bosses. Since women share all those conversational habits of the less powerful, even across the many lines of class and status that divide us, how accidental can that be?

Even the new feminist-influenced research has a long way to go in neutralizing the masculine bias of existing studies. For instance, *talking* is assumed to be the important and positive act, while *listening,* certainly a productive function, is the subject of almost no studies at all.

Nonetheless, there is enough new scholarship to document different styles, to point out some deficiencies in the masculine model of communicating, and to give us some ideas on how to create a synthesis of both that could provide a much wider range of alternatives for women *and* for men.

I

*Have you assumed that women talk more than men—and thus may dominate in discussion if nowhere else?* If so, you're not alone. Researchers of sex differences in language started out with that assumption. So did many feminists, who often explained women's supposedly greater penchant for talking as compensation for a lack of power to act.

In fact, however, when Dale Spender, an English feminist and scholar, surveyed studies of talkativeness for her recent book, *Man Made Language,* she concluded that "perhaps in more than any other research area, findings were in complete contradiction with the stereotype....There has not been one study which provides evidence that women talk more than men, and there have been numerous studies which indicate that men talk more than women."

Her conclusion held true regardless of whether the study in question asked individuals to talk into a tape recorder with no group interaction; or compared men and women talking on television; or measured amounts of talk in mixed groups (even among male and female state legislators); or involved group discussions of a subject on which women might be expected to have more expertise. (At a London workshop on sexism and education, for instance, the five men present managed to talk more than their thirty-two female colleagues combined.)

Some studies of male silence in heterosexual couples might seem to counter these results, but Spender's research supports their conclusion that a major portion of female talk in such one-to-one situations is devoted to drawing the man out, asking questions, introducing multiple subjects until one is accepted by him, or demonstrating interest in the subjects he introduces. Clearly, male silence (or silence from a member of any dominant group) is not necessarily the same as listening. It might mean a rejection of the speaker, a refusal to become vulnerable through self-revelation, or a decision that this conversation is not worthwhile. Similarly, talking by the subordinate group is not necessarily an evidence of power. Its motive may be a Scheherazade-like need to intrigue and thus survive, or simply to explain and justify one's actions.

In addition to a generally greater volume of talk, however, men interrupt women more often than vice versa. This is true both in groups and in couples. Male interruptions of women also bring less social punishment than female interruptions of men. Men also interrupt women more often than women interrupt each other.

Moreover, males are more likely to police the subject matter of conversation in mixed-sex groups. One study of working-class families showed that women might venture into such "masculine" topics as politics or sports, and men might join "feminine" discussions of domestic events, but in both cases, it was the men who ridiculed or otherwise straightened out nonconformers who went too far. Even in that London workshop on sexism, for instance, the concrete experiences of the female participants were suppressed in favor of the abstract, general conclusions on sexism that were preferred by the men. The few males present set the style for all the females.

How did the myth of female talkativeness and conversational dominance get started? Why has this supposed female ability been so accepted that many sociologists, and a few battered women themselves, have even accepted it as a justification for some men's violence against their wives?

The uncomfortable truth seems to be that the amount of talk by women has been measured less against the amount of men's talk than against the expectation of female silence.

Indeed, women who accept and set out to disprove the myth of the talkative woman may pay the highest price of all. In attempting to be the exceptions, we silence ourselves. If that is so, measuring our personal behavior against real situations and real studies should come as a relief, a confirmation of unspoken feelings.

We are not crazy, for instance, if we feel that, when we finally do take the conversational floor in a group, we are out there in exposed verbal flight, like fearful soloists plucked from the chorus. We are not crazy to feel that years of unspoken thoughts are bottled up inside our heads, and come rushing out in a way that may make it hard to speak calmly, even when we finally have the chance.

Once we give up searching for approval by stifling our thoughts, or by imitating the male norm of abstract, assertive communicating, we often find it easier to simply say what needs to be said, and thus to earn respect and approval. Losing self-consciousness and fear allows us to focus on the content of what we are saying instead of on ourselves.

Women's well-developed skill as listeners, perhaps the real source of our much vaunted "intuition," should not be left behind. We must retain it for ourselves and teach it to men by bringing it with us into our work and daily lives, but that will only happen if we affirm its value. Female culture does have a great deal to contribute to the dominant one. Furthermore, women might feel better about talking equally, selecting subjects, and even interrupting occasionally if we took the reasonable attitude that we are helping men to become attentive and retentive listeners, too. We are paying them the honor of communicating as honestly as we can and treating them as we would want to be treated. After all, if more men gained sensitive listening skills, they would have "intuition," too.

*These are practical exercises for achieving a change in the balance of talk.* Try tape-recording a dinner-table conversation or meeting (in the guise of recording facts, so participants don't become self-conscious about their talk politics), then play the tape back to the same group, and ask them to add up the number of minutes talked, interruptions, and subject introductions for each gender. Or give a dozen poker chips to each participant in a discussion, and require that one chip be given up each time a person speaks. Or break the silence barrier for those who rarely talk by going around the room once at the beginning of each meeting, consciousness-raising-style, with a question that each participant must answer personally, even if it's only a self-introduction. (It is said that the British Labor party was born only after representatives of its warring factions spent an hour moving their conference table into a larger room. That one communal act broke down individual isolation, just as one round of communal speaking helps break the ice.)

If such methods require more advance planning or influence on the group than you can muster, or if you're trying to sensitize just one person, try some individual acts. Discussing the results of studies on who talks more can produce some very healthy self-consciousness in both women and men. If one group member speaks rarely, try addressing more of your own remarks to her (or him) directly. On the other hand, if one man (or woman) is a domineering interrupter, try objecting directly, interrupting in return, timing the minutes of his or her talk, or just being inattentive. If someone cuts you off, say with humor, "That's one," then promise some conspicuous act when the interruptions get to three. Keep score on "successful" topic introductions, add them up by gender, and announce them at the discussion's end.

If questions and comments following a lecture come mostly from men, stand up and say so. It may be a learning moment for everyone. The prevalence of male speakers in mixed audiences has caused some feminist lecturers to reserve equal time for questions from women only.

To demonstrate the importance of listening as a positive act, try giving a quiz on the content of female and male speakers. Hopefully you *won't* discover the usual: that men often remember what male speakers say better than they remember female speakers' content; that women often remember male content better, too, but that women listen and retain the words of *both* sexes somewhat better than men do.

Check the talk politics concealed in your own behavior. Does your anxiety level go up (and your hostess instincts quiver) when women are talking and men are listening, but not the reverse? For instance, men often seem to feel okay about "talking shop" for hours while women listen, but women seem able to talk in men's presence for only a short time before feeling anxious, apologizing, and encouraging the men to speak. If you start to feel wrongly uncomfortable about making males listen, try this exercise: *keep on talking,* and encourage your sisters to do the same. Honor men by treating them as honestly as you treat women. You will be allowing them to learn.

II

*Here are three popular assumptions: (1) Women talk about themselves, personally, and gossip more than men do. (2) Men would rather talk to groups of men than to mixed groups, and women prefer mixed groups to all-female ones. (3) Women speakers and women's issues are hampered by the feminine style of their presentation.* As you've probably guessed by now, most evidence is to the contrary of all three beliefs.

After recording the conversational themes of single-sex and mixed-sex groups, for instance, social psychologist Elizabeth Aries found that men in all-male groups were more likely to talk about themselves than were women in all-female ones. Men were also more likely to use self-mentions to demonstrate superiority or aggressiveness, while women used them to share an emotional reaction to what was being said by others.

Phil Donahue, one of the country's most experienced interviewers, capsulizes the cultural difference between men and women this way: "If you're in a social situation, and women are talking to each other, and one woman says, 'I was hit by a car today,' all the other women will say, 'You're kidding! What happened? Where? Are you all right?' In the same situation with males, one male says, 'I was hit by a car today.' I guarantee you that there will be another male in the group who will say, 'Wait till I tell you what happened to *me.*'"

If quantity of talking about oneself is a measure of "personalizing," and self-aggrandizement through invoking the weakness of others is one characteristic of gossip, then men may be far more "gossipy" than women—especially when one includes sexual bragging.

In addition, subjects introduced by males in mixed groups are far more likely to "succeed" than subjects introduced by women, and, as Aries concluded, women in mixed groups are more likely to interact with men than with other women. Thus, it's not unreasonable to conclude that mixed groups spend more time discussing the lives and interests of male participants than of female ones.

On the other hand, research by Aries and others shows that women are more likely to discuss human relationships. Since "relationships" often fall under "gossip" in men's view, this may account for the frequent male observation that women "personalize" everything. Lecturers often comment, for instance, that women in an audience ask practical questions about their own lives, while men ask abstract questions about groups or policies. When the subject is feminism, women tend to ask about practical problems. Men are more likely to say something like, "But how will feminism impact the American family?"

To quote Donahue, who deals with mostly female audiences: "I've always felt a little anxious about the possibility of a program at night with a male audience. The problem as I perceive it—and this is a generalization—is that men tend to give you a speech, whereas women will ask a question and then listen for the answer and make another contribution to the dialogue. In countless situations I have a male in my audience stand up and say in effect, 'I don't know what you're arguing about; here's the answer to this thing.' And then proceed to give a mini-speech."

Aries also documented the more cooperative, rotating style of talk and leadership in women-only groups: the conscious or unconscious habit of "taking turns." As a result, women actually prefer talking in their own single-sex groups for the concrete advantages of both having a conversational turn and being listened to. On the other hand, she confirmed research that shows male-only groups to have more stable hierarchies, with the same one or several talkers dominating most of the time.

As Aries points out, no wonder men prefer the variation and opportunity of mixed-sex audiences. They combine the seriousness of a male presence with more choice of styles—and, as Spender adds caustically, the assurance of at least some noncompetitive listeners.

Women's more gentle delivery, "feminine" choice of adjectives, and greater attention to grammar and politeness have been heavily criticized. Linguist Robin Lakoff pioneered the exposure of "ladylike" speech as a double bind that is both required of little girls, and used as a reason why, as adults, they may not be seen as forceful or serious. (Even Lakoff seems to assume, however, that female speech is to be criticized as the deficient form, while male speech is the norm and thus escapes equal comment.) Sociologist Arlie Hochschild also cites some survival techniques of racial minorities that women of all races seem to share: playing dumb and dissembling, for instance, or expressing frequent approval of others.

But whether this criticism of female speech patterns is justified or not, there is also evidence that a rejection of the way a woman speaks is often a way of blaming or dismissing her without dealing with the content of what she is saying.

For instance, women speakers are more likely to hear some version of "You have a good point, but you're not making it effectively," or "Your style is too aggressive/weak/loud/quiet." It is with such paternalistic criticisms that male politicians often dismiss the serious message of a female colleague, or that husbands turn aside the content of arguments made by their wives.

It is also such criticisms that allow women candidates to be rejected without dealing with the substance of the issues they raise. When Bella Abzug of New York and Gloria Schaeffer of Connecticut both ran for political office in one recent year, each was said to have a personal style that would prevent her from being an effective senator: Abzug because she was "too abrasive and aggressive," and Schaeffer because she was "too ladylike and quiet." Style was made the central issue by the press, and thus became one in the public-opinion polls. Both were defeated.

There are three anomalies that give away this supposedly "helpful" criticism. First, it is rarely used when a woman's message is not challenging to male power. (How often are women criticized for being too fierce in defense of their families? How often was Phyllis Schlafly criticized for being too aggressive in her opposition to the Equal Rights Amendment?) Second, the criticism is rarely accompanied by real support, even when the critic presents himself (or herself) as sympathetic. (Women political candidates say they often get critiques of their fund-raising techniques instead of cash, even from people who agree with them on issues.) Finally, almost everyone, regardless of status, feels a right to criticize. (Women professors report criticism of their teaching style from young students, as do women bosses from their employees.)

Just as there is a conversational topic that men in a group often find more compelling than any introduced by a woman (even when it's exactly the same topic, but *re*introduced by a man), or a political issue that is "more important" than any of concern to women, so there is usually a better, more effective style than the one a woman happens to be using.

Men *would* support us, we are told, if only we learned how to ask for their support in the right way. It's a subtle and effective way of blaming the victim.

*What can we do to break through these stereotypes?* Keeping notes for one meeting or one week on the male/female ratio of gossip or self-mentions could be educational. Declaring a day's moratorium on all words that end in "-tion" and all generalities might encourage men to state their personal beliefs *without* disguising them as general conclusions.

As a personal exercise, try countering slippery abstractions with tangible examples. When David Susskind and Germaine Greer were guests on the same television talk show, for instance, Susskind used general, pseudoscientific statements about women's monthly emotional changes as a way of excusing the injustices cited by this very intelligent woman. Finally, Greer turned politely to Susskind and said, "Tell me, David. Can you tell if I'm menstruating right now—or not?" She not only eliminated any doubts raised by Susskind's statements, but subdued his pugnacious style for the rest of the show.

Men themselves are working to break down the generalities and competitiveness that a male-dominant culture has imposed on them. Some are meeting in all-male consciousness-raising groups, learning how to communicate more openly and personally among themselves.

Many women are also trying to break down the barriers we ourselves maintain. For instance, women's preference for talking to one another has a great deal to do with the shorthand that shared experience provides. Furthermore, the less powerful group usually knows the powerful one much better than vice versa—blacks have had to understand whites in order to survive, women have had to know men—yet the powerful group can afford to regard the less powerful one as a mystery. Indeed, the idea of differentness and the Mysterious Other may be necessary justifications for the power imbalance and the lack of empathy it requires.

One result is that, even when the powerful group *wants* to listen, the other may despair of talking: it's just too much trouble to explain. Recognizing this unequal knowledge encourages women to talk about themselves to men, at least to match the time they spend talking about themselves. After all, they cannot read our minds.

On issues of style, role reversals are enlightening. For instance, ask a man who is critical of "aggressive" women to try to argue a serious political point while speaking "like a lady." A woman candidate might also ask critics to write a speech in the style they think she should use. Responding in kind can create a quick reversal. There's a certain satisfaction to saying, in the middle of a man's impassioned speech: "I suppose you have a point to make, but you're not expressing it well. Now, if you just used more personal examples. If you changed your language, your timing, and perhaps your suit...."

Finally, if all talk fails, try putting the same message in writing. The point is to get your message across, whether or not the man in question can separate it from the medium.

### III

*Women's higher-pitched voices and men's lower ones are the result of physiology. Because deep voices are more pleasant and authoritative ,women speakers will always have a problem. Besides, female facial expressions and gestures aren't as forceful...and so on.* It's true that tone of voice is partly created by throat-construction and the resonance of bones. Though there is a big area of male–female overlap in voice tone as well as in size, strength, and other physical attributes, we assume that all men will have a much deeper pitch than all women.

In fact, however, no one knows exactly how much of our speaking voices are imitative and culturally produced. Studies of young boys before puberty show that their vocal tones may deepen *even before physiological changes can account for it.* They are imitating the way the males around them speak. Dale Spender cites a study of males who were not mute, but who were born deaf and thus unable to imitate sound. Some of them never went through an adolescent voice change at all.

Whatever the mix of physiological and cultural factors, however, the important point is that the *acceptance* of vocal tone is definitely cultural and therefore subject to change.

In Japan, for instance, a woman's traditionally high-pitched, soft speaking voice is considered a very important sexual attribute. (When asked in a public-opinion poll what attribute they found most attractive in women, the majority of Japanese men said "voice.") Though trained to speak in upper registers, Japanese women, like many of their sisters around the world, often speak in lower tones when men are not present. They may even change their language as well. (A reporter's tapes of Japanese schoolgirls talking among themselves caused a scandal. They were using masculine word endings and verbs in a country where the language is divided into formally masculine and feminine forms.) Thus,

Japanese men may find a high voice attractive not for itself but for its tribute to a traditional subservience.

Some American women also cultivate a high, childish, or whispery voice à la Marilyn Monroe. We may sense that a woman is talking to a man on the other end of the phone, or a man to a woman, because she lightens her normal tone and he deepens his.

A childlike or "feminine" vocal style becomes a drawback, however, when women try for any adult or powerful role. Female reporters were kept out of television and radio for years by the argument that their voices were too high, grating, or nonauthoritative to speak the news credibly. Even now, women's voices may be thought more suitable for human interest and "soft news"' while men still announce "hard news." In the early days of television, women were allowed to do the weather reports—very sexily. When meteorology and weather maps became the vogue, however, most stations switched to men. Even now, 85 percent of all voice-overs on television ads, including those for women's products, are done by men. Even on floor wax and detergents, men are likely to be the voices of expertise and authority.

In the long run, however, men may suffer more from cultural restrictions on tone of voice than women do. Linguist Ruth Brend's study of male and female intonation patterns in the United States, for instance, disclosed four contrasting levels used by women in normal speech, but only three levels used by men. This isn't a result of physiology; men also have at least four levels available to them, but they rarely use the highest one. Thus, women may speak publicly in both high and low tones with some degree of social acceptability, but men must use their lower tones only. It's okay to flatter the ruling class with imitation, just as it's okay for women to wear pants or for blacks to speak and dress like Establishment whites, but it's less okay for men to wear feminine clothes, for whites to adopt black speech and street style, or for men to imitate or sound like women. (Such upper-class exceptions as the female-impersonating shows put on by the Hasty Pudding Club at Harvard or by the very rich men of the Bohemian Grove in California seem to indicate that even ridicule of women requires security. It's much less likely to happen at the working-class level of bowling clubs and bars.)

As the price of "masculinity," men as a group are losing variety in their speech and an ability to express a full range of emotions. The higher proportion of masculine monotones is also a penalty to the public ear.

In the same way, physical expressiveness may be viewed as "feminine." Women can be vivacious. We are allowed more varieties of facial expression and gestures. Men must be rocklike. Certainly, some emotive and expressive men are being imprisoned by that belief.

The down side is that women's greater range of expression is also used to ridicule females as emotionally unstable. That sad point is made by Nancy Henley in *Body Politics: Power, Sex, and Nonverbal Communication.* "Women's facial expressivity," she explains, "has been allowed a wider range than men's, encompassing within the sex stereotype not only pleasant expressions, but negative ones like crying." Since males are encouraged to leave crying and other emotional expression in their childhoods, females who retain this human ability are often compared to children.

Nonetheless, women's wider range also allows us to recognize more physical expression when we see it. Henley refers to a study showing that women of all races and black men usually do better than white men at identifying nonverbal clues. We're both less imprisoned by the rocklike mask of being in control, and more needful of the survival skill of paying attention.

In short, women need to affirm and expand expressiveness, but men are also missing some major ways of signaling the world and getting signals back.

*You can't change vocal cords (theirs or ours), but you can make sure they're being well used.* Tape-record women talking together, then record the same people talking to men. It's a good way to find out whether we're sending out geishalike tonal clues. Some women are neglecting our lower range. Others, especially when trying to be taken seriously, are overcompensating for supposed emotionalism by narrowing to a "reasonable" monotone. Men may also change under pressure of taped evidence: for instance, the contrast between their dullness when talking with men and their expressiveness when talking to children. Many actors, female and male, are living testimonials to how much and how quickly—with effort, exercise, and freedom—a vocal range can change.

Most important, remember that there is nothing *wrong* with women's voices, and no subject or emotion they cannot convey. This is especially important for women who are lonely tokens. The first women in law and business schools, the board room, or the assembly line often report that the sound of their own voices comes as a shock—a major barrier to reciting in class, speaking up on policy, or arguing in union meetings. It may take a while for words said in a female voice to be taken seriously, but a head-turning response to the unusual sound is also a tribute to its owner as a courageous pioneer.

The advent of video recorders is a major breakthrough in understanding and changing our nonverbal expressions. Watching the incontrovertible evidence of how we come across to others can be more useful than years of psychiatry. Many men and boys could also benefit from such expressiveness exercises as a game of charades, or communicating with children. Women and girls can free body movements through sports, a conscious effort to take up more space when sitting or standing, and using body language we may now use only when relaxed with other women. Many of us could benefit from watching female impersonators and learning the many ways in which we have been trained to be female impersonators, too.

The point is not that one gender's cultural style is superior to the other's. The current "feminine" style of communicating may be better suited to, say, the performing arts, medical diagnosis, and conflict resolution. It has perfected emotional expressiveness, careful listening, and a way of leaving an adversary with dignity intact. The current "masculine" style may be better suited to, say, procedural instruction, surgical teams and other situations requiring hierarchical command, and job interviews. It has perfected linear and abstract thinking, quick commands, and a willingness to speak well of oneself or present views with assertiveness. But we will never achieve this full human circle of expression if women imitate the male "adult" style. We have to teach as well as learn.

A feminist assault on the politics of talking, and listening, is a radical act. It's a way of transforming the cultural vessel in which both instant communication and long-term anthropological change are carried. Unlike the written word, or visual imagery, or any form of communication divorced from our presence, talking and listening won't allow us to hide. There is no neutral page, image, sound or even a genderless name to protect us. We are demanding to be accepted and understood by all the senses and for our whole selves.

That's precisely what makes the change so difficult. And so crucial.

## For discussion

*Content*

1. Steinem says that listening "is the subject of almost no studies at all" (paragraph eight). To you, how important a skill is listening? Do you think you listen more than you talk? Because of your status and your gender, are you expected to listen or to talk?

2. Why do people repeat "Women talk too much" or "Women talk all the time," even though, as Steinem reports in the second paragraph of Section I, "there have been numerous studies which indicate that men talk more than women"?

3. What kinds of specific support does Steinem use to illustrate her ideas? Is it enough support? What do you think of her referral to several linguists' research as support?

4. Steinem suggests at the end of Section I that women should "[h]onor men by treating them as honestly as you treat women." In what particular linguistic ways have women not treated men honestly, according to Steinem? In what particular linguistic ways have men not treated women honestly?

5. Steinem suggests practical ways to balance the amount of talk-time each person gets in a discussion. Evaluate those methods.

6. At the beginning of Section II, Steinem lists three popular assumptions about women and men talking, and Section III starts with another assumption. What does Steinem say about each assumption? Have you held any of these assumptions? Does Steinem's evidence help you to re-evaluate any of those assumptions?

7. What does it mean to "talk like a lady"? When you learned that phrase, what did you take it to mean? Do women's answers to this question differ from men's answers? If so, do the differences matter in how women and men communicate with each other? Do the differences create expectations that we should examine?

*Style*

1. Look at the transitions at the beginnings of paragraphs four, six, and seven, and of Section III paragraphs nine, ten, 11, and 12. What directions do those transitions give you?

2. Do the numbers of the essay's main blocks help you as a reader or do they get in your way? Explain.

3. Would Steinem have done better to state her thesis at the beginning instead of at the end of the essay? Why or why not?

4. What is the effect of Steinem's ending the essay with a sentence fragment?

**For writing**

1. Observe the talking styles of women and men in your college classes, and write a paragraph in which you support a point about women's or men's talking styles.

2. Write a paragraph in which you state and disprove one assumption about women's or men's talking or listening styles.

# Chapter Two:

# Take Your Choice

# Take Your Choice

## Introduction

ALMOST EVERYONE is born into one complex verbal language or another. English is such a verbal language. "Verbal" means "of words" ("oral" means "of the mouth," spoken words), and our study in this book is verbal language—words written, spoken and thought. Certainly, humans communicate with non-verbal methods—body language and language of flowers, for example—but verbal language is our focus here.

One complexity of our verbal language is that some of its vocabulary is purely conventional, allowing us to make appropriate noises; and some of its vocabulary is literal, allowing us to state ideas and information. For example, "Good morning" is simply a greeting, an appropriate noise; "Oh phooey" is a mild expletive, an appropriate noise in some circumstances. Words we use in these conventional ways are very important to us, even though we do not use them to convey specific information or to discuss ideas and events. On the other hand, "This course is Composition One" conveys information. The words in this paragraph form a discussion of an idea. Words we use in these literal ways are also very important to us.

Understanding the difference between conventional language and literal language is an important first step in examining our language inheritance and our language habits. In addition, we need to understand that we can change our language habits, and to some extent, the language itself. But to change or to decide not to change, we must have additional information about our complex language. Most of the remainder of our discussion in this book will be about the language of literal meaning—words we use when we intend to convey information or to discuss ideas and events.

Our verbal language is also complex because while English allows us to use more words than we need, it also allows us to be economical. Because we learn language by listening to other people and by reading others' words, and because we often use language more from habit than from careful thought, we learn and we use redundant phrases. For example, "at this time," "general consensus of opinion," "widow woman," "on a regular basis," "the use of," and "throughout the entire" use two or three times as many words as they need. A single word will do in each case. But we hear and read these phrases and we use them out of habit, without thinking what each word means. If we think about what we want to say and if we want to be precise and economical, we can choose the single word for our meaning.

Perhaps we have the notion that the phrase is better than the word, that it says more, or that it makes us sound more intelligent or better educated. That notion leads us to pretentiousness. And our language allows us to be pretentious, to use larger words than we need; it also allows us to be unpretentious if we choose the exact word rather than simply the large one. A large word is not inherently pretentious; sometimes the large word is exactly the right one for the meaning. A word is pretentious only when the speaker or writer chooses it to impress. If I want to try to impress you, I might say, "It is my hope that you will successfully pass this course of study and that the parameters of the designed curriculum will impact in a positive nature on you." I might also use those words out of lazy habit. But if I want to give you a clear message and to save your time, I will choose the more economical "I hope you will learn the content and pass this course."

We might also choose to use more and larger words than we need if we want to baffle a listener or a reader. For example, a United States Senator who cannot or will not tell me directly that he represents his interests rather than mine may choose to spew forth four times as many words as he needs and larger words than he needs, hoping to confuse me. If I ask my Senator to vote for a women's freedom-of-choice-bill or for a bill to lift the ban on homosexuals in the military, he may respond with a three-page form letter that finally *means* nothing more than "No. I won't vote for that bill because I think men should control women's bodies," or "No. I won't vote for that bill because I think that heterosexual people should have all the educational, retirement, and other economic benefits of military service." Suppose the Senator writes:

> I am hopeful that you will come to agree with my humanitarian views regarding our society's future generations, their prosperity in a democratic nation, the viability of their choices for which I am and always have been a staunch supporter and ally, and therefore, understand why I am compelled to raise my voice and indeed my vote against any legislation that might encourage federal law to mitigate against the rights of individual states.

He is trying to baffle me. It works if I don't recognize pretension and excess verbiage.

In addition to our using wordy phrases and pretentious diction from habit or from a wish to hide our thoughts or to confuse a reader or listener, we may be wordy and pretentious for another reason. We may think that we are supposed to be. The linguistic environment in which we live is a part of our larger social environment. Part of our learning to function in the social environment is learning to function in its language, which means that all of us are caught in the ways of the language. We saw in Chapter One that men are "supposed" to use language in strong, authoritative ways (they discuss, debate, argue) and that women are "supposed" to use language in weak trivial ways (they chatter, natter, gossip). We grew up learning how we are "supposed" to use language if we are women or if we are men. In *Women in American Society*, Virginia Sapiro argues that in hierarchical relationships between women and men, men are usually in the superior spot, and that "the traffic rules of communication and interaction are governed in part by...patterns of dominance and deference and a male right-of-way" (257). Sapiro quotes Victor A. Thompson's theory about hierarchy and communication, saying that one right of communication of the superior is to "'speak out on all sorts of matters from a position of almost complete ignorance'" (257). Is it possible, then, that a man, knowing that he is "supposed" to "speak out on all sorts of matters," even if "from a position of almost complete ignorance," uses more and larger words than he needs so that he can sound authoritative? Is it possible that a woman, knowing that she is "supposed" to use trivial language, uses more and larger words than she needs, thinking that her words don't matter anyway? As we consider those two questions, we must keep in mind that not all men are in superior positions and that some women sometimes are. What situations can you think of in which a man is not in the position of authority or superiority? What situations can you think of in which a woman is in the position of authority or superiority?

We live in a linguistic environment that includes wordiness and pretentiousness. Although we cannot erase that fact about our language, we can decide how we will use language. I might choose to be wordy and pretentious to try to fool listeners and readers. If they are inattentive or uninformed, my language may fool them. In that case, my language was effective—it accomplished my purpose. But if my wordy and pretentious language makes me think that I have said something profound when in fact I have not, I am the fool. On the other hand, we might choose not to contribute additional wordiness and pretension. We can think about our words and habits and we can decide to use only those words we need and only the exact words whether they are large or small. Because other people learn language from us—just as we have learned it by imitating people—our more precise language may influence others to use language more economically. We cannot erase the fact that we all learn the ways of our society any more than we can erase the fact that English includes wordiness and pretension. But, as we can choose how we will use language, we can choose to recognize the influence of social learning on us; and we can change our behavior. If men refuse to speak in ignorance simply because they feel pressured to be authoritative, and if women refuse to sound trivial simply because they are "supposed" to sound that way, perhaps we can change the language behaviors others learn.

If we are to make informed choices about how we use language and if we are to exert some control over language, a third complexity of English that we must be aware of is that English allows us to make active-voice or passive-voice sentences. In passive-voice sentences, the subject receives the action of the verb. For example, in "Women are thought to be lousy drivers," "women" is the subject. In that sentence, "women" are not doing the action, the thinking; someone else is thinking about them. And passive voice hides who *is* doing the action. Is it men who think women are lousy drivers? Do people who sell car insurance think that? Does the whole society think that? In active-voice sentences, the subject does the action of the verb. In "The man raped his daughter," the subject, "man," does the action. Active voice clarifies blame and responsibility.

If we don't know the difference between active and passive voice, we use one or the other without being aware of what we do and without knowing the effects our sentences may have on readers or listeners. If we know the difference, we can choose active voice to clarify information or to assign blame, or we can choose passive voice to conceal information, to indicate that we don't know who did the action, or to emphasize a result more than who caused it. Knowing the difference between active and passive structures, I can write, "The United States does not guarantee equal rights in its constitution because too few state legislatures ratified the Equal Rights Amendment," to place responsibility for our lack of equal rights on the legislators who did not ratify the amendment, and to clarify my opinion that the federal government should guarantee equal rights. If I want to pretend or to make you think that no one is responsible, I could choose to write, "Equal rights are not guaranteed in the United States because the ERA was not ratified by enough states." In this passive structure, no entity is responsible for seeing to it that citizens have equal rights. And by using "states," I conceal the fact that it was people, legislators, who refused to ratify the ERA.

We cannot do anything about the fact that our linguistic environment includes both active and passive voice, but we can choose which to use, and we can know that other people may use passive structures intentionally to conceal information from us.

And if we are to assert choice and control of language, a fourth complexity of English that we need to understand is that English allows us to use euphemisms, but it also allows us to use precise words. Most of us have grown up in a language that includes two or more words or sets of words for the same action, event, fact, or idea. One word or group of words names or describes in a blunt, straightforward, sometimes painful, but usually very clear and precise way. The other word or set of words names or describes in a more pleasant or less abrupt and often ambiguous or unclear way. Words that fit into the second group are called euphemisms; they are words and phrases that make harsh, embarrassing, or unpleasant realities sound less harsh. Euphemisms give us a way to avoid using technical or clinical or blunt words for subjects we are uncomfortable talking about. For example, "menstruation," the technical term for natural, cyclical uterine change, names an event so embarrassing for some people that they cannot say the word. Instead, people use euphemisms like "period," "that time of the month," "curse," and "Aunt Flo" to avoid saying "menstruation." Euphemisms do not change the facts, but they may incline people to have distorted ideas about women and about what is natural and healthy for women. On the other hand, when we can use the technical and usually very clear term, we recognize that language can help us to be very precise.

Precise terms can also help us recognize social biases built into euphemisms. Why does a society make euphemisms for women used in prostitution?[1] What euphemisms do you know for women used in prostitution? Do we create the euphemisms because we do not want to recognize that we use people in that specific sexual way? Do we create them to hide the people who use women in that specific way, and to put the blame on the women themselves? Do we create euphemisms for old people because we are biased against them and do not want to think clearly enough about them to find solutions to some of the problems of being old? Do we think that senior citizens have fewer health and financial problems than do old people? Do we create euphemisms for women's physical processes because our culture is biased against women? Do we as a society think that women going through the change of life deserve or need less information about their bodies than women in menopause? "Menopause" sounds almost medical; would using "menopause" encourage the medical profession to do more research for women's benefit?

We often use words without knowing that they are euphemisms, and in those cases, we are not trying consciously to lie or to mislead. But when we say "period," thinking that somehow it sounds better than "menstruation," we may be fooling ourselves into thinking that the word changes the situation. Words do not have that kind of magic. Calling a woman used in prostitution "a working girl" or "a woman of the evening" does not change the fact that she is often subjected to violence and it does not make her life glamorous and romantic. Calling a man who exploits women sexually a "manager" or a "pimp," a "john" or a "date" does not change the fact that he exploits women sexually.

On the other hand, we may carefully choose euphemisms to avoid embarrassing or offending a reader or listener. I may choose "she is very ill" rather than "she's dying of cancer" to spare my listener's feelings for the moment. Or we may choose euphemisms to confuse listeners or readers, to lie. I may choose "collateral damage" to confuse a reader who doesn't recognize that phrase as euphemism for "human death in nuclear war."

A third reason to choose euphemism, according to Carol E. Barringer, is to bridge the chasm between experiences too horrible to think and talk about, and talking about such experiences. Barringer argues that some abuse survivors can think and speak about their experiences *only* by using euphemisms. In those cases, Barringer says, euphemism "places distance between the survivor and the raw facts of her experiences...[and] define[s] a space within which the survivor feels safe enough to speak" (11). Barringer states, "euphemism reveals the struggle to gain control, of both the experience of abuse and of the telling about it" (11).

We have grown up in a language that includes euphemisms, and we can't do anything about that fact. But we can choose to be aware of euphemisms so that we can decide whether to use them or not and so that we are not misled by them. And we can analyze euphemisms to learn whether or not they harm us, by making us think, for example, that we should be ashamed of our natural physical functions, or by allowing us to see drunkenness as funny or violence as acceptable. We can consider whether euphemisms help us by allowing us a way to report violence against us and to discuss experiences we should not have had to endure. Using euphemisms does not change facts or make them go away; not talking at all about facts doesn't make them change or go away either. If we have the direct, blunt words, we can choose not to use euphemisms so that we can think more accurately and realistically. We can choose not to repeat euphemisms without thinking and we can let them wither from the language. We can choose to use euphemism for specific reasons. We can choose if we know what our choices are.

English is a complex verbal language. Beyond the complexities of language itself are the complexities of the social environment in which we learn about ourselves as language users and in which we make linguistic choices—whether to be economical, to be unpretentious, to be as honest as we can be. And beyond those complexities are the complex issues of audience, purpose, and specific situation for which we choose our words. Chapter Two has begun our discussion of the complexities and subtleties that direct our linguistic choices. We will pursue the discussion of these complications throughout this book.

The euphemism exercise that follows will call your attention to subjects for which we use several euphemisms, and the active-passive structure exercise will give you some practice manipulating active and passive sentences.

The essays in this chapter examine, from a variety of angles, the complexities of language that we have been discussing. As you read each essay, consider not only its content but how each author handles language.

**Notes**

1.    I thank Dr. Patricia Murphy for teaching me the phrase "women used in prostitution," which has helped me to see the women and the social issue in a new light.

## Works Cited

Barringer, Carol E. "The Survivor's Voice: Breaking the Incest Taboo." *NWSA Journal* 4:1 (Spring 1992): 4–22.

Sapiro, Virginia. *Women in American Society*. Second Edition. Mountain View, California: Mayfield Publishing Company, 1990.

## Euphemism Exercise 1

Write as many euphemisms as you can think of for each term below. Remember that different age groups have different euphemisms; what seems blunt to you may be euphemism to the generation older or younger than you.

Failure:

_____

_____

Death:

_____

_____

Drunkenness:

_____

_____

Murder:

_____

_____

Sexual intercourse:

_____

_____

Rape of children:

_____

_____

Violence against women:

_____

_____

## Euphemism Exercise 2

For what other subjects do people typically use euphemisms?

_____

_____

_____

_____

_____

What do you make of the fact that the euphemism is almost always longer than the word or phrase it replaces?

## Passive/Active Sentence Structure Exercise

Change each subject-verb combination below into an active structure. How does the information change in each sentence when you change passive structure to active structure?

My car was wrecked. _____

It was found by the committee... _____

The child was abused. _____

The candidate was elected. _____

It is generally thought... _____

The ERA amendment was defeated. _____

Change each subject-verb combination below into a passive structure. How does responsibility or blame shift in each sentence?

The vice-president fired her. _____

The man shot a wolf. _____

Her live-in boyfriend beat her to death. _____

Women earn about 70 cents for every dollar men earn. _____

Governments do not consider women's unpaid labor in their homes
       as work. _____

# Habit Is Useful and Dangerous

## Arlene Larson

....IN ONE CAPACITY, words provide us a way of handling social exchange, venting emotions, and operating linguistic systems. We shall call this language "language of convention." Conventional language conveys—in an easy, conventional way—rather complicated mental reactions, and knowing what we do when we participate in successful exchange of this kind makes us effective members of the society.

Try to define the words "but" and "in." Probably you cannot do so; I cannot. But we understand well the relationship implied by each of these words. Nearly all our conjunctions (but, and, because, when), our prepositions (in, over, through), and our articles (a, an, the) are indefinable, but they are all essential in making sentences. If you have studied a foreign language, you know the difficulties in learning the idiomatic use of these function words....If you can recognize now the indefinable quality of these function words, and at the same time recognize their importance in the linguistic system, you can move easily to the next category of conventional language.

We have equal difficulty defining the words of social exchange (hello, hi, goodbye, thank you, please, you're welcome); however these words are important in our day-to-day lives. If you do not greet a friend, you will be thought snobbish: you would find it difficult to plunge into a conversation without some kind of opener; and you might experiment to see what happens to you and to the other person if you try to walk away from a conversation without some kind of ending phrase. "Please" and "thank you" acknowledge our awareness of the polite forms.

These words originally had literal meaning; you might check the Oxford English Dictionary for the etymology of certain social phrases. Though the original "meaning," or definition, has been lost, the words serve us perfectly well to convey our general goodwill to another person. Occasionally a linguistic novice will complain that these are words of habit—as indeed they are—and that they are insincere because they do not have meaning. In a well-intended attempt to correct this, many people a few years ago adopted the phrase "Have a nice day" as a sincere farewell; nowadays we can hear that phrase used as habitually as "goodbye," and even corrupted to a conventional "havanice." That shift from meaning to convention merely indicates that for certain purposes language habits are our best means of conveying impressions. If we want to say something specifically designed for the person and the time, we have to construct an original sentence, but "goodbye" and "have a nice day" are equally effective to convey our sincere intent to show good will.

English is rich in language of convention, giving us many choices of greetings and polite phrases. We learn the conventions very early. We learn that we are not meant to answer "How are you?" with a summary of health problems; we learn that "hi" is appropriate for a casual friend, but that "Good afternoon, Aunt Miriam" would be better for a different situation. "Hi" is a brief salutation, suitable for passing a friend on campus, but other occasions call for an equally conventional, but much longer salutation: "Good afternoon, Mrs. Smith," "Good afternoon, Mr. Brown. How are you today?" "Just fine, thank you; and you?" "Just fine." Some groups of close friends and some fraternal groups have long, elaborate, highly stylized conventional greetings and farewells. Any of these choices recognizes the relationship between the two people, the formality of the situation, the intent to pass by or the intent to stop to talk.

Some social exchange goes beyond the greetings, farewells, and polite phrases. If you and I meet between classes for a cup of coffee just to be friendly, not to exchange information, we might have a whole conversation of habit phrases. ("How was your test?" "A bummer. Yours?" "Ich." That conveys impressions but not information.) We could go bowling and spend two-thirds of our conversation on habit phrases such as "Shoulda been!" Some people, in fact, so dislike silence that they talk at length without any attempt to communicate ideas but rather with the intent of showing good will to one another.

We also vent emotions with habitual words, words called expletives. (Technically an expletive is a word that fills a hole in the linguistic structure: "there is"—an indefinable phrase—is an expletive construction.) "Ouch" is an expletive; we cannot define it, but it serves us well. "Oh," "well," "my goodness," and "damn" are conventional phrases, expletives with which we fill holes in our sentences. Some expletives, such as "my goodness" and "damn" have a literal meaning, but in their habitual use that meaning has been lost. In an individual's language, one might be able to gauge the extent of the emotion by the expletive employed, but some people use "damn" as casually as others use "gee," so one has to know the individual before deciding whether "damn" conveys intense anger or mild annoyance. Since these words are not used literally, arguing about what one "means to say" or "ought to say" is as fruitless as arguing about the meaning of "hello." Expletives are merely handy.

Nevertheless, there are social conventions governing the use of expletives, conventions that we learn at a very early age. We know perfectly well which expletives are acceptable within our families, among our own friends, in a formal speech. We know perfectly well which expletives will gain our acceptance in a church youth group or on an oil-rig crew. We know perfectly well what impressions we create by our choice of expletives. We do not gather this information by using a dictionary, but by paying attention to language in our society.

In using these three forms—linguistic function words, social exchanges, and expletives—we choose words not to convey meaning but to conform to the conventions of our linguistic society, and recognizing the intent behind words used this way is part of our fitting into our society. Though people vary, a large part of each person's language is language of convention. That kind of language is essential to us and it serves us very well in its limited uses; we could not do without it and we would be silly to try.

There is, however, a more complex use of language where words afford a way of describing experience and communicating ideas. To serve us this way, a word must convey literal meaning rather than merely be a convention, and to use words proficiently for this purpose, we must first recognize the relationship between words and their referents.

In the literal language, words are names for, or symbols of, referents. They have meaning only because people give them exchange value. We agree, for example, that "beer" will be the name for an alcoholic drink, but we might just as well agree to call the drink "plix" or "blonk." The important point is that the word "beer" has an exchange value that we have not given to "blonk" or "plix," neither of which is associated in our language with a real object. If you insist upon being different from others, you can call the drink "blonk"; you probably will not do any harm, but neither will you be understood. A word is not chosen as a symbol because of any intrinsic value in its sound or in its orthography; rather a word comes to stand for an object in a purely arbitrary way. Perhaps in class several people can supply from French, German, Spanish, Chinese and other languages the equivalent for the English "chair." Such an exercise will demonstrate that one sound is as good as another to stand for an object, providing the society has agreed upon its exchange value. When we learn vocabulary, at the age of two or the age of sixty-two, we are learning which symbols our society has agreed upon. If we want to communicate clearly in our society, we will use words to stand for objects in the same sense that other knowledgeable people use them.

Understanding literal meaning is not as easy as the previous paragraph might indicate. Because thought is more than sense images and concrete objects, command of language demands more than recognizing a material referent. If one is stuck in trying to define "chair," a concrete noun, she can always point to a chair, but some nouns stand for concepts; trying to define such an abstract noun—"love" for example—illustrates the difficulty of exact communication. Nevertheless each of us has an idea of what "love" stands for; we seldom confuse it with "like," "hate," "beauty," or "emotion"—all abstract nouns that bear some relation to "love"; and your idea of the concept is close enough to mine to allow us to communicate fairly well. In other words, if we adhere to society's generally accepted meanings, we can communicate ideas to one another using even abstract nouns, abstract adjectives, verbs and adverbs, and we can do so with surprising success.

But society's agreements change. Because language is a human phenomenon, words shift their meaning from time to time. Tracing shifting meanings—the narrowing of "coast" or the broadening of "butcher" for example—demonstrates further complications in our agreeing on a word's exchange value. Because we learn words within our society, though, we usually learn the current use and seldom mistakenly use a word in its archaic sense. As long as we remain functioning members of our society, we keep up with slight shifts in meaning or application and only rarely do we find that our individual use of a term is out of date with society's generally accepted use. (It does happen. You can easily see the problem in slang where "cool" has undergone several shifts in the last 50 years.)

After we know enough to use one, a dictionary helps us check on a word's generally accepted meaning in our culture and our time, but we gain most of our language skill simply from exposure to the society; indeed we acquire the bulk of our everyday vocabulary before we are old enough to use a dictionary.

Once we have acquired a word, it becomes an integral part of our mentality. The word "chair" and the object chair are so closely linked in our minds that we seldom have to consider consciously that particular word choice or search for the word for that object. Even when we are speaking of abstractions like love and beauty, we choose the word automatically when we are certain of our thought. This storing of words is a complex mental feat; to simplify for now, let us say that uttering "chair" or "love" or "coast"—even when we are using language to communicate meaning—is the result of deeply ingrained linguistic habit. Without that habit, we would have to search and experiment before every word of every sentence.

At the same time, habit can be a hindrance to effective communication.

Because language is such deeply ingrained habit, people sometimes fail to recognize words for what they are: an arbitrary set of symbols. Instead, people sometimes ascribe to language characteristics that it does not possess. We may have the deep feeling—not quite a thought—that the concept is made concrete in the word. Some primitive people refrained from saying their word for a god, fearing that the word would invoke the presence. Though we scoff at that, we are familiar with the notion that "if I don't say it, it won't happen" or we may feel that "passing on" is not as bad as "dying." But the word is not the thing. We may also feel that a word has intrinsic value. Though commonly heard, the phrase "bad word" is most often a misnomer, for words have no morals, conscience or intent. The writer's intent may be to harm, or his ideas may be invalid, but the word itself has neither vice nor virtue. When we remember that the word is not the thing and that words have no intrinsic value, we realize that we can alter and control our habits; we free ourselves to be masters of the language.

We also need to distinguish between habits that serve us—using language of convention easily and effectively; selecting and saying a word without conscious search—and habits that hinder us—using the handy phrase instead of finding the one that expresses the meaning we want to state.

When a speaker has no clear idea of what he wants to say, or when he needs to think too hard to find the words which exactly express a meaning, he often settles for handy, habitual phrases. Expletives often become handy phrases to fill the blank spots. In "I broke my damn pencil," for instance, "damn" does not convey literal meaning, but it does fill a hole in the sentence. For some people it fills out a comfortable rhythm pattern. What adjectives might replace "damn"? What would any one of them add to meaning? How do you feel about simply "I broke my pencil"? Does it lack anything or is it better than a sentence that contains an adjective for pencil?

Even more dangerous than using an expletive to fill blank spots is using a phrase that we feel expresses a literal meaning even when it does not. Our language is full of such catchwords. A catchword is a word (or phrase) that has been used so often that it comes readily to mind. We learn it the same way we learn all our language, by exposure to our society. The difference between conventional language and a catchword is that we use the first for social intercourse and it serves us well, but we use the second when we intend to be saying something but it fails us. The difference between an effective word and a catchword is that the effective word retains meaning (a generally accepted referent), but the catchword has been used so often and so loosely that it has shifted from a word of meaning to a mere habit word, useful for filling in the blank spots. "A meaningful relationship" sounds good, it is handy, and perhaps once, in a given context, it had a meaning, but it is no longer useful. Applied to everything from a business acquaintance to a love affair to a mystical event, it no longer says anything about experience. Such catchwords do little harm in our brief social conversation over coffee, but they hinder, rather than aid, communication and are especially dangerous if we think we are saying something which our listener comprehends clearly.

Why a catchword gains popularity is a sociological mystery. Perhaps the first speaker to use the phrase was respected or envied; perhaps the phrase had a nice rhythm; perhaps it was particularly effective in its original use and was repeated by people who wanted to mimic the effectiveness; perhaps in its original context, the word evoked a common emotional response. In any case, the word is repeated, gains current popularity, becomes mere habit, then works to conceal a lack of meaning. Like slang, the popular catchwords come and go in our language. Only careful examination of the language we hear/read and the language we use will identify those phrases that have lost effectiveness.

Our society also provides us with some handy words to avoid naming reality; those words are euphemisms. A euphemism is a word deliberately chosen in place of another word because the speaker thinks the euphemism somehow softens fact. We learn euphemisms just as we learn other words—by hearing them. A writer who does not want to describe her friend as a thief might say the friend "ripped-off" an article. Some subjects, such as bodily functions, are nearly always discussed in euphemistic terms because technical terms sound too clinical and few other terms are available. Sometimes the euphemism is, indeed, the better word choice; euphemisms concerning death might be kinder to the bereaved in his first shock. Like catchwords, euphemisms are sometimes handy, but, if the habitual use of euphemisms causes us to forget that stealing is wrong or to ignore death as a part of life, that habit inhibits clear thinking and clear communications. That habit might restrict an individual's thinking; when it becomes widespread it can restrict clear discussion within the society and, perhaps, alter the cultural view of topics like theft, death, or war.

Euphemisms and catch phrases can be deliberately chosen to deceive. When the writer successfully misleads, he has made the language work for him; however, the reader who pays so little attention as to be misled has been enslaved by language. To avoid being slaves, we must read, as well as write, with careful, critical attention to the words, to what they say and to what they fail to say.

This essay has probably not introduced you to any uses of language with which you were totally unfamiliar. Each of us uses language of convention and language of literal meaning; each of us lets easy habit get in the way of thinking; each of us resorts to catchword and euphemism. The purpose of this essay has been to make you consciously aware of the difference between habit and considered choice because moving language from subconscious to conscious activity insures attentive use....

**For discussion**

*Content*

1. Larson says that we learn at an early age which expletives are acceptable in our groups. What expletives were acceptable for you to use when you were a child? Which are acceptable for you to use now? Do women and men follow different rules about which expletives are acceptable?

2. What are the three uses of "language of convention" Larson names and explains? Are the explanations clear to you? What makes them clear?

3. In your understanding, how does language of convention (what I referred to on page 37 as "appropriate noise") differ from language of literal meaning?

4. Larson's example of a catchword is "meaningful relationship." What other examples of catchwords can you think of?

5. What is Larson's thesis or main point?

6. What is the difference between stating a thesis and stating a purpose? What difference do you see between these two sentence beginnings: "The essay's thesis is that..." and "The essay's purpose is to..." ?

*Style*

1. What is the purpose or function of paragraphs nine and 10? How do they guide you as a reader?

2. In paragraph 12 ("Understanding literal meaning..."), Larson uses "she" to refer to an indefinite "one." In paragraph 17 ("Because language is..."), she refers to an indefinite writer as "he." What do you think of alternating "she" and "he" as a deliberate attempt to avoid using the false generic "he" all the time to refer to an indefinite antecedent?

3. Do you find any unnecessary or pretentious words in Larson's essay? Do you find economical sentences, those with only the necessary words? Give specific examples.

**For writing**

1. Write a paragraph about greetings or about cursing: Do women and men use different greetings? Do they curse differently? Do women and men learn different rules about polite exchange?

2. Write a paper about euphemisms: Are they harmful or beneficial to you and to other people? Develop your paragraph with euphemisms you have actually heard people use.

3. If you know a language other than English, write a paragraph in which you explain how any one of the complexities discussed in Chapter Two (ritual/literal language, wordiness, pretentious language, active/passive structures, euphemism) functions in the other language.

# The Passive Voice, or The Secret Agent

## Rita Mae Brown

AVOID THE PASSIVE VOICE WHENEVER POSSIBLE. University term papers bleed with the passive voice. It seems to be the accepted style of Academia. Dump it.

The times you need to use the passive voice are as follows: 1. You don't know the active subject or you can't easily state that subject. Hence, "The store was robbed." 2. The subject is plainly evident from the context. 3. Tact or social delicacy prevents you from identifying the active subject. This also allows you or your character to pass the buck. 4. The passive connects one sentence with another. "She rose to sing and was listened to with enthusiasm by the crowd."

Deleted agents teach us how devious people can be. Let's look at a benign example: "The murderer was caught yesterday." Who caught him/her? Perhaps the writer doesn't know. On the other hand, perhaps the murderer is the writer's brother and she doesn't want you to know. Knock out the agent and you're fine until someone has the brains to question you.

Our government displays unusual genius in its official style. They have sanctified the deleted agent. Here are two ripe examples.

"Secret commitments to other nations *are* not *sensed* as infringing on the treaty-making powers of the Senate, because they are not publicly *acknowledged*."[1] (Italics mine.)

How about this one? "It was there thought best to commence with the addition of 25,000 regulars to the existing establishment of 10,000."[2]

Dear reader, tell me, who thought it best to add 25,000 regulars? Who decided on 25,000? Same person? Different people? Squadrons of people?

The use of deleted agents in government documents demonstrates vividly that language has a moral function. Language, supposedly, should tell us something. In these examples the opposite is true: Language is used to obscure. What is the difference then between the authors of the Pentagon Papers and the authors of Soviet documents? When a government seeks to evade responsibility, it no longer governs by consent; it governs by guile and possibly by the club. I am not suggesting that our government is analogous to the Soviet Union's. Let's just say that when it comes to accepting responsibility, both systems leave something to be desired. The irony of government duplicity via its choice of writing style is that removing the agents of responsibility contributes to making people feel powerless, alienated. They fall away from the system. Don't then turn around, Mr. Elected Official, and squeal and holler that voter turnout is low. Participation depends on a sense of responsibility. If government people are unwilling to take responsibility, why should the public?

Language exerts hidden power, like the moon on the tides. You can think, "Hell, so government documents are loaded with deleted agents. So what? You're making a big deal out of it because you're a writer, so you see writing as the basis for everything." Not exactly. I see language as the basis for civilization. Without language we couldn't form governments. We're doing a piss-poor job of it with language but it's still better than being controlled by the physically strongest person in the tribe. The abuse and debasement of English in government documents has serious long-range consequences. It creates public cynicism and eventually encourages disrespect for the government and for law. You and I have a right to know who does what to whom, when, and where. If we don't start to demand that, we deserve what we get.

Another infamous trick with deleted agents is to appeal to the "generic person." Journalists do this a lot. You get this construction: "It is known" or "It is understood" or "It is thought." Who knows? Who understands? Who thinks? What's going on is a con job. The suppressed deleted agent is really "All right-thinking people know" or, closer to the truth, "All people who agree with me understand." You'd be surprised how often people fall for that because no one wants to be out in the cold. Agreeing with the speaker or writer means that you're "in the know."

Passive adjectives give you another opportunity to lie. They occur immediately before a noun. The agent can't show up in this type of construction, so an assertion can slip by unchallenged. Here's a good example: "Men regard as amusing this *exaggerated* fad of trying to substitute 'Ms.' for 'Mrs.'"[3] Exaggerated by whom?

Nominalized passive provides us with yet another twist. Here a verb becomes a noun. So *refuse* now becomes *refusal*; *destroy/destruction*; *enjoy/enjoyment*; *use/use*, and so on. You can obscure responsibility with the nominalized passive. "*Impoundment* of billions of dollars of allocated funds represents an unparalleled *seizure* of power by the White House. How can a structure impound money? It looks as though we've been given an agent, but we've been duped. A house can't seize money. Yeah, well, it's the White House. What does that mean? Does it mean the President? The agent of responsibility is halfway obscured. It could be the President but it could also be the downstairs maid. Does the President know what his minion has done? See what I mean?

In this example of using the nominalized passive, the agent isn't expressed at all: "What is needed is more intentional control, not less." Control by whom?

Experiencer deletion is one of my favorites. Putting this technique in the mouth of a gossipy character yields humorous or vituperative results. Politically, of course, it serves exactly the same function. What you do here is, you remove the person responsible for the perception. In most usage this perception is understood to belong to the speaker/writer. When the experiencer pronoun is stated it is usually a first-person pronoun.

"You seem to me to be getting careless." The speaker is taking responsibility for her/his perception. But "You seem to be getting careless" removes the perceiver. This implies that other people share this perception. What other people? The entire world knows you are careless. Mercy.

Try attributive adjectives. Those are *appropriate/inappropriate; proper, effective, acceptable, clear*, and the like. "The outlines of an effective technology are already clear." Clear and effective for whom? Imagine this sentence buried in a paper before your city's planning commission. The presenters of the paper want to tear down low-income housing and put up a high-rise for upper-middle-income people. Attributor adjectives seek to suppress the emotive element in any conflict and present information in a "scientific" manner.

When all else fails, why take responsibility? Try the flat-out lie. Here is my absolute favorite. When a reporter pointed out to Ron Ziegler, Nixon's press secretary, that Nixon's statements were considerably contradictory, Ziegler calmly stated before God and America that the President's previous statements were "inoperative."[4]

The passive voice, while grammatically useful, must be handled with care. Aside from the above usages of the passive, that voice can also signify a withdrawal from the world. Not feeling responsible is a form of withdrawal. If you want to think of it as grammatical existentialism, okay. Of course, I think when existentialism came over here from France it should have been packed right back to Paris. Let the French suffer with it. Americans have better things to do with their time.

A good example of passive voice being consciously used to illustrate withdrawal comes from Hemingway's *Old Man and the Sea*. (Another writer, Bertha Harris, brought it to my attention.) "He did not like to look at the fish anymore since he had *been mutilated*. When the fish had been *hit* it was as though he himself *were hit*." and "'But man *is* not *made* for defeat,'" he said. "'A man can be *destroyed* and not *defeated*'" (Italics mine).

Reading that passage makes me sad, not only because of what Hemingway is writing about but because such a talent belittled himself with his he-man charade. When you're as good as Hemingway, gender is irrelevant—informative but irrelevant.

Being alert to the passive voice makes you technically stronger. It also sharpens your senses for everyday life.

**Notes**

1.  Neil Sheehan, Hedrick Smith, E.W. Kenworthy, and Fox Butterfield, *The Pentagon Papers* (New York: Bantam Books, 1971).

2.  Gaillard Hunt, ed. *The Writings of James Madison* (New York: G. P. Putnam's Sons, 1900).

3.  For this and other examples, I am indebted to the pioneering work of Julia Penelope (Stanley), and in particular to her groundbreaking discussions of the passive voice in "The Stylistics of Beliefs" in *Teaching About Doublespeak*, edited by Daniel J. Dietrich (the National Council of Teachers, 1976) and "Passive Motivation" in *Foundations of Language* 13 (1975).

4.  *Facts on File,* Vol. 33, No. 1694 (April 15-21), 1973.

**For discussion**

*Content*

1.  What is Brown's thesis? Explain how each paragraph illustrates that point.

2.  In what situations would you choose to use passive voice?

3.  In what situations would you choose to use active voice?

*Style*

1.  Identify the subject in each sentence of Brown's first paragraph. Is she following her own advice to use the active voice whenever possible? Does she follow that advice throughout the essay? (Is "her own" in my question a wordy phrase?)

2. Examine and describe the essay's overall organization. What is the effect of Brown's manner of leading up to "the flat-out lie" and then "withdrawal from the world"? What would be the effect of starting with "the flat-out lie"?

3. This essay is a chapter from Brown's book of advice to writers, *Starting from Scratch.* When Brown says "you," she is speaking directly to her reading audience, as I do in this book. Is that an effective choice? When is "you" not an effective choice for a writer?

4. Explain the essay's title: how is the passive voice the secret agent?

## For writing

1. Analyze a newspaper story. If the writer uses passive voice, has she or he used it for one of the reasons Brown cites, or has the writer used passive voice carelessly, for no reason?

# Problems of Language
# in a Democratic State: 1982

## June Jordan

IN AMERICA, YOU CAN SEGREGATE THE PEOPLE, but the problems will travel. From slavery to equal rights, from state suppression of dissent to crime, drugs and unemployment, I can't think of a single supposedly Black issue that hasn't wasted the original Black target group and then spread like the measles to outlying white experience.

If slavery was all right, for example, if state violence and law could protect property rights against people, then the Bossman could call out the state against striking white workers. And he did. And nobody bothered to track this diseased idea of the state back to the first victims: Black people. Concepts of the state as the equal servant of all the people, as the resource for jobs or subsistence income; concepts of the state as a regulator of the economy to preserve the people from hunger and sickness and doom, these are ideas about a democratic state that have been raised, repeatedly, by minority Americans without majority support.

Most Americans have imagined that problems affecting Black life follow from pathogenic attributes of Black people and not from malfunctions of the state. Most Americans have sought to identify themselves with the powerful interests that oppress poor and minority peoples, perhaps hoping to keep themselves on the shooting side of the target range.

Nevertheless and notwithstanding differences of power, money, race, gender, age and class, there remains one currency common to all of us. There remains one thing that makes possible exchange, shared memory, self-affirmation and collective identity. And isn't that currency known and available to everybody regardless of this and that? And isn't that common currency therefore the basis for a democratic state that will not discriminate between the stronger and the weak? And isn't that indispensable, indiscriminate, or non-discriminating, currency our language? Isn't that so?

I remember very clearly how, when I first became a teacher, back in the 60s, popular wisdom had it that the only American boys and girls who could neither read nor write were Black. This was a function of the poverty of culture or vice versa: I forget which. But anyway, Black children had something wrong with them. They couldn't talk right. They couldn't see straight. They never heard a word you said to them. They seemed to think that they should throw their books around the room or out the windows. And another thing, their parents were no good or they were alcoholics or illiterate or, anyhow, uninterested, inept, and rotten role models.

Obviously, school was cool. It was just the students who kept messing up. In those days teachers were frequently brave, depressed, dedicated, idealistic, tireless, and overworked, but they were never accountable for their failures to teach Black children how to read and write. That was not their responsibility. That was a minority problem of language, in a democratic state.

At the least, most Americans have tried to avoid what they call trouble: opposition to the powerful is a pretty sure way to get yourself in trouble.

But lately these same Americans have begun to understand that trouble does not start somewhere on the other side of town. It seems to originate inside the absolute middle of the homemade cherry pie. In our history, the state has failed to respond to the weak. State power serves the powerful. You could be white, male, Presbyterian and heterosexual besides, but if you get fired or if you get sick tomorrow, you might as well be Black, for all the state will want to hear from you. More and more of the majority is entering that old minority experience of no power: unless you stay strong, state power does not want to sweetly wait upon you.

And when minority problems become the problems of the majority, or when the weak stay weak and the strong become weak, then something does seem to be mighty wrong with the whole situation.

I suggest that as long as state power serves the powerful, more and more of the people of this democracy will become the powerless. As long as we have an economic system protected by the state rather than state protection against economic vagaries and depredations, then your and my welfare become expendable considerations.

Less than two decades after the 60s and I find national reports of a dismal discovery occurring at Harvard, at the nearby community college and on the state campus where I teach. Apparently the minority problem of language has become a majority problem of low-level reading and writing skills. Every university in the nation now recognizes that most of its students seriously lack those analytical abilities that devolve from disciplined and critical and confident and regular exercise of the mind. Students cannot express themselves, clearly. They cannot judge if any essay is gibberish or coherent. They cannot defend a point of view. They cannot examine a written document and then accurately relate its meaning or uncover its purpose. And, either they have nothing to say, or else they talk funny. How did this happen?

I know what went down for Black kids, the ones people dismissed as unruly, unteachable. What those children brought into the classroom: their language, their style, their sense of humor, their ideas of smart, their music, their need for a valid history and a valid literature—history and literature that included their faces and their voices—and serious teachers who would tell them "C'mon, I see you. Let me give you a hand,"—all of this was pretty well ridiculed and rejected, or denied to them.

Mostly Black kids ran into a censorship of their living particular truth, past and present. Nobody wanted to know what they felt or to teach them to think for themselves. Nobody wanted to learn anything from them. Education was a one-way number leading from the powerful teacher to the trapped parolee. Nobody wanted to hear any more political arguments raised by the fact of certain children whom the compulsory school system consistently failed. Not too many people wanted to grant that maybe schools really are political institutions teaching power to the powerful and something unpalatable and self-destructive to the weak. Not too many people wanted to reexamine their fantasies about the democratizing function of American education.

And when Black dropout rates across the country soared and stabilized at irreversible tragic heights because the kids figured, "If you don't know and don't care about who I am then why should I give a damn about what you say you do know about?" The popular wisdom smiled, satisfied: Good riddance to a minority uproar.

But meanwhile, white youngsters fared only somewhat better. These are American kids required to master something described as the English language. These are American kids required to study what's accurately described as English literature. When will a legitimately American language, a language including Nebraska, Harlem, New Mexico, Oregon, Puerto Rico, Alabama and working-class life and freeways and Pac-Man become the language studied and written and glorified in the classroom?

When will a legitimate American literature rightfully supplant nostalgia for Queen Mary? Who teaches white kids to think for themselves? Who has ever wanted white children to see their own faces, clearly, to hear their own voices, clearly?

I believe Americans have wanted their sons and daughters to write just well enough to fill out a job application. Americans have wanted their children to think just well enough to hold that job. Not too many people have wanted to start trouble, or get into it.

So I would say that our schools have served most of us extremely well. We have silenced or eliminated minority children. We have pacified white children into barely competent imitations of their fear-ridden parents.

But now there are no jobs and, consequently, somebody needs to write aggressive new editorials. Somebody needs to write aggressive new statements of social design and demand. More and more Americans finally want to hear new sentences, new ideas, to articulate this unprecedented, and painful, *majority* situation. But is there anybody new around the house? Someone who can think and organize a solution to this loss of privilege, this loss of power?

I am talking about majority problems of language in a democratic state, problems of a currency that someone has stolen and hidden away and then homogenized into an official "English" language that can only express non-events involving nobody responsible, or lies. If we lived in a democratic state our language would have to hurtle, fly, curse, and sing, in all the common American names, all the undeniable and representative participating voices of everybody here. We would not tolerate the language of the powerful and, thereby, lose all respect for words, *per se*. We would make our language conform to the truth of our many selves and we would make our language lead us into the equality of power that a democratic state must represent.

This is not a democratic state. And we put up with that. We do not have a democratic language. And we put up with that. We have the language of the powerful that perpetuates that power through the censorship of dissenting views.

This morning I watched tv. Four white men sat around talking about some ostensibly important public issue. Everyone of them was wealthy, powerful, unaccountable to you and me and also accustomed to the nationwide delivery of his opinions on a lot of subjects. Except for Tom Wicker, who can't shake his trembling southern drawl for the life of him, they might be quadruplets from an identical Ma and Pa. After about half an hour of this incestuous display, the moderator announced that, after the commercial, he'd send these "experts" out of the studio and replace them with quote a free for all unquote.

I could hardly wait.

After the break, the moderator returned with his new guests: four white men, everyone of them wealthy, powerful, unaccountable to you and me, and also accustomed to the nationwide delivery of his opinions! So much for a quote free for all unquote.

When I say that those particular white men all sounded alike, I am not exaggerating. All of them used the language of the state seeking to transcend accountability to the people, as in: "The Federal Reserve has been forced to raise interest rates" or "It is widely believed..." or "While I can't comment on that I would like to emphasize that it has been said, many times..." or "When you take all of these factors into consideration it is obvious..." or "Unemployment has emerged as a number one concern." Is somebody really saying those words? Is any real life affected by those words? Should we really just relax into the literally non-descript, the irresponsible language of the passive voice? Will the passive voice lead us safely out of the action? Will the action and the actors behind it leave us alone so long as we do not call them by their real names?

We have begun to live in the land of Polyphemus. Poor Polyphemus! He was this ugly and gigantic, one-eyed Cyclops who liked to smash human beings on rocks and then eat them. But one day he happened to capture the wily and very restless Ulysses who, one night, gave Polyphemus so much wine that the poor lunk fell into a drunken sleep. Taking advantage of his adversary's discomposure, Ulysses and a couple of his buddies seized a great stick and heated its tip in the nearby, handily burning, fire. When the tip was glowing hot, Ulysses and his buddies stuck that thing into the one eye of Polyphemus, twisting it deeply into that socket, and blinding him.

Polyphemus howled a terrible loud howl. He was in much pain. "What is the name of the man who has done this to me?" he cried. And the wily Ulysses answered him, "My name is No One."

Later, several other Cyclops raced up to Polyphemus, because they had heard him howling.

"Who did this to you?" they asked.

Polyphemus screamed his accusation for the world to hear: "No One has done this to me!"

Well, when the fellow Cyclops heard that they decided that if No One had done this to Polyphemus, it must be the will of the gods. Hence nothing could or should be done about the blinding of Polyphemus. And so nothing was done.

And after a while, Ulysses and his men escaped, unnoticed by the blinded Cyclops.

I share this story with you because it remains one of my favorites and because it was the only reason I stayed awake during my second year of Latin.

And I tell you about Polyphemus because we seem determined to warp ourselves into iddy-biddy imitations of his foolishness. To repeat: The other Cyclops decided that if no one had done anything then nothing was to be done. What happened to him represented the will of the gods.

I worry about that notion of a democratic state. Do we really believe 11.5% unemployment represents God's will? Is that why the powerful say, "Unemployment has emerged?" If that construction strikes your ear as somehow ridiculous because, quite rightly, it conjures up the phenomenon of unemployment as if it emerges from nowhere into nothing, then what sense do you make of this very familiar construction used, very often, by the power-*less*: "I lost my job." Who in his or her right mind loses a job? What should I understand if you say something like that to me? Should I suppose that one morning you got up and drank your coffee and left the house but, then, you just couldn't find your job? If that's not what anybody means then why don't we say, "GM laid off half the night shift. They fired me."

Who did what to whom? Who's responsible?

We have a rather foggy mess and not much hope for a democratic state when the powerless agree to use a language that blames the victim for the deeds of the powerful.

As in: "I was raped." What should we conclude from that most sadly passive use of language? By definition, nobody in her right mind can say that, and mean it. For rape to occur, somebody real has to rape somebody else, equally real. Rape presupposes a rapist and his victim. The victim must learn to make language tell her own truth: He raped me.

But the victim accommodates to power. The victim doesn't want anymore trouble; someone has already fired him or someone has already raped her, and so the victim uses words to evade a further confrontation with the powerful.

By itself, our language cannot refuse to reflect the agonizing process of alienation from ourselves. If we collaborate with the powerful then our language will lose its currency as a means to tell the truth in order to change the truth.

In our own passive ways, we frequently validate the passive voice of a powerful state that seeks to conceal the truth from us, the people. And this seems to me an ok situation only for a carnivorous idiot like Polyphemus.

I would not care if, for example, instead of bashing men's heads against the rock, Polyphemus decided to watch tv, every evening. I wouldn't even care if he, consequently, became addicted to that ultimate passive experience, although maybe that's why he thought that when you murder somebody it's not such a big deal: the agony will last only a couple of minutes until the much more exciting drama of Ajax the Foaming Cleanser takes over the screen. Some people *should* be pacified. Polyphemus was one of those.

But I really think that a democratic state presupposes a small number of psychopathic giants and a rather huge number of ordinary men and women who cannot afford to resemble Polyphemus.

In September of this year, a huge number of ordinary men and women came out of their houses to make an outcry against the language of the state. Four hundred thousand Israelis plunged into the streets of Tel Aviv to demand an investigation of the massacre in Lebanon. They insisted. They must know: who did what to whom?

Against official pronouncements such as: "Security measures have been taken," or "It seems that an incident has taken place inside the camps," nearly half a million Israelis, after the massacre at Sabra and Shatilah, demanded another kind of language: an inquiry into the truth, an attribution of responsibility, a forcing of the powerful into an accountability to the people. As Jacobo Timmerman writes in his Israeli *Journal of the Longest War*, it did seem to him that the democratic nature of the state lay at risk.

All the summer leading to Sabra and Shatilah I lived with the Israeli invasion of Lebanon. It did not kill me. As Timmerman has described our remarkable endurance of the unendurable, "...nobody has yet died of anguish." But that invasion killed other people: tens of thousands died and I watched it happen. I sat down and I read the newspaper accounts or I listened to the nightly news. The uniformity of official state language appalled me. How could this be 1984 in 1982?

I saw American reporters respectfully quote Philip Habib as having proclaimed, "This is a ceasefire" even as the whistling bombs drowned out the broadcast. When Menachem Begin declared, "This is not an invasion," his statement appeared in print and on the screen, everywhere as the world news of the day, even as the Israeli tanks entered Beirut.

During that same September, 1982, and shortly before Sabra and Shatilah, Israeli planes bombed the houses and the hospitals and the schools of West Beirut for twenty-two hours, unceasingly. But this was something, evidently, other than a massacre. Our American newspapers and newsmen told us that this was a "tightening of the noose" in order to "speed negotiations at the peace table."

But when one word finally burst through that foggy mess of American mass media, and when that word was *massacre*, who took it to the streets? Who called for an investigation of the government and moved to put the leadership on trial? Who said *stop*?

It happened in another country where the citizens believe it matters when the state controls the language. It didn't happen here. It happened when the citizens decided that the passive voice in a democracy means something evil way beyond a horribly mixed metaphor. It didn't happen here.

It happened in Israel. And we Americans should be ashamed.

But we were looking for a language of the people; we were wondering why our children do not read or write.

Last week a delegation of Black women graduate students invited me to address a large meeting that loud yellow flyers described as "A Black Sisters Speak-Out" followed by two exclamation points. I went to the gathering with great excitement. Obviously, we would deal with one or another crisis; whether national or international, I simply wondered which enormous and current quandary would be the one most of the women wanted to discuss.

During the warm-up period one of the women announced that we should realize our debt to the great Black women who have preceded us in history. "We are here," she said, "because of the struggle of women like," and here her sentence broke down. She tried again. "We have come this far because of all the Black women who fought for us like, like..." and, here, only one name came to her mouth: "Sojourner Truth!" she exclaimed, clearly relieved to think of it, but, also embarrassed because she couldn't keep going. "And," she tried to continue, nevertheless, "the other Black women like"...but here somebody in the audience spoke to her rescue, by calling aloud the name of Harriet Tubman. At this point I interrupted to observe that now we had *two* names for 482 years of our Afro-American history.

"What about Mary McLeod Bethune?" somebody else ventured at last. "That's three!" I remarked, in the manner of a referee: "Do we have a fourth?"

There was silence. Thoroughly embarrassed, the first woman looked at me and said, "Listen. I could come up with a whole list of Black women if my life depended on it."

"Well," I had to tell her, "It does."

But even this official erasure of their faces and their voices was not what those students wanted to discuss. Something more hurtful than that was bothering them. As one by one these Black women rose to express themselves, the problem was this:

> A lotta times and I'm walking on campus and I see another Black woman and so I'll say *"Hi"* but then she won't answer me and I don't understand it because I don't mean we have to get into a conversation or do all of that like talking to me but you could say, *"Hi."* If you see me you could say, *"Hi."*

I was stunned. From looking around the room I knew there were Black women right there who face critical exposure to bodily assault, alcoholic mothers, and racist insults and graffiti in the dorms. I knew that the academic curriculum omitted the truth of their difficult lives. I knew that they certainly would not be found welcome in the marketplace after they got their degrees.

But the insistent concern was more intimate and more pitiful and more desperate than any of those threatening conditions might suggest. The abject plea of those Black women students was ruthlessly minimal: "If you see me, you could say, '*Hi.*' Let me know that you see me; let me know I exist. Never mind a conversation between us, but, please, if you see me, you could say, '*Hi.*'"

Who can tell these Americans that they should trust the language available to them? Who will presume to criticize their faltering, their monosyllables, their alienation from a literature that condemns them to oblivion?

If you choose, you can consider this desperation a minority problem in America, today, and then try to forget about it. But I believe this invisibility and this silence of the real and various peoples of our country is a political situation of language that every one of us must move against, because our lives depend on it.

I believe we will have to eliminate the passive voice from our democracy. We will have to drown out the official language of the powerful with our own mighty and conflicting voices or we will perish as a people. Until we can tell our children that the powerful people are the children, themselves, then I do not see why we should expect our children to read or write anything.

Until we can tell our children that truth is the purpose of our American language, and that the truth is what they know and feel and need, then I believe our children will continue to act as though the truth is just something that will get you into trouble.

I believe that somebody real has blinded America in at least one eye. And, in the same way that so many Americans feel that "we have lost our jobs," we suspect that we have lost our country.

*We know that we do not speak the language.*

And I ask you: well, what are we going to do about it?

### For discussion

*Content*

1. What is your considered response to Jordan's statement, "maybe schools really are political institutions teaching power to the powerful and something unpalatable and self-destructive to the weak (paragraph 13)?

2. Identify Jordan's sentences that indicate that people can make important choices about their language. Do you agree that people have linguistic choices? What differences do the choices make?

3. What is Jordan's thesis? How does the incident at the African-American women students' gathering that Jordan relates at the end of the essay illustrate her thesis?

*Style*

1. Examine Jordan's sentences in paragraph two for parallel structure and for variety in length. Is the three-word sentence effective?

2. Rewrite the examples of passive structures in paragraph 25 so that each is an active structure. What main changes do you see in the sentences and in what they convey in active voice?

3. Do you know "unpalatable"? Does your not knowing a word make it a pretentious word? Is "unpalatable" (paragraph 13) a pretentious word in that context?

4. Do you find economical sentences in Jordan's essay? Give specific examples.

**For writing**

1. Watch an issues program (about unemployment, interest rates, taxes, education, nuclear waste siting, homosexuals in the military, for example) on television and write about the language of the people who analyze the issue. Which speakers use what Jordan calls "the language of the state"? Which speakers don't? Why do you think the speakers chose the language they chose?

# Speaking Out

## Julia Penelope

....EUPHEMISMS PRETTY UP PEOPLE, objects, behaviors, and events perceived by members of a culture as bad, immoral, or terrible, and they allow us to distance ourselves conceptually from "them." We forget that we are "they." To gauge the degree of repugnance with which people perceive someone or something, we need only count how many euphemisms are available in the language. Death and dying, for example, aren't perceived as celebratory events in western cultures, and we have numerous euphemisms to avoid mentioning death explicitly: "pass away," "gone to one's reward," "pushing up daisies," "gone to heaven," "meeting St. Peter," "crossed the final bridge."

Poverty and aging are also aspects of the real world speakers euphemize. In a society that boasts of the wealth only a few actually enjoy, poor people are a repugnant embarrassment, and expressions that suppress explicit reference to the people who live in poverty proliferate apace with superficial attempts to provide them with better living conditions: "the poor," "the poverty-stricken," "the homeless," "the economically disadvantaged." These descriptions make both victims and agents invisible as people and hide the fact that the structure of u.s. society perpetuates poverty. Poverty itself is an abstraction made purposeful agent in *poverty-stricken*, in which the human agents and victims are suppressed, as though the conditions "struck" the unnamed. Because PUD [ed:. Patriarchal Universe of Discourse] values youth, or the appearance of youth, especially in women, English provides euphemisms for aging that hide our underlying fear of the process: "the elderly," "senior citizens," "advanced in age," and "over the hill." Many people believe that whatever they refuse to talk about doesn't exist or is less real and euphemism is one device for avoiding whatever realities they wish to deny.

Neil Postman has maintained that "euphemisms are a means through which a culture may alter its imagery and by doing so change its style, its priorities, and its values" (1982, 262), but, as the editors of *Time* magazine observed, "the persistent growth of euphemism...represents a danger to thought and action, since its fundamental intent is to deceive" (1982, 256).[1] But western culture perceives some aspects of reality as so horrible that euphemizing them is virtually impossible, and the descriptions that follow these negative concepts dehumanize the people victimized by them. One of those things-that-cannot-be-euphemized is the idea of being incapacitated or disabled in some way. The words and phrases that describe physical limitations reflect the negative attitudes we've learned. We think of being able to do something as normal, and being incapable as inherently negative. Mobility is positively valued; immobility is negative. Conceptually, *able/not able* are fixed in a binary, either/or relation in which ability to perform is assumed. The way we conceptualize abilities focuses our vocabulary negatively on what we cannot do, on what we lack, rather than what we can do. When all or part of our bodies can't perform in ways thought of as normal, we are described as *dis*abled. There are no positive ways of thinking or talking about the abilities of people who have physical or anatomical limitations; what they can't do becomes their only identifying characteristic and their many other qualities are conceptually suppressed.

People who cannot perform one physical activity or another are thought of as "defective" or "deformed." They are "disabled," "crippled," "handicapped," or "physically-challenged." We have no positive ways to describe something we cannot do. There aren't even any neutral terms in the English vocabulary. The only phrases that point us toward a different way of thinking about the range of human abilities are "differently abled," and the acronym T.A.B.s, 'temporarily able-bodied', which reminds the able-bodied that an automobile accident, a fire or disease may make them suddenly unable to perform acts they take for granted. Being able is good; being unable is bad, and the idea that there are events in our lives we cannot control frightens us. Yet, there are areas of our lives over which we don't have control, and some disabled people consider the phrase "*differently abled*" to be a ridiculous euphemism because there are things they cannot do and this fact is a reality of their lives they have to deal with every day. Euphemizing their reality doesn't change their lives; shifting the focus away from what they can't do to what they can is a useless pretense. As Catherine Odette has commented, saying that she is "differently abled" suggests that she's able to perform differently, that, instead of walking up a hill, she can fly to the top.

Yet, we must confront how we think and examine the meaning of what we say. Recognizing how our language hurts others and admitting that we don't know how to change begin the process of confronting the conceptual restrictions that determine the language we use. We can certainly refuse to use words and phrases that extend the language of disability metaphorically as negative descriptions of events and situations. In common usage, both *cripple* and *paralyze* are used negatively to describe an inability to act: "Losing their best wide receiver has *crippled* Chicago's offense," "I was *paralyzed* by fear." Chicago's offense wasn't crippled; it wasn't as good as it would have been with their best wide receiver in the line-up. We may be unable to move or act because we're afraid, but we aren't paralyzed. Similarly, because both seeing and hearing metaphorically represent knowledge or understanding in common expressions (e.g., "I see what you mean," "I hear you") *blind* and *deaf* are frequently used metaphorically to mean ignorant or unaware.[2] Such changes aren't difficult, and thinking about what we say commits us to changing how we think.

Less obvious immediately are syntactic maneuvers in descriptions of disabilities. One in particular, the phrase "hidden disabilities," was brought to my attention by Anne Leighton when she gave a workshop on the subject called "Who's Doing the Hiding?" Her title challenges the distortion created by the agentless passive *hidden* which seems to "modify" *disabilities* as though someone were hiding a disability. The buried proposition of *hidden* suggests that individuals purposely hide their disabilities and implies a secretive intent on their part. In fact, this passive modifier functions as a perceptual reversal, making disabled people responsible for the act of hiding when what is meant is that others are unable to perceive the disability. That is, there are no apparent visual signals to cue people who are strangers to someone who is deaf or chronically ill or has heart trouble, diabetes, or arthritis. The description reflects the assumption that everyone is able-bodied unless they tell us otherwise, and puts responsibility for declaring the existence of disabilities on those who have them rather than on the individuals who don't perceive them. As more and more of us are disabled by chemicals in our food, poisons in our water, and the toxicity of our environment, the practice of assuming able-bodiedness becomes less supportable as the probability increases that we, or someone we know, has Epstein-Barr Syndrome or some other type of environmental illness (EI).

Regardless of the specifics of disabilities, this area of our vocabulary requires complete restructuring, as my own descriptive efforts indicate. There is probably no good reason to think positively of disabilities, but perpetuating negative descriptions serves no useful purpose either. As the numbers of those disabled by war, automobile accidents, job-related illnesses, malnutrition, drugs, and neurological diseases increase, the most feasible approach is accepting the idea that being disabled is a permanent aspect of our reality. Although I've tried to avoid the negative descriptions of PUD, I haven't succeeded nearly as well as I wanted to, at least in part because I am writing *generally*. Kate Moran has pointed out to me that one way of avoiding the negative structures I'm discussing is to speak specifically—"She has cerebral palsy," "The child was born with club feet," "I use sign language to communicate with those who can't hear." If we're to change our thinking about physical inabilities, we'll have to change the way we describe them, and my futile efforts should convince readers of the need to unlearn PUD ways of thinking as well as illustrating the difficulties involved. Until we achieve that, however, we must seek ways of describing our bodies that acknowledge the existence of disabilities without attempting to euphemize or ignore them. We may not be able to learn to think differently about abilities immediately, but we can refuse to use words like *blind, deaf, cripple*, and *lame* as negative metaphors. We don't need to call someone "blind" when we mean they're unaware of something, or to talk about "lame excuses" and a "crippled economy."

Euphemism may properly fail as a way to describe people who are disabled, but in other areas of our lives, equally insupportable euphemistic expressions proliferate. In my analysis of sex-specific nouns and verbs, I showed how actions and behaviors attributed to women are thought of as inherently negative. Yet, there are certain acts and behaviors identified as both negative and primarily male, such as rape and battering. In contrast to the negative vocabularies that describe women and physical abilities, euphemisms abound for male violence. In these cases, men have created a plethora of euphemisms to downplay their violence and hide their sexual exploitation of women and children, and these expressions quickly find their way into common usage. Men beat their wives, but the media talk about *spouse abuse, battered spouses,* and *domestic violence.* In the last phrase, *domestic* hides male agency and focuses our attention on the places where men beat their wives and children, dwellings, disguising violent acts as well as erasing the male agents. Men rape children, but we talk about *incest, sexual abuse* and *molestation*, making the men who commit crimes of violence against children invisible. The most euphemistic word for describing how men exploit children sexually we inherited from the Greeks: *pedophilia.* Translated literally, it means 'love of children'; 'love' not only euphemizes sexual activities but disguises male predation.

Men create euphemisms to control how we perceive and interpret their actions. These aren't descriptions we should emulate because they distort reality, making the bad seem good and the merely innocuous seem wonderful. Yet, some women prefer euphemisms for the same reason. A booth selling turkey-basters at the Michigan Women's Music Festival, for example, advertised "parthenogenetic wands" for sale, fostering the illusion that sperm aren't involved in Lesbian pregnancies. Sado-masochists are now describing themselves as "differently pleasured," a description that accomplishes several conceptual tricks at once. First, it exploits the positive phrase "differently abled" and the oppressed people it refers to by linking sado-masochists to them. Because being differently abled isn't a matter of choice, "differently pleasured" suggests that sado-masochists haven't chosen their sexual behaviors and they are oppressed for something they can't help. Second, it obliterates the fact that pain is the defining element of sado-masochism, and that its sexuality requires humiliation, degradation, and elaborate "scenes" based on stereotyped power-over relationships: teacher/student, parent/child, master/slave, nazi/Jew. Third, the phrase uses women's attempts to value differences (such as class, race, and ethnic background) positively to suggest that sado-masochism is nothing more than another difference we should not only tolerate but think of as a good thing.

There is a point at which we identify the function of euphemism in our speech with politeness and kindness because PUD describes truth-telling as making waves or being mean and rude. Honesty is not valued positively, so we increasingly use an oblique mode of speaking in which we disconnect what we say from what we are thinking or what we mean. In public discourse, rape has become "unconsented sexual activity," murder is "neutralizing someone," and a man who beats his wife commits "domestic violence." We are so numbed to dishonest uses of language that the oblique mode permeates our private discourse, too. Sometimes speaking obliquely is harmful, sometimes it's not. But it is always dishonest, even when it is a defensive tactic for avoiding emotional conflict and physical violence.

A couple of examples will illustrate my point. A friend casually described a pleasant phone conversation with an acquaintance, saying, "I had a warm encounter with her." She didn't "have an encounter." Two women talked to each other by telephone, perhaps with mutual pleasure. What the speaker avoided saying was that she had *enjoyed* her conversation with the other woman. No one was harmed by her description, but the lack of motivation for it shows how thoroughly the oblique mode has become our linguistic habit.

My next example is more complex. I arranged to have lunch with an acquaintance to discuss her comments on a manuscript of mine. A couple of days after we'd made the appointment, the manuscript and her comments appeared in my mailbox with a note that said, "Thought I'd just send these and make it easier all around." Because I wanted to be sure that I was accurately interpreting the meaning of her statement, I called her to confirm my guess that what she'd meant was, "I'm cancelling our lunch date."

What factors do we consider when we choose to say something other than exactly what we mean? I can understand why men prefer the word "pedophilia" to saying "I rape children," why generals talk about "neutralizing the enemy" instead of how many soldiers were killed, why politicians prefer legislation that deals with "domestic violence" rather than "wife beating." Euphemism and other forms of oblique discourse serve the interests of the powerful. Any use of language that directs our attention away from the violence men do when they assert their power over other people enables them to deny their agency and responsibility for what they do. At the same time, oblique language enables women to pretend that they don't know what men are doing. If we remain "unaware" of male violence, we don't have to challenge them and, in this way, avoid the possibility of yet more male violence.

But what motivates us to use oblique language among ourselves, particularly in private situations where there is no audience to judge the relative merits of our behaviors? Why should those of us who are without social and political power perpetuate male forms of discourse? What is our investment in not saying what we mean? Using my friend's statement, I'll speculate. We don't say what we mean when we don't want to be honest. We don't want to be honest if we believe we won't like the results. Lying is a way of avoiding conflict. My friend didn't want to discuss whether or not we'd have lunch. As a discourse tactic, not saying what she meant was a way of exercising power over me without having to be responsible for her decision. She had decided she didn't want to have lunch with me, knew that she had to inform me of her decision without giving me an opportunity to ask her why she'd changed her mind, and was confident that I'd decipher her intention accurately. Being oblique gave her a way to inform me of her decision without discussing it; she made a unilateral decision that involved both of us without giving me an opportunity to argue whether we should have lunch. She reserved to herself all the power in the situation and invalidated any idea I might have had that we had a relationship in which we could discuss the pros and cons of having lunch together.

The meanings and results of her language are clearer than her motivations for it, but indicating some of the possibilities will illustrate why we have to say what we mean to each other. Two elements of her statement alerted me to hidden meaning: *just*, which downplayed the significance of her decision, and *make it easier all around*. With "all around" she suppressed explicit mention of the two of us. Her omission of explicit reference to her own agency was also important, but it didn't affect my interpretation. It was her choice of the adjective *easier*, because she didn't explain who her decision made "it easier" for, that told me she was trying to avoid saying something. Since I had had no part in the decision, I wasn't the beneficiary of *easier*. She was. How did her decision make "it" easier for her, though? Maybe she didn't want to have lunch on that day, or something more important had come up and she didn't want to discuss the change in plans. Maybe she thought I'd be angry, disappointed, or annoyed by a change in plans, and she didn't want to deal with how I might feel about her decision. Maybe she doesn't like me and spoke obliquely to put me off; that way, she didn't have to be responsible for what she felt. Maybe she was angry at me about something I'd done or said and being oblique enabled her to cancel our lunch without discussing her feelings with me. Perhaps she thought I didn't want to have lunch with her, and using *easier* was her way of claiming that her decision was motivated by concern for me. Or, her self-esteem may be so low that she thought I didn't want to have lunch with her and, in order to avoid my hypothetical rejection, she cancelled our lunch before I could. Whatever her motivation, her goal was avoiding a situation she believed would be painful for her, and she succeeded.

**Notes**

1.     There are several excellent collections of articles on the relationship between language and thought, class, race, and sex, and any one of them will provide interested readers with more information about how language reflects the way we think. Among the most readable are *Language,* ed. Virginia P. Clark, Paul A. Eschholz, and Alfred A. Rosa, 4th ed. (New York: St. Martin's Press, 1985); *Language Awareness*, ed. Paul Eschholz, Alfred Rosa, and Virginia Clark, 3rd. ed. (New York: St. Martin's Press, 1982); *Language Power*, ed. Carol J. Boltz and Dorothy U. Seyler (New York: Random House, 1982); *Speaking of Words: A Language Reader*, ed. James MacKillop and Donna Woolfolk Cross, 2nd ed. (New York: Holt, Rinehart and Winston, 1982); and *Exploring Language,* ed. Gary Goshgarian (Boston: Little, Brown and Co., 1983). There are also single-author books analyzing contemporary language use: *How Language Works* by Madelon E. Heatherington (Cambridge, MA: Winthrop Publishers, 1980) and *Language: The Loaded Weapon* by Dwight Bolinger (London: Longman, 1980).

2.     Words like *crippled* and *blind* continue to be used as metaphors in contexts where one might hope for more sensitivity to the implications of language use. In the January 23, 1989, issue of *Time*, for example, Susan Tifft quoted the trustees of Dartmouth College as denouncing the editors of *Dartmouth Review* for "ignorance and moral *blindness*" ("Bigots in the Ivory Tower," 56), and, in a letter soliciting contributions, a lobbyist for the National Gay and Lesbian Task Force described Jesse Helms as wanting "to add *crippling* amendments" to the congressional bill against hate crimes (August, 1989). Apparently, sensitivity to prejudiced language in one situation doesn't carry over into other contexts.

**For discussion**

*Content*

1. State Penelope's thesis in your words. Where in the essay does she state her thesis?

2. How can euphemism be a danger to thought and action?

3. How might our attitudes change if we had "positive ways of thinking or talking about the abilities of people who have physical or anatomical limitations" (paragraph three)?

4. In paragraphs five and seven, Penelope suggests that we stop using disability metaphors as "negative descriptions of events and situations" (paragraph five). Cite her examples, and supply other examples. How might those metaphors sound to a disabled person?

5. How are the euphemisms Penelope names in paragraph eight harmful? To whom are they harmful? Whom do they protect? How do those euphemisms influence thought and action?

6. Imagine Julia Penelope, Carol Barringer (I referred to her on pages 41–42, and June Jordan (see her essay in Chapter Two) discussing euphemisms. What examples and ideas would be part of their discussion?

*Style*

1. The lower-case "u.s." in paragraph two is not a typing error; Penelope deliberately uses lower-case initials to indicate her disapproval of U.S. policies. Is this an effective device?

2. How do the transitions at the beginnings of paragraphs five and six direct you as a reader? Are those transitions helpful to you?

3. Paragraph nine begins with an active-voice sentence—"Men create euphemisms to control how we perceive and interpret their actions." Change that sentence to passive voice. What is the main difference between the two sentences? Which requires more words? What does each sentence accomplish?

4. Do you find unnecessary or pretentious words in Penelope's essay? Give specific examples of unnecessary or pretentious words if you find them, or of precise words if you find them.

**For writing**

1. Analyze a piece of political writing that uses one or more of these language possibilities: pretentious words, euphemisms, unnecessary words, passive voice. Cite examples, explain them, and show ways the writer might have changed those passages. Was the writer using language carelessly or carefully?

2. Analyze a piece of writing in which the writer uses precise diction and avoids unnecessary passive structures and euphemisms. Cite and explain examples. Why do you think the writer made those choices? For either writing assign-

ment, you will find examples of women's political speeches/writing in *Outspoken Women* (Anderson), *American Voices* (Andrews and Zarefsky), *Man Cannot Speak for Her* (Campbell), *Great Speakers and Speeches* (Lucaites). Your instructor can direct you to other sources.

# Chapter Three:

# Why Do You Think That?

# Why Do You Think That?

## Introduction

JUST AS WE LEARN TO FUNCTION in the family and society we grow up in, we learn to think in the language we grow up in; and that language influences how we think and what we think about. As members of families and society, we can influence the ways of our social groups; similarly, we can influence our language to some degree.

In Chapter One, you read about and remembered some of the conventional wisdom passed along to you through language. You read and thought about inherited sayings that tell us how women and men are thought to use language, and you read and thought about statements that tell us how women and men are "supposed" to conduct themselves. That part of our language inheritance is more than simply the words we know and say; it shapes our thoughts, our behavior and expectations, and our perceptions.

Do we believe that women's talk is only gossip, as our language inheritance tells us it is, or do women gossip because that is what the language tells us we are supposed to do? Is it even possible for us to define "gossip" positively, as that talk which allows people to know each other and to regulate behavior? Do men never gossip, or do we call men's gossip another name and therefore not perceive any of men's talk as gossip? Do women really talk too much, or does the linguistic inheritance make us think women talk too much? How much is too much? Do women think that we are supposed to talk a lot because the language tells us that is what women do? Are men really as silent as the linguistic inheritance tells us they are, or does the phrase "strong and silent type" make us see and believe something that isn't there? If men are silent, are they suppressing words they would like to say but don't because the language tells them they are supposed to be silent?

Language allows us to form questions and to wonder and think beyond what language has already taught us. Contemporary feminist linguistic researchers, asking questions about linguistic habits and language use, have found in one study after another that women do not talk as much as men do, that people who think women talk too much measure the amount of women's talk against silence (not talking at all) and not against men's talk, that men interrupt and silence women more than women interrupt and silence men, and that women do not use tag-questions more than men do. The results of such studies suggest that the research was limited to a single cultural group, a homogeneous group of women and men, and was not cross-cultural. For example, the studies may have been limited to a group of middle-class white women and men. What results do you think the researchers would have found if they had asked whether African-American men interrupt white women, or if they had asked whether Native American women use more modifiers than do Puerto Rican-American women, or if they had asked whether working-class men, in conversation with upper-class women, talk more than women do?

Researchers continue to raise questions about women's and men's linguistic ways: Do women talk differently with other women than they do with men? Do men talk differently with other men than they do with women? And researchers are becoming more and more aware of researcher biases influencing hypotheses and conclusions. For example, most linguistic researchers before the 1970s were men; if those men assumed (because their linguistic inheritance told them to) that women's talk was trivial and that men's talk was important, it would no doubt have seemed to them that women talk too much. Further, those early researchers did not examine women's talk to find out what it was about; they studied men's talk which they assumed to be about "important" subjects. By the time we have reason to ask questions about language, language has already shaped our minds in some ways.

You learned in Chapter Two that we are born into a complex verbal language. That language allows us to use words to make appropriate noises and to convey information. It lets us use more and bigger words than we need, and it provides us with precise and non-pretentious words as well. It allows us to make sentences in passive and in active structures. Language allows us to mislead and lie, and it allows us to be as honest and direct as we can be. Chapter Two suggests that in all these cases, we can choose how we will use language and that our choices affect language itself. As we shall see, those complexities of language are but a part of a much larger picture.

What we have seen so far suggests that thinking in the language into which one is born means more than learning the vocabulary of that language. In complex ways, in its vocabulary, its structure, and its metaphors, language affects the way we think.

The vocabulary of the language in which we grow up influences what we think about. The English language includes thousands of words. No doubt, the more words we know, the more we can think about, because in most cases, if we don't have the word to name an idea, an event, or an object, we do not think about that idea, event, or object. Was "euphemism" a new word for you when you read it in Chapter Two? If it was, you broadened your range of thought by learning a word and what it stands for. If you hadn't known about euphemisms before you knew a name for them, you probably had not thought specifically about that aspect of language. Do you know "racism," "homophobia," "misogyny"? If you know these words, you probably think in some detail about social conditions of which you might not otherwise even be aware.

If I don't have a word to name sexual harassment, I probably do not think specifically about sexual harassment. I may be uneasy about a situation, but until I have a name for it, I cannot think and talk clearly and efficiently about it. Having words to name that social condition allows us to talk efficiently about unwanted sexual attention without having to define it or describe it in every sentence. Further, having the phrase "sexual harassment" allows people to be aware of situations that they might otherwise overlook. In fact, until a few years ago, when women created the name for that specific kind of discrimination and began to call attention to it, many people did not know that sexual harassment existed.

We live in a linguistic environment that allows us to learn enormous amounts of information and to have a wide range of thought by learning words—nouns and verbs that name both concrete and abstract, conjunctions and other function words that name connections and relationships, adverbs and adjectives that describe and define. As we saw in Chapter Two, if we acquire a large vocabulary, we must then decide whether to use it to communicate clearly or to show off with it.

But vast as it is, the English vocabulary does not name or identify everything. And here the discussion becomes difficult: how can we talk about what we do not know about? How can we know about objects or occurrences if we do not have words for them? Can we even think about events or objects if we do not have words for them? Of course, people imagine and invent new things and name them (the dozens of new words that name computer parts and functions are good examples), and people make new words and phrases for new ideas, as we saw with "sexual harassment."

Comparing English to other languages lets us see what English lacks. For example, English has a few words to identify kin relationships—sister, mother, aunt, grandmother, brother, father, uncle, grandfather, cousin. If I want to talk about my male sibling, I refer to him as my brother. But English does not give me a specific noun to designate whether my brother is older or younger than I. Other languages, Lakota Sioux, for example, have nouns to specify birth order. According to Bea Medicine (see her essay in this chapter), in Lakota, my younger brother is *mi-sunka-la*; an older brother is *tiblo*. If I want to talk about my grandmother on my mother's side of the family, I can call her "my grandmother on my mother's side of the family," or "my maternal grandmother," or "my mother's mother," but English does not give me a specific noun to designate that particular grandmother. Other languages provide words to identify clearly and economically specific kin relationships because the people who created those languages needed the words. In matrilineal and matrilocal cultures, people need specific words for mothers' families and for kinship relationships

that people in patriarchal cultures do not need. Different cultures think differently about the importance of women's family lines.

Not having a specific noun for "younger brother" or "mother's mother"
does not mean that I cannot know or think about *which* brother or *which* grandmother, but it does mean that I have to add modifying words to nouns. And it
probably means that I do not habitually think about kin relations in quite the
same way as do people who grew up in languages with large and specific kinship vocabularies. My English vocabulary does not constantly call my attention
to birth order or to maternal blood lines.

The vocabulary of the language in which we grow up encourages us to think
about those ideas, events, objects, and distinctions our language names. And it
may discourage our thinking about ideas, occurrences, objects, and distinctions
for which our language has no words. Inside that large cultural vocabulary,
American society encourages women and men to learn somewhat different
vocabularies. It encourages most men and boys to learn the vocabularies of math
and sciences, of technology and machinery, of politics and business, and of
sports, for examples. American culture encourages women and girls to learn the
vocabularies of emotion, of cooking and cleaning and nurturing, of child-
rearing, of personal relationships, for examples. That social encouragement and
discouragement affect all of us, often in negative ways. If women are discouraged from learning the vocabularies of science and technology, they are
handicapped in that world. If men are discouraged from learning the vocabulary
of personal relationships, they are handicapped in that world. Excluding either
women or men from a part of human endeavor diminishes human endeavor. Of
course, women can learn—and in increasing numbers are learning—the
vocabularies of the sciences and of politics and of technology; men can learn—
do learn—the language of child-rearing and of nurturing. Knowing the vocabulary, the words, allows women and men not only to know about what the
words name; it allows them to participate more fully in discussions and decisions
about those subjects. And in the same way that any of us can learn a specific
vocabulary, whether or not our society encourages us to learn it, we can learn
languages other than English and we can learn the ways other languages name
the world. We can learn to see the world from other perspectives.

In its structure, particularly its sentence structure, the language in which we
grow up also influences the way we think. For example, English sentences must
have verbs; that means that we cannot make an English sentence without
indicating time—past, present, or future. That prescribed structure probably
inclines English users to be constantly aware of linear time; an action is going
on, is finished, or will occur. But not all languages encourage that view of
action or of time. Nootka, a Native North American language used on Van-
couver Island, makes no distinction between nouns and verbs, and views the
world as constantly in process. In Nootka, instead of "a fire," there is "a

burning." How would our thinking differ from the thinking English encourages if we did not have to have verbs and verb tense in our sentences?

The English verb "be" (and all its forms) implies fixedness, absolutes. What difference do you see between "This rose is red" and "I see this rose as red"? English encourages us to make structures like the first, although it allows us to make structures like the second. How do you think our thought processes would differ if our language did not have "be" and the structures we make with it? Do languages other than English encourage different thought patterns? Do languages other than English have verbs that only women can use and different verbs that only men can use, for example?

The typical English sentence structure puts the subject before the verb, as in "She works." Usually, the subject or the noun does the action of the verb. We saw in Chapter Two that English also allows us to make passive structures in which the subject does not do the verb's action, but the typical construction makes the subject the active agent. That structure probably encourages, and perhaps comes from, the notion that people are in control of their actions and of the world. But not all languages encourage that world view. How would our thinking be different if English did not allow us to make active structures? How would our thinking be different if we could not make passive structures? Do you know of a language in which women cannot be the active subjects of verbs? How would such a language shape people's thoughts about women's and men's capabilities and roles?

In its structure and in its vocabulary, language creates and reflects habitual ways of thinking and of making statements. In its metaphors, a language also creates and reflects habitual thought and statement patterns.

A metaphor is a figurative statement that equates two basically unlike items to make one or both more vivid. A simile does the same thing. The difference between metaphor and simile is technical and minor; metaphor equates and simile compares. For example, "education is an octopus" is metaphor and "education is like an octopus" is simile. We often learn about metaphor and simile when we study poetry, and therefore we have the notion that simile and metaphor are the exclusive language of poets. Indeed, poets use metaphor because it is condensed and imaginative, but metaphor is not limited to poetry. In fact, metaphor is common to our language and to our thought. It is not the language of poetry only.

English allows us to make fresh, new metaphors; it also allows us to use the old ones that are part of our linguistic inheritance. Those old metaphors become grooves for our minds, habitual ways of thinking. Making new metaphors requires thought, and it can be fun. I enjoyed making the octopus metaphor, but creating it was more work than using an old one would have been. The octopus metaphor suggests some qualities about education, and it also suggests some attitudes about education. If I use that metaphor over and over, it begins to shape the way I think about education.

The metaphors that are part of our linguistic inheritance and that we use repeatedly also shape our thinking. For example, a common contemporary metaphor in North America equates nearly every kind of undertaking with a game. In talking about work and employment, political campaigns, war, personal relationships, and education, we use metaphors such as "She's a team player," "We have a game plan," "It's time to punt," and "What's the score?" When these game metaphors were new, they were effective. Now they are so old that they do not create vivid images for us; but because we continue to use them, they probably influence the way we think. If I repeatedly refer to my plans for this course as a "game plan," perhaps I am simply too lazy to think of a new metaphor. On the other hand, perhaps I use "game plan" because, in the back of my mind, I think of the course as a game. Whether or not I think of it as a game, I give you the impression that the course is a game. How does that affect your attitude, your attendance, your work? A man who talks about "scoring" with his lover gives the impression that intimate relationships are a game. Does he use that metaphor because he doesn't want to take the time to make a new one, because he doesn't know that he can make a new one, or because intimate relationships *are* a game for him? Is he always the one who scores? Can his lover score on him? Does the familiar metaphor trap men into thinking of sex in ways that they would rather not think of it? Does the metaphor trap women in the same way?

Recently, some New England Patriots football team members sexually harassed a sports writer in their locker room. The team owner apparently found the situation amusing and told this "joke" for which he later apologized: "What do the Iraqis have in common with Lisa Olson [the writer]? They've both seen Patriot missiles up close." That may look like a harmless metaphor until we realize that metaphors are not simply figures of speech. They reflect and betray thoughts. They are statements that mirror the images of the mind. Does the team owner, the boss, think of players on his team as destroyers that he owns? Missiles and many other weapons of destruction are destroyed as they are used. Do some men think of their penises as weapons? If so, how do they think of sexual intercourse and of their partners in sex?

The men who created and tested atomic and hydrogen bombs referred to themselves as the "fathers" of the bombs, and they called the bombs that worked "Little Boy," "Fat Boy," "George," and "Mike." They called the bombs that didn't work, the duds, "girls." The metaphors are more than innocent words. They reveal attitudes about sex, war, and science. As part of the English language inheritance, these metaphors influence our thoughts; they create a view of the world and perpetuate that view through repetition.

English perpetuates an image of the earth as female in the metaphors "Mother Earth" and "Mother Nature." Do these metaphors encourage American culture to treat the earth as the culture treats females, especially women and girls? Violence against women increases annually in the United States. Those who keep statistics about violence against women estimate that men rape one woman/girl in every four in the U.S. every year, that husbands and male partners beat three to four million American women annually, that women are 95 per cent of domestic violence victims. Does English include the earth-as-female metaphor to justify treating the earth violently, or do we treat the earth violently because we have the metaphor? I do not have an answer to that question. I pose the question to indicate that, even with metaphor, as with vocabulary and with structure, language influences our thoughts. And our thoughts influence our language. The essays in this chapter continue the discussion of the complex relationships between thought and language. As you read them, consider how your language has influenced not only what you think about, but how you think about those subjects. If you are bilingual, consider different thoughts your languages allow you to have. If you are monolingual, consider ways your language might be constricting your thoughts.

# Politics and the English Language

## George Orwell

MOST PEOPLE WHO BOTHER WITH THE MATTER at all would admit that the English language is in a bad way, but it is generally assumed that we cannot by conscious action do anything about it. Our civilization is decadent and our language—so the argument runs—must inevitably share in the general collapse. It follows that any struggle against the abuse of language is a sentimental archaism, like preferring candles to electric light or hansom cabs to aeroplanes. Underneath this lies the half-conscious belief that language is a natural growth and not an instrument which we shape for our own purposes.

Now, it is clear that the decline of a language must ultimately have political and economic causes: it is not due simply to the bad influence of this or that individual writer. But an effect can become a cause, reinforcing the original cause and producing the same effect in an intensified form, and so on indefinitely. A man may take to drink because he feels himself to be a failure, and then fail all the more completely because he drinks. It is rather the same thing that is happening to the English language. It becomes ugly and inaccurate because our thoughts are foolish, but the slovenliness of our language makes it easier for us to have foolish thoughts. The point is that the process is reversible.

Modern English, especially written English, is full of bad habits which spread by imitation and which can be avoided if one is willing to take the necessary trouble. If one gets rid of these habits one can think more clearly, and to think clearly is a necessary first step towards political regeneration: so that the fight against bad English is not frivolous and is not the exclusive concern of professional writers. I will come back to this presently, and I hope that by that time the meaning of what I have said here will have become clearer. Meanwhile, here are five specimens of the English language as it is now habitually written.

These five passages have not been picked out because they are especially bad—I could have quoted far worse if I had chosen—but because they illustrate various of the mental vices from which we now suffer. They are a little below the average, but are fairly representative samples. I number them so that I can refer back to them when necessary.

(1)  I am not, indeed sure whether it is not true to say that the Milton who once seemed not unlike a seventeenth-century Shelley had not become, out of an experience ever more bitter in each year, more alien (sic) to the founder of that Jesuit sect which nothing could induce him to tolerate.

Professor Harold Laski (Essay in Freedom of Expression)

(2)  Above all, we cannot play ducks and drakes with a native battery of idioms which prescribes such egregious collocations of vocables as the Basic *put up with* for *tolerate* or *put at a loss* for *bewilder*.

Professor Lancelot Hogben (Interglossa)

(3)  On the one side we have the free personality: by definition it is not neurotic, for it has neither conflict nor dream. Its desires, such as they are, are transparent, for they are just what institutional approval keeps in the forefront of consciousness; another institutional pattern would alter their number and intensity; there is little in them that is natural, irreducible, or culturally dangerous. But on the other side, the social bond itself is nothing but the mutual reflection of these self-secure integrities. Recall the definition of love. Is not this the very picture of a small academic? Where is there a place in this hall of mirrors for either personality or fraternity?

Essay on psychology in Politics (New York)

(4)  All the "best people" from the gentlemen's clubs, and all the frantic fascist captains, united in common hatred of Socialism and bestial horror of the rising tide of the mass revolutionary movement, have turned to acts of provocation, to foul incendiarism, to medieval legends of poisoned wells, to legalize their own destruction of proletarian organizations, and rouse the agitated petty-bourgeoisie to chauvinistic fervour on behalf of the fight against the revolutionary way out of the crisis.

Communist pamphlet

(5)  If a new spirit is to be infused into this old country, there is one thorny and contentious reform which must be tackled, and that is the humanization

and galvanization of the B.B.C. Timidity here will bespeak canker and atrophy of the soul. The heart of Britain may be sound and of strong beat, for instance, but the British lion's roar at present is like that of Bottom in Shakespeare's *Midsummer Night's Dream*—as gentle as any sucking dove. A virile new Britain cannot continue indefinitely to be traduced in the eyes or rather ears, of the world by the effete languors of Langham Place, brazenly masquerading as "standard English." When the Voice of Britain is heard at nine o'clock, better far and infinitely less ludicrous to hear aitches honestly dropped than the present priggish, inflated, inhibited, schoolma'amish arch braying of blameless bashful mewing maidens!

Letter in Tribune

Each of these passages has faults of its own, but, quite apart from avoidable ugliness, two qualities are common to all of them. The first is staleness of images: the other is lack of precision. The writer either has a meaning and cannot express it, or he inadvertently says something else, or he is almost indifferent as to whether his words mean anything or not. This mixture of vagueness and sheer incompetence is the most marked characteristic of modern English prose, and especially of any kind of political writing. As soon as certain topics are raised, the concrete melts into the abstract and no one seems able to think of turns of speech that are not hackneyed: prose consists less and less of words chosen for the sake of their meaning, and more and more of phrases tacked together like the sections of a prefabricated hen-house. I list below, with notes and examples, various of the tricks by means of which the work of prose-construction is habitually dodged:

**Dying Metaphors**. A newly invented metaphor assists thought by evoking a visual image, while on the other hand a metaphor which is technically "dead" (e.g., *iron resolution*) has in effect reverted to being an ordinary word and can generally be used without loss of vividness. But in between these two classes there is a huge dump of worn-out metaphors which have lost all evocative power and are merely used because they save people the trouble of inventing phrases for themselves. Examples are: *Ring the changes on, take up the cudgels for, toe the line, ride roughshod over, stand shoulder to shoulder with, play into the hands of, no axe to grind, grist to the mill, fishing in troubled waters, on the order of the day, Achilles' heel, swan song, hotbed.* Many of these are used without knowledge of their meaning (what is a "rift," for instance?), and incompatible metaphors are frequently mixed, a sure sign that the writer is not interested in what he is saying. Some metaphors now current have been twisted out of their original meaning without those who use them even being aware of the fact. For example, *toe the line* is sometimes written *tow the line*. Another example is *the hammer and the anvil*, now always used with the implication that the anvil gets the worst of it. In real life it is always the anvil that breaks the hammer, never the other way about: a writer who stopped to think what he was saying would be aware of this, and would avoid perverting the original phrase.

**Operators or Verbal False Limbs.** These save the trouble of picking out appropriate verbs and nouns, and at the same time pad each sentence with extra syllables which give it an appearance of symmetry. Characteristic phrases are: *render inoperative, militate against, make contact with, be subjected to, give rise to, give grounds for, have the effect of, play a leading part (role) in, make itself felt, take effect, exhibit a tendency to, serve the purpose of,* etc., etc. The keynote is the elimination of simple verbs. Instead of being a single word, such as *break, stop, spoil, mend, kill,* a verb becomes a phrase, made up of a noun or adjective tacked on to some general-purpose verb such as *prove, serve, form, play, render.* In addition, the passive voice is wherever possible used in preference to the active, and noun constructions are used instead of gerunds (*by examination of* instead of *by examining*). The range of verbs is further cut down by means of the *-ize* and *de-* formations, and the banal statements are given an appearance of profundity by means of the *not un-* formation. Simple conjunctions and prepositions are replaced by such phrases as *with respect to, having regard to, the fact that, by dint of, in view of, in the interests of, on the hypothesis that*; and the ends of sentences are saved from anticlimax by such resounding commonplaces as *greatly to be desired, cannot be left out of account, a development to be expected, in the near future, deserving of serious consideration, brought to a satisfactory conclusion,* and so on and so forth.

**Pretentious Diction.** Words like *phenomenon, element, individual* (as noun), *objective, categorical, effective, virtual, basic, primary, promote, constitute, exhibit, exploit, utilize, eliminate, liquidate,* are used to dress up simple statements and give an air of scientific impartiality to biased judgments. Adjectives like *epoch-making, epic, historic, unforgettable, triumphant, age-old, inevitable, inexorable, veritable* are used to dignify the sordid processes of international politics, while writing that aims at glorifying war usually takes on an archaic colour, its characteristic words being *realm, throne, chariot, mailed fist, trident, sword, shield, buckler, banner, jackboot, clarion.* Foreign expressions such as *cul de sac, ancien régime, deux ex machina, mutatis mutandis, status quo, gleichschaltung, weltanschauung,* are used to give an air of culture and elegance. Except for the useful abbreviations, *i.e., e.g.,* and *etc.,* there is no real need for any of the hundreds of foreign phrases now current in English. Bad writers, and especially scientific, political and sociological writers, are nearly always haunted by the notion that Latin or Greek words are grander than Saxon ones, and unnecessary words like *expedite, ameliorate, predict, extraneous, deracinated, clandestine, subaqueous* and hundreds of others constantly gain ground from their Anglo-Saxon opposite numbers.[1] The jargon peculiar to Marxist writing (*hyena, hangman, cannibal, petty bourgeois, these gentry, lacquey, flunkey, mad dog, White Guard, etc.*) consists largely of words and phrases translated from Russian, German or French; but the normal way of coining a new word is to use a Latin or Greek root with the appropriate affix and, where necessary, the -ize formation. It is often easier to make up words of this kind (*deregionalize, impermissible, extramarital, non-fragmentary* and so forth) than to think up the English words that will cover one's meaning. The result, in general, is an increase in slovenliness and vagueness.

**Meaningless Words.** In certain kinds of writing, particularly in art criticism and literary criticism, it is normal to come across long passages which are almost completely lacking in meaning.[2] Words like *romantic, plastic, values, human, dead, sentimental, natural, vitality*, as used in art criticism, are strictly meaningless, in the sense that they not only do not point to any discoverable object, but are hardly ever expected to do so by the reader. When one critic writes, "The outstanding feature of Mr. X's work is its living quality," while another writes, "The immediately striking thing about Mr. X's work is its peculiar deadness," the reader accepts this as a simple difference of opinion. If words like *black* and *white* were involved, instead of the jargon words *dead* and *living*, he would see at once that language was being used in an improper way. Many political words are similarly abused. The word *Fascism* has now no meaning except in so far as it signifies "something not desirable." The words *democracy, socialism, freedom, patriotic, realistic, justice,* have each of them several different meanings which cannot be reconciled with one another. In the case of a word like *democracy,* not only is there no agreed definition, but the attempt to make one is resisted from all sides. It is almost universally felt that when we call a country democratic we are praising it: consequently the defenders of every kind of régime claim that it is a democracy, and fear that they might have to stop using the word if it were tied down to any one meaning. Words of this kind are often used in a consciously dishonest way. That is, the person who uses them has his own private definition, but allows his hearer to think he means something quite different. Statements like *Marshal Pétain was a true patriot, The Soviet Press is the freest in the world, The Catholic Church is opposed to persecution,* are almost always made with intent to deceive. Other words used in variable meanings, in most cases more or less dishonestly, are: *class, totalitarian, science, progressive, reactionary, bourgeois, equality.*

Now that I have made this catalogue of swindles and perversions, let me give another example of the kind of writing that they lead to. This time it must of its nature be an imaginary one. I am going to translate a passage of good English into modern English of the worst sort. Here is a well-known verse from *Ecclesiastes*:

> I returned and saw under the sun, that the race is not to the swift, nor the battle to the strong, neither yet bread to the wise, nor yet riches to men of understanding, nor yet favour to men of skill: but time and chance happeneth to them all.

Here it is in modern English:

Objective consideration of contemporary phenomena compels the conclusion that success or failure in competitive activities exhibits no tendency to be commensurate with innate capacity, but that a considerable element of the unpredictable must invariably be taken into account.

This is a parody, but not a very gross one. Exhibit (3), above, for instance, contains several patches of the same kind of English. It will be seen that I have not made a full translation. The beginning and ending of the sentence follow the original meaning fairly closely, but in the middle the concrete illustrations—race, battle, bread—dissolve into the vague phrase "success or failure in competitive activities." This had to be so, because no modern writer of the kind I am discussing—no one capable of using phrases like "objective consideration of contemporary phenomena"—would ever tabulate his thoughts in that precise and detailed way. The whole tendency of modern prose is away from concreteness. Now analyze these two sentences a little more closely. The first contains forty-nine words but only sixty syllables, and all its words are those of everyday life. The second contains thirty-eight words of ninety syllables: eighteen of its words are from Latin roots, and one from Greek. The first sentence contains six vivid images, and only one phrase ("time and chance") that could be called vague. The second contains not a single fresh, arresting phrase, and in spite of its ninety syllables it gives only a shortened version of the meaning contained in the first. Yet without a doubt it is the second kind of sentence that is gaining ground in modern English. I do not want to exaggerate. This kind of writing is not yet universal, and outcrops of simplicity will occur here and there in the worst-written page. Still, if you or I were told to write a few lines on the uncertainty of human fortunes, we should probably come much nearer to my imaginary sentence than to the one from *Ecclesiastes*.

As I have tried to show, modern writing at its worst does not consist in picking out words for the sake of their meaning and inventing images in order to make the meaning clearer. It consists in gumming together long strips of words which have already been set in order by someone else, and making the results presentable by sheer humbug. The attraction of this way of writing is that it is easy. It is easier—even quicker, once you have the habit—to say *In my opinion it is a not unjustifiable assumption that* than to say *I think*. If you use ready-made phrases, you not only don't have to hunt about for words; you also don't have to bother with the rhythms of your sentences, since these phrases are generally so arranged as to be more or less euphonious. When you are composing in a hurry—when you are dictating to a stenographer, for instance, or making a public speech—it is natural to fall into a pretentious, Latinized style. Tags like *a consideration which we should do well to bear in mind* or *a conclusion to which all of us would readily assent* will save many a sentence from coming down with a bump. By using stale metaphors, similes and idioms, you save much mental effort, at the cost of leaving your meaning vague, not only for your reader but for yourself. This is the significance of mixed metaphors. The sole aim of a metaphor is to call up a visual image. When these images clash—as in *The Fascist octopus has sung its swan song, the jackboot is thrown into the melting pot*—it can be taken as certain that the writer is not seeing a mental image of the objects he is naming; in other words he is not really thinking. Look again at the examples I gave at the beginning of this essay, Professor Laski (1) uses five negatives in fifty-three words. One of these is superfluous, making nonsense of the whole passage, and in addition there is the slip *alien* for akin, making further nonsense, and several avoidable pieces of clumsiness which increase the general vagueness. Professor Hogben (2) plays ducks and drakes with a battery which is able to write prescriptions, and, while disapproving of the everyday phrase *put up with*, is unwilling to look *egregious* up in the dictionary and see what it means. (3), if one takes an uncharitable attitude towards it, is simply meaningless: probably one could work out its in-tended meaning by reading the whole of the article in which it occurs. In (4), the writer knows more or less what he wants to say, but an accumulation of stale phrases chokes him like tea leaves blocking a sink. In (5), words and meaning have almost parted company. People who write in this manner usually have a general emotional meaning—they dislike one thing and want to express solidarity with another—but they are not interested in the detail of what they are saying. A scrupulous writer, in every sentence that he writes, will ask himself at least four questions, thus: What am I trying to say? What words will express it? What image or idiom will make it clearer? Is this image fresh enough to have an effect? And he will probably ask himself two more: Could I put it more shortly? Have I said anything that is avoidably ugly? But you are not obliged to go to all this trouble. You can shirk it by simply throwing your mind open and letting the ready-made phrases come crowding in. They will construct your sentences for you—even think your thoughts for you, to a certain extent—and at need they will perform the important service of partially concealing your meaning even from yourself. It is at this point that the special connection between politics and the debasement of language becomes clear.

In our time it is broadly true that political writing is bad writing. Where it is not true, it will generally be found that the writer is some kind of rebel, expressing his private opinions and not a "party line." Orthodoxy, of whatever colour, seems to demand a lifeless, imitative style. The political dialects to be found in pamphlets, leading articles, manifestos, White Papers and the speeches of undersecretaries do, of course vary from party to party, but they are all alike in that one almost never finds in them a fresh, vivid, home-made turn of speech. When one watches some tired hack on the platform mechanically repeating the familiar phrases—*bestial atrocities, iron heel, bloodstained tyranny, free peoples of the world, stand shoulder to shoulder*—one often has a curious feeling that one is not watching a live human being but some kind of dummy: a feeling which suddenly becomes stronger at moments when the light catches the speaker's spectacles and turns them into blank discs which seem to have no eyes behind them. And this is not altogether fanciful. A speaker who uses that kind of phraseology has gone some distance towards turning himself into a machine. The appropriate noises are coming out of his larynx, but his brain is not involved as it would be if he were choosing his words for himself. If the speech he is making is one that he is accustomed to make over and over again, he may be almost unconscious of what he is saying, as one is when one utters the responses in church. And this reduced state of consciousness, if not indispensable, is at any rate favourable to political conformity.

In our time, political speech and writing are largely the defence of the indefensible. Things like the continuance of British rule in India, the Russian purges and deportations, the dropping of the atom bombs on Japan, can indeed be defended, but only by arguments which are too brutal for most people to face, and which do not square with the professed aims of political parties. Thus political language has to consist largely of euphemism, question-begging and sheer cloudy vagueness. Defenceless villages are bombarded from the air, the inhabitants driven out into the countryside, the cattle machine-gunned, the huts set on fire with incendiary bullets; this is called *pacification*. Millions of peasants are robbed of their farms and sent trudging along the roads with no more than they can carry: this is called *transfer of population* or *rectification of frontiers*. People are imprisoned for years without trial, or shot in the back of the neck or sent to die of scurvy in Arctic lumber camps: this is called *elimination of unreliable elements*. Such phraseology is needed if one wants to name things without calling up mental pictures of them. Consider for instance some comfortable English professor defending Russian totalitarianism. He cannot say outright, "I believe in killing off your opponents when you can get good results by doing so." Probably, therefore, he will say something like this:

> While freely conceding that the Soviet régime exhibits certain features which the humanitarian may be inclined to deplore, we must, I think agree that a certain curtailment of the right to political opposition is an unavoidable concomitant of transitional periods, and that the rigours which the Russian people have been called upon to undergo have been amply justified in the sphere of concrete achievement.

The inflated style is itself a kind of euphemism. A mass of Latin words falls upon the facts like soft snow, blurring the outlines and covering up all the details. The great enemy of clear language is insincerity. When there is a gap between one's real and one's declared aims, one turns as it were instinctively to long words and exhausted idioms, like a cuttlefish squirting out ink. In our age there is no such thing as "keeping out of politics." All issues are political issues, and politics itself is a mass of lies, evasions, folly, hatred and schizophrenia. When the general atmosphere is bad, language must suffer. I should expect to find—this is a guess which I have not sufficient knowledge to verify—that the German, Russian and Italian languages have all deteriorated in the last ten or fifteen years, as a result of dictatorship.

But if thought corrupts language, language can also corrupt thought. A bad usage can spread by tradition and imitation, even among people who should and do know better. The debased language that I have been discussing is in some ways very convenient. Phrases like *a not unjustifiable assumption, leaves much to be desired, would serve no purpose, a consideration which we should do well to bear in mind* are a continuous temptation, a packet of aspirins always at one's elbow. Look back through this essay, and for certain you will find that I have again and again committed the very faults I am protesting against. By this morning's post I have received a pamphlet dealing with conditions in Germany. The author tells me that he "felt impelled" to write it. I open it at random, and here is almost the first sentence that I see: "(The Allies) have an opportunity not only of achieving a radical transformation of Germany's social and political structure in such a way as to avoid a nationalistic reaction in Germany itself, but at the same time of laying the foundations of a cooperative and unified Europe." You see, he "feels impelled" to write—feels, presumably, that he has something new to say—and yet his words, like cavalry horses answering the bugle, group themselves automatically into the familiarly dreary pattern. This invasion of one's mind by ready-made phrases (*lay the foundations, achieve a radical transformation*) can only be prevented if one is constantly on guard against them, and every such phrase anesthetizes a portion of one's brain.

I said earlier that the decadence of our language is probably curable. Those who deny this would argue, if they produced an argument at all, that language merely reflects existing social conditions, and that we cannot influence its development by any direct tinkering with words and constructions. So far as the general tone or spirit of a language goes, this may be true, but it is not true in detail. Silly words and expressions have often disappeared, not through any evolutionary process but owing to the conscious action of a minority. Two recent examples were *explore every avenue* and *leave no stone unturned*, which were killed by the jeers of a few journalists. There is a long list of flyblown metaphors which could similarly be got rid of if enough people would interest themselves in the job; and it should also be possible to laugh the *not un-* formation out of existence,[3] to reduce the amount of Latin and Greek in the average sentence, to drive out foreign phrases and strayed scientific words, and, in general, to make pretentiousness unfashionable. But all these are minor points. The defence of the English language implies more than this, and perhaps it is best to start by saying what it does not imply.

To begin with it has nothing to do with archaism, with the salvaging of obsolete words and turns of speech, or with the setting up of a "standard English" which must never be departed from. On the contrary, it is especially concerned with the scrapping of every word or idiom which has outworn its usefulness. It has nothing to do with correct grammar and syntax, which are of no importance so long as one makes one's meaning clear, or with the avoidance of Americanisms, or with having what is called a "good prose style." On the other hand it is not concerned with fake simplicity and the attempt to make written English colloquial. Nor does it even imply in every case preferring the Saxon word to the Latin one, though it does imply using the fewest and shortest words that will cover one's meaning. What is above all needed is to let the meaning choose the word, and not the other way about. In prose, the worst thing one can do with words is to surrender to them. When you think of a concrete object, you think wordlessly, and then, if you want to describe the thing you have been visualizing you probably hunt about till you find the exact words that seem to fit it. When you think of something abstract you are more inclined to use words from the start, and unless you make a conscious effort to prevent it, the existing dialect will come rushing in and do the job for you, at the expense of blurring or even changing your meaning. Probably it is better to put off using words as long as possible and get one's meaning as clear as one can through pictures or sensations. Afterwards one can choose—not simply accept—the phrases that will best cover the meaning, and then switch round and decide what impression one's words are likely to make on another person. This last effort of the mind cuts out all stale or mixed images, all prefabricated phrases, needless repetitions, and humbug and vagueness generally. But one can often be in doubt about the effect of a word or a phrase, and one needs rules that one can rely on when instinct fails. I think the following rules will cover most cases:

(i) Never use a metaphor, simile or other figure of speech which you are used to seeing in print.
(ii) Never use a long word where a short one will do.
(iii) If it is possible to cut a word out, always cut it out.
(iv) Never use the passive where you can use the active.
(v) Never use a foreign phrase, a scientific word or a jargon word if you can think of any everyday English equivalent.
(vi) Break any of these rules sooner than say anything outright barbarous.

These rules sound elementary, and so they are, but they demand a deep change of attitude in anyone who has grown used to writing in the style now fashionable. One could keep all of them and still write bad English, but one could not write the kind of stuff that I quoted in those five specimens at the beginning of this article.

I have not here been considering the literary use of language, but merely language as an instrument for expressing and not for concealing or preventing thought. Stuart Chase and others have come near to claiming that all abstract words are meaningless, and have used this as a pretext for advocating a kind of political quietism. Since you don't know what Fascism is, how can you struggle against Fascism? One need not swallow such absurdities as this, but one ought to recognize that the present political chaos is connected with the decay of language, and that one can probably bring about some improvement by starting at the verbal end. If you simplify your English, you are freed from the worst follies of orthodoxy. You cannot speak any of the necessary dialects, and when you make a stupid remark its stupidity will be obvious, even to yourself. Political language—and with variations this is true of all political parties, from Conservatives to Anarchists—is designed to make lies sound truthful and murder respectable, and to give an appearance of solidity to pure wind. One cannot change this all in a moment, but one can at least change one's own habits, and from time to time one can even, if one jeers loudly enough, send some worn-out and useless phrase—some *jackboot, Achilles' heel, hotbed, melting pot, acid test, veritable inferno* or other lump of verbal refuse—into the dustbin where it belongs.

**Notes**

1.   An interesting illustration of this is the way in which the English flower names which were in use till very recently are being ousted by Greek ones, *snapdragon* becoming *antirrhinum, forget-me-not* becoming *myosotis*, etc. It is hard to see any practical reason for this change of fashion; it is probably due to an instinctive turning-away from the more homely word and a vague feeling that the Greek word is scientific.

2.   "Comfort's catholicity of perception and image, strangely Whitmanesque in range, almost the exact opposite in aesthetic compulsion, continues to evoke that trembling atmospheric accumulative hinting at a cruel, an inexorably serene timelessness...Wrey Gardiner scores by aiming at simple bull's-eyes with precision. Only they are not so simple, and through this contented sadness runs more than the surface bitter-sweet of resignation." (*Poetry Quarterly.*)

3.   One can cure oneself of the *not un-* formation by memorizing this sentence: *A not unblack dog was chasing a not unsmall rabbit across a not ungreen field.*

**For discussion**

*Content*

1.  Restate Orwell's thesis in your words. Which of Orwell's sentences are his thesis statement?

2.  Explain how language can corrupt thought and how thought can corrupt language.

3. Identify sentences in which Orwell tells us what we can do about thought and language corruption. What can we do?

4. Does Orwell provide enough examples to illustrate his ideas clearly? Is the analogy in paragraph two a clear illustration?

5. Discuss each of the "tricks" Orwell lists. How is each "trick" a barrier to clear thinking?

6. Orwell states that all issues are political issues. Whether you agree with his statement depends upon how you define "politics" and "political." Does Orwell seem to define "politics" as public and government policy-making? How do you define "politics" and "political"? Is it possible for you to see private or personal issues as political issues? For example, are violence against women, contraception and abortion, sexuality, and child rearing political issues? Is education a political issue? Are issues that are of particular concern to women political issues?

*Style*

1. Discuss the organization of main points in the essay, and the transitions Orwell uses to move a reader from one point to the next. What is the effect of Orwell's giving five examples of bad writing early in the essay and withholding his analysis of those examples until later? What is the effect of stating the thesis early and of withholding until near the end specific rules for improving language and thought ?

2. Discuss the new metaphors Orwell creates for this essay (not the dying ones he quotes). What effect do the new metaphors have on you as a reader?

**For writing**

All suggestions for writing for Chapter Three follow the discussion suggestions for the chapter's final essay. (See page 175.)

# Pronoun Envy

## Alette Olin Hill

"PRONOUN ENVY" was the title of an article that appeared in *Newsweek*, December 6, 1971, but it was coined by a linguist, Professor Calvert Watkins, eminent Indo-Europeanist and at that time Chairman of the Department of Linguistics at Harvard. He and sixteen of his colleagues in the department had written a letter to *The Harvard Crimson*, which was published November 16, 1971, and said, in part:

> For people and pronouns in English *the masculine is the unmarked and hence is used as a neutral or unspecified term...*The fact that the masculine is the unmarked gender in English...is simply a feature of grammar. It is unlikely to be an impediment to any change in the patterns of the sexual division of labor toward which our society may wish to evolve. There is really no cause for anxiety or pronoun-envy on the part of those seeking such changes. (p. 17; my italics)

This letter from the "authorities" was prompted by an article that had appeared in *The Harvard Crimson* on November 11 entitled "Two Women Liberate Church Course." The two women—Harvard Divinity School students—had called for an end to sexist language in a course they were enrolled in. The teacher, Professor Harvey G. Cox, polled the class about this request, which specifically called for a halt to the use of the nouns *man* and *men* as well as the masculine pronouns to refer to all people. The proposal also asked that masculine names and pronouns be avoided when referring to God. The class voted for these linguistic reforms, which would have remained an intramural matter were it not for the fact that the articles in *The Harvard Crimson* were picked up by *Newsweek*. This lively bit of history can be found in Chapter Five, "The Language of Religion," in *Words and Women* by Casey Miller and Kate Swift.[1]

Miller and Swift did not take Watkins to task for his calling the masculine pronoun "unmarked...hence...a neutral or unspecified term." I would have challenged him on this assertion and on another part of his letter that said, "This reflects the ancient pattern of the Indo-European languages...." Since my Ph.D. is in Indo-European linguistics, I was particularly struck by this statement, for an ancient Indo-European pattern seldom has a bearing on English usage today. It is enlightening to learn about the history of a given locution, but it does not follow that whatever has been established as the norm since prehistoric times should be maintained without "anxiety." In other words, descriptive linguistics has been turned into prescriptive linguistics. Mary Ritchie Key, an anthropological linguist, represents a more liberated point of view. After amassing data from various cultures on how language reflects society, she concludes:

> Serious and responsible people can experiment in areas that will encourage rational changes based on patterns of human behavior. Such a process may bring stability to the seeming chaos. Research in languages and linguistic studies allied with male/female social behavior should be undertaken in depth. There is much to be done yet in understanding the universalities of gender systems in all languages of the world. *We don't even understand the gender system in English yet.*[2]

Yet despite our lack of data and our failure to understand the cultural origins of various linguistic phenomena, she does not hesitate to recommend alternatives to sexist expressions.

Miller and Swift argued more persuasively and succinctly than I would have done: they merely quoted Watkins to Watkins and caught him out in an internal inconsistency:

> Professor Watkins was apparently ignoring his own insights on the interaction of language and culture already quoted in Chapter 4.[3]

Chapter 4 includes the following statement by Watkins: "The lexicon of a language remains the single most effective way of approaching and understanding the culture of its speakers."[4] And "[language] is at once the expression of culture and a part of it."[5]

Miller and Swift also quote the shrewd insight of James C. Armagost of the Department of Linguistics at the University of Washington:

> A reasonably inquisitive person might wonder why the masculine is un-

marked. The question deserves a better answer than: "What a coincidence that the masculine is unmarked in the language of a people convinced that men are superior to women."[6]

Ann Bodine, a sociologist at Rutgers, wrote in 1975 that some grammarians lamented the lack of a sex-indefinite third person singular pronoun in English; others declared that *he* must serve this function; still others said that the masculine *is* the sex-indefinite pronoun.[7] This last position seems to have been the one adopted by Calvert Watkins when he called the masculine pronoun "unmarked," and therefore "neutral" and "unspecified." Bodine wrote that feminists objected to the use of *he* when it might be referring to women and that they thought a substitute ought to be found. "The reaction to this demand has ranged from agreement, to disagreement, to ridicule, to horror, but invariably the feminists' demand is viewed as an attempt to alter the English language."[8] Bodine maintained that the opposite was true: it is the prescriptive grammarians who have been trying to alter the language for 250 years. The third person plural has been widely used for a long time because it is sex-indefinite, unlike the third person singular, e.g.: "(1) anyone can do it if *they* try hard enough." "(2) Who dropped *their* ticket?" and "(3) Either Mary or John should bring a schedule with *them*."[9] Prescriptive grammarians and the entire publishing industry (wrote Bodine) have attempted to "eradicate" such locutions on the grounds of lack of agreement. Note that in each of the three examples the subject of the main clause is singular and sex-indefinite. The pronouns *they, their,* and *them* (being plural) do not agree in number with their antecedents (*anyone, who,* and *either Mary or John*). *They, their*, and *them* are sex-indefinite like *anyone, who,* and *someone*, yet grammarians insisted that the pronoun must agree in number with its antecedent. Therefore, the only "correct" form to use was *he, his,* or *him*.

Why? wondered Bodine. She did not think it was a coincidence that gender agreement was ignored. "Surprising as it may seem in the light of the attention later devoted to the issue, prior to the nineteenth century 'they' was widely used in written, therefore presumably also in spoken, English."[10] Usage, however, has not been the yardstick for prescriptive grammarians since the eighteenth century up to the present, even if some of the users were illustrious writers. "A non-sexist 'correction' would have been to advocate 'he or she' but rather than encourage this usage the grammarians actually tried to eradicate it also, claiming 'he or she' is 'clumsy', 'pedantic', or 'unnecessary.'"[11] Neither sex-indefinite *they* nor *he* or *she* was allowed: only *he* was "correct." For a current definition of "correctness" in American English, see the interesting debate between Dwight Bolinger and William F. Buckley, Jr., "Usage and Acceptability in Language," *The American Heritage Dictionary*, Second College Edition (Boston: Houghton Mifflin, 1982), pp. 30–33. Buckley writes: "mere usage, however prolonged, does not baptize. Providence in due course sometime accepts into its bosom sinners, but usually only after time served in the ante-chambers. And how will we know just when that dispensation is granted? Well, to answer that only in part in jest: by asking me" (p.32). Pope William decides. But I caught His Holiness in an error once on "Firing Line": men (or horses, I can't remember which) were "gam.-bŏl.ing" around. The correct pronunciation is "gám.bəl.ing"; perhaps Pope William thought hoi polloi would confuse it with "gambling" and therefore supplied a spelling pronunciation (a habit of the semi-learned). For a less pontifical opinion, see Dwight Bolinger, ibid., pp. 30–32.

Bodine summarized her findings thus:

> Although the grammarians felt they were motivated by an interest in logic, accuracy, and elegance, the above analysis reveals that there is no rational, objective, basis for their choice, and therefore the explanation must lie elsewhere. It would appear that their choice was dictated by an androcentric worldview; linguistically, human beings were to be considered male unless proven otherwise.[12]

She proved her case with ease and demonstrated that linguistic chauvinism (my phrase) was rampant in 1975. Of thirty-three grammar books being used in American junior and senior high schools, twenty-eight "condemn both 'he or she' and singular 'they', the former because it is clumsy and latter because it is inaccurate."[13] One of the grammar books she consulted made this astonishing explanation as to why the "awkwardness" of *he* or *she* should be shunned: "grammatically, men are more important than women."[14] However, if you follow this prescription to its logical conclusion, you may fall into ludicrous hypercorrection. The following sentence was written by a twelve-year-old boy after a "dunking" by classmates: "When I came up, everybody was laughing at me, but I was glad to see him just the same."[15]

Of course, this and similar sentences can be corrected by supplying a plural subject, such as "all the children," for *everyone*, but Bodine has made her point. The use of singular *they* is widespread, but since we have been brainwashed into not using it because of lack of agreement in number, we shrug and assume that usage must be wrong. Even feminist linguists have thought that the pronoun system was too entrenched to be changed—the opinion of Robin Lakoff and also of Nancy Faires Conklin, author of "Perspectives on the Dialects of Women."[16]

Bodine thought that the pronoun had changed in favor of singular *they* more than most people (including linguists) realize. Her proof is in the second person: we now use *you* for both singular and plural. Earlier English had singular *thou-thee* (nominative and accusative) and plural *yé-you* (nominative and accusative). Eventually the accusative plural *you* supplanted the other forms of the second person, proving that pronouns can change after all.

Bodine believed that English developed its second person singular form in the feudal age to be used by persons of superior rank. When the need for a familiar vs. formal second person died out with the feudal system, the plural *you* swept in. She took this explanation from Otto Jespersen's *Growth and Structure of the English Language* (1938; reprinted 1968), but it is not historically convincing. Old English had a well-developed pronoun system in place before the rise of feudalism. The second person alone had twelve forms:

|      | Singular | Dual | Plural |
|------|----------|------|--------|
| Nom. | $^x$oū | git | gē |
| Gen. | $^x$oīn | incer | ēower (lower) |
| Dat. | $^x$oē | inc | ēow (low) |
| Acc. | $^x$oec, $^x$oē | incit, inc | ēowic, ēow (low)[17] |

That most of these forms dropped out of use (notably the entire dual) indicates a drive toward simplification that is paralleled by the loss of the oblique cases in nouns and adjectives.* Nouns and adjectives also lost their gender (English used to have masculine, feminine, and neuter, like ancient Latin and modern German). I cannot see the simplification of the second person pronouns as a consequence of the rise and decline of the feudal system since other kinds of simplification (including verb conjugations) were also under way that have no particular connection with hierarchical social structure.

Nevertheless, Bodine is convincing in her argument that if the second person pronoun made such a significant alteration, so could the third, if prescriptive grammarians would let it alone. She does not insist that we should switch over to "everyone...their" in the name of Women's Liberation. What she does is to suggest that we observe this construction closely over the next few years, since the locution in question has been in our speech and writing for more than 250 years. Even Buckley should think that is enough time in the antechambers waiting for an audience, if not a dispensation.

If Ann Bodine's cautious optimism is prophetic and *vox populi* becomes *vox dei*, singular *they* could replace generic *he* in sentences beginning with *someone, anyone, somebody, anybody, any student, the person who*, etc. At the moment, singular *they* is not so sanctioned. Advice from McGraw–Hill includes the following:

> The English language lacks a generic singular pronoun signifying *he* or *she*, and therefore it has been customary and grammatically sanctioned to use masculine pronouns in expressions such as "one...*he*," "anyone...*he*," and "each child opens *his* book." Nevertheless, avoid when possible the pro-

---

* The oblique cases include all but the nominative. In addition to the nominative, genitive, dative, and accusative cases, nouns and adjectives had a fifth case—the instrumental.

nouns *he, him,* and *his* in reference to the hypothetical person or humanity in general.[18]

Suggestions for avoiding these traps include excision of *his* where it is not necessary, recasting the subject as a plural, and replacing the masculine pronoun with "*one, you,* or *he* or *she, her* or *his*, as appropriate. (Use *he* or *she* and its variations sparingly to avoid clumsy prose.)"[19] Singular *they* is missing.

Bodine rightly said that not only the grammarians but also the publishing industry had condemned he or she as "awkward." McGraw–Hill gives additional interesting advice:

> To avoid severe problems of repetition or inept wording, it may sometimes be best to use the generic *he* freely, but to add, in the preface and as often as necessary in the text, *emphatic statements to the effect that the masculine pronouns are being used for succinctness and are intended to refer to both females and males.*[20]

George F. Will, who found the whole document "depressing," is correct only about this particular section, which he didn't cite. For a set of guidelines aimed at "equal treatment of the sexes," this lapse into *he* as the final solution strikes me as backsliding. It reminds me of the textbook I had for modern European history as an undergraduate, R. R. Palmer's *A History of the Modern World* (New York: Alfred A. Knopf, 1950). There wasn't much about women in it, only a few female monarchs. A new edition (the fifth) appeared in 1978 with Joel Colton as co-author. I glanced at the index to see if there was now an entry for *women*. There was! I turned to the main pages cited (915–916). (There were eight other entries under *women*, but this was the longest—the "in-depth" survey, as it were.) In one and one-half pages the first and second women's movements were mentioned, with references to the Third World as well. These few paragraphs stressed the importance of women more than once, but the fact that women were allotted so little space in a textbook of 1100 pages tells more about the significance of women than the authors' glowing sentences would lead the reader to believe.

Similarly, when McGraw–Hill says that recourse to generic *he* is sometimes necessary so long as the author stresses in the preface and throughout that *he* is only being used for succinctness and that *he* means both *he* and *she*, the publisher is acknowledging a debt to history and tradition. I do not accuse them of "bad faith" or assume that McGraw–Hill is/are a fink.[**] For most people trained

---

[**] It is worth noting that the option "McGraw-Hill is" and "McGraw-Hill are" is not only acceptable but *de rigueur* in the British Isles. "The government prefers to postpone their decision" and "The government prefer to postpone their decision" can both be found because the first statement emphasizes government as a collectivity where-

to write in a certain way (including me), breaking with tradition can be both painful and awkward. Take the case of *like*. I was taught that under no circumstances was it to be used as a conjunction. The phrase "like I say" was ruthlessly purged from our prose in those dismal six weeks before the New York State Regents Exams. Then Winston cigarettes came out with a new slogan: "Winstons taste good like a cigarette should!" I couldn't believe my eyes and ears. I don't remember the year, but I suspect it was in the early fifties, yet to this day I cannot hear the phrase "like I say" without wincing, nor can I bring myself to use it. "As I say" is what I was taught, and "like I say" affects me about the same way that "ain't" does. It sounds uncouth; it grates on my eardrums. In short, I think there is an esthetic factor to be discussed before we accept "anyone...their." It doesn't make me wince when I see it or hear it, and I believe Bodine was right when she asserted that singular *they* was far more widespread than we might have suspected, widespread among outstanding writers as well as among the public at large. I predict that it will eventually enter the canons of sanctioned locutions, whereas *he* or *she* (which is perfectly correct in both number and gender) will not, at least not in writing. If you begin a paragraph with *someone* or *anyone* and continue on for several sentences, each one requiring either *he* or *she, his* or *her, him* or *her*, the paragraph does sound clumsy. Singular *they* (patiently waiting in the antechambers) appears tempting by contrast.

On the other hand, to take McGraw–Hill's advice and "to boldly go" where every man has gone before is fraught with peril. I could not forego the opportunity to quote a well-known split infinitive. If you haven't heard it on "Star Trek," you are probably an alien. Prescriptive grammarians have cautioned against the split infinitive with as much zeal as they have labored in behalf of generic he. The reason seems to lie in the fact that you do not split infinitives in Latin and therefore you shouldn't do so in English. The Latin infinitive consists of a single world (e.g., *vincere*, "to conquer") and therefore is incapable of being split. This proves that all older grammarians are not necessarily sexists, since the infinitive contains no hint of gender. (Actually when used as a substantive, the Latin infinitive is considered to be neuter in gender.) That the unfounded taboo against splitting infinitives is still alive is illustrated by columnist Jill Scott, who reported a letter she had received from a "gentleman lawyer who calls himself an 'amateur grammatical purist'": "This letter was painstakingly done and rather charming, even if his criticisms were out to lunch. He included reminiscences of his own high school English teacher—who '...would have condoned adultery in the school hallways before he would suffer the anguish of a split infinitive!'" Jill Scott's column is called "Essays on Educa-

as the second stresses it as a group of individuals. That government and other collective nouns may be singular or plural at will though the word is grammatically singular shows that usage among the most literate can defy the convention of numerical agreement.

tion," and this particular item appeared under the title "Fan Mail: Welcome to the Grammar Lonely Hearts Club," *The Sunday Denver Post, Contemporary,* July 22, 1984, p. 46.

We should heed the warnings of psychologists, philosophers, and educators before slouching reverently back toward HE.[21] We should consider the effect of so-called "generic *he*" upon children as well as upon adults. Do school girls perceive any females in *he*? No. Do women feel left out when books contain only the masculine (but supposedly "neutral") pronoun? Definitely.

Psychologist Wendy Martyna has published results of experimental tests that should convince the most hardened linguistic chauvinist.[22] In a paper before the American Psychological Association she explained that of seventy-two students she tested (thirty-six males, thirty-six females) nearly 20 percent did not infer *she* from *he* in comprehending the generic masculine. (She used both statements and accompanying pictures for part of the test.)

> When given a sentence such as "When someone listens to the record player, he will often sing along," and presented with the female version of the appropriate picture, these students responded that the picture did not apply to the sentence. There were no sex differences: eight females and six males returned this judgment.[23]

The explanation of the experimental set-up and its results are somewhat complex to one not trained in social science research (generic me), but I found 20 percent to be a significantly large number of students choosing "not apply" to a generic sentence accompanied by a female picture. All of the grammatical comfort about the "neutral," "unspecified," and "unmarked" character of the masculine pronoun proffered by Calvert Watkins and other members of the Harvard Linguistics Department skirts an important issue: The actual perception of hearers and readers.

Martyna continues:

> The ambiguity of generic "he" is doubly evident. Not only do some students comprehend it as specifically male, and other students as a human referent: but the same students render contradictory judgments, deciding in one instance that "he" includes "she," and in another, that it does not.[24]

She supplies some of the explanations the students gave, first those who chose "not apply" for generic he sentences accompanied by a female picture. "Recall," she says, "that *all of these students noticed the generic 'he' and said that it entered as a conscious factor into their decision to respond 'not apply.'*"[25]

Here are three of those responses:

—I said "not apply," because it was a lady. The "he" didn't agree. (Male)

—I said "not apply," because I expected a male and that's a female. (Male)
—I said "not apply," because it's a "he" and I couldn't decide whether a "she" would be appropriate. There was a clash between my mental image and the word. It could apply because of "someone," and "he" could be for no particular gender. I still pushed "not apply" because it was a girl. (Female)[26]

This last comment seems particularly enlightening as to the thought processes of a person asked to make a complex decision. Even knowing that generic *he* is *supposed* to be neutral has not been internalized as a reality by this student.

Among those students who pushed the "apply" button, many seem to have been taught the generic *rule* rather than responding spontaneously: "I guess I'm just so used to seeing 'he' meaning 'one', like in analytical English, that I let it go. Right after I answered, I realized it was a woman, but then I thought, 'Well, OK.' (Female)"[27]

In the "Discussion" portion of the paper, Martyna remarks that some defenders of the generic masculine might use her data as proof that it was "doing its generic duty quite well" (80 percent). Such a conclusion would be mistaken inasmuch as the "study was deliberately designed to facilitate the drawing of a generic interpretation."[28]

Our actual encounters with "he" rarely take place in a generic context as clear as that devised for this study. In the language perhaps most familiar to this student population, that of educational materials, the sex-specific "he" appears five to ten times for every generic "he..."[29]

One scholar whom Martyna cites considered "he" and "man" so restricted by context that she called them "pseudo-generics."[30] This is a word for grammarians to ponder—both prescriptivists and descriptivists. After more than two centuries of insistence upon *he* as the "unmarked," "unspecified," and "neutral" pronoun, 20 percent of a test group of college students rejected the rule. The only feature of the generic masculine that is truly consistent is its history as a cornerstone of "correctness" in grammars written by men. Without the bolstering (one is tempted to call it boosterism) in the grammars and textbooks, would we have slid wholeheartedly into Bodine's "singular *they*" by now? In light of Martyna's research, it seems quite possible.

E.B. White ignored both Martyna and Bodine when he updated *Elements of Style* in the late seventies. A form of "they" is still wrong after such pronouns as "everyone," "anybody," and "someone." A form of "he" is obligatory since "he or she" is "awkward." White's explanation dismisses any other solution:

The use of *he* as pronoun for nouns embracing both genders is a simple, practical convention rooted in the beginnings of the English language. *He* has lost all suggestion of maleness in these circumstances. The word was unquestionably biased to begin with (the dominant male), but after hundreds of years it has become seemingly indispensable. It has no pejorative connotations; it is never incorrect.[31]

In another publication Martyna writes:

Some would say that such [psychological] consequences are minor, since ambiguity is common in our language and creates nothing more than mild confusion. The specific/generic ambiguities of *he* and *man*, however, lead to far more than confusion. Examinations of the "he/man approach" to language have focused on the social and psychological significance of the generic masculine usage.[32]

For example,

Marguerite Ritchie has surveyed the legal implications of the generic masculines as it appears in Canadian law, concluding that its ambiguity has allowed either generic or specific interpretations to be drawn, depending on the judge's personal prejudices and the climate of the times.[33]

South of the border there are also indications that the masculine pronoun has been used against women. Take the case of Susan B. Anthony, who cast a vote in 1872 in Rochester, New York. She was arrested for "knowingly, wrongfully, and unlawfully" voting in the election. She had deliberately put the law to the test to see if she was a citizen (as defined in the 14th Amendment, 1868) and a voter (as defined in the 15th, 1870). She was convicted and fined $100 but refused to pay in the hope that she could then appeal the decision to a higher court. However, she was denied this opportunity since her failure to pay the fine was simply ignored.

Between the election in 1872 and her trial in 1873, Anthony toured the state lecturing on women's rights, or lack thereof, and she said the following about pronouns and the law:

It is argued that the use of the masculine pronouns *he, his* and *him* in all the constitutions and laws, is proof that only men were meant to be included in their provisions. If you insist on this version of the letter of the law, we shall insist that you be consistent and accept the other horn of the dilemma, which would compel you to exempt women from taxation for the support of the government and from penalties for the violations of laws. There is no *she* or *her* in the tax laws, and this is equally true of all the criminal laws.

Take for example the civil rights laws, which I am charged with having violated; not only are all the pronouns in the masculine, but everybody knows that it was intended expressly to hinder the rebel men from voting. It reads, "If any person shall knowingly vote without *his* having a lawful right." It was precisely so with all the papers served on me—the United States marshal's warrant, the bail-bond, the petition for habeas corpus, the bill of indictment—not one of them had a feminine pronoun; but to make them applicable to me, *the clerk of the court prefixed an "s" to the "he" and made "her" out of "his" and "him;"* and I insist if government officials may thus manipulate the pronouns to tax, fine, imprison and hang women, it is their duty to thus change them in order to protect us in our right to vote.[34]

Why is it if *he* is considered generic that in 1872 the male pronouns were all changed to female in order to avoid any ambiguity in Anthony's case? If Anthony and Ritchie are right—that the masculine pronoun has been used both generically and specifically in order to discriminate against women—then Geraldine Ferraro should have been on her guard in 1984, for Article II, Section 1, of the Constitution reads as follows: "The executive power shall be vested in a President of the United States of America. *He* shall hold *his* office during the term of four years, and, together with the Vice-President, chosen for the same term...."[35] I found no argument in the press against Ferraro's choice by Mondale as his running mate on the grounds that the constitutional *he* prevented her nomination. There seems to be no pronoun qualification in running for President or Vice President.

Susan B. Anthony tested the pronoun qualification for voting and lost. It is probably because the 14th Amendment—the foundation of civil rights, the amendment that is used so often because it contains the words "due process" and "equal protection of the laws"—also contains the first instance of the use of the word *male* in the Constitution:

Section 2.    Representatives shall be apportioned among the several states according to their respective numbers, counting the whole number of persons in each state, excluding Indians not taxed. But when the right to vote at any election for the choice of electors for President and Vice-President of the United States, representatives in Congress, the executive and judicial officers of a state, or the members of the legislature thereof, is denied to any of the *male* inhabitants of such state, being twenty-one years of age, and citizens of the United States, or in any way abridged, except for participation in rebellion, or other crime, the basis of representation therein shall be reduced in the proportion which the number of such *male* citizens shall bear to the whole number of *male* citizens twenty-one years of age in such state.[36]

There is nothing generic about *male*, and the assumption that all voters must be male was retained until ratification of the 19th Amendment in 1920:

Section 1.    The right of citizens of the United States to vote shall not be denied or abridged by the United States or by any states on account of sex.

Section 2.    The Congress shall have the power to enforce this article by appropriate legislation.[37]

Phyllis Schlafly has claimed that she approved of the 19th Amendment, but was against the 27th (ERA) because of Section 2, which (as in the 19th) gives the federal government the right to enforce it.[38] Other opponents of the ERA have said that women are sufficiently protected by the 14th Amendment, that there is no need for yet another amendment prohibiting infringement of rights on the basis of sex. Yet the 14th is the very one that contains the word *male* thereby implicitly denying that women were part of the electorate. Schlafly's emphasis on Section 2 of the Equal Rights Amendment scared women who feared loss of "protection" under state law through interference from the federal government. Such an argument goes beyond the scope of this book since each state has its own statutes concerning divorce, child custody, and property.

Before leaving the pronoun problem, with or without envy, we should take a look at the first person. Although most of the linguistic skirmishing has focused upon generic *he*, feminists have also reviewed the situation with respect to how they speak of themselves collectively. Simone de Beauvoir wrote in 1949: "...women do not say 'We,' except at some congress of feminists or similar formal demonstration; men say 'women,' and women use the same word in referring to themselves."[39] Her point is proof of her argument that men think of themselves as "Self" and women as "Other" and that women have internalized this male view so that they think of themselves as "Other" also. Women do not (wrote Beauvoir) band together like other oppressed groups—Jews, blacks, the proletariat—and proudly say "we." Instead, they use the third person, demonstrating that they consider themselves secondary, subordinate, and inessential (as well as inauthentic).

Beauvoir's book is a cornerstone of modern feminism; hence, her assertions about how women refer to themselves have been taken seriously by women writers. One example of the current agonizing reappraisal is to be found in an introductory textbook for women's studies courses called *Women's Realities, Women's Choices* by the Hunter College Women's Studies Collective.[40] The preface explains how the book was conceived and put together over a period of years; it also addresses the pronoun problem directly and at some length:

Throughout this book, we its authors use the pronoun "we" to refer to women everywhere, in any period of history. The choice requires an explanation and some personal history.

We, the authors, originally decided to try to take the point of view of women, to speak for women as subjects (we) rather than as objects (them), to speak, that is, for all of "us." The device of the pronoun, using "women... we" rather than "women...they" appealed to us, so we tried using it.

We immediately ran into difficulties. The device struck some readers as awkward and artificial: "we the authors" did not take part in the French Revolution or suffer the indignities of slavery; how could we presume to speak for all women? Was it not either disrespectful or silly to pretend to do so?

We decided that the manuscript should be rewritten, using "they" to refer to women collectively and in the contexts we were describing, and "we" refer only to us the authors.

It was at this stage that the chapters were put together and that many of us authors saw the book as a whole for the first time. As we read it over, we realized what had been lost in relegating women, again, to the voiceless "they," the "other," where patriarchy has always tried to put all of us.

After much re-thinking and lengthy discussion of fresh criticism and reactions from new readers, we the authors revised the perspectives of the book yet again, again trying to speak, however haltingly, for all women. We the authors do not presume for a minute to be able to do so. We are only a small number of women with restricted backgrounds and limited experiences. We are of course not pretending to be able to give adequate voice to the experiences of all women. But the authors of this book together with all those who read it and teach with it may be quite a large number of women with more varied backgrounds. We hope that women can be encouraged to see the world from the point of view of *women*, from the point of view of all of us, from *our* perspective. We hope the device of identifying with whatever women are being discussed in this book will help in this shift of perspective.[41]

If this preface had been published in the mid-seventies, some male columnist would doubtless have made fun of it, as George F. Will ridiculed McGraw-Hill's nonsexist guidelines, as William F. Buckley sneared [sic] at those of the publisher Scott, Foresman, and as Stefan Kanfer attacked the whole concept of women interfering with the language in an article called "Sispeak: A Msguided Attempt to change Herstory."[42] This last is a very witty title, but all three of these normally urbane authors appear more condescending than understanding of the language problems involved in women's new awareness of themselves as human beings. It seemed to embarrass them, and they offered a helping hand to the poor ladies so that they would not further disgrace themselves meddling with English. But their helpfulness and comfort appear thoroughly hypocritical. By trivializing women's attempts to grope toward a more equitable language, they only drew attention to their own assumed status as judges and authorities. Sarcasm permeates their advice. If men are so logical, so reasonable, and ahysterical as we have been led to believe, we should expect a more objective statement, such as:

> Thinking about profound social change, conservatives always expect disaster, while revolutionaries confidently anticipate utopia. Both are wrong.

This logical, reasonable, one might say "classical," statement was made by a woman—Carolyn G. Heilbrun.[43] She has a wider audience under the pseudonym Amanda Cross, author of many delightful detective novels. One of them—*Death in a Tenured Position*—deals with sexist discrimination in faculty appointments at Harvard. (Heilbrun is Professor of English at Columbia.)

Mary Daly used the first-person plural pronoun in 1973, under the influence of Simone de Beauvoir, for the following appeared two paragraphs after a reference to woman as "the Other":

> Women may judge that in some cases the names imposed upon reality by male-dominated society and sanctified by the religion are basically oppressive and must be rejected. In other instances, it may be that partial truth has been taken for the whole in the past, and that the symbols and conceptualizations that are biased have to be liberated from their partiality. Women will free traditions, thought, and customs only by hearing each other and thus making it possible to speak *our* word.[44]

## Notes

1. "The Language of Religion," in *Words and Women*, eds. Casey Miller and Kate Smith (Garden City, N.Y.: Doubleday/Anchor, 1976).

2. Mary Ritchie Key, *Male/Female Language* (Metuchen, N.J.: Scarecrow Press, 1975), p. 142. The chapter in which the quotation occurs is entitled "An Androgynous Language: The Future Tense." (My italics).

3. Miller and Swift, *Words and Women*, p. 76.

4. Ibid., p. 55.

5. Ibid., p. 57. Both quotes from Watkins were taken from "Indo-European and the Indo-Europeans," *The American Heritage Dictionary of the English Language* (New York: American Heritage Publishing Company, 1969), p. 1498.

6. Miller and Swift, *Words and Women*, pp. 76–77, quoting Armagost's Letter to the Editor in *Newsweek*, December 27, 1971.

7. Ann Bodine, "Androcentrism in Prescriptive Grammar: Singular 'They,' Sex-Indefinite 'He,' and 'He or She,'" *Language in Society*, 4 (1975): 129–146.

8. Ibid., pp. 130–131.

9. Ibid., p. 131. (My italics.)

10. Ibid., pp. 131–133.

11. Ibid., p. 133.

12. Ibid.

13. Ibid., p. 138.

14. Ibid., p. 139, quoting Paul Roberts, *The Roberts English Series* (New York: Harcourt, Brace, and World, 1967), p. 355.

15. Bodine, "Androcentrism," p. 140.

16. Ibid., p. 141. Conklin presented her "perspectives" paper at a meeting of the American Dialect Society, Ann Arbor, in 1973.

17. James R. Hulbert, ed. *Bright's Anglo-Saxon Reader* (New York: Henry Holt, 1957; original copyright 1891), p. liii.

18. "Guidelines," p. 8.

19. It seems to me that *or* should be italicized in the phrase *"he or she."*

20. Ibid. (My italics.)

21. For two philosophers' opinions on both generic *he* and the noun *man*, see Janice Moulton, "The Myth of the Neutral 'Man,'" in *Sexist Language: A Modern Philosophical Analysis*, ed. Mary Vetterling-Braggin (n.p.: Littlefield, Adams, 1981), pp. 115–199, and a counter argument by Jane Durance, "Gender-Neutral Terms," ibid., pp. 147–154.

22. Martyna's doctoral dissertation is entitled "Using and Understanding the Generic Masculine: A Social-Psychological Approach to Language and the Sexes" (Ph.D. Stanford 1978), but she had begun publishing before receiving her degree.

23. Wendy Martyna, "Comprehension of the Generic Masculine: Inferring 'She' from 'He,'" paper presented at the American Psychological Association, 85th Annual Convention, San Francisco, California, August, 1977, p. 9. I am indebted to the author for having sent me a copy of this paper in December, 1977.

24. Ibid., p. 9.

25. Ibid., p. 14. (My italics.)

26. Ibid., pp. 14–15.

27.  Ibid., p. 16.

28.  Ibid., p. 17.

29.  Ibid., p. 19.

30.  Ibid., quoting and paraphrasing J. P. Stanley, "Gender-marking in American English: Usage and Reference," in *Sexism and Language*, ed. A. P. Nilsen et al. (Urbana: National Council of Teachers of English, 1977).

31.  William Strunk, Jr., With Revisions an Introduction, and a Chapter on Writing by E.B. White, *The Elements of Style*, 3rd. ed. (New York: Macmillan, 1979).

32.  Wendy Martyna, "The Psychology of the Generic Masculine," in *Women and Language in Literature and Society*, eds. Sally McConnell-Ginet, Ruth Borker, and Nelly Furman (New York: Praeger, 1980), pp. 69–78. Quotation from p. 75.

33.  Martyna, "Psychology," drawing upon Ritchie's article "Alice through the Statutes," *McGill Law Journal*, 21 (1975), 685–707.

34.  Ida Husted Harper, *The Life and Work of Susan B. Anthony* (Indianapolis: Bowen–Merrill, 1898), II, 982.

35.  *Webster's New World Dictionary with Student Handbook,* Concise Edition (Nashville, Tenn.: The Southwestern Company, 1975), *Student Handbook*, p. 17. (My italics.)

36.  Webster, *Handbook*, p. 25. (My italics).

37.  Ibid., p. 26.

38.  Carol Felsenthal, *The Sweetheart of the Silent Majority: The Biography of Phyllis Schlafly* (Garden City, N.Y.: Doubleday, 1981).

39.  Simone de Beauvoir, *The Second Sex,* trans. and ed. H. M. Parshley (New York: The Modern Library, 1968), p. xix. Originally published in France in two volumes as *La Deuxième Sexe* (Librairie Gallimard, 1949).

40.  Hunter College Women's Studies Collective, *Women's Realities, Women's Choices* (New York: Oxford University Press, 1983). The eight members of the Collective are identified on pp. v–vi.

41.  Collective, *Women's Realities*, pp. x–xi.

42.  George F. Will, "Sexist Guidelines and Reality," *The Washington Post*, September 20, 1974; William F. Buckley, Jr., "On the Right: Who's Beautiful?" Middleton (Conn.) *Press*, November 30, 1972; Kanfer's article appeared in *Time,* October 23, 1972, p. 79.

43.  Carolyn G. Heilbrun, *Toward a Recognition of Androgyny* (New York: W. W. Norton, 1982; originally published by Alfred A. Knopf, 1964), p. x.

44.    Mary Daly, *Beyond God the Father: Toward a Philosophy of Women's Liber-ation* (Boston: Beacon Press, 1973), pp. 10–11. (My italics.) Daly's first book, published in 1968, was entitled *The Church and the Second Sex.*

**For discussion**

*Content*

1. Hill carefully documents her evidence. How is that practice helpful to you as a reader? What is its effect? Is the evidence specific and sufficient? Does it cover an adequate range?

2. What did you learn in junior high or high school grammar or English classes about using "he" and "him"? What did you learn about noun and pronoun agreement? Did any of your texts or teachers mention sex agreement of noun and pronoun? What do you think about the pronoun question that so interests so many people? How do "he" and "man" affect our thoughts and perceptions?

3. Who created the rules of grammar to which Watkins refers in paragraph one and to which McGraw-Hill refer in paragraph 12? What difference does the origin of the rules make?

4. Which is more important—what the grammar rules say *should* be, or what people's perceptions of "he" or of "man" *are*?

5. Do you consider "he or she" awkward? How does "she or he" or "s/he" look, instead of "he"? How much of the reaction against alternatives to "he" is simply that people are used to seeing and hearing "he"? What do you think of the possibility of alternating "she" and "he"? Some scholars advocate using "she" as the singular generic pronoun for the next three hundred years to balance three hundred years of "he." What do you think of that alternative to the false generic "he"?

*Style*

Does Hill choose words and sentence structures appropriate for readers who are not experts in linguistic study? Give several examples to support your answer.

**For writing**

All suggestions for writing for Chapter Three follow the discussion suggestions for the chapter's final essay. (See page 175.)

# The Role of American Indian Women in Cultural Continuity and Transition

## Bea Medicine

AMERICAN INDIAN AND ALASKAN NATIVE WOMEN are perhaps the most neglected and grossly treated in the literature of minority women. This is true especially in research on speech forms and patterns of language usage in American Indian and Alaskan Native communities. Research on the language patterns of women in these communities suffers from the mistaken notion that such an entity as "the monolithic American Indian" exists. To speak of speech patterns typical of "the American Indian" and to make generalizations across tremendously complex and varied linguistic differences is obviously dangerous. There are an estimated 206 distinct languages being spoken by natives of North America which reflect totally distinct language stocks, with many of them being as dissimilar as English and Chinese (Chafe 1962). Such multiplicity of languages makes it extremely difficult to speak of the linguistic aspects of "the American Indian woman."

It is important to point out, however, that although there is great variation in American Indian languages, traditions, and customs, there is a common experience which these communities share historically as a result of language policies and practices imposed by various political institutions and education systems governing them. For example, many of the unique language systems of American Indians have been obliterated through the education policies of a federal government which often has sought to eliminate the cultural and linguistic differences of the indigenous tribes in order to pressure them into becoming part of the dominant culture. In some cases, this suppression of language has resulted in their decline or their death. Today, language retrieval and revitalization are seeking to undo the results of this linguistic oppression. In other cases, this oppression has had less devastating effects on American Indian communities and instead resulted in varying degrees of native language use among contemporary native peoples. As a result, one finds that there are extreme variations in the communicative skills in native languages from one tribal community to another on reservations or in urban areas.

The power of linguistic domination by the superimposition of an alien tongue—English—and an education system, both of which serve as instruments of social control, have markedly affected the structures, uses and attitudes of the languages of subordination. Indian women are particularly affected by these sociohistorical circumstances for a variety of reasons to be discussed below. American Indian women perform at least three distinctive social roles through their patterns of language use in their communities. They maintain cultural values through the socialization of children; they serve as evaluators of language use by setting the normative standards of the native or ancestral tongue and English; and they are effective as agents of change through mediation strategies with the White society.

## Enforcers of Tradition

The historical pattern of English language domination has been especially significant for Indian women—the primary socializers of children.

The introduction of the majority language—English—placed and continues to place a heavy burden on Indian women because adopting the English language often has meant losing linguistic symbols of culture and gaining male bias carried by the semantic system of English. One example is found in the very different way gender is handled in some American Indian languages and English.

Standard English with its male bias has often obviated the rich gender-based distinctions which exist in the ancestral language. To cite one example, Lakota Sioux, in any of its three dialects—Lakota, Dakota, or Nakota—has significant obligatory structural markers to indicate first person women's speech as opposed to men's speech. For the most part these markers consist of suffixes. For example, *Hanta yo* would be a command muttered by males to indicate "Get out!" *Hanta ye* would be the equivalent referential meaning for female speakers.

Aside from the more obvious linguistic obligatory markers which exist in American Indian ancestral languages and which do not in English, there are [sic] also an entire set of kinship terms serving to depict social and familial relationships in American Indian culture. Again, these do not exist in their English translation. Women are indirectly affected here again.

For example, in Lakota, gender-specific terms exist to indicate birth order and vocative designations, so that for females the simple English term "brother" would be distinguished in one of two ways depending on age: *tiblo* "older brother" versus *mi-sunka-la* "younger brother." Conversely, similar terms are used by males to indicate feminine gender and age (or birth order). Moreover, in the bilateral kinship system, the terms are extended to parallel cousins or cross cousins, depending on the sex of the speaker. As a result, one can understand the confusion a superimposed kinship system, such as English, brought to social structures and reciprocal relationships in this particular American Indian culture and to others. In those cases where the ancestral language has literally died or barely continues to exist, often even linguistic marking of female-female relationships, feminine bonds, and responsive relationships have been obliterated.

Building on these ancestral kinship designations, mothers usually indicate proper behavior to daughters and other "daughters" in kinship equivalencies, such as female parallel cousins. One may commonly hear such affective assessment given to daughters as, "White persons don't have proper kinship names for brothers. But you know you respect your older brother, and take care of your younger one."

It may be that some Lakota persons as well as other American Indian groups have accepted or have been forced to accept the new kinship models imposed by the white culture and language. Although specific linguistic designations may no longer exist, other culturally revealing patterns of language usage remain. One such vestige is the "joking relationship." Such verbal interaction with its sexual connotation which an older sister's husband often extends towards his wife's younger sister or her younger female cousin reflect a language usage pattern which denotes the continuity of an ancient cultural form. Perhaps English or the ways of white people have not been effective in destroying core cultural values. In Lakota communities, women continue to participate in joking relationships, usually at public events. These jokes are always stated in Lakota, for it is felt that this type of humor is best expressed in the native tongue. Nuance and repartee reflect skillful manipulation of language and add to the enjoyment of the group. Some women are known for their remarkable wit and subtlety in "joking" and "putting men down" by their verbal skills.

There are other instances where women of an older generation who stayed at home and attended local schools rather than going away to governmental or parochial boarding schools are known to have greater knowledge in oral history or knowledge of traditional techniques and material items. These women are often envied for this unique and valued information, not only by other women but by Lakota males as well. It is in the rich folklore and legendary domain that much knowledge is being lost in cultural transmission to children, especially grandchildren. These youngsters tend to be monolingual in English and thus stories detailing "how it was in the old days" are usually told in English. Folktales and proverbs which have traditionally served as prescriptive devices are not totally significant in contemporary communities in the native idiom. Cultural retrieval programs have succeeded in collecting folktales and legends in English. Folktales have also been recorded in the native language. Whether in English or the native language, these have relied heavily on women's contribution, both as storytellers and translators of native oratory.

## Cultural Brokers

One particular role which women have played and continue to play in many American Indian cultures is that of mediator between their own community and White society. They are often vested with this role because of their facility with the English language. In many communities, women acquire English more readily than men, and this resulting competence often places them in the role of mediator. One can hear statements such as the following made by a Brule Sioux male from the Rosebud reservation: "*They* (BIA administrators, county welfare workers, judges, and police officers) listen to women when they talk to them."

Yet, while there is a realization of the need for such mediators on the part of Indian men, there is at the same time a great deal of dislike, criticism, and frustration. Males often criticize women for learning the English tongue "too well," since getting too close to the White society is taken as a sign of assimilation and consequent rejection of one's own cultural values. But the fact that women are put in the role of mediators becomes a point of frustration for males. They envy them for their bilingual skill and especially the power associated with it in the dominant society. In a sense, such language usage patterns make males feel helpless in the face of oppression and racism in a dominant White society. This emasculation often leads to conflict between males and females, exhibited too often toward wives in verbal or physical battering. Such conflict is an especially onerous position to men in Northern Plains Indian societies, which have been labeled "Warrior" societies. Since male self-valuation has produced a sense of male superiority, the "macho" image is eroded by such speech usage patterns, and the locus of control in male/female relationships is seen by males as being usurped.

Lakota Sioux adults can be seen in dual roles as cultural conservators and cultural innovators in the area of language use. This traditional role of cultural guardian is seen vividly in this example from Ella Deloria (1945:43) who uses it to include all adults:

> Nor was it any wonder that small children rapidly learned their social duties, since the training constantly given them was calculated to condition them and direct them in that way. All grown-ups by tacit consent seemed to "gang up" for that purpose. Even before a child was aware of his kinship obligations they make sentences and put the correct words and formal speeches into his mouth for him to repeat to this or that relative. It was their informal but constant system of education in human relations and social responsibility.

But it was acknowledged that the major socializers of children were the Lakota females, even though both men and women taught the proper kin terms which guaranteed smoothly working *tiospaye* (extended family) relationships in a traditional setting. It was this sharing of child training which was quickly submerged in a new superimposed system of patriarchal orientations, a system foisted on the Lakota in the acculturational process which held to the ideal that the training of children was entirely in the woman's domain. Along with the demolition of the warrior role among the Sioux, and the fact that women were often sent to get the rations which were doled out in the early reservation period, women began a subtle but functional assumption of the role of cultural broker or mediator. In addition, women were often recruited to work in the houses of missionaries and of other agents of change. In order to interact on this level, women learned the English language as a means of survival in a rapidly changing situation. Women also taught the children that interaction in two different worlds required entirely different languages and subsumed a new behavioral pattern.

Interestingly, women were recruited along with the men to attend off-reservation schools in such far-removed places as Hampton, Virginia, and Carlisle, Pennsylvania. It was in these schools that the native language was suppressed and both sexes learned to excel in reading and writing English. It was usually the Indian men who said that they had completely lost their ability to speak the native tongue after returning to the reservation. On the other hand, oral history accounts, such as those of the Standing Rock Reservation, substantiate that women were often called on to deliver speeches in community events such as Christmas and New Year's celebrations, weddings, and other public events.

In the public sphere as well as the private ones, Lakota women are groomed to be expressive. Even today when I return home, I am expected to address the crowds at Pow Wow celebrations and other community events. The skill of public speaking was and is now equally accessible and available to both Lakota males and females.

At the time when Tribal Councils were first functioning on reservations, some Lakota members often took their daughters to observe the meetings, and they thus became aware of the *Pogo* (political climate of a new institution). Since meetings were conducted in English and Lakota, fluency in both languages was enhanced. It was not surprising that Standing Rock had a female Tribal Chair in the 1940s and another in the 1950s. This may have been unusual, but the thrust to biculturalism and bilingualism was seen as a means to understanding the superimposed culture with a strong background in the native one. The females fulfilled both.

As mothers, women have played an important role in educating their children in the proper usage of the English language through games devised for this purpose. Such training has added a great deal to the success of their children in school. Often contextual situations were pointed out to indicate to the child the proper vernacular mode. Students who lived at home had parental surrogates within the kinship network as well as parents who supported their efforts.

Speech-making was still part of the expected behavior pattern. More important, before the days of relevant Indian curricula, many of the mothers encouraged the use of oral history, legends, and native materials to write histories of the various villages or towns on the reservation as a means of interesting students in improving writing competency in English.

## Evaluators of Language

Women in American Indian communities hold a wide variety of different attitudes toward language usage. They range from very traditional ones in which ancestral language and values are tenaciously adhered to, even though English is also used, to a more assimilationist one in which children are not even spoken to in their ancestral language. Some families try to maintain a truly bilingual home. As mothers, women play a decisive role in the whole matter of language choice, since it is often their decision that determines which language the child will acquire naturally. Some continue speaking the ancestral language to the child but send the child to a school in which English is the only language of instruction. Others speak English only. Still others follow a bilingual model through the use of more modern bilingual schooling. For example, some Southeastern groups such as Lumbee or Pamunkey, although claiming to be native, do not have a cultural or linguistic base which reflects a tribal character. On the other hand, such groups in the Northeast as the Passamaquody or the Penobscot have retained a native language base. In the Southwest, the Navajo evidence a high degree of monolingualism in their native language. It could be argued that women have contributed greatly to these variations in bilingualism. A long-distinguished "Indian" trait seems to center on native autonomy; the choice is usually made by the mother or maternal surrogate as to which language or languages will be used and consequently learned by the child. It is often the case, however, that one hears statements regarding the loss of language, such as, "I'm sorry that my mother did not teach me my native language."

This paper has discussed various aspects of women's role in American Indian communities as manifested by the use of the ancestral language and English. As males and females within these communities have acknowledged, the impact and importance of native women in cultural and linguistic continuity is noteworthy.

## References

Chafe, Wallace L. 1962. "Estimates Regarding the Present Speakers of North American Indian Languages," *International Journal of American Linguistics* 28: 161–171.

Deloria, Ella. 1945. *Speaking of Indians*. New York: Friendship Press.

Dumont, Robert V. 1972. "Learning English and How to be Silent-Studies in Sioux and Cherokee Classrooms." In *Functions of Language in the Classroom*, edited by C. Cazden, V. John, and D. Hymes. New York: Teacher's College Press.

Hill, Ruth Beebe. 1979. *Hanta Yo.* New York: Macmillan.

Leap, William T., ed. 1977. *Studies in Southwestern English.* San Antonio: Trinity University Press.

Malancon, Richard, & Mary Jo Malancon, 1977. "Indian English at Haskell, 1915." In *Studies in Southwestern English*, edited by William Leaf. San An-tonio: Trinity University Press.

Medicine, Bea. " 'Speaking Indian': Parameters of Language Use Among American Indians." *FOCUS*, March 6 (1981), 1–8.

——. 1979a. "Native American Speech Patterns: The Case of the Lakota Speakers." In *Handbook of Intercultural Communications*, edited by Molefi Ashante, Eileen New-mark & Cecil Blake. Beverly Hills, CA: Sage Publications.

——. 1979b. "Bilingual Education and Public Policy: The Cases of the American Indians." In *Bilingual Education and Public Policy in the United States*, edited by Raymond Padilla. Ypsilanti, Michigan: Eastern Michigan University.

——. 1979c. "Issues in the Professionalization of Indian Women." Paper presented to the American Psychological Association, Toronto.

Metcalf, Ann. December 1978. "A Model for Treatment in a Native American Family Service Center." Oakland, CA: Urban Indian Child Resource Center.

Phillips, Susan. 1972. "Participant Structures and Communicative Competence: Warm Springs Children in Community and Classroom." In *Functions of Language in the Classroom*, edited by C. Cazden, V. John, & D. Hymes. New York: Teacher's College Press.

## For discussion

*Content*

1. Cite the information in Medicine's essay that gives you a new way to think about Native North American women.

2. In paragraph three, Medicine mentions "male bias" in English. From your study of English, give several examples of male bias in the language, examples that illustrate male biases in our thoughts.

3. Explain, with several examples from this essay and from your experience or knowledge, how a language imposed over a people's native language or language of birth might obscure the people's ideas and customs.

4. If you have been forbidden to use your birth language, explain the constrictions that situation placed on you. Were there ideas you could not think because the imposed language did not have words for those ideas? Were there thoughts you could not express in the imposed language? If you have not been forbidden to use your birth language, imagine what your world would

been forbidden to use your birth language, imagine what your world would be like if tomorrow you were forbidden to use that language.

5.  Medicine points out that Native North American men may see Native women's learning English as a sign of rejecting Native cultural values. Explain how learning a language could be tied so closely to cultural values.

*Style*

1.  What is the function of paragraph two? Having read that paragraph, do you need or appreciate the subheadings?

# Nuclear Language and How We Learned to Pat the Bomb

## Carol Cohn

MY CLOSE ENCOUNTER with nuclear strategic analysis started in the summer of 1984. I was one of 48 college teachers attending a summer workshop on nuclear weapons, strategic doctrine, and arms control that was held at a university containing one of the nation's foremost centers of nuclear strategic studies, and that was co-sponsored by another institution. It was taught by some of the most distinguished experts in the field, who have spent decades moving back and forth between academia and governmental positions in Washington. When at the end of the program I was afforded the chance to be a visiting scholar at one...defense studies center, I jumped at the opportunity.

I spent the next year immersed in the world of defense intellectuals—men (and indeed, they are virtually all men) who, in Thomas Powers' words, "Use the concept of deterrence to explain why it is safe to have weapons of a kind and number it is not safe to use." Moving in and out of government, working sometimes as administrative officials or consultants, sometimes in universities and think tanks, they create the theory that underlies U.S. nuclear strategic practice.

My reason for wanting to spend a year among these men was simple, even if the resulting experiences were not. The current nuclear situation is so dangerous and irrational that one is tempted to explain it by positing either insanity or evil in our decision makers. That explanation is, of course, inadequate. My goal was to gain a better understanding of how sane men of goodwill could think and act in ways that lead to what appear to be extremely irrational and immoral results.

*From* Signs: Journal of Women in Culture and Society. *12 (Summer 1987): 687–718. Copyright© University of Chicago. Reprinted by permission of The University of Chicago Press.*

I attended lectures, listened to arguments, conversed with defense analysts, interviewed graduate students throughout their training, obsessed by the question, "How *can* they think this way?" But as I learned the language, as I became more and more engaged with their information and their arguments, I found that my own thinking was changing, and I had to confront a new question: How can *I* think this way? Thus, my own experience becomes part of the data that I analyze in attempting to understand not only how "they" can think that way, but how any of us can.

This article is the beginning of an analysis of the nature of nuclear strategic thinking, with emphasis on the role of a specialized language that I call "technostrategic." I have come to believe that this language both reflects and shapes the American nuclear strategic project, and that all who are concerned about nuclear weaponry and nuclear war must give careful attention to language—with whom it allows us to communicate and what it allows us to think as well as say.

I had previously encountered in my reading the extraordinary language used to discuss nuclear war, but somehow it was different to hear it spoken. What hits first is the elaborate use of abstraction and euphemism, which allows infinite talk about nuclear holocaust without ever forcing the speaker or enabling the listener to touch the reality behind the words.

Anyone who has seen pictures of Hiroshima burn victims may find it perverse to hear a class of nuclear devices matter-of-factly referred to as "clean bombs." These are weapons which are largely fusion rather than fission; they therefore release a somewhat higher proportion of their energy as prompt radiation, but produce less radioactive fallout than fission bombs of the same yield. Clean bombs may provide the perfect metaphor for the language of defense analysts and arms controllers. This language has enormous destructive power, but without the emotional fallout that would result if it were clear one was talking about plans for mass murder, mangled bodies, human suffering. Defense analysts talk about "countervalue attacks" rather than about incinerating cities. Human death, in nuclear parlance, is most often referred to as "collateral damage." While Reagan's renaming the MX missile "the Peacekeeper" was the object of considerable scorn in the community of defense analysts, the same analysts refer to the missile as a "damage limitation weapon."

These phrases, only a few of the hundreds that could be chosen, exemplify the astounding chasm between image and reality that characterizes technostrategic language. They also hint at the terrifying way the existence of nuclear devices has distorted our perceptions and redefined the world. "Clean bombs" as a phrase tells us that radioactivity is the only "dirty" part of killing people.

It is hard not to feel that one function of this sanitized abstraction is to deny the uncontrolled messiness of the situations one contemplates creating. So that we not only have clean bombs but also "surgically clean strikes": "counterforce" attacks that can purportedly "take out"—that is, accurately destroy—an opponent's weapons or command centers, without causing significant injury to anything else. The image is unspeakably ludicrous when the surgical tool is not a delicately controlled scalpel but a nuclear warhead.

Feminists have often suggested that an important aspect of the arms race is phallic worship; that "missile envy," to borrow Helen Caldicott's phrase, is a significant motivating force in the nuclear buildup. I have always found this an uncomfortably reductionist explanation and hoped that observing at the center would yield a more complex analysis. Still, I was curious about the extent to which I might find a sexual subtext in the defense professionals' discourse. I was not prepared for what I found.

I think I had naively imagined that I would need to sneak around and eavesdrop on what men said in unguarded moments, using all my cunning to unearth sexual imagery. I had believed that these men would have cleaned up their acts, or that at least at some point in a long talk about "penetration aids," someone would suddenly look up, slightly embarrassed to be caught in such blatant confirmation of feminist analyses.

I was wrong. There was no evidence that such critiques had ever reached the ears, much less the minds, of these men. American military dependence on nuclear weapons was explained as "irresistible, because you get more bang for the buck." Another lecturer solemnly and scientifically announced, "To disarm is to get rid of all your stuff." A professor's explanation of why the MX missile is to be placed in the silos of the newest Minuteman missiles, instead of replacing the older, less accurate missiles, was "because they're in the nicest hole—you're not going to take the nicest missile you have and put it in a crummy hole." Other lectures were filled with discussion of vertical erector launchers, thrust-to-weight ratios, soft lay downs, deep penetration, and the comparative advantages of protracted versus spasm attacks—or what one military adviser to the National Security Council has called "releasing 70 to 80 percent of our megatonnage in one orgasmic whump."[1]

But if the imagery is transparent, its significance may be less so. I do *not* want to assert that it somehow reveals what defense intellectuals are really talking about, or their motivations; individual motives cannot necessarily be read directly from imagery, which originates in a broader cultural context. The history of the atomic bomb project itself is rife with overt images of competitive male sexuality, as is the discourse of the early nuclear physicists, strategists, and members of the Strategic Air Command.[2] Both the military itself and the arms manufacturers are constantly exploiting the phallic imagery and promise of sexual domination that their weapons so conveniently suggest. Consider the following, from the June 1985 issue of *Air Force Magazine:* Emblazoned in bold letters across the top of a two-page advertisement for the AV-8B Harrier II—"Speak Softly and Carry a Big Stick." The copy below boasts "an exceptional thrust-to-weight ratio," and "vectored thrust capability that makes the...unique rapid response possible."

Another vivid source of phallic imagery is to be found in descriptions of nuclear blasts themselves. Here, for example, is one by journalist William Laurence, who was brought by the Army Air Corps to witness the Nagasaki bombing.

> Then, just when it appeared as though the thing had settled down into a state of permanence, there came shooting out of the top a giant mushroom that increased the size of the pillar to a total of 45,000 feet. The mushroom top was even more alive than the pillar, seething and boiling in a white fury of creamy foam, sizzling upward and then descending earthward, a thousand geysers rolled into one. It kept struggling in an elemental fury, like a creature in the act of breaking the bonds that held it down.[3]

Given the degree to which it suffuses their world, the fact that defense intellectuals use a lot of sexual imagery is not especially surprising. Nor does it, by itself, constitute grounds for imputing motivation. The interesting issue is not so much the imagery's possible psychodynamic origins as how it functions—its role in making the work world of defense intellectuals feel tenable. Several stories illustrate the complexity.

At one point a group of us took a field trip to the New London Navy base where nuclear submarines are home-ported, and to the General Dynamics Electric Boat yards where a new Trident submarine was being constructed. The high point of the trip was a tour of a nuclear-powered submarine. A few at a time, we descended into the long, dark, sleek tube in which men and a nuclear reactor are encased underwater for months at a time. We squeezed through hatches, along neon-lit passages so narrow that we had to turn and press our backs to the walls for anyone to get by. We passed the cramped racks where men sleep, and the red and white signs warning of radioactive materials. When we finally reached the part of the sub where the missiles are housed, the officer accompanying us turned with a grin and asked if we wanted to stick our hands through a hole to "pat the missile." *Pat the missile?*

The image reappeared the next week, when a lecturer scornfully declared that the only real reason for deploying cruise and Pershing II missiles in Western Europe was "so that our allies can pat them." Some months later, another group of us went to be briefed at NORAD (the North American Aerospace Defense Command). On the way back, the Air National Guard plane we were on went to refuel at Offut Air Force Base, the Strategic Air Command headquarters near Omaha, Nebraska. When word leaked out that our landing would be delayed because the new B-1 bomber was in the area, the plane became charged with a tangible excitement that built as we flew in our holding pattern, people craning their necks to try to catch a glimpse of the B-1 in the skies, and climaxed as we touched down on the runway and hurtled past it. Later, when

I returned to the center I encountered a man who, unable to go on the trip, said to me enviously, "I hear you got to pat a B-1."

What is all this patting? Patting is an assertion of intimacy, sexual possession, affectionate domination. The thrill and pleasure of "patting the missile" is the proximity of all that phallic power, the possibility of vicariously appropriating it as one's own. But patting is not only an act of sexual intimacy. It is also what one does to babies, small children, the pet dog. The creatures one pats are small, cute, harmless—not terrifyingly destructive. Pat it, and its lethality disappears.

Much of the sexual imagery I heard was rife with the sort of ambiguity suggested by "patting the missiles." The imagery can be construed as a deadly serious display of the connections between masculine sexuality and the arms race. But at the same time it says that the whole thing is not very serious—it is just what little boys or drunk men do.

Sanitized abstraction and sexual imagery, even if disturbing, seemed to fit easily into the masculine world of nuclear war planning. What did not fit was another set of words that evoked images that can only be called domestic.

Nuclear missiles are based in "silos." On a Trident submarine, which carries 24 multiple-warhead nuclear missiles, crew members call the part of the sub where the missiles are lined up in their silos ready for launching "the Christmas tree farm." In the friendly, romantic world of nuclear weaponry, enemies "exchange" warheads; weapons systems can "marry up." "Coupling" is sometimes used to refer to the wiring between mechanisms of warning and response, or to the psychopolitical links between strategic and theater weapons. The patterns in which a MIRVed missile's nuclear warheads land is known as a "footprint." These nuclear explosives are not dropped, a "bus" "delivers" them. These devices are called "reentry vehicles," or "RVs for short, a term not only totally removed from the reality of a bomb but also resonant with the image of the recreational vehicles of the ideal family vacation.

These domestic images are more than simply one more way to remove oneself from the grisly reality behind the words; ordinary abstraction is adequate to that task. Calling the pattern in which bombs fall a "footprint" almost seems a willful distorting process, a playful, perverse refusal of accountability—because to be accountable to reality is to be unable to do this work.

The images evoked by these words may also be a way to tame the uncontrollable forces of nuclear destruction. Take the fire-breathing dragon under the bed, the one who threatens to incinerate your family, your town, your planet, and turn it into a pet you can pat. Or domestic imagery may simply serve to make everyone more comfortable with what they're doing. "PAL" (permissive action links) is the carefully constructed, friendly acronym for the electronic system designed to prevent the unauthorized firing of nuclear warheads. The president's annual nuclear weapons stockpile memorandum, which outlines both short- and long-range plans for production of new nuclear weapons, is benignly referred to as "the shopping list." The "cookie cutter" is a phrase used to describe a particular model of nuclear attack.

The imagery that domesticates, that humanizes insentient weapons, may also serve, paradoxically, to make it all right to ignore sentient human beings. Perhaps it is possible to spend one's time dreaming up scenarios for the use of massively destructive technology, and to exclude human beings from that technological world, because that world itself now includes the domestic, the human, the warm and playful—the Christmas trees, the RVs, the things one pats affectionately. It is a world that is in some sense complete in itself; it even includes death and loss. The problem is that all things that get "killed" happen to be weapons, not humans. If one of your warheads "kills" another of your warheads, it is "fratricide." There is much concern about "vulnerability" and "survivability," but it is about the vulnerability and survival of weapons systems, rather than people.

Another set of images suggests men's desire to appropriate from women the power of giving life. At Los Alamos, the atomic bomb was referred to as "Oppenheimer's baby"; at Lawrence Livermore, the hydrogen bomb was "Teller's baby," although those who wanted to disparage Teller's contribution claimed he was not the bomb's father but its mother. In this context, the extraordinary names given to the bombs that reduced Hiroshima and Nagasaki to ash and rubble—"Little Boy" and "Fat Man"—may perhaps become intelligible. These ultimate destroyers were the male progeny of the atomic scientists.

The entire history of the bomb project, in fact, seems permeated with imagery that confounds humanity's overwhelming technological power to destroy nature with the power to create: imagery that converts men's destruction into their rebirth. Laurence wrote of the Trinity test of the first atomic bomb: "One felt as though he had been privileged to witness the Birth of the World." In a 1985 interview, General Bruce K. Holloway, the commander in chief of the Strategic Air Command from 1968 to 1972, described a nuclear war as involving "a big bang, like the start of the universe."

Finally, the last thing one might expect to find in a subculture of hard-nosed realism and hyper-rationality is the repeated invocation of religious imagery. And yet, the first atomic bomb test was called Trinity. Seeing it, Robert Oppenheimer thought of Krishna's words to Arjuna in the *Bhagavad Gita*: "I am become death, destroyer of worlds." Defense intellectuals, when challenged on a particular assumption, will often duck out with a casual, "Now you're talking about matters of theology." Perhaps most astonishing of all, the creators of strategic doctrine actually refer to their community as "the nuclear priesthood." It is hard to decide what is most extraordinary about this: the arrogance of the claim, the tacit admission that they really are creators of dogma; or the extraordinary implicit statement about who, or rather what, has become god.

Although I was startled by the combination of dry abstraction and odd imagery that characterizes the language of defense intellectuals, my attention was quickly focused on decoding and learning to speak it. The first task was training the tongue in the articulation of acronyms.

Several years of reading the literature of nuclear weaponry and strategy had not prepared me for the degree to which acronyms littered all conversations, nor for the way in which they are used. Formerly, I had thought of them mainly as utilitarian. They allow you to write or speak faster. They act as a form of abstraction, removing you from the reality behind the words. They restrict communication to the initiated, leaving the rest both uncomprehending and voiceless in the debate.

But being at the center revealed some additional, unexpected dimensions. First, in speaking and hearing, a lot of these terms are very sexy. A small supersonic rocket "designed to penetrate any Soviet air defense" is called a SRAM (for short-range attack missile). Submarine-launched cruise missiles are referred to as "slick'ems" and ground-launched cruise missiles are "glick'ems." Air-launched cruise missiles are magical "alchems."

Other acronyms serve in different ways. The plane in which the president will supposedly be flying around above a nuclear holocaust, receiving intelligence and issuing commands for where to bomb next, is referred to as "Kneecap" (for NEACP—National Emergency Airborne Command Post). Few believe that the president would really have the time to get into it, or that the communications systems would be working if he were in it—hence the edge of derision. But the very ability to make fun of a concept makes it possible to work with it rather than reject it outright.

In other words, what I learned at the program is that talking about nuclear weapons is fun. The words are quick, clean, light, they trip off the tongue. You can reel off dozens of them in seconds, forgetting about how one might interfere with the next, not to mention with the lives beneath them. Nearly everyone I observed—lecturers, students, hawks, doves, men, and women—took pleasure in using the words; some of us spoke with a self-consciously ironic edge, but the pleasure was there nonetheless. Part of the appeal was the thrill of being able to manipulate an arcane language, the power of entering the secret kingdom. But perhaps more important, learning the language gives a sense of control, a feeling of mastery over technology that is finally not controllable but powerful beyond human comprehension. The longer I stayed, the more conversations I participated in, the less I was frightened of nuclear war.

How can learning to speak a language have such a powerful effect? One answer, discussed earlier, is that the language is abstract and sanitized, never giving access to the images of war. But there is more to it than that. The learning process itself removed me from the reality of nuclear war. My energy was focused on the challenge of decoding acronyms, learning new terms, developing competence in the language—not on the weapons and wars behind the words. By the time I was through, I had learned far more than an alternate, if abstract, set of words. The content of what I could talk about was monumentally different.

Consider the following descriptions, in each of which the subject is the aftermath of a nuclear attack:

> Everything was black, had vanished into the black dust, was destroyed. Only the flames that were beginning to lick their way up had any color. From the dust that was like a fog, figures began to loom up, black, hairless, faceless. They screamed with voices that were no longer human. Their screams drowned out the groans rising everywhere from the rubble, groans that seemed to rise from the very earth itself.[4]

> [You have to have ways to maintain communications in a] nuclear environment, a situation bound to include EMP blackout, brute force damage to systems, a heavy jamming environment, and so on.[5]

There is no way to describe the phenomena represented in the first with the language of the second. The passages differ not only in the vividness of their words, but in their content: the first describes the effects of a nuclear blast on human beings; the second describes the impact of a nuclear blast on technical systems designed to secure the "command and control" of nuclear weapons. Both of these differences stem from the difference of perspective: the speaker in the first is a victim of nuclear weapons, the speaker in the second is a user. The speaker in the first is using words to try to name and contain the horror of human suffering all around her; the speaker in the second is using words to insure the possibility of launching the next nuclear attack....

While I believe that the language is not the whole problem, it is a significant component and clue. What it reveals is a whole series of culturally grounded and culturally acceptable mechanisms that make it possible to work in institutions that foster the proliferation of nuclear weapons, to plan mass incinerations of millions of human beings for a living. Language that is abstract, sanitized, full of euphemisms; language that is sexy and fun to use; paradigms whose referent is weapons; imagery that domesticates and deflates the forces of mass destruction; imagery that reverses sentient and nonsentient matter, that conflates birth and death, destruction and creation—all of these are part of what makes it possible to be radically removed from the reality of what one is talking about, and from the realities one is creating through the discourse.

Close attention to the language itself also reveals a tantalizing basis on which to challenge the legitimacy of the defense intellectuals' dominance of the discourse on nuclear issues. When defense intellectuals are criticized for the cold-blooded inhumanity of the scenarios they plan, their response is to claim the high ground of rationality. They portray those who are radically opposed to the nuclear status quo as irrational, unrealistic, too emotional—"idealistic activists." But if the smooth, shiny surface of their discourse—its abstraction and technical jargon—appears at first to support these claims, a look below the surface does not. Instead we find strong currents of homoerotic excitement, heterosexual domination, the drive toward competence and mastery, the pleasures of membership in an elite and privileged group, of the ultimate importance and meaning of membership in the priesthood. How is it possible to point to the pursuers of these values, these experiences, as paragons of cool-headed objectivity?

While listening to the language reveals the mechanisms of distancing and denial and the emotional currents embodied in this emphatically male discourse, attention to the experience of learning the language reveals something about how thinking can become more abstract, more focused on parts disembedded from their context, more attentive to the survival of weapons than the survival of human beings.

Because this professional language sets the terms for public debate, many who oppose current nuclear policies choose to learn it. Even if they do not believe that the technical information is very important, some believe it is necessary to master the language simply because it is too difficult to attain public legitimacy without it. But learning the language is a transformative process. You are not simply adding new information, new vocabulary, but entering a mode of thinking not only about nuclear weapons but also about military and political power, and about the relationship between human ends and technological means.

The language and the mode of thinking are not neutral containers of information. They were developed by a specific group of men, trained largely in abstract theoretical mathematics and economics, specifically to make it possible to think rationally about the use of nuclear weapons. That the language is not well suited to do anything but make it possible to think about using nuclear weapons should not be surprising.

Those who find U.S. nuclear policy desperately misguided face a serious quandary. If we refuse to learn the language, we condemn ourselves to being jesters on the sidelines. If we learn and use it, we not only severely limit what we can say but also invite the transformation, the militarization, of our own thinking.

I have no solutions to this dilemma, but I would like to offer a couple of thoughts in an effort to push it a little further—or perhaps even to reformulate its terms. It is important to recognize an assumption implicit in adopting the strategy of learning the language. When we outsiders assume that learning and speaking the language will give us a voice recognized as legitimate and will give us greater political influence, we assume that the language itself actually articulates the criteria and reasoning strategies upon which nuclear weapons development and deployment decisions are made. This is largely an illusion. I suggest that technostrategic discourse functions more as a gloss, as an ideological patina that hides the actual reasons these decisions are made. Rather than informing and shaping decisions, it far more often legitimizes political outcomes that have occurred for utterly different reasons. If this is true, it raises serious questions about the extent of the political returns we might get from using it, and whether they can ever balance out the potential problems and inherent costs.

I believe that those who seek a more just and peaceful world have a dual task before them—a deconstructive project and a reconstructive project that are intimately linked. Deconstruction requires close attention to, and the dismantling of, technostrategic discourse. The dominant voice of militarized masculinity and decontextualized rationality speaks so loudly in our culture that it will remain difficult for any other voices to be heard until that voice loses some of its power to define what we hear and how we name the world.

The reconstructive task is to create compelling alternative visions of possible futures, to recognize and develop alternative conceptions of rationality, to create rich and imaginative alternative voices—diverse voices whose conversations with each other will invent those futures.

## Notes

1.    General William Odom, "C³I and Telecommunications at the Policy Level," incidental paper from a seminar, *Command, Control, Communications and Intelligence* (Cambridge, Mass., Harvard University Center for Information Policy Research, Spring 1980), p. 5.

2.    See Brian Easlea, *Fathering the Unthinkable: Masculinity, Scientists and the Nuclear Arms Race* (London: Pluto Press, 1983).

3.    William L. Laurence, *Dawn Over Zero: The Study of the Atomic Bomb* (London: Museum Press, 1974), pp. 198–99.

4.    Hisako Matsubara, *Cranes at Dusk* (Garden City, New York: Dial Press, 1985).

5.    Gen. Robert Rosenberg, "The Influence of Policy Making on C³I." Speaking at the Harvard Seminar, *Command, Control and Intelligence,* p. 59.

**For discussion**

*Content*

1. How does Cohn establish her credentials? Why is it necessary for her to do that early in the essay?

2. Name the characteristics of "technostrategic" language. How do the characteristics of that language affect the thoughts of the people who use it?

3. What are the functions of "technostrategic"?

4. Examine the specific vocabulary people use to discuss a current war of whatever scope. Does that language have the same basic function "technostrategic" has?

5. Cohn states that we cannot read a person's motives directly from the metaphors or images the person uses because those metaphors and images originate "in a broader cultural context" (paragraph 13). But people make the cultural context. What are the motives of the people who create the metaphors and images? Do the images perpetuate thoughts of male sexual dominance? Who would want to use those metaphors and images, and who would benefit from using them?

6. Explain how using a particular language could be fun, how it could give access to "the secret kingdom," how it could give a sense of control.

7. Explain how a language about nuclear war and destruction could cover up nuclear war and destruction and could keep its speakers from thinking about nuclear war and destruction. What influences might such a language have on a nation's policy decisions or on a people's accepting of those policies? What influences might such a language have on the way people think about nuclear destruction?

8. State Cohn's thesis in your words.

*Style*

1. In paragraph four, Cohn announces that her experience is part of her data. Is that kind of data acceptable to you as a reader? Is personal experience effective specific development?

2. What is the allusion in "missile envy" (paragraph ten) and in "Pronoun En-

vy" (Alette Olin Hill's essay title)? What does the allusion add for a reader who understands it?

3.  What is the function of paragraph 20? Is that paragraph necessary to you as a reader? How important are the first sentence of paragraph 25 and the first sentence of paragraph 27 to your following the essay's organization?

4.  Is Cohn's overall organization effective? What makes it effective or not?

# Patriarchy, Scientists, and Nuclear Warriors

## Brian Easlea

IN A LECTURE AT THE UNIVERSITY OF CALIFORNIA in 1980, the Oxford historian Michael Howard accused the world's scientific community, and particularly the Western scientific community, of an inventiveness in the creation and design of weapons that has made, he believes, the pursuit of a "stable nuclear balance" between the superpowers virtually impossible. At the very least, he found it curious that a scientific community that had expressed great anguish over its moral responsibility for the development of the first crude fission weapons "should have ceased to trouble itself over its continuous involvement with weapons-systems whose lethality and effectiveness make the weapons that destroyed Hiroshima and Nagasaki look like clumsy toys."[1] On the other hand, in the compelling pamphlet *It'll Make a Man of You: A Feminist View of the Arms Race*, Penny Strange expresses no surprise at the militarization of science that has occurred since the Second World War. While acknowledging that individual scientists have been people of integrity with a genuine desire for peace, she tersely states that "weapons research is consistent with the attitudes underlying the whole scientific worldview" and that she looks forward to "an escape from the patriarchal science in which the conquest of nature is a projection of sexual dominance."[2] My aim in this article is to explore the psychological attributes of patriarchal science, particularly physics, that contribute so greatly to the apparent readiness of scientists to maintain the inventive momentum of the nuclear arms race.

My own experiences as a physicist were symptomatic of the problems of modern science. So I begin with a brief account of these experiences followed by a look at various aspects of the masculinity of science, particularly physics, paying special attention to the ideology surrounding the concept of a scientific method and to the kinds of sexual rhetoric used by physicists to describe both their "pure" research and their contributions to weapons design. I conclude with some thoughts on the potential human integrity of a life in science—once patriarchy and its various subsystems have become relics of history.

## A Personal Experience of Physics

Growing up in the heart of rural England, I wanted in my early teens to become a professional birdwatcher. However, at the local grammar school I was persuaded that boys who are good at mathematics become scientists: people just don't become birdwatchers. I did in fact have a deep, if romantic, interest in physics, believing that somehow those "great men" like Einstein and Bohr truly understood a world whose secrets I longed to share. So I went to University College London in 1954 to study physics and found it excruciatingly boring. But I studied hard and convinced myself that at the postgraduate level it would be different if only I could "do research"—whatever that mysterious activity really was. It didn't seem remarkable to me at the time that our class consisted of some forty men and only three or four women. At that time, I was both politically conservative and politically naive, a situation not helped by the complete absence of any lectures in the physics curriculum on "science and society" issues.

In my final year it was necessary to think of future employment. Not wanting to make nuclear weapons and preferring to leave such "dirty" work to other people, I considered a career in the "clean and beautiful" simplicity of the electronics industry. I came very close to entering industry but in the end, to my great happiness, was accepted back at University College to "do research" in mathematical physics. It was while doing this research that I was to begin my drift away from a career in physics.

One event in my graduate years stands out. As an undergraduate I had only twice ever asked about the nature of reality as presented by modern physics, and both times the presiding lecturer had ridiculed my question. However, one day a notice appeared announcing that a famous physicist, David Bohm, together with a philosopher of science were inviting physics students to spend a weekend in a large country house to discuss fundamental questions of physics. That weekend was an enlightening experience that gave me the confidence to believe that physics was not solely a means for manipulating nature or a path to professional mundane achievement through the publication of numerous, uninteresting papers, but ideally was an essential part of human wisdom.

In the early 1960s, while I was on a two-year NATO Fellowship at the Institute of Theoretical Physics in Copenhagen, the first cracks and dents began to appear in my worldview. I met scientists from around the world, including the Soviet Union, who engaged me in animated political discussions. With a group of physicists I went on a ten-day tour of Leningrad and Moscow and, equipped with a smattering of Russian, I left the group to wander about on my own and kept meeting people who, at this high point of the Cold War, implored me to believe Russia wanted peace. I couldn't square this image of Russia and the Russian people with what I had become accustomed to in Britain and would soon be exposed to while teaching at the University of Pittsburgh.

It seemed to be a world gone mad: my new university in Pittsburgh awarded honorary degrees to Werner von Braun, the former Nazi missile expert, and to Edward Teller, the father of the H-bomb. The Cuban blockade followed; Kennedy, Khrushchev, and physics were going to bring about the end of the world. I kept asking myself how the seemingly beautiful, breathtaking physics of Rutherford, Einstein, Heisenburg, and Niels Bohr had come to this.

New experiences followed which deepened my frustration with physics and increased my social and philosophic interests. University appointments in Brazil gave me a first-hand experience with the type of military regime that the United States so liked to support to save the world from communism. In the end I returned to the University of Sussex, where I taught "about science" courses to non-science students and "science and society" courses to science majors.

The more I learned, the more I became convinced that the reason physics was so misused and the reason the nuclear arms race existed was the existence of capitalistic societies, principally the United States, that are based on profit making, permanent war economies, and the subjugation of the Third World. My pat conclusion was that if capitalism could be replaced by socialism, human behavior would change dramatically. But I felt uneasy with this belief since oppression and violence had not first appeared in the world in the sixteenth century. As the years went by and the feminist movement developed, I came to explore the profound psychological connections between the discipline of physics and the world of the warriors—connections that are ultimately rooted in the social institutions of patriarchy. That is the focus of this paper.

## The Masculinity of Physics

Indisputably, British and American physics is male-dominated. In Britain in the early 1980s, women made up only 4 percent of the membership of the Institute of Physics, and in the United States women made up only 2 percent of the faculty of the 171 doctorate-awarding physics departments.[3] This male domination of physics has obviously not come about by chance; not until recently have physicists made serious attempts to encourage women to study the discipline and enter the profession. Indeed, in the first decades of the twentieth century strenuous attempts by physicists to keep women out of their male preserve were not unknown. Symbolic of such attempts in the 1930s was that of no less a man than the Nobel laureate Robert Millikan, who in 1936 wrote to the President of Duke University questioning the wisdom of the University's appointment of a woman to a full physics professorship.[4] As the statistics amply demonstrate, the male domination of physics continues despite publicized attempts by physicists to eliminate whatever prejudice still exists against the entry of women into the profession.

A second aspect of the masculinity of physics is that men who inhabit this scientific world—particularly those who are successful in it—behave in culturally masculine ways. Indeed, as in other hierarchical male-dominated activities, getting to the top invariably entails aggressive, competitive behavior. Scientists themselves recognize that such masculine behavior, though it is considered unseemly to dwell upon it, is a prominent feature of science. The biologist Richard Lewontin even goes so far as to affirm that "science is a form of competitive and aggressive activity, a contest of man against man that provides knowledge as a side-product."[5] Although I wouldn't agree with Lewontin that knowledge is a mere "side-product" of such competition, I would, for example, agree with the anthropologist Sharon Traweek, who writes that those most prestigious of physicists—the members of the high-energy physics "community"—display the highly masculine behavioral traits of "aggressive individualism, haughty self-confidence, and a sharp competitive edge."[6] Moreover, Traweek's verdict is supported by the remarks of the high-energy physicist Heinz Pagels, who justifies such masculine behavior by explaining that a predominant feature in the conduct of scientific research has to be intellectual aggression, since, as he puts it, "no great science was discovered in the spirit of humanity."[7] Scientists, then, physicists included, behave socially in a masculine manner.

A third aspect of the masculinity of physics is the pervasiveness of the ideology and practice of the conquest of nature rather than a human goal of respectful interaction and use. Although, of course, many attitudes (including the most gentle) have informed and continue to inform the practice of science, nevertheless a frequently stated masculine objective of science is the conquest of nature. This was expressed prominently by two of the principal promoters and would-be practitioners of the "new science" in the seventeenth century, Francis Bacon and René Descartes, the former even claiming that successful institutionalization of his method would inaugurate the "truly masculine birth of time." Although modern scientists usually attempt to draw a distinction between "pure" and "applied" science, claiming that pure science is the attempt to discover the fundamental (and beautiful) laws of nature without regard to possible application, it is nevertheless widely recognized that it is causal knowledge of nature that is sought, that is, knowledge that in principle gives its possessors power to intervene successfully in natural processes. In any case, most "pure" scientists know very well that their work, if successful, will generally find application in the "conquest of nature." We may recall how the first investigators of nuclear energy wrote enthusiastically in the early years of the twentieth century that their work, if successful, would provide mankind with an almost limitless source of energy. Both the "pure" and the technological challenges posed by the nucleus proved irresistible: the nucleus was there to be conquered and conquest was always incredibly exciting. Even in today's beleaguered domain of nuclear power for "peaceful" purposes, the ideology and practice of the conquest of nature has not disappeared. Thus, rallying the troops in 1979 at the twenty-fifth anniversary of the formation of the UK Atomic Energy Authority, the physicist chairman of the Authority, Sir John Hill, said that we will be judged "upon our achievements and not upon the plaintive cries of the faint-hearted who have lost the courage and ambitions of our forefathers, which made mankind the master of the earth."[8]

The masculine goal of conquest undoubtedly makes its presence felt in our images of nature and beliefs about the nature of reality; this constitutes a fourth aspect of the masculinity of physics and of science in general. That which is to be conquered does not usually emerge in the conqueror's view as possessing intrinsically admirable properties that need to be respected and preserved. Much, of course, could be written on specific images of nature, particularly with respect to "pure" and "applied" research objectives, and the subject does not lend itself to obvious generalizations. Nevertheless, it is clear that from the seventeenth century onwards, natural philosophers, men of science, and scientists tended to see the "matter" of nature as having no initiating, creative powers of its own (a point of view maintained only with some difficulty after the development of evolutionary theory in the nineteenth century). The historian of science, R.S. Westfall, is certainly not wrong when he writes that "whatever the crudities of the seventeenth century's conception of nature, the rigid exclusion of the psychic from physical nature has remained as its permanent legacy."[9] No matter what the cognitive arguments in favor of science's generally reductionist conception of "matter" and nature, it is clear that a nature that is seen as "the mere scurrying of matter to and fro" is a nature not only amenable to conquest but also one that requires no moral self-examination on the part of its would-be conqueror. "Man's place in the physical universe," declared the Nobel laureate physical chemist (and impeccable Cold-War warrior) Willard Libby, "is to be its master...to be its king through the power he alone possesses—the Principle of Intelligence."[10]

A fifth aspect of the masculinity of physics lies in the militarization the discipline has undergone in the twentieth century. Optimistically, Francis Bacon had expressed the hope in the seventeenth century that men would cease making war on each other in order to make collective warfare on nature. That hope has not been realized, nor is it likely to be. We may, after all, recall C. S. Lewis's opinion that "what we call Man's power over nature turns out to be a power exercised by some men over other men [and women] with nature as its instrument."[11] In the overall militarization of science that has occurred largely in this century and that was institutionalized during and after the Second World War, physics and its associated disciplines have indeed been in the forefront. For example, in a courageous paper to the *American Journal of Physics*, the physicist E.L. Woollett reported that at the end of the 1970s some 55 percent of physicists and astronomers carrying out research and development in the United States worked on projects of direct military value and he complained bitterly that physics had become a largely silent partner in the nuclear arms race.[12] It is estimated that throughout the world some half million physical scientists work on weapons design and improvement. As the physicist Freeman Dyson has reported, not only is the world of the scientific warriors overwhelmingly male-dominated but he sees the competition between physicists in weapons creation, allied to the (surely masculine) thrill of creating almost limitless destructive power, as being in large part responsible for the continuing qualitative escalation of the nuclear arms race.[13] Moreover, competition between weapons physicists is still a powerful motivating force in the nuclear arms race. Commenting on the rivalry at the Livermore Weapons Laboratory between two physical scientists, Peter Hagelstein and George Chapline, as to who would be the first to achieve a breakthrough in the design of a nuclear-bomb-powered X-ray laser, the head of the Livermore "Star Wars" Group, Lowell Wood, alleged: "It was raw, unabashed competitiveness. It was amazing—even though I had seen it happen before...two relatively young men...slugging it out for dominance in this particular technical area."[14] And he then went on to agree with Richard Lewontin's unflattering description of motivation throughout the world of science:

> I would be very surprised if very many major scientific endeavors, maybe even minor ones, happen because a disinterested scientist coolly and dispassionately grinds away in his lab, devoid of thoughts about what this means in terms of competition, peer esteem, his wife and finally, prizes and recognition. I'm afraid I'm sufficiently cynical to think that in excess of 90 percent of all science is done with these considerations in mind. Pushing back the frontiers of knowledge and advancing truth are distinctly secondary considerations.[15]

One might, no doubt naively, like to believe that male scientists do not compete among themselves for the privilege of being the first to create a devastating new weapon. That belief would certainly be quite wrong.

Given such a sobering description of the masculine world of physics in Britain and North America, it isn't altogether surprising if girls, whose gender social-ization is quite different from that of boys, are reluctant to study physics at school. What's more, it is in no way irrational, as British science teacher Hazel Grice points out, for girls to reject a subject that appears to offer "as the apex of its achievement a weapon of mass annihilation."[16]

## Scientific Method for Scientists and Warriors

One common description of physics is that it is a "hard," intellectually difficult discipline, as opposed to "soft" ones, such as English or history. The hard–soft spectrum spanning the academic disciplines is, of course, well-known, and within the sciences themselves there is also a notorious hard–soft spectrum, with physics situated at the hard end, chemistry somewhere toward the middle, biology toward the soft end, and psychology beyond. Insofar as mind, reason, and intellect are (in a patriarchy) culturally seen as masculine attributes, the hard–soft spectrum serves to define a spectrum of diminishing masculinity from hard to soft.

But what is held to constitute intellectual difficulty? It seems that the more mathematical a scientific discipline, the more intellectually difficult it is believed to be and hence the "harder" it is. Mathematics not only makes a discipline difficult, it seems: it also makes it rigorous; and the discipline is thus seen to be "hard" in the two connecting senses of difficult and rigorous. The fact that physics, and especially theoretical physics, makes prodigious use of sophisticated mathematics no doubt contributes to their enviable position at the masculine end of the hard–soft spectrum. It is perhaps of more relevance, however, that mathematics and logical rigor are usually seen as essential components of the "scientific method" and it is the extent to which a discipline is able to practice the "scientific method" that determines its ultimate "hardness" in the sense of intellectual difficulty, the rigor of its reasoning, and the reliability and profundity of its findings. Physics, it is widely believed, is not only able to but does make excellent use of the "scientific method," which thus accounts for its spectacular successes both in the understanding of physical processes and in their mastery. While, of course, all the scientific disciplines aspire to practice the "scientific method," it is physics and related disciplines that are held to have succeeded best.

But does such a procedure as the "scientific method" really exist? If it does, it is deemed to enjoy masculine rather than feminine status insofar as it rigorously and inexorably arrives at truth about the natural world and not mere opinion or wishful thinking. Such a method must therefore, it seems, be ideally characterized by logically rigorous thinking aided by mathematics and determined by experimental, that is, "hard" evidence with no contamination by feminine emotion, intuition, and subjective desires. "The scientific attitude of mind," explained Bertrand Russell in 1913, "involves a sweeping away of all other desires in the interest of the desire to know—it involves the suppression of hopes and fear, loves and hates, and the whole subjective emotional life, until we become subdued to the material, able to see it frankly, without preconceptions, without biases, without any wish except to see it as it is."[17] Such a view of the scientific method remains incredibly influential. In 1974 the sociologist Robert Bierstedt could confirm that "the scientist, *as such,* has no ethical, religious, political, literary, philosophical, moral, or marital preferences....As a scientist he is interested not in what is right or wrong, or good and evil, but only in what is true or false."[18] Numerous examples could be given. Emotion, wishful thinking, intuition, and other such apparent pollutants of cognition are held to betray and subvert the objectivity of the scientific method, which is the hard, ruthless application of logic and experimental evidence to the quest to understand and master the world. Thus while the philosopher of science Hans Reichenbach could tell the world in 1951 that "the scientific philosopher does not want to belittle the value of emotions, nor would he like to live without them" and that the philosopher's own life could be as passionate and sentimental as that of any literary man, nevertheless the truly scientific philosopher "refuses to muddle emotion and cognition, and likes to breathe the pure air of logical insight and penetration."[19] Perhaps that is why the Nobel laureate physicist, Isidor Rabi, then eighty-four years of age, could confide in the early 1980s to Vivian Gornick that women were temperamentally unsuited to science, that the female nervous system was "simply different." "It makes it impossible for them to stay with the thing," he explained. "I'm afraid there's no use quarrelling with it, that's the way it is."[20]

Now the view of successful "scientific method" as masculine logic, rigor, and experimentation necessarily untainted and uncontaminated with feminine emotion, intuition, and wishful thinking is completely and hopelessly wrong. Such a scientific method is as elusive as "pure" masculinity. If nothing else, the invention of theories demands considerable intuition and creative imagination, as every innovative scientist knows and often has proclaimed. Does this therefore mean that the masculine "objectivity" of scientific method is intrinsically compromised? The philosopher of science, Carl Hempel, explains that it doesn't, since "scientific objectivity is safeguarded by the principle that while hypotheses and theories may be freely invented and *proposed* in science [the so-called context of discovery], they can be *accepted* into the body of scientific knowledge only if they pass critical scrutiny [the context of justification], which includes in particular the checking of suitable test implications by careful observation and experiment."[21] Alas for this typical defense of scientific objectivity, for ever since the work of Thomas Kuhn in his 1962 essay *The Structure of Scientific Revolutions*, it is generally accepted that no hard and fast distinction can be readily drawn between such a feminine context of discovery and a masculine context of justification.[22]

For this is what seems to be at issue. Not only does the notion of scientific objectivity appear to entail a clear-cut distinction between the masculine investigator and the world of "feminine" or "female" matter, within the psyche of the masculine investigator there also appears to be a pressing need to establish an inviolable distinction between a masculine mode of "hard," rigorous reasoning determined by logic and experimental evidence and, should it operate at all, a feminine mode characterized by creative imagination, intuition, and emotion-linked preferences. However, such clear-cut distinctions neither exist nor are possible in scientific practice, no matter how much the masculine mode appears paramount in normal research. What certainly does exist (although not uniformly so) is a very impassioned commitment to deny an evaluative subjective component to scientific practice; we may see such a masculine commitment as stemming from an emotional rejection and repudiation of the feminine within masculine inquiry. In other words, the impassioned claim that there exists an unemotional, value-free scientific method (or context of justification) may be interpreted as an emotional rejection and repudiation of the feminine and, if this is so, it would mean that scientific practice carried out (supposedly) in an "objective," value-free, unemotional way is in fact deeply and emotionally repressive of the feminine. This is a hornets' nest with all kinds of implications, but it may help to explain why much of modern science has, I shall argue, been embraced so uncritically by a society that is misogynistic and, in the case of war industries, misanthropic as well. It is partly because patriarchal science is fundamentally antifeminine that its practitioners are psychologically vulnerable to the attractions of the "defense" industry.

We learn from Freeman Dyson that the world of the warriors, which comprises military strategists, scientists, and Pentagon officials, is ostentatiously defined by a "deliberately cool," quantitative style that explicitly excludes "overt emotion and rhetoric"—it is a style modelled on "scientific method" and directly opposed to, for example, the emotional, "anecdotal" style of the anti-nuclear campaigner Helen Caldicott, whose arguments, according to Dyson, the warriors find unacceptable even when they manage to take them seriously.[23] For her part, Helen Caldicott believes that great rage and hatred lie suppressed behind the seemingly imperturbable, "rational" mask of scientific military analysis.[24] The military historian Sue Mansfield has posed the problem at its starkest: the stress placed in the scientific world on "objectivity" and a quantitative approach as a guarantee of truth, together with the relegation of emotions to a peripheral and unconscious existence, has, she maintains, carried "from its beginnings in the seventeenth century the burden of an essential hostility to the body, the feminine, and the natural environment."[25]

## Sexual Rhetoric by Scientists and Warriors

The stereotype of the sober male scientist dispassionately investigating the properties of matter with, obviously, not a single sexual thought in mind is singularly undermined by the extent to which scientists portray nature as female in their informal prose, lectures, and talks. Indeed, according to the historian of science, Carolyn Merchant, the most powerful image in Western science is "the identification of nature with the female, especially a female harboring secrets."[26] Physicists often refer to their "pure" research as a kind of sexual exploration of the secrets of nature—a female nature that not only possesses great subtlety and beauty to be revealed only to her most skillful and determined admirers and lovers, but that is truly fearsome in her awesome powers.

"Nature," wrote the high-energy physicist Frank Close in the *Guardian*, "hides her secrets in subtle ways." By "probing" the deep, mysterious, unexpectedly beautiful submicroscopic world, "we have our eyes opened to her greater glory."[27] The impression is given of a non-violent, male exploration of the sexual secrets of a mysterious, profoundly wonderful female nature. From the end of the nineteenth century to the middle 1980s, such sentiments have frequently been expressed by famous physicists. Thus, addressing the annual meeting of the British Association in 1898, the physicist Sir William Crookes announced to his audience, "Steadily, unflinchingly, we strive to pierce the inmost heart of nature, from what she is to reconstruct what she has been, and to prophesy what she yet shall be. Veil after veil we have lifted, and her face grows more beautiful, august, wonderful, with every barrier that is withdrawn."[28]

But no matter how many veils are lifted, ultimately the fearsome and untameable "femaleness" of the universe will remain.[29] Even if female nature is ultimately untameable, scientific research and application can reveal and make usable many of nature's comparatively lesser secrets. It is striking how successful scientific research is frequently described in the language of sexual intercourse, birth, and claims to paternity in which science or the mind of man is ascribed the phallic role of penetrating or probing into the secrets of nature— with the supposed hardness of successful scientific method now acquiring an obvious phallic connotation. Accounts of the origins of quantum mechanics and nuclear physics in the first decades of the twentieth century illustrate this well. In 1966 the physicist, historian, and philosopher of science, Max Jammer, admiringly announced that those early achievements of physicists in quantum mechanics clearly showed "how far man's intellect can penetrate into the secrets of nature on the basis of comparatively inconspicuous evidence"; indeed, Victor Weisskopf, Nobel laureate, remembers how the physicists at Niels Bohr's institute were held together "by a common urge to penetrate into the secrets of nature."[30] While Frederick Soddy was already proudly convinced by 1908 that "in the discovery of radioactivity...we had penetrated one of nature's innermost secrets,"[31] it was Soddy's collaborator in those early years, Sir Ernest Rutherford, who has been adjudged by later physicists and historians to have been the truly masculine man behind nuclear physics' spectacular advances in this period. Referring to Rutherford's triumphant hypothesis in 1911 that the atom consisted of an extremely concentrated nucleus of positively charged matter surrounded by a planetary system of orbiting electrons, one of Rutherford's assistants at the time, C. G. Darwin, later wrote that it was one of the "great occurrences" of his life that he was "actually present half-an-hour after the nucleus was born."[32] Successful and deep penetration, birth, and ensuing paternity: these are the hallmarks of great scientific advance.

At first sight it might seem that there is little untoward in such use of sexual, birth, and paternity metaphors, their use merely demonstrating that nuclear research, like scientific research in general, can be unproblematically described by its practitioners as a kind of surrogate sexual activity carried out by male physicists on female nature. However, not only did all the early nuclear pioneers (Rutherford included) realize that enormous quantities of energy lay waiting, as it were, to be exploited by physicists—"it would be rash to predict," wrote Rutherford's collaborator, W. C. D. Whetham, "that our impotence will last for ever"[33]—but, ominously, some of the sexual metaphors were extremely aggressive, reminding one forcibly of the ideology of (masculine) conquest of (female) nature. Indeed, since Rutherford's favorite word appears to have been "attack," it does not seem startling when one of the most distinguished physicists in the United States, George Ellery Hale, who was convinced that "nature has hidden her secrets in an almost impregnable stronghold," wrote admiringly to Rutherford in astonishingly military-sexual language. "The rush of your advance is overpowering," he congratulated him, "and I do not wonder that nature has retreated from trench to trench, and from height to height, until she is now capitulating in her inmost citadel."[34]

The implications of all this were not lost on everyone. Well before the discovery of uranium fission in 1939, the poet and Cambridge historian Thomas Thornely expressed his great apprehension at the consequences of a successful scientific assault on nature's remaining nuclear secrets:

*Well may she start and desperate strain,*
*To thrust the bold besiegers back;*
*  If they that citadel should gain,*

*What grisly shapes of death and pain*
*May arise and follow in their track!*[35]

Not surprisingly, just as military scientists and strategists have adopted the formal "scientific style" of unemotional, quantitative argument, so they also frequently make informal use of sexual, birth, and paternity metaphors in their research and testing. Now, however, these metaphors become frighteningly aggressive, indeed obscene: military sexual penetration into nature's nuclear secrets will, the metaphors suggest, not only shake nature to her very foundations, but at the same time demonstrate indisputable masculine status and military paternity. We learn that the first fission bomb developed at the Los Alamos laboratory was often referred to as a "baby"—a baby boy if a successful explosion, a baby girl if a failure. Secretary of War Henry Stimson received a message at Potsdam after the successful Trinity test of an implosion fission weapon which (after decoding) read:

*Doctor has just returned most enthusiastic and confident that the little boy*
*[the uranium bomb] is as husky as his big brother [the tested plutonium*
*bomb]. The light in his eyes discernible from here to Highhold and I could*
*have heard his screams from here to my farm.*[36]

Examples are abundant: the two bombs (one uranium and one plutonium) exploded over Japanese cities were given the code names "Little Boy" and "Fat Man"; a third bomb being made ready was given the name "Big Boy." Oppenheimer became known as the Father of the A-Bomb and indeed the National Baby Institution of America made Oppenheimer its Father of the Year. Edward Teller, publicly seen as the principal physicist behind the successful design of the first fusion weapon or H-bomb, seemingly takes pains in his memoirs to draw readers' attention to the fact that it was a "phallic" triumph on his part.[37] After the enormous blast of the first H-bomb obliterated a Pacific island and all its life, Teller sent a triumphant telegram to his Los Alamos colleagues, "It's a boy."[38] Unfortunately, for Teller, his paternity status of "Father of the H-Bomb" has been challenged by some physicists who claim that the mathematician Stanislaw Ulam produced the original idea and that all Teller did was to gestate the bomb after Ulam had inseminated him with this idea, thus, they say, making him the mere Mother.

Following the creation of this superbomb, a dispute over two competing plans for a nuclear attack against the Soviet Union occurred between strategists in the RAND think tank and the leading generals in the Strategic Air Command (SAC) of the U.S. Air Force. In a circulated memorandum the famous strategist Bernard Brodie likened his own RAND plan of a limited nuclear strike against military targets while keeping the major part of the nuclear arsenal in reserve to the act of sexual penetration but with withdrawal before ejaculation; he likened the alternative SAC plan to leave the Soviet Union a "smoking radiating ruin at the end of two hours" to sexual intercourse that "goes all the way."[39] His colleague Herman Kahn coined the term "wargasm" to describe the all-out "orgastic spasm of destruction" that the SAC generals supposedly favored.[40] Kahn's book *On Escalation* attempts, like an elaborate scientific sex manual, a precise identification of forty-four (!) stages of increasing tension culminating in the final stage of "spasm war."[41] Such sexual metaphors for nuclear explosions and warfare appear to be still in common use. In 1980 General William Odom, then a military adviser to Zbigniew Brzesinski on the National Security Council, told a Harvard seminar of a strategic plan to release 70 to 80 percent of America's nuclear megatonnage "in one orgasmic whump"[42] while at a London meeting in 1984, General Daniel Graham, a former head of the Defense Intelligence Agency and a prominent person behind President Reagan's Strategic Defense Initiative, brought some appreciative chuckles from his nearly all-male audience in referring to all-out nuclear "exchange" as the "wargasm."[43]

What is one to make of such metaphors and in particular of an analogy that likens ejaculation of semen during sexual intercourse (an act, one hopes, of mutual pleasure and possibly the first stage in a new creation of life) with a nuclear bombardment intended to render a huge country virtually lifeless, perhaps for millennia to come? And what conception of pleasure was foremost in Kahn's mind when he coined the term "wargasm"—surely the most obscene word in the

English language—to describe what he sees as the union between Eros and Thanatos that is nuclear holocaust? I find such comparisons and terminology almost beyond rational comment. Simone de Beauvoir's accurate observation that "the erotic vocabulary of males" has always been drawn from military terminology becomes totally inadequate.[44] Brodie's and Kahn's inventiveness has surely eclipsed Suzanne Lowry's observation in the *Guardian* that "'fuck' is the prime hate word" in the English language.[45] Indeed, given the sexual metaphors used by some of the nuclear warriors, one can understand Susan Griffin's anguished agreement with Norman Mailer's (surprising) description of Western culture as "drawing a rifle sight on an open vagina"—a culture, Griffin continues, "that even within its worship of a female sex goddess hates female sexuality."[46] We may indeed wonder why a picture of Rita Hayworth, "the ubiquitous pinup girl of World War II," was stenciled on the first atomic bomb exploded in the Bikini tests of 1946.[47]

## Unconscious Objectives of Patriarchy and Patriarchal Physics

There has been much analysis of the Catholic Church's dichotomization of women into the stereotypes: the unattainable, asexual, morally pure virgin to which the Christian woman could aspire but never reach and the carnal whore–witch representing uncontrollable sexuality, depravity, wickedness, and the threat of universal chaos and disorder. During the sixteenth and seventeenth centuries such a fear and loathing of women's apparent wickedness came to a head in the European witch craze that was responsible for the inquisition and execution of scores of thousands of victims, over 80 percent of them female. A major historian of the witch craze, H.C.E. Midelfort, has noted that "one cannot begin to understand the European witch craze without recognizing that it displayed a burst of misogyny without parallel in Western history."[48]

Whatever the causes of the European witch craze, what may be particularly significant is that it coincided with the first phase of the scientific revolution, the peak of the witch craze occurring during the decades in which Francis Bacon, René Descartes, Johannes Kepler, and Galileo Galilei made their revolutionary contributions. In *one* of its aspects, I believe that the scientific revolution may be seen as a secularized version of the witch craze in which sophisticated men either, like Francis Bacon, projected powerful and dangerous "femaleness" onto nature or, like René Descartes, declared nature to be feminine and thus totally amenable to manipulation and control by (the mind of) man. We recall how Simone de Beauvoir declared that woman is seemingly "represented, at one time, as pure passivity, available, open, a utensil"—which is surely Descartes's view of "feminine" matter—while "at another time she is regarded as if possessed by alien forces: there is a devil raging in her womb, a serpent lurks in her vagina, eager to devour the male's sperm"—which has more affinity to Francis Bacon's view of "female" matter.[49] Indeed, Bacon likened the experimental investigation of the secrets of "female" nature to the inquisition of witches on the rack and looked forward to the time when masculine science would shake "female" nature to her very foundations. It is, I believe, the purified natural magical tradition advocated by Bacon (with considerable use of very aggressive sexual imagery) that contributed in a major way to the rise of modern science. Believing firmly in the existence of the secrets of nature that could be penetrated by the mind of man, Bacon predicted that eventually the new science would be able to perform near miracles. And indeed the momentous significance of the scientific revolution surely lies in the fact that, unlike the rituals of the preliterate societies which in general failed to give their practitioners power over nature (if this is what they sought), the male practitioners of modern science have been awarded with truly breathtaking powers to intervene successfully in natural phenomena (we have become blasé about the spectacular triumphs of modern science, but what a near miracle is, for example, a television picture). Bacon's prediction that the new science he so passionately advocated would inaugurate the "truly masculine birth of time" and eventually shake nature to her very foundations has been triumphantly borne out by the achievements of modern physics and the sad possibility of devastating nature with environmental destruction, nuclear holocaust, and nuclear winter.

Clearly modern science possesses what might be called a rational component. In this article I am taking for granted the fact that modern science produces knowledge of nature that "works" relative to masculine (and other) expectations and objectives and that the intrinsic interest and fascination of scientific inquiry would render a non-patriarchal science a worthy and central feature of a truly human society. What I am here concerned with is the "truly masculine" nature of scientific inquiry involving the discipline's would-be rigid separation between the masculine science and "female" nature and the possibility of an underlying, if for the most part unconscious, hostility to "dangerous femaleness" in the minds of some, or many, of its practitioners—a hostility presumably endemic to patriarchal society. A case can be made—and has been both by Carolyn Merchant and myself—that a powerful motivating force, but not the only one, behind the rise of modern science was a kind of displaced misogyny.[50] In addition a case can be made that a powerful motivating force behind some (or much) modern science and particularly weapons science is a continuation of the displaced misogyny that helped generate the scientific revolution.

Certainly a counterclaim is possible that modern science might have had some misogynistic origins, but that this has no relevance today. In disagreement with such a counterclaim, however, it can be plausibly argued that the industrialized countries have remained virulently misogynistic, as seen in the prevalence of violence practiced and depicted by men against women. If there is indeed a link between misogyny, insecure masculinity, and our conceptions of science, particularly weapons science, then we are given a way to understand why nuclear violence can be associated in warrior's minds with sexual intercourse and ejaculation. Moreover, not only does Sue Mansfield suggest that at a deep level the scientific mentality has carried from its inception in the seventeenth century "the burden of an essential hostility to the body, the feminine, and the natural environment," but she also points out that, if human life survives at all after a nuclear holocaust, then it will mean the total restoration of the power of arm-bearing men over women. This leads her to make a significant comment that "though the reenslavement of women and the destruction of nature are not conscious goals of our nuclear stance, the language of our bodies, our postures, and our acts is a critical clue to our unexamined motives and desires."[51]

Of course, at the conscious level the scientific warrior today can, and does, offer a "rational" explanation for his behavior: his creation of fission and fusion weapons, he maintains, has made the deliberate starting of world war unthinkable and certainly has preserved peace in Europe for the last forty years. Whatever financial gain comes his way is not unappreciated but is secondary to the necessity of maintaining his country's security; likewise whatever scientific interest he experiences in the technological challenge of his work is again secondary to the all-important objective of preserving the balance of terror until world statesmen achieve multilateral disarmament. While well-known arguments can be made against the coherence of such a typical rationalization, what I am suggesting is that at a partly conscious, partly unconscious level the scientific warrior experiences not only an almost irresistible need to separate his (insecure) masculinity from what he conceives as femininity but also a compulsive desire to create the weapons that unmistakably affirm his masculinity and by means of which what is "female" can, if necessary and as a last resort, be annihilated. (And it must be noted that scientific warriors can be supported by women or even joined by female warriors in their largely unconscious quest to affirm masculine triumph over the feminine and female.)

## Conclusion

Looking over the history of humanity—the "slaughter-bench of history" as Hegel called it—I feel compelled to identify a factor—beyond economic and territorial rationales—that could help explain this sorry escalation of weaponry oppression, and bloodshed. It seems to me of paramount importance to try to understand why men are generally the direct oppressors, oppressing other men and women, why in general men allow neither themselves nor women the opportunity to realize full humanity.

While the political scientist Jean Bethke Elshtain may well be correct when she writes skeptically that no great movement will ever be fought under the banner of "androgyny," I suggest that it could well be fought under the banner of "a truly human future for everyone."[52] And that would entail the abolition of the *institutionalized* sexual division of labor. Men and women must be allowed the right to become complete human beings and not mutilated into their separate masculine and feminine gender roles. At the same time, I agree with Cynthia Cockburn when she writes in her book *Machinery of Dominance* that "men need more urgently to learn women's skills than women need to learn men's" and that "the revolutionary step will be to bring men down to earth, to domesticate technology and reforge the link between making and nurturing."[53]

In such a world "education" could not remain as it is now in Britain and the United States (and elsewhere). Certainly there would be no "physics" degree as it exists today, although there would be studies that would eventually take "students" to the frontiers of research in "physics." Needless to say, such an educational system would not be male-dominated (or female-dominated), it would not institutionalize and reward socially competitive aggressive behavior, and there would be no objective in "physics" education of the "conquest of nature," although it would certainly recognize the need to find respectful, ecologically sound ways of making use of nature. Moreover, images of nature would, I suspect, undergo some profound changes (with probably major changes to some theories as well), and clearly in a truly human world there would be no militarization of physics. As for the "scientific method," this would be recognized to be a somewhat mysterious activity, perhaps never completely specifiable, certainly an activity making use of the full range of *human* capacities from creative intuition to the most rigorous logical reasoning.

As for sexual imagery, that would surely thrive in the new truly human activity of scientific research, given that sexual relations—deprived of the hatred that now so greatly distorts sexuality—would continue to provide not only much of the motivation but also the metaphors for describing scientific activity (and much else). Consider, for example, the language of a woman who was awarded just about every honor the discipline of astrophysics could bestow (but only after she spent years challenging blatant sexism and discrimination). The images invoked by Cecilia Payne-Gaposchkin are more directly erotic than the "equivalent" sexual imagery used by male scientists and physicists (not to mention their frequent aggressive imagery); her language was of her friendship, her love, her delight, her ecstasy with the world of "male" stars and galaxies. Writing of nature as female, Payne-Gaposchkin advises her fellow researchers: "Nature has always had a trick of surprising us, and she will continue to surprise us. But she has never let us down yet. We can go forward with confidence,

*Knowing that nature never did betray*
*The heart that loved her.*[54]

But it was an embrace of relatedness that Payne-Gaposchkin sought and which had given her great satisfaction throughout her life, the satisfaction arising, in the words of Peggy Kidwell, from a sustained impassioned, loving endeavor "to unravel the mysteries of the stars."[55] In a truly human world, the principal purpose and result of science, as Erwin Schrödinger once said, will surely be to enhance "the general joy of living."[56]

## Notes

I am most grateful to Michael Kaufman for his extremely skillful pruning of a very long manuscript.

1. Michael Howard, "On Fighting a Nuclear War," in Michael Howard, *The Causes of War and Other Essays* (London: Temple Smith, 1983), 136.

2. Penny Strange, *It'll Make a Man of You* (Nottingham, England: Mushroom Books with Peace News, 1983), 24–5.

3. These statistics are taken from *Girls and Physics: A Report by the Joint Physics Education Committee of the Royal Society and the Institute of Physics* (London, 1982), 8, and Lilli S. Hornig, "Women in Science and Engineering: Why So Few?" *Technology Review 87* (November/December, 1984), 41.

4. See Margaret W. Rossiter, *Women Scientists in America: Struggles and Strategies to 1940* (Baltimore: Johns Hopkins University Press, 1982), 190–1.

5. Richard Lewontin, "'Honest Jim' Watson's Big Thriller, about DNA," Chicago *Sun Times*, 25 Feb. 1968, 1–2, reprinted in James D. Watson, *The Double Helix...A New Critical Edition*, edited by Gunther S. Stent (London: Weidenfeld, 1981), 186.

6. Sharon Traweek, "High-Energy Physics: A Male Preserve," *Technology Review* (November/December, 1984), 42–3; see also her *Particle Physics Culture: Buying Time and Taking Space* (1987), forthcoming.

7. Heinz Pagels, *The Cosmic Code: Quantum Physics as the Language of Nature* (London: Michael Joseph, 1982), 338.

8. Sir John Hill, "The Quest for Public Acceptance of Nuclear Power," *Atom*, no. 273 (1979): 166–72.

9. Richard S. Westfall, *The Construction of Modern Science* (1971; Cambridge: Cambridge University Press, 1977), 41. It should be noted, however, that quantum mechanics is essentially an antireductionist theory; see, for example, the (controversial) book by Fritjof Capra, *The Tao of Physics* (London: Fontana, 1976).

10. Willard Libby, "Man's Place in the Physical Universe," in John R. Platt, ed., *New Views of the Nature of Man* (Chicago: University of Chicago Press, 1965), 14–15.

11. C.S. Lewis, *The Abolition of Man* (1943; London: Geoffrey Bles, 1946), 40.

12. E. L. Woollett, "Physics and Modern Warfare: The Awkward Silence," *American Journal of Physics* 48 (1980): 104–11.

13. Freeman Dyson, *Weapons and Hope* (New York: Harper and Row, 1984), 41–2.

14.     William J. Broad, *Star Warriors: A Penetrating Look into the Lives of the Young Scientists Behind Our Space Age Weaponry* (New York: Simon and Schuster, 1985), 204.

15.     Ibid.

16.     Hazel Grice, letter to the *Guardian*, 9 Oct. 1984, 20.

17.     Bertrand Russell, "Science in a Liberal Education," the *New Statesman* (1913) reprinted in *Mysticism and Logic and Other Essays* (Harmondsworth: Penguin, 1953), 47-8.

18.     Robert Bierstedt, *The Social Order* (1957; New York: McGraw-Hill, 1974), 26.

19.     Hans Reichenbach, *The Rise of Scientific Philosophy* (1951; Berkeley and Los Angeles: California University Press, 1966), 312.

20.     Vivian Gornick, *Women in Science: Portraits from a World in Transition* (New York: Simon and Schuster, 1984), 36.

21.     Carl Hempel, *Philosophy of Natural Science* (Englewood Cliffs, N.J.: Prentice-Hall, 1966), 16.

22.     See, for example, Imre Lakotas and Alan Musgrave, eds., *Criticism and the Growth of Knowledge* (Cambridge: Cambridge University Press, 1970), Sandra Harding, "Is Gender a Variable in Conceptions of Rationality? A Survey of Issues," *Dialectica: International Journal of Philosophy of Knowledge* 36 (1982): 225-42, and Harry M. Collins, ed., special issue of *Social Studies of Science* 11 (1981): 3-158, "Knowledge and Controversy: Studies of Modern Natural Science."

23.     Freeman Dyson, *Weapons and Hope*, 4-6.

24.     Helen Caldicott, "Etiology: Missile Envy and Other Psychopathology," in her *Missile Envy: The Arms Race and Nuclear War* (New York: William Morrow, 1984).

25.     Sue Mansfield, *The Gestalts of War: An Inquiry into Its Origins and Meaning as a Social Institution* (New York: Dial Press, 1982), 224.

26.     Carolyn Merchant, "Isis' Consciousness Raised," *Isis* 73 (1982): 398-409.

27.     Frank Close, "And now at last, the quark to top them all," the *Guardian*, 19 July 1984, 13 , and "A shining example of what ought to be impossible," the *Guardian*, 8 Aug. 1985, 13.

28.     Sir William Crookes, quoted in E. E. Fournier d'Albe, *The Life of Sir William Crookes* (London: Fisher Unwin, 1923), 365.

29.     See, for example, the physicist Paul Davies's account of "black holes," "naked singularities," and "cosmic anarchy" in his *The Edge of Infinity: Naked Singularities and the Destruction of Space-time* (London: Dent, 1981), especially 92-3, 114, 145.

30. Max Jammer, *The Conceptual Development of Quantum Mechanics* (New York: McGraw–Hill, 1966), 61, and Victor Weisskopf, "Niels Bohr and International Scientific Collaboration," in S. Rozenthal, ed., *Niels Bohr: His Life and Work as Seen by His Friends and Colleagues* (Amsterdam: North Holland, 1967), 262.

31. Frederick Soddy, *The Interpretation of Radium* (London, 1909), 234.

32. C.G. Darwin quoted in A.S. Eve, *Rutherford* (Cambridge: Cambridge University Press, 1939), 199, 434.

33. W.C.D. Whetham, *The Recent Development of Physical Science* (London: Murray, 1904), 242.

34. G.E. Hale quoted in Helen Wright, *Explorer of the Universe: A Biography of George Ellery Hale* (New York: Dutton, 1966), 283, and in A.S. Eve, *Rutherford*, 231.

35. "The Atom" from *The Collected Verse of Thomas Thornely* (Cambridge: W. Heffer, 1939), 70-1, reprinted in John Heath-Stubbes and Phillips Salmon, eds., *Poems of Science* (Harmondsworth: Penguin, 1984), 245.

36. Richard G. Hewlett and Oscar E. Anderson, *A History of the United States Atomic Energy Commission* (Pennsylvania State University Press, 1962), vol. 1, *The New World*, 1939–1946, 386.

37. Edward Teller with Allen Brown, *The Legacy of Hiroshima* (London: Macmillan, 1962), 51-3.

38. Edward Teller, *Energy from Heaven and Earth* (San Francisco: W. H. Freeman, 1979), 151. See also Norman Moss, *Men Who Play God* (Harmondsworth: Penguin, 1970), 78. For general detail see my *Fathering the Unthinkable: Masculinity, Scientists and the Nuclear Arms Race* (London: Pluto Press, 1983), ch. 3.

39. Bernard Brodie's memorandum is referred to by Fred Kaplan in *The Wizards of Armageddon* (New York: Simon and Schuster, 1983), 222. I have not seen the text of Brodie's memorandum. The chilling phrase "smoking, radiating ruin at the end of two hours" comes from a declassified Navy memorandum on a SAC briefing held in March 1954; see David Alan Rosenburg, "'A Smoking Radiation Ruin at the End of Two Hours': Documents on American Plans for Nuclear War with the Soviet Union 1954-55," *International Security* 6 (1981/82), 3–38.

40. Herman Kahn, *On Escalation: Metaphors and Scenarios* (London: Pall Mall, 1965), 194.

41. Note that Gregg Herken in *Counsels of War* (New York: Knopf, 1985), 206, writes that Bernard Brodie objected to Herman Kahn's "levity" in coining the term "wargasm."

42. Quoted in Thomas Powers, "How Nuclear War Could Start," *New York Review of Books*, 17 Jan. 1985, 34.

43. Roger Hutton (personal communication), who attended the meeting when researching the Star Wars project.

44. Simone de Beauvoir, *The Second Sex* (1949; Harmondsworth: Penguin, 1972), 396.

45. Suzanne Lowry, "O Tempora, O Mores," the *Guardian*, 24 May 1984, 17.

46. Susan Griffin, *Pornography and Silence: Culture's Revenge Against Nature* (London: Women's Press, 1981), 217.

47. Paul Boyer, *By the Bomb's Early Light: American Thought and Culture at the Dawn of the Atomic Age* (New York: Pantheon, 1985), 83.

48. H.C.E. Midelfort, "Heartland of the Witchcraze: Central and Northern Europe," *History Today* 31 (February 1981): 28.

49. Simone de Beauvoir, *The Second Sex*, 699.

50. See, for example, Carolyn Merchant, *The Death of Nature: Women, Ecology and the Scientific Revolution* (San Francisco: Harper and Row, 1980), and my *Science and Sexual Oppression: Patriarchy's Confrontation with Women and Nature* (London: Weidenfeld, 1981), ch. 3, and *Fathering the Unthinkable*, ch. 1.

51. Sue Mansfield, *The Gestalts of War*, 223.

52. Jean Bethke Elshtain, "Against Androgyny," *Telos* 47 (1981), 5–22.

53. Cynthia Cockburn, *Machinery of Dominance* (London: Pluto Press, 1985), 256–7.

54. Katherine Haramundanis, ed., *Cecilia Payne-Gaposchkin: An Autobiography and Other Recollections* (Cambridge: Cambridge University Press, 1984), 237.

55. *Ibid*, 28.

56. "Science, Art and Play," reprinted in E.C. Schrödinger, *Science, Theory and Man* (New York: Dover, 1957), 29; see, for example, Euan Squires, *To Acknowledge the Wonder: The Story of Fundamental Physics* (Bristol: Adam Hilger, 1985).

## For discussion

*Content*

1. What new information does Easlea give you about language, about science, about patriarchy, about nuclear warriors? How does that new information help you to rethink any ideas?

2. Discuss the notions of "feminine" (emotion, intuition) and "masculine" (logic, experiment) status in "the sciences," and the ways these notions perpetuate cultural thought about women and men.

3. Discuss the significance of "scientific" imagery or metaphor in our habitual ways of thinking. Consider, for example, Easlea's statement, "It is striking how successful scientific research is frequently described in the language of sexual intercourse, birth and claims to paternity..." ("Sexual Rhetoric by Scientists and Warriors," paragraph three).

4. Does it seem strange or contradictory to you that "scientific" language, which scientists usually tell us is objective, unemotional, and quantitative, is so often metaphoric, and that the metaphors are sexual ones? Does it seem unusual that the metaphors are "frighteningly aggressive, indeed obscene" ("Sexual Rhetoric by Scientists and Warriors," paragraph six)?

5. Easlea quotes and/or refers to a number of scientists and historians. Are those quotations and references effective specific development? Why or why not?

6. Speculate about how scientists might work and might view their work if their language used metaphors of Father Nature, nature as powerful male, nature as pimp, nature as rapist, nature as big brother, instead of nature as female images.

7. What does Easlea's essay teach you about relationships between language and thought?

*Style*

1. Is it necessary or helpful that Easlea outlines the main blocks of the essay in paragraph two?

2. Is Easlea's "A Personal Experience of Physics" section effective or necessary? Why do you think that section is so close to the beginning of the essay? What does the section establish about Easlea as a writer, a physicist, a human?

3. Examine the paragraph-to-paragraph transitions in "The Masculinity of Physics" section. Are they necessary? Is the order of "aspects of masculinity" in that section effective?

4. Do you think Easlea's concluding section is effective? What makes it so or not?

# The Egg and the Sperm: How Science has Constructed a Romance Based on Stereotypical Male–Female Roles

## Emily Martin

> The theory of the human body is always a
> part of a world-picture...The theory of the
> human body is always a part of a *fantasy*.
> [James Hillman, *The Myth of Analysis*][1]

AS AN ANTHROPOLOGIST, I am intrigued by the possibility
that culture shapes how biological scientists describe what they discover about
the natural world. If this were so, we would be learning about more than the
natural world in high school biology class; we would be learning about cultural
beliefs and practices as if they were part of nature. In the course of my research
I realized that the picture of egg and sperm drawn in popular as well as scientific accounts of reproductive biology relies on stereotypes central to our cultural
definitions of male and female. The stereotypes imply not only that female biological processes are less worthy than their male counterparts but also that
women are less worthy than men. Part of my goal in writing this article is to
shine a bright light on the gender stereotypes hidden within the scientific
language of biology. Exposed in such a light, I hope they will lose much of their
power to harm us.

## Egg and Sperm: A Scientific Fairy Tale

At a fundamental level, all major scientific textbooks depict male and female
reproductive organs as systems for the production of valuable substances, such

*From* Signs: Journal of Women in Culture and Society *16:3 (1991): 485–501.*
*Copyright © University of Chicago. Reprinted by permission of University of*
*Chicago Press.*

as eggs and sperm.[2] In the case of women, the monthly cycle is described as being designed to produce eggs and prepare a suitable place for them to be fertilized and grown—all to the end of making babies. But the enthusiasm ends there. By extolling the female cycle as a productive enterprise, menstruation must necessarily be viewed as a failure. Medical texts describe menstruation as the "debris" of the uterine lining, the result of necrosis, or death of tissue. The descriptions imply that a system has gone awry, making products of no use, not to specification, unsalable, wasted, scrap. An illustration in a widely used medical text shows menstruation as a chaotic disintegration of form, complementing the many texts that describe it as "ceasing," "dying," "losing," "denuding," "expelling."[3]

Male reproductive physiology is evaluated quite differently. One of the texts that sees menstruation as failed production employs a sort of breathless prose when it describes the maturation of sperm: "The mechanisms which guide the remarkable cellular transformation from spermatid to mature sperm remain uncertain....Perhaps the most amazing characteristic of spermatogenesis is its sheer magnitude: the normal human male may manufacture several hundred million sperm per day."[4] In the classic text *Medical Physiology*, edited by Vernon Mountcastle, the male/female, productive/destructive comparison is more explicit: "Whereas the female *sheds* only a single gamete each month, the seminiferous tubules *produce* hundreds of millions of sperm each day" (emphasis mine).[5] The female author of another text marvels at the length of the microscopic seminiferous tubules, which, if uncoiled and placed end to end, "would span almost one-third of a mile!" She writes, "In an adult male these structures produce millions of sperm cells each day." Later she asks, "How is this feat accomplished?"[6] None of these texts expresses such intense enthusiasm for any female processes. It is surely no accident that the "remarkable" process of making sperm involves precisely what, in the medical view, menstruation does not: production of something deemed valuable.[7]

One could argue that menstruation and spermatogenesis are not analogous processes and, therefore, should not be expected to elicit the same kind of response. The proper female analogy to spermatogenesis, biologically, is ovulation. Yet ovulation does not merit enthusiasm in these texts either. Textbook descriptions stress that all of the ovarian follicles containing ova are already present at birth. Far from being *produced*, as sperm are, they merely sit on the shelf, slowly degenerating and aging like overstocked inventory: "At birth, normal human ovaries contain an estimated one million follicles [each], and no new ones appear after birth. Thus, in marked contrast to the male, the newborn female already has all the germ cells she will ever have. Only a few, perhaps 400, are destined to reach full maturity during her active productive life. All the others degenerate at some point in their development so that few, if any, remain by the time she reaches menopause at approximately 50 years of age."[8] Note the "marked contrast" that this description sets up between male and female, who has stockpiled germ cells by birth and is faced with their degeneration.

Nor are the female organs spared such vivid descriptions. One scientist writes in a newspaper article that a woman's ovaries become old and worn out from ripening eggs every month, even though the woman herself is still relatively young: "When you look through a laparoscope... at an ovary that has been through hundreds of cycles, even in a superbly healthy American female, you see a scarred, battered organ."[9]

To avoid the negative connotations that some people associate with the female reproductive system, scientists could begin to describe male and female processes as homologous. They might credit females with "producing" mature ova one at a time, as they're needed each month, and describe males as having to face problems of degenerating germ cells. This degeneration would occur throughout life among spermatogonia, the undifferentiated germ cells in the testes that are the long-lived, dormant precursors of sperm.

But the texts have an almost dogged insistence on casting female processes in a negative light. The texts celebrate sperm production because it is continuous from puberty to senescence, while they portray egg production as inferior because it is finished at birth. This makes the female seem unproductive, but some texts will also insist that it is she who is wasteful.[10] In a section heading for *Molecular Biology of the Cell*, a best-selling text, we are told that "Oogenesis is wasteful." The text goes on to emphasize that of the seven million oogonia, or egg germ cells, in the female embryo, most degenerate in the ovary. Of those that do go on to become oocytes, or eggs, many also degenerate, so that at birth only two million eggs remain in the ovaries. Degeneration continues throughout a woman's life: by puberty 300,000 eggs remain, and only a few are present by menopause. "During the 40 or so years of a woman's reproductive life only 400 to 500 eggs will have been released," the authors write. "All the rest will have degenerated. It is still a mystery why so many eggs are formed only to die in the ovaries."[11]

The real mystery is why the male's vast production of sperm is not seen as wasteful.[12] Assuming that a man "produces" 100 million ($10^8$) sperm per day (a conservative estimate) during an average reproductive life of sixty years, he would produce well over two trillion sperm in his lifetime. Assuming that a woman "ripens" one egg per lunar month, or thirteen per year, over the course of her forty-year reproductive life, she would total five hundred eggs in her lifetime. But the word "waste" implies an excess, too much produced. Assuming two or three offspring, for every baby a woman produces, she wastes only around two hundred eggs. For every baby a man produces, he wastes more than one trillion ($10^{12}$) sperm.

How is it that positive images are denied to the bodies of women? A look at language—in this case, scientific language—provides the first clue. Take the egg and the sperm.[13] It is remarkable how "femininely" the egg behaves and how "masculinely" the sperm.[14] The egg is seen as large and passive.[15] It does not *move* or *journey*, but passively "is transported," "is swept,"[16] or even "drifts"[17] along the fallopian tube. In utter contrast, sperm are small, "streamlined,"[18] and invariably active. They "deliver" their genes to the egg, "activate the developmental program of the egg,"[19] and have a "velocity" that is often remarked upon.[20] Their tails are "strong" and efficiently powered.[21] Together with the forces of ejaculation, they can "propel the semen into the deepest recesses of the vagina."[22] For this they need "energy," "fuel,"[23] so that with a "whiplashlike motion and strong lurches"[24] they can "burrow through the egg coat"[25] and "penetrate" it.[26]

At its extreme, the age-old relationship of the egg and the sperm takes on a royal or religious patina. The egg coat, its protective barrier, is sometimes called its "vestments," a term usually reserved for sacred, religious dress. The egg is said to have a "corona,"[27] a crown, and to be accompanied by "attendant cells."[28] It is holy, set apart and above, the queen to the sperm's king. The egg is also passive, which means it must depend on sperm for rescue. Gerald Schatten and Helen Schatten liken the egg's role to that of Sleeping Beauty: "a dormant bride awaiting her mate's magic kiss, which instills the spirit that brings her to life."[29] Sperm, by contrast, have a "mission,"[30] which is to "move through the female genital tract in quest of the ovum."[31] One popular account has it that the sperm carry out a "perilous journey" into the "warm darkness," where some fall away "exhausted." "Survivors" "assault" the egg, the successful candidates "surrounding the prize."[32] Part of the urgency of this journey, in more scientific terms, is that "once released from the supportive environment of the ovary, an egg will die within hours unless rescued by a sperm."[33] The wording stresses the fragility and dependency of the egg, even though the same text acknowledges elsewhere that sperm also live for only a few hours.[34]

In 1948, in a book remarkable for its early insights into these matters, Ruth Herschberger argued that female reproductive organs are seen as biologically interdependent, while male organs are viewed as autonomous, operating independently and in isolation:

At present the functional is stressed only in connection with women: it is in them that ovaries, tubes, uterus, and vagina have endless interdependence. In the male, reproduction would seem to involve "organs" only.

Yet the sperm, just as much as the egg, is dependent on a great many related processes. There are secretions which mitigate the urine in the urethra before ejaculation, to protect the sperm. There is the reflex shutting off of the bladder connection, the provision of prostatic secretions, and various types of muscular propulsion. The sperm is no more independent of its milieu than the egg, and yet from a wish that it were, biologists have lent their support to the notion that the human female, beginning with the egg, is congenitally more dependent than the male.[35]

Bringing out another aspect of the sperm's autonomy, an article in the journal *Cell* has the sperm making an "existential decision" to penetrate the egg: "Sperm are cells with a limited behavioral repertoire, one that is directed toward fertilizing eggs. To execute the decision to abandon the haploid state, sperm swim to an egg and there acquire the ability to effect membrane fusion."[36] Is this a corporate manager's version of the sperm's activities—"executing decisions" while fraught with dismay over difficult options that bring with them very high risk?

There is another way that sperm, despite their small size, can be made to loom in importance over the egg. In a collection of scientific papers, an electron micrograph of an enormous egg and tiny sperm is titled "A Portrait of the Sperm."[37] This is a little like showing a photo of a dog and calling it a picture of the fleas. Granted, microscopic sperm are harder to photograph than eggs, which are just large enough to see with the naked eye. But surely the use of the term "portrait," a word associated with the powerful and wealthy, is significant. Eggs have only micrographs or pictures, not portraits.

One depiction of sperm as weak and timid, instead of strong and powerful—the only such representation in western civilization, so far as I know—occurs in Woody Allen's movie *Everything You Always Wanted To Know About Sex\* \*But Were Afraid to Ask*. Allen, playing the part of an apprehensive sperm inside a man's testicles, is scared of the man's approaching orgasm. He is reluctant to launch himself into the darkness, afraid of contraceptive devices, afraid of winding up on the ceiling if the man masturbates.

The more common picture—egg as damsel in distress, shielded only by her sacred garments; sperm as heroic warrior to the rescue—cannot be proved to be dictated by the biology of these events. While the "facts" of biology may not *always* be constructed in cultural terms, I would argue that in this case they are. The degree of metaphorical content in these descriptions, the extent to which differences between egg and sperm are emphasized, and the parallels between cultural stereotypes of male and female behavior and the character of egg and sperm all point to this conclusion.

## New Research, Old Imagery

As new understandings of egg and sperm emerge, textbook gender imagery is being revised. But the new research, far from escaping the stereotypical representations of egg and sperm, simply replicates elements of textbook gender imagery in a different form. The persistence of this imagery calls to mind what Ludwig Fleck termed "the self-contained" nature of scientific thought. As he described it, "the interaction between what is already known, what remains to be learned, and those who are to apprehend it, go to ensure harmony within the system. But at the same time they also preserve the harmony of illusions, which is quite secure within the confines of a given thought style."[38] We need to understand the way in which the cultural content in scientific descriptions changes as biological discoveries unfold, and whether that cultural content is solidly entrenched or easily changed.

In all of the texts quoted above, sperm are described as penetrating the egg, and specific substances on a sperm's head are described as binding to the egg. Recently, this description of events was rewritten in a biophysics lab at Johns Hopkins University—transforming the egg from the passive to the active party.[39]

Prior to this research, it was thought that the zona, the inner vestments of the egg, formed an impenetrable barrier. Sperm overcame the barrier by mechanically burrowing through, thrashing their tails and slowly working their way along. Later research showed that the sperm released digestive enzymes that chemically broke down the zona; thus, scientists presumed that the sperm used mechanical and chemical means to get through to the egg.

In this recent investigation, the researchers began to ask questions about the mechanical force of the sperm's tail. (The lab's goal was to develop a contraceptive that worked topically on sperm.) They discovered, to their great surprise, that the forward thrust of sperm is extremely weak, which contradicts the assumption that sperm are forceful penetrators.[40] Rather than thrusting forward, the sperm's head was now seen to move mostly back and forth. The sideways motion of the sperm's tail makes the head move sideways with a force that is ten times stronger than its forward movement. So even if the overall force of the sperm were strong enough to mechanically break the zona, most of its force would be directed sideways rather than forward. In fact, its strongest tendency, by tenfold, is to *escape* by attempting to pry itself off the egg. Sperm, then, must be exceptionally efficient at escaping from any cell surface they contact. And the surface of the egg must be designed to trap the sperm and prevent their escape. Otherwise, few if any sperm would reach the egg.

The researchers at Johns Hopkins concluded that the sperm and egg stick together because of adhesive molecules on the surfaces of each. The egg traps the sperm and adheres to it so tightly that the sperm's head is forced to lie flat against the surface of the zona, a little bit, they told me, "like Br'er Rabbit getting more and more stuck to tar baby the more he wriggles." The trapped sperm continues to wiggle ineffectually side to side. The mechanical force of its tail is so weak that a sperm cannot break even one chemical bond. This is where the digestive enzymes released by the sperm come in. If they start to soften the zona just at the tip of the sperm and the sides remain stuck, then the weak, flailing sperm can get oriented in the right direction and make it through the zona—provided that its bonds to the zona dissolve as it moves in.

Although this new version of the saga of the egg and the sperm broke through cultural expectations, the researchers who made the discovery continued to write papers and abstracts as if the sperm were the active party who attacks, binds, penetrates, and enters the egg. The only difference was that the sperm were now seen as performing these actions weakly.[41] Not until August 1987, more than three years after the findings described above, did these researchers reconceptualize the process to give the egg a more active role. They began to describe the zona as an aggressive sperm catcher, covered with adhesive molecules that can capture a sperm with a single bond and clasp it to the zona's surface.[42] In the words of their published account: "The innermost vestment, the *zona pellucida*, is a glycoprotein shell, which captures and tethers the sperm before they penetrate it....The sperm is captured at the initial contact between the sperm tip and the *zona*....Since the thrust [of the sperm] is much smaller than the force needed to break a single affinity bond, the first bond made upon the tip-first meeting of the sperm and *zona* can result in the capture of the sperm."[43]

Experiments in another lab reveal similar patterns of data interpretation. Gerald Schatten and Helen Schatten set out to show that, contrary to conventional wisdom, the "egg is not merely a large, yolk-filled sphere into which the sperm burrows to endow new life. Rather, recent research suggests the almost heretical view that sperm and egg are mutually active partners."[44] This sounds like a departure from the stereotypical textbook view, but further reading reveals Schatten and Schatten's conformity to the aggressive-sperm metaphor. They describe how "the sperm and egg first touch when, from the tip of the sperm's triangular head, a long, thin filament shoots out and harpoons the egg." Then we learn that "remarkably, the harpoon is not so much fired as assembled at great speed, molecule by molecule, from a pool of protein stored in a specialized region called the acrosome. The filament may grow as much as twenty times longer than the sperm head itself before its tip reaches the egg and sticks."[45] Why not call this "making a bridge" or "throwing out a line" rather than firing a harpoon? Harpoons pierce prey and injure or kill them, while this filament only sticks. And why not focus, as the Hopkins lab did, on the stickiness of the egg, rather than the stickiness of the sperm?[46] Later in the article, the Schattens replicate the common view of the sperm's perilous journey into the warm darkness of the vagina, this time for the purpose of explaining its journey into the egg itself: "[The sperm] still has an arduous journey ahead. It must penetrate farther into the egg's huge sphere of cytoplasm and somehow locate the nucleus, so that the two cells' chromosomes can fuse. The sperm dives down into the cytoplasm, its tail beating. But it is soon interrupted by the sudden and swift migration of the egg nucleus, which rushes toward the sperm with a velocity triple that of the movement of chromosomes during cell division, crossing the entire egg in about a minute."[47]

Like Schatten and Schatten and the biophysicists at Johns Hopkins, another researcher has recently made discoveries that seem to point to a more interactive view of the relationship of egg and sperm. This work, which Paul Wassarman conducted on the sperm and eggs of mice, focuses on identifying the specific molecules in the egg coat (the zona pellucida) that are involved in egg-sperm interaction. At first glance, his descriptions seem to fit the model of an egalitarian relationship. Male and female gametes "recognize one another," and "interactions...take place between sperm and egg."[48] But the article in *Scientific American* in which those descriptions appear begins with a vignette that presages the dominant motif of their presentation: "It has been more than a century since Hermann Fol, a Swiss zoologist, peered into his microscope and became the first person to see a sperm penetrate an egg, fertilize it and form the first cell of a new embryo."[49] This portrayal of the sperm as the active party—the one that *penetrates* and *fertilizes* the egg and *produces* the embryo—is not cited as an example of an earlier, now outmoded view. In fact, the author reiterates the point later in the article: "Many sperm can bind to and penetrate the zona pellucida, or outer coat, of an unfertilized mouse egg, but only one sperm will eventually fuse with the thin plasma membrane surrounding the egg proper (*inner sphere*), *fertilizing the egg and giving rise to a new embryo.*"[50]

The imagery of sperm as aggressor is particularly startling in this case: the main discovery being reported is isolation of a particular molecule *on the egg coat* that plays an important role in fertilization! Wassarman's choice of language sustains the picture. He calls the molecule that has been isolated, ZP3, a "sperm receptor." By allocating the passive, waiting role to the egg, Wassarman can continue to describe the sperm as the actor, the one that makes it all happen: "The basic process begins when many sperm first attach loosely and then bind tenaciously to receptors on the surface of the egg's thick outer coat, the zona pellucida. Each sperm, which has a large number of egg-binding proteins on its surface, binds to many sperm receptors on the egg. More specifically, a site on each of the egg-binding proteins fits a complementary site on a sperm receptor, much as a key fits a lock."[51] With the sperm designated as the "key" and the egg the "lock," it is obvious which one acts and which one is acted upon. Could this imagery not be reversed, letting the sperm (the lock) wait until the egg produces the key? Or could we speak of two halves of a locket matching, and regard the matching itself as the action that initiates the fertilization?

It is as if Wassarman were determined to make the egg the receiving partner. Usually in biological research, the protein member of the pair of binding molecules is called the receptor, and physically it has a pocket in it rather like a lock. As the diagrams that illustrate Wassarman's article show, the molecules on the sperm are proteins and have "pockets." The small, mobile molecules that fit into these pockets are called ligands. As shown in the diagrams, ZP3 on the egg is a polymer of "keys"; many small knobs stick out. Typically, molecules in the sperm would be called receptors and molecules on the egg would be called ligands. But Wassarman chose to name ZP3 on the egg the receptor and to create a new term, "the egg-binding protein," for the molecule on the sperm that otherwise would have been called the receptor.[52]

Wassarman does credit the egg coat with having more functions than those of a sperm receptor. While he notes that "the zona pellucida has at times been viewed by investigators as a nuisance, a barrier to sperm and hence an impediment to fertilization," his new research reveals that the egg coat "serves as a sophisticated biological security system that screens incoming sperm, selects only those compatible with fertilization and development, prepares sperm for fusion with the egg and later protects the resulting embryo from polyspermy [a lethal condition caused by fusion of more than one sperm with a single egg]."[53] Although this description gives the egg an active role, that role is drawn in stereotypically feminine terms. The egg *selects* an appropriate mate, *prepares* him for fusion, and then *protects* the resulting offspring from harm. This is courtship and mating behavior as seen through the eyes of a sociobiologist: woman as the hard-to-get prize, who, following union with the chosen one, becomes woman as servant and mother.

And Wassarman does not quit there. In a review article for *Science*, he outlines the "chronology of fertilization."[54] Near the end of the article are two subject headings. One is "Sperm Penetration," in which Wassarman describes how the chemical dissolving of the zona pellucida combines with the "substantial propulsive force generated by sperm." The next heading is "Sperm-Egg Fusion." This section details what happens inside the zona after a sperm "penetrates" it. Sperm "can make contact with, adhere to, and fuse with (that is, fertilize) an egg."[55] Wassarman's word choice, again, is astonishingly skewed in favor of the sperm's activity, for in the next breath he says that sperm *lose* all motility upon fusion with the egg's surface. In mouse and sea urchin eggs, the sperm enters at the *egg's* volition, according to Wassarman's description: "Once fused with egg plasma membrane [the surface of the egg], how does a sperm enter the egg? The surface of both mouse and sea urchin eggs is covered with thousands of plasma membrane-bound projections, called microvilli [tiny 'hairs']. Evidence in sea urchins suggests that, after membrane fusion, a group of elongated microvilli cluster tightly around and interdigitate over the sperm head. As these microvilli are resorbed, the sperm is drawn into the egg. Therefore, sperm motility, which ceases at the time of fusion in both sea urchins and mice, is not required for sperm entry."[56] The section called "Sperm Penetration" more logically would be followed by a section called "The Egg Envelopes," rather than "Sperm-Egg Fusion." This would give a parallel—and more accurate—sense that both the egg and the sperm initiate action.

Another way that Wassarman makes less of the egg's activity is by describing components of the egg but referring to the sperm as a whole entity. Deborah Gordon has described such an approach as "atomism" ("the part is independent of and primordial to the whole") and identified it as one of the "tenacious assumptions" of Western science and medicine.[57] Wassarman employs atomism to his advantage. When he refers to processes going on within sperm, he consistently returns to descriptions that remind us from whence these

activities came: they are part of sperm that penetrate an egg or generate propulsive force. When he refers to processes going on within eggs, he stops there.
As a result, any active role he grants them appears to be assigned to the parts
of the egg, and not to the egg itself. In the quote above, it is the microvilli that
actively cluster around the sperm. In another example, "the driving force for
engulfment of a fused sperm comes from a region of cytoplasm just beneath an
egg's plasma membrane."[58]

## Social Implications

All three of these revisionist accounts of egg and sperm cannot seem to escape
the hierarchical imagery of older accounts. Even though each new account gives
the egg a larger and more active role, taken together they bring into play another cultural stereotype: woman as a dangerous and aggressive threat. In the
Johns Hopkins lab's revised model, the egg ends up as the female aggressor who
"captures and tethers" the sperm with her sticky zona, rather like a spider lying
in wait in her web.[59] The Schatten lab has the egg's nucleus "interrupt" the
sperm's dive with a "sudden and swift" rush by which she "clasps the sperm
and guides its nucleus to the center."[60] Wassarman's description of the surface
of the egg "covered with thousands of plasma membrane–bound projections,
called microvilli" that reach out and clasp the sperm adds to the spiderlike
imagery.[61]

   These images grant the egg an active role but at the cost of appearing disturbingly aggressive. Images of woman as dangerous and aggressive, the femme
fatale who victimizes men, are widespread in Western literature and culture.[62]
More specific is the connection of spider imagery with the idea of an engulfing,
devouring mother.[63] New data did not lead scientists to eliminate gender stereotypes in their descriptions of egg and sperm. Instead, scientists simply began to
describe egg and sperm in different, but no less damaging, terms.

   Can we envision a less stereotypical view? Biology itself provides another
model that could be applied to the egg and the sperm. The cybernetic model—
with its feedback loops, flexible adaptation to change, coordination of the parts
within a whole, evolution over time, and changing response to the environment—is common in genetics, endocrinology, and ecology and has a growing
influence in medicine in general.[64] This model has the potential to shift our
imagery from the negative, in which the female reproductive system is castigated
both for not producing eggs after birth and for producing (and thus wasting) too
many eggs overall, to something more positive. The female reproductive system
could be seen as responding to the environment (pregnancy or menopause),
adjusting to monthly changes (menstruation), and flexibly changing from re-
productivity after puberty to nonreproductivity later in life. The sperm and egg's
interaction could also be described in cybernetic terms. J.F. Hartman's research
in reproductive biology demonstrated fifteen years ago that if an egg is killed by
being pricked with a needle, live sperm cannot get through the zona.[65] Clearly,

this evidence shows that the egg and sperm do interact on more mutual terms, making biology's refusal to portray them that way all the more disturbing.

We would do well to be aware, however, that cybernetic imagery is hardly neutral. In the past, cybernetic models have played an important part in the imposition of social control. These models inherently provide a way of thinking about a "field" of interacting components. Once the field can be seen, it can become the object of new forms of knowledge, which in turn can allow new forms of social control to be exerted over the components of the field. During the 1950s, for example, medicine began to recognize the psychosocial *environment* of the patient: the patient's family and its psychodynamics. Professions such as social work began to focus on this new environment, and the resulting knowledge became one way to further control the patient. Patients began to be seen not as isolated, individual bodies, but as psychosocial entities located in an "ecological" system: management of "the patient's psychology was a new entrée to patient control."[66]

The models that biologists use to describe their data can have important social effects. During the nineteenth century, the social and natural sciences strongly influenced each other: the social ideas of Malthus about how to avoid the natural increase of the poor inspired Darwin's *Origin of Species*.[67] Once the *Origin* stood as a description of the natural world, complete with competition and market struggles, it could be reimported into social science as social Darwinism, in order to justify the social order of the time. What we are seeing now is similar: the importation of cultural ideas about passive females and heroic males into the "personalities" of gametes. This amounts to the "implanting of social imagery on representations of nature so as to lay a firm basis for reimporting exactly that same imagery as natural explanations of social phenomena."[68]

Further research would show us exactly what social effects are being wrought from the biological imagery of egg and sperm. At the very least, the imagery keeps alive some of the hoariest old stereotypes about weak damsels in distress and their strong male rescuers. That these stereotypes are now being written in at the level of the cell constitutes a powerful move to make them seem so natural as to be beyond alteration.

The stereotypical imagery might also encourage people to imagine that what results from the interaction of egg and sperm—a fertilized egg—is the result of deliberate "human" action at the cellular level. Whatever the intentions of the human couple, in this microscopic "culture" a cellular "bride" (or femme fatale) and a cellular "groom" (her victim) make a cellular baby. Rosalind Petchesky points out that through visual representations such as sonograms, we are given "*images* of younger and younger, and tinier and tinier, fetuses being 'saved.'" This leads to "the point of visibility being 'pushed back' *indefinitely*."[69] Endowing egg and sperm with intentional action, a key aspect of personhood in our culture, lays the foundation for the point of viability being pushed back to the

moment of fertilization. This will likely lead to greater acceptance of technological developments and new forms of scrutiny and manipulation, for the benefit of these inner "persons": court-ordered restrictions on a pregnant woman's
activities in order to protect her fetus, fetal surgery, amniocentesis, and rescind-
ing of abortion rights, to name but a few examples.[70]

Even if we succeed in substituting more egalitarian, interactive metaphors
to describe the activities of egg and sperm, and manage to avoid the pitfalls of
cybernetic models, we would still be guilty of endowing cellular entities with
personhood. More crucial, then, than what *kinds* of personalities we bestow on
cells is the very fact that we are doing it at all. This process could ultimately
have the most disturbing social consequences.

One clear feminist challenge is to wake up sleeping metaphors in science,
particularly those involved in descriptions of the egg and the sperm. Although
the literary convention is to call such metaphors "dead," they are not so much
dead as sleeping, hidden within the scientific content of texts—and all the more
powerful for it.[71] Waking up such metaphors, by becoming aware of when we
are projecting cultural imagery onto what we study, will improve our ability to
investigate and understand nature. Waking up such metaphors, by becoming
aware of their implications, will rob them of their power to naturalize our social
conventions about gender.

### Notes

1.      James Hillman, *The Myth of Analysis* (Evanston, Ill.: Northwestern University
        Press, 1972), 220.

2.      The textbooks I consulted are the main ones used in classes for undergraduate
        premedical students or medical students (or those held on reserve in the library
        for these classes) during the past few years at Johns Hopkins University. These
        texts are widely used at other universities in the country as well.

3.      Arthur C. Guyton, *Physiology of the Human Body*, 6th ed. (Philadelphia:
        Saunders College Publishing, 1984), 624.

4.      Arthur J. Vander, James H. Sherman, and Dorothy S. Luciano, *Human
        Physiology: The Mechanisms of Body Function*, 3rd ed. (New York: McGraw
        Hill, 1980), 483–84.

5.      Vernon B. Mountcastle, *Medical Physiology*, 14th ed. (London: Mosby, 1980),
        2:1624.

6.      Eldra Pearl Solomon, *Human Anatomy and Physiology* (New York: CBS
        College Publishing, 1983), 678.

7.      For elaboration, see Emily Martin, *The Woman in the Body: A Cultural Anal-
        ysis of Reproduction* (Boston: Beacon, 1987), 27–53.

8.      Vander, Sherman, and Luciano, 568.

9.      Melvin Konner, "Childbearing and Age," *New York Times Magazine* (December 27, 1987), 22–23, esp. 22.

10.     I have found but one exception to the opinion that the female is wasteful: "Smallpox being the nasty disease it is, one might expect nature to have designed antibody molecules with combining sites that specifically recognize the epitopes on smallpox virus. Nature differs from technology, however: it thinks nothing of wastefulness. (For example, rather than improving the chance that a spermatozoon will meet an egg cell, nature finds it easier to produce millions of spermatozoa.)" (Niels Kaj Jerne, "The Immune System," *Scientific American* 229, no. 1 [July 1973]: 53.) Thanks to a *Signs* reviewer for bringing this reference to my attention.

11.     Bruce Alberts et al., *Molecular Biology of the Cell* (New York: Garland, 1983), 795.

12.     In her essay "Have Only Men Evolved?" (in *Discovering Reality: Feminist Perspectives on Epistemology, Metaphysics, Methodology, and Philosophy of Science*, ed. Sandra Harding and Merrill B. Hintikka [Dordrecht: Reidel, 1983], 45–69, esp. 60–61), Ruth Hubbard points out that sociobiologists have said the female invests more energy than the male in the production of her large gametes, claiming that this explains why the female provides parental care. Hubbard questions whether it "really takes more 'energy' to generate the one or relatively few eggs than the large excess of sperms required to achieve fertilization." For further critique of how the greater size of eggs is interpreted in sociobiology, see Donna Haraway, "Investment Strategies for the Evolving Portfolio of Primate Females," in *Body/Politics*, ed. Mary Jacobus, Evelyn Fox Keller, and Sally Shuttleworth (New York: Routledge, 1990), 155–56.

13.     The sources I used for this article provide compelling information on interactions among sperm. Lack of space prevents me from taking up this theme here, but the elements include competition, hierarchy, and sacrifice. For a newspaper report, see Malcolm W. Browne, "Some Thoughts on Self Sacri-fice," *New York Times* (July 5, 1988), C6. For a literary rendition, see John Barth, "Night-Sea Journey," in his *Lost in the Funhouse* (Garden City, N.Y.: Doubleday, 1968), 3–13.

14.     See Carol Delaney, "The Meaning of Paternity and the Virgin Birth Debate," *Man* 21, no. 3 (September 1986): 494–513. She discusses the difference between this scientific view that women contribute genetic material to the fetus and the claim of long-standing Western folk theories that the origin and identity of the fetus comes from the male, as in the metaphor of planting a seed in soil.

15.     For a suggested direct link between human behavior and purportedly passive eggs and active sperm, see Erik H. Erikson, "Inner and Outer Space: Reflections on Womanhood," *Daedalus* 93, no. 2 (Spring 1964): 582–606, esp. 591.

16.     Guyton (n. 3 above), 619; and Mountcastle (n. 5 above), 1609.

17.     Jonathan Miller and David Pelham, *The Facts of Life* (New York: Viking Penguin, 1984), 5.

18.    Alberts et al., 796.

19.    Ibid., 796.

20.    See, e.g., William F. Ganong, *Review of Medical Physiology*, 7th ed. (Los Altos, Calif.: Lange Medical Publications, 1975), 322.

21.    Alberts et al. (n. 11 above), 796.

22.    Guyton, 615.

23.    Solomon (n. 6 above), 683.

24.    Vander, Sherman, and Luciano (n. 4 above), 4th ed. (1985), 580.

25.    Alberts et al., 796.

26.    All biology texts quoted above use the word "penetrate."

27.    Solomon, 700.

28.    A. Beldecos et al., "The Importance of Feminist Critique for Contemporary Cell Biology," *Hypatia* 3, no. 1 (Spring 1988): 61–76.

29.    Gerald Schatten and Helen Schatten, "The Energetic Egg," *Medical World News* 23 (January 23, 1984): 51–53, esp. 51.

30.    Alberts et al., 796.

31.    Guyton (n. 3 above), 613.

32.    Miller and Pelham (n. 17 above), 7.

33.    Alberts et al. (n. 11 above), 804.

34.    Ibid., 801.

35.    Ruth Herschberger, *Adam's Rib* (New York: Pelligrini & Cudaby, 1948), esp. 84. I am indebted to Ruth Hubbard for telling me about Herschberger's work, although at a point when this paper was already in draft form.

36.    Bennett M. Shapiro. "The Existential Decision of a Sperm," *Cell* 49, no. 3 (May 1987): 293–94, esp. 293.

37.    Lennart Nilsson, "A Portrait of the Sperm," in *The Functional Anatomy of the Spermatozoan*, ed. Bjorn A. Afzelius (New York: Pergamon, 1975), 79–82.

38.    Ludwik Fleck, *Genesis and Development of a Scientific Fact*, ed. Thaddeus J. Trenn and Robert K. Merton (Chicago: University of Chicago Press, 1979), 38.

39.    Jay M. Baltz carried out the research I describe when he was a graduate student in the Thomas C. Jenkins Department of Biophysics at Johns Hopkins University.

40.    Far less is known about the physiology of sperm than comparable female substances, which some feminists claim is no accident. Greater scientific scrutiny of female reproduction has long enabled the burden of birth control to be

placed on women. In this case, the researchers' discovery did not depend on development of any new technology: The experiments made use of glass pipettes, a manometer, and a simple microscope, all of which have been available for more than one hundred years.

41.  Jay Baltz and Richard A. Cone, "What Force Is Needed to Tether a Sperm?" (abstract for Society for the Study of Reproduction, 1985), and "Flagellar Torque on the Head Determines the Force Needed to Tether a Sperm" (abstract for Biophysical Society, 1986).

42.  Jay M. Baltz, David F. Katz, and Richard A. Cone, "The Mechanics of the Sperm-Egg Interaction at the Zona Pellucida," *Biophysical Journal 54*, no. 4 (October 1988): 643–54. Lab members were somewhat familiar with work on metaphors in the biology of female reproduction. Richard Cone, who runs the lab, is my husband, and he talked with them about my earlier research on the subject from time to time. Even though my current research focuses on biological imagery and I heard about the lab's work from my husband every day, I myself did not recognize the role of imagery in the sperm research until many weeks after the period of research and writing I describe. Therefore, I assume that any awareness the lab members may have had about how underlying metaphor might be guiding this particular research was fairly inchoate.

43.  Ibid., 643, 650.

44.  Schatten and Schatten (n. 29 above), 51.

45.  Ibid., 52.

46.  Surprisingly, in an article intended for a general audience, the authors do not point out that these are sea urchin sperm and note that human sperm do not shoot out filaments at all.

47.  Schatten and Schatten, 53.

48.  Paul M. Wassarman, "Fertilization in Mammals," *Scientific American 259*, no. 6 (December 1988): 78–84, esp. 78, 84.

49.  Ibid., 78.

50.  Ibid., 79.

51.  Ibid., 78.

52.  Since receptor molecules are relatively *immotile* and the ligands that bind to them relatively *motile*, one might imagine the egg being called the receptor and the sperm the ligand. But the molecules in question on egg and sperm are immotile molecules. It is the sperm as a *cell* that has motility, and the egg as a cell that has relative immotility.

53.  Wassarman, 78–79.

54.  Paul M. Wassarman, "The Biology and Chemistry of Fertilization," *Science 235*, no. 4788 (January 30, 1987): 553–60, esp. 554.

55.  Ibid., 557.

56.    Ibid, 557–58. This finding throws into question Schatten and Schatten's description (n. 29 above) of the sperm, its tail beating, diving down into the egg.

57.    Deborah R. Gordon, "Tenacious Assumptions in Western Medicine,: in *Biomedicine Examined*, ed. Margaret Lock and Deborah Gordon (Dordrecht: Kluwer, 1988), 19–56, esp. 26.

58.    Wassarman, "The Biology and Chemistry of Fertilization," 558.

59.    Baltz, Katz, and Cone (n. 42 above), 643, 650.

60.    Schatten and Schatten, 53.

61.    Wassarman, "The Biology and Chemistry of Fertilization," 557.

62.    Mary Ellman, *Thinking about Women* (New York: Harcourt Brace Jovanovich, 1968), 140; Nina Auerbach, *Woman and the Demon* (Cambridge, Mass.: Harvard University Press, 1982), esp. 186.

63.    Kenneth Alan Adams, "Arachnophobia: Love American Style," *Journal of Psychoanalytic Anthropology* 4, no. 2 (1981): 157–97.

64.    William Ray Arney and Bernard Bergen, *Medicine and the Management of Living* (Chicago: University of Chicago Press, 1984).

65.    J. F. Hartman, R. B. Gwatkin, and C. F. Hutchison, "Early Contact Interactions between Mammalian Gametes In Vitro," *Proceedings of the National Academy of Sciences* (U.S.) 69, no. 10 (1972): 2767–69.

66.    Arney and Bergen, 68.

67.    Ruth Hubbard, "Have Only Men Evolved?" (n. 12 above), 51–52.

68.    David Harvey, personal communication, November 1989.

69.    Rosalind Petchesky, "Fetal Images: The Power of Visual Culture in the Politics of Reproduction," *Feminist Studies* 13, no. 2 (Summer 1987): 263–92, esp. 272.

70.    Rita Arditti, Renate Klein, and Shelley Minden, *Test-Tube Women* (London: Pandora, 1984); Ellen Goodman, "Whose Right to Life?" *Baltimore Sun* (November 17, 1987); Tamar Lewin, "Courts Acting to Force Care of the Unborn," *New York Times* (November 23, 1987), A1 and B10; Susan Irwin and Brigitte Jordon, "Knowledge, Practice, and Power: Court Ordered Cesarean Sections," *Medical Anthropology Quarterly 1*, no. 3 (September 1987): 319–34.

71.    Thanks to Elizabeth Fee and David Spain, who in February 1989 and April 1989, respectively, made points related to this.

**For discussion**

*Content*

1. Explain how cultural stereotypes and definitions could influence scientific language. Isn't scientific language "supposed" to be objective? If sexist bias exists in scientific descriptions of egg and sperm, in what other "scientific" descriptions do you suspect similar biases exist?

2. Explain how words like "sheds," "waste," "debris," "degenerate," "produce," and "feat" shape our view of female and male physical processes. How could such words and their connotations create researcher bias among scientists?

3. Explain how passive and active voice structures in scientific writing about egg and sperm perpetuate a notion of female passivity and male aggression.

4. In paragraph 16, Martin quotes Ruth Herschberger's 1948 comments about female and male reproductive organs. Why do you suppose Herschberger's view wasn't taken up as a standard, textbook description of reproductive organs?

5. Explain how scientists can be so trapped by old metaphors that they cannot describe facts without biases, even when their research gives them new information, contradicts some old information, and might suggest new interpretations.

6. Martin suggests several images alternative to the typical description of egg-sperm meeting. Cite those alternative images and discuss the different view of women and men those images might create.

7. How can a scientist or anyone else free herself from thought-shaping cultural metaphors in order to see the world from a different view, perhaps a view without sex bias?

8. State Martin's thesis in your words.

9. Martin states, near the end of the essay, "cybernetic imagery is hardly neutral." Is any of the other imagery scientists use to describe reproduction neutral? Discuss the implications for social policy, a society's thinking, and social influences of biased language.

10. Evaluate Martin's evidence. Does she provide enough specific support to make her point convincing?

*Style*

1. Discuss the essay's overall organization. Does Martin organize information and ideas effectively?

2. Look at the transitions from paragraph to paragraph in the "New Research, Old Imagery" section. Discuss the effectiveness of those transitions.

3. Is it effective for Martin to place "Social Implications: Thinking Beyond" at the end of the essay, as a concluding section? Would that section have been more effective as an introduction? Why or why not?

4. Is Martin's title effective? Why or why not?

5. Both Martin and Easlea discuss difficult "scientific" subjects. Do they use language (diction, sentence structures, organization, evidence) that non-scientists can understand? Give several examples.

**For writing**

1. Write a paper in which you explain the advantages and disadvantages of growing up in a bilingual home or of growing up in a monolingual home.

2. If you know American Sign Language, write a paper in which you discuss differences and similarities of expressions and thoughts between American Sign Language and English. Can ASL express ideas that English cannot express?

3. Add rule #vii to Orwell's list of six rules: Don't use sexist false generic pronouns and nouns. Analyze any of the papers you have written this semester according to the seven rules. Or analyze a piece of published writing according to the seven rules.

4. Find and analyze some of the old grammar rules that cover "he," "his," and "man." Consider who wrote the rules and when. Good sources of information are Dale Spender's *Man Made Language*, Casey Swift and Kate Miller's *A Handbook for Nonsexist Writing*, and Julia Penelope's *Speaking Freely*. Your instructor can direct you to other sources of information.

5. Discuss the language of science and its influence on thought. Carol Cohn, Brian Easlea, and Emily Martin analyze some aspects of scientific language. Your instructor can suggest other sources of information, such as Evelyn Fox Keller's writing.

6. Analyze a piece of scientific writing for its assumptions and biases disguised in metaphors and images.

# Chapter Four:

# Is Anybody Out There?

# Is Anybody Out There?

## Introduction

AS WE HAVE SEEN IN THE PRECEDING THREE CHAPTERS, language affects all of us. Language is everybody's business. It is not the business only of English teachers or professional writers. Because you think, speak, read, write, and listen, the language is your concern no matter what your major is or what your particular interests are. The language is your business because it is part of the environment in which you live. And, as we have seen, each of us can exert some influence on language because we can choose whether to use it carefully or carelessly.

Using language carefully, choosing to create a new metaphor, for example, or choosing to make an active structure, is not the same as using "proper" or "correct" language. "Proper" and "correct" are hard to define because they depend on audience, purpose, and situation. When they think of "proper, correct language," most people are probably thinking of formal standard language, the language of textbooks, professional journals, many periodicals and newspapers, and of formal speech. But for our purposes, "correct and proper" means effective language—language that is appropriate for the audience, the purpose, and the situation.

If I am golfing with friends and miss a birdie putt by half an inch, it is appropriate for me to say, "Aw, damn!" If I am golfing in a tournament with people I don't know well, I choose a milder expletive if I miss the putt. In both situations, I simply want to vent frustration. Even with conventional language, we can choose words carefully for situation, audience, and purpose.

If I am speaking to a class of sixth-grade children about women of the American Revolution, I shift to language of literal meaning because I want to convey information. For that audience, I deliberately build sentences and choose words that I think children of that age will understand. "Sybil Luddington rode her horse 40 miles at night to warn people that the British were coming" is more appropriate for that audience than is: "Although we don't hear as much about her as we do about Paul Revere, sixteen-year-old Sybil Luddington rode horseback 40 miles through the New England country at night to alert patriots about the British," a sentence I would make for an audience of educated adults. What differences do you see in length, content, and word choice (diction) in these two sentences? What differences do you see in sentence structure? I did not over-simplify my sentence for the sixth-graders, but I probably do not have any vocabulary in that sentence that would challenge a sixth-grader to learn a new word. Neither did I sound pretentious in my sentence for the adults. I chose "proper" language for each situation.

Choosing words and crafting sentences for a specific audience, though, means more than finding words the audience will know and making grammatically complete sentences. Let's look first at one of the complications of word choice. Most words in English have two layers of meaning, denotation and connotation. A word's denotation is its dictionary definition, its flat, literal meaning. A word's connotation is what the word suggests beyond its denotation, the images and the emotional associations we attach to the word. Connotation makes denotatively similar words different from each other. "Country" and "countryside" mean just about the same thing, according to dictionary definition, but their connotations add meanings that make us see quite different pictures. If I had wanted listeners to see Sybil Luddington riding safely over hill and dale, I would have chosen "countryside" because that word suggests a pastoral, pleasant scene. Because I wanted listeners to see a sixteen-year-old girl on a more dangerous mission, riding through a large rural area, I chose "country." I chose "her horse," and "horseback," "warn" and "alert," and "people" and "patriots" for their denotations and connotations. What differences in connotation do you recognize between each pair?

Now let's look at sentence structure, the way a sentence is put together, the number of sentence parts, and the way the parts connect. "Sybil Luddington rode her horse 40 miles at night to warn people that the British were coming" is a complex sentence structure (it has an independent clause and a dependent clause), but it is not a difficult sentence. Sixth-graders and even younger children can make and understand complex sentence structures. My sentence has six details including the subject-verb combination, and I have put them together in an easy order, with subject and verb at the beginning and with independent clause at the beginning so that the main idea is clear right away; less important information follows. "Although we don't hear as much about her as we do about Paul Revere, sixteen-year-old Sybil Luddington rode horseback 40 miles through the New England country at night to alert patriots about the British" is also a complex sentence (it has one independent clause and two dependent clauses), but it is more difficult to follow than is the other sentence. This second sentence has 10 pieces of information, including the subject-verb combination, and the order is different. Because I put the two dependent clauses before the independent clause, the audience doesn't know the main point immediately. And because "her" has no antecedent, the audience has to wait for "Sybil Luddington" for the pronoun to become clear. To put emphasis on "at night," I withheld it until after "the country," again expecting my audience to hold details in mind until I had completed the sentence.

The organization of a sentence and the amount of information in a sentence are miniatures of the overall organization and development of a speech or an essay. For a young audience with a short attention span and limited experience, knowledge, and interests, I would organize the paragraphs of a speech or an essay in a simple pattern. If the subject permitted, I would use a chronology. No matter what organizational pattern I chose, I would use clear and direct transitions to let my young audience know when I was going to change directions and where I would lead them next. I would use transitions like "first," "next," "and," and "for example"; if those were the exact connections I wanted to make, I would also use those transitions for an adult audience. But for an adult audience with a mature attention span and knowledge, I would also need more complicated transitions to fit more complicated ideas and the organization I would choose to satisfy that audience. I might need "consequently," "in contrast," "furthermore," and "more significant" to clarify more complex relationships between and among ideas, but I would choose transitions for precision—to let my audience know when I intended to add more examples, when I intended to detour and when I got back on the main trail, where I wanted to lead them next.

As I planned an overall organization, I would think carefully about a beginning—a title and an introductory paragraph. Should I make my title a question to get attention, or should I use a phrase to describe the content? Should I make a controversial statement in the title, or does that kind of title turn people away? In my first paragraph, should I state my thesis or should I hope to interest my audience with a narrative? In my first paragraph, should I create a hypothetical situation connected to my thesis, or should I quote a famous line? My title and first paragraph will create a first impression. I want the first impression to get my audience on my side, hearing what I have to say, and I want it to make me look good.

Then I would consider how much and what kind of information my audience wants and needs. For an educated adult audience, I would provide more development of ideas than I would for an audience of children because educated adults expect and require more and can comprehend more than children can. For any audience, I would want to satisfy curiosity. For children, a few details will satisfy; for educated adults, I will need many details. To illustrate for a young audience the point that women of the American Revolution were heroic, I would tell the stories of four or five heroes including Sybil Luddington. To illustrate that point for an educated adult audience, I would analyze the actions of eight or ten women including Abigail Adams, Mercy Otis Warren, Elizabeth Drinker, Nancy Shippen Livingston, and Eliza Lucas Pinckney. I would choose a somewhat different kind of information as well as a different quantity of it, depending on audience.

I have used two quite different audiences as examples—children and educated adults—to emphasize language choices a careful writer or speaker makes. Between children and educated adults is a range of audiences (bright children and dull adults, 10-year-old children with twelfth-grade reading abilities and adults with fourth-grade reading abilities, literate children and illiterate adults). And beyond children who are learning and adults who are educated (who read habitually and have a range of interests and information) are adults who are experts in their disciplines.

If I were writing for that audience of experts, I would consider the same language choices we have just examined: diction, sentence structure, organization, quantity and quality of development. If, as a scholar of women of the American Revolution, I were writing a paper for a professional journal of American history, I would choose diction and sentence structure, organization and introduction, and amount and kind information to fit my audience. I would assume that such an audience would not appreciate pretension any more than I do; even though I might choose larger and more technical words than I would use for an audience of educated adults who are not historians of the American Revolution, I would choose words and sentence structures for precision and meaning and not to show off. A listening audience does not have the opportunity to look back over a complicated sentence structure, but readers have that opportunity. If, in a paper, I needed a complicated structure to fit a complicated idea, I would not hesitate to make such a sentence; for a listening audience, I would perhaps need two less complicated sentences to make the same point. I assume that a reading audience of experts in a discipline has the reading ability to follow a complex organization. Even so, that audience appreciates clear transitions. Readers of a professional journal may not especially want cute introductory devices, but they do not want to be bored either. Such an audience would want more information than I could present to children in 20 minutes or to informed adults in an hour. I would provide enough specific support of my thesis to satisfy my audience, but I would not attempt to impress that audience with my erudition. Someone always knows more than I do.

The choices I have been considering are choices any writer or speaker can make. Most of the writing you do as a college student will be for an audience of your classmates and your instructors, people whose reading abilities and knowledge may be as advanced as or more advanced than your own. (Your college probably has a reading lab or other facility where you can find out what your reading level is.) After your college years, you may write for audiences who read the same professional journals you read and whose reading ability and knowledge are as advanced as or more advanced than yours. You may write for audiences who know very little about your subject and whose reading abilities are minimal. You may learn the special skills necessary to write for children, or you may spend most of your professional writing time writing for your supervisors as audience. Most likely during your college years and after, you will be in situations in which you adapt your speech for different audiences. Knowing that you can adapt your language to fit audience, purpose, and situation allows you to be a more effective speaker and writer.

Knowing that other writers adapt their language for specific audiences also makes us more effective readers. Not only can we decide what reading is too easy for us and what challenges us, we can analyze language choices other writers have made and learn from and appreciate those choices. The selections that follow illustrate choices writers have made for specific audiences. As you read them, look at word choices, sentence structures and sentence lengths, and paragraph size, including how many sentences and how much specific development each paragraph has. Describe the reading ability of each audience as precisely as you can, and decide whether you think the authors have made appropriate choices for their audiences.

Read also for content—information and ideas. The first essay, "Selection, Slanting, and Charged Language," for a general adult audience, discusses some of the language choices I have examined in this chapter. The subject of the next two essays, "Dictionaries" and "From Discourse to Dictionary," as you would guess, is dictionaries, but the essays provide quite different discussions, one for an audience of children and the other for an informed adult audience. The final essay, "Making Changes," for an expert adult audience, discusses some technical aspects of language that affect all of us. As you read each essay, consider whether the authors have made appropriate choices for their audiences.

And consider what kind of audience you are. What is your reading ability, attention span, comprehension, interest in a range of issues? What kind of audience do you aspire to be?

# Selection, Slanting, and Charged Language

## Newman P. Birk and Genevieve B. Birk

### A. The Principle of Selection

*BEFORE* IT IS EXPRESSED IN WORDS, our knowledge, both inside and outside, is influenced by the principle of selection. What we know or observe depends on what we notice; that is, what we select, consciously or unconsciously, as worthy of notice or attention. As we observe, the principle of selection determines which facts we take in.

Suppose, for example, that three people, a lumberjack, an artist, and a tree surgeon, are examining a large tree in a forest. Since the tree itself is a complicated object, the number of particulars or facts about it that one could observe would be very great indeed. Which of these facts a particular observer will notice will be a matter of selection, a selection that is determined by his interests and purposes. A lumberjack might be interested in the best way to cut the tree down, cut it up and transport it to the lumber mill. His interest would then determine his principle of selection in observing and thinking about the tree. The artist might consider painting a picture of the tree, and his purpose would furnish his principle of selection. The tree surgeon's professional interest in the physical health of the tree might establish a principle of selection for him. If each man were now required to write an exhaustive, detailed report on everything he observed about the tree, the facts supplied by each would differ, for each would report those facts that his particular principle of selection led him to notice.[1]

The principle of selection holds not only for the specific facts that people observe but also for the facts they remember. A student suddenly embarrassed may remember nothing of the next ten minutes of class discussion but may have a vivid recollection of the sensation of the blood mounting, as he blushed, up his face and into his ears. In both noticing and remembering, the principle of selection applies, and it is influenced not only by our special interest and point of view but by our whole mental state of the moment.

The principle of selection then serves as a kind of sieve or screen through which our knowledge passes before it becomes our knowledge. Since we can't notice everything about a complicated object or situation or action or state of our own consciousness, what we do notice is determined by whatever principle of selection is operating for us at the time we gain the knowledge.

It is important to remember that what is true of the way the principle of selection works for us is true also of the way it works for others. Even before we or other people put knowledge into words to express meaning, that knowledge has been screened or selected. Before an historian or an economist writes a book, or before a reporter writes a news article, the facts that each is to present have been sifted through the screen of a principle of selection. Before one person passes on knowledge to another, that knowledge has already been selected and shaped, intentionally or unintentionally, by the mind of the communicator.

## B. The Principle of Slanting

When we put our knowledge into words, a second process of selection, the process of slanting, takes place. Just as there is something, a rather mysterious principle of selection, which chooses for us what we will notice, and what will then become our knowledge, there is also a principle which operates, with or without our awareness, to select certain facts and feelings from our store of knowledge, and to choose the words and the emphasis that we shall use to communicate our meaning.[2] Slanting may be defined as the process of selecting (1) knowledge—factual and attitudinal; (2) words; and (3) emphasis, to achieve the intention of the communicator. Slanting is present in some degree in all communication: one may slant for (favorable slanting), slant against (unfavorable slanting), or slant both ways (balanced slanting)....

## C. Slanting by Use of Emphasis

Slanting by use of the devices of emphasis is unavoidable,[3] for emphasis is simply the giving of stress to subject matter, and so indicating what is important and what is less important. In speech, for example, if we say that Socrates was *a wise old man*, we can give several slightly different meanings, one by stressing *wise*, another by stressing *old*, another by giving equal stress to *wise* and *old*, and still another by giving chief stress to *man*. Each different stress gives a different slant (favorable or unfavorable or balanced) to the statement because it conveys a different attitude toward Socrates or a different judgment of him. Connectives and word order also slant by the emphasis produced by *old but wise, old and wise, wise but old.* In writing, we cannot indicate subtle stresses on words as clearly as in speech, but we can achieve our emphasis and so we can slant by the use of more complex patterns of word order, by choice of connectives, by underlining heavily stressed words, and by marks of punctuation that indicate short or long pauses and so give light or heavy emphasis. Question marks, quotation marks, and exclamation points can also contribute to slanting.[4] It is impossible either in speech or in writing to put two facts together without giving some slight emphasis or slant. For example, if we have in mind only two facts about a man, his awkwardness and his strength, we subtly slant those facts favorably or unfavorably in whatever way we may choose to join them:

| More Favorable Slanting | Less Favorable Slanting |
| --- | --- |
| He is awkward and strong. | He is strong and awkward. |
| He is awkward but strong. | He is strong but awkward. |
| Although he is somewhat awkward, he is very strong. | He may be strong, but he's very awkward. |

With more facts and in longer passages it is possible to maintain a delicate balance by alternating favorable emphasis and so producing a balanced effect.

All communication, then, is in some degree slanted by the *emphasis* of the communicator.

## D. Slanting by Selection of Facts

To illustrate the technique of slanting by selection of facts, we shall examine three passages of informative writing which achieve different effects simply by the selection and emphasis of material. Each passage is made up of true statements or facts about a dog, yet the reader is given three different impressions. The first passage is an example of objective writing or balanced slanting, the second is slanted unfavorably, and the third is slanted favorably.

### 1. Balanced Presentation

Our dog, Toddy, sold to us a cocker, produces various reactions in various people. Those who come to the back door she usually growls and barks at (a milkman has said that he is afraid of her); those who come to the front door, she whines at and paws: also she tries to lick people's faces unless we have forestalled her by putting a newspaper in her mouth. (Some of our friends encourage these actions; others discourage them. Mrs. Firmly, one friend, slaps the dog with a newspaper and says, "I know how hard dogs are to train.") Toddy knows and responds to a number of words and phrases, and guests sometimes remark that she is a "very intelligent dog." She has fleas in the summer, and she sheds, at times copiously, the year round. Her blonde hairs are conspicuous when they are on people's clothing or on rugs or furniture. Her color and her large brown eyes frequently produce favorable comment. An expert on cockers would say that her ears are too short and set too high and that she is at least six pounds too heavy.

The passage above is made up of facts, verifiable facts,[5] deliberately selected and emphasized to produce a *balanced* impression. Of course not all the facts about the dog have been given—to supply *all* the facts on any subject, even such a comparatively simple one, would be an almost impossible task. Both favorable and unfavorable facts are used, however, and an effort has been made to alternate favorable and unfavorable details so that neither will receive greater emphasis by position, proportion, or grammatical structure.

## 2. Facts Slanted Against

That dog put her paws on my white dress as soon as I came in the door, and she made so much noise that it was two minutes before she had quieted down enough for us to talk and hear each other. Then the gas man came and she did a great deal of barking. And her hairs are on the rug and on the furniture. If you wear a dark dress they stick to it like lint. When Mrs. Firmly came in, she actually hit the dog with a newspaper to make it stay down, and she made some remark about training dogs. I wish the Birks would take the hint or get rid of that noisy, short-eared, overweight "cocker" of theirs.

This unfavorably slanted version is based on the same facts, but now these facts have been selected and given a new emphasis. The speaker, using her selected facts to give her impression of the dog, is quite possibly unaware of her negative slanting.

Now for a favorably slanted version:

## 3. Facts Slanted For

What a lively and responsive dog! When I walked in the door, there she was with a newspaper in her mouth, whining and standing on her hind legs and wagging her tail all at the same time. And what an intelligent dog. If you suggest going for a walk, she will get her collar from the kitchen and hand it to you, and she brings Mrs. Birk's slippers whenever Mrs. Birk says she is "tired" or mentions slippers. At a command she catches balls, rolls over, "speaks," or stands on her hind feet and twirls around. She sits up and balances a piece of bread on her nose until she is told to take it; then she tosses it up and catches it. If you are eating something, she sits up in front of you and "begs" with those big dark brown eyes set in that light, buff-colored face of hers. When I got up to go and told her I was leaving, she rolled her eyes at me and sat up like a squirrel. She certainly is a lively and intelligent dog.

Speaker 3, like Speaker 2, is selecting from the "facts" summarized in balanced version 1, and is emphasizing his facts to communicate his impression.

All three passages are examples of *reporting* (i.e., consist only of verifiable facts), yet they give three very different impressions of the same dog because of the different ways the speakers slanted the facts. Some people say that figures don't lie, and many people believe that if they have the "facts," they have the "truth." Yet if we carefully examine the ways of thought and language, we see that any knowledge that comes to us through words has been subjected to the double screening of the principle of selection and the slanting of language....

Wise listeners and readers realize that the double screening that is produced by the principle of selection and by slanting takes place even when people honestly try to report the facts as they know them. (Speakers 2 and 3, for instance, probably thought of themselves as simply giving information about a dog and were not deliberately trying to mislead.) Wise listeners and readers know too that deliberate manipulators of language, by mere selection and emphasis, can make their slanted facts appear to support almost any cause.

In arriving at opinions and values we cannot always be sure that the facts that sift into our minds through language are representative and relevant and true. We need to remember that much of our information about politics, governmental activities, business conditions, and foreign affairs comes to us selected and slanted. More than we realize, our opinions on these matters may depend on what newspaper we read or what news commentator we listen to. Worthwhile opinions call for knowledge of reliable facts and reasonable arguments for and against—and such opinions include beliefs about morality and truth and religion as well as about public affairs. Because complex subjects involve knowing and dealing with many facts on both sides, reliable judgments are at best difficult to arrive at. If we want to be fairminded, we must be willing to subject our opinions to continual testing by new knowledge, and must realize that after all they are opinions, more or less trustworthy. Their trustworthiness will depend on the representativeness of our facts, on the quality of our reasoning, and on the standard of values that we choose to apply.

We shall not give here a passage illustrating the unscrupulous slanting of facts. Such a passage would also include irrelevant facts and false statements presented as facts, along with various subtle distortions of fact. Yet to the uninformed reader the passage would be indistinguishable from a passage intended to give a fair account. If two passages (2 and 3) of casual and unintentional slanting of facts about a dog can give such contradictory impressions of a simple subject, the reader can imagine what a skilled and designing manipulation of facts and statistics could do to mislead an uninformed reader about a really complex subject. An example of such manipulation might be the account of the United States that Soviet propaganda has supplied to the average Russian. Such propaganda, however, would go beyond the mere slanting of the facts: it would clothe the selected facts in charged words and would make use of the many other devices of slanting that appear in charged language.

## E. Slanting by Use of Charged Words

In the passages describing the dog Toddy, we were illustrating the technique of slanting by the selection and emphasis of facts. Though the facts selected had to be expressed in words, the words chosen were as factual as possible, and it was the selection and emphasis of facts and not of words that was mainly responsible for the two distinctly different impressions of the dog. In the passages below we are demonstrating another way of slanting—by the use of charged words. This time the accounts are very similar in the facts they contain; the different impressions of the subject, Corlyn, are produced not by different facts but by the subtle selection of charged words.

The passages were written by a clever student who was told to choose as his subject a person in action, and to write two descriptions, each using the "same facts." The instruction required that one description be slanted positively and the other negatively, so that the first would make the reader favorably inclined toward the person and the action, and the second would make him unfavorably inclined.

Here is the favorably charged description. Read it carefully and form your opinion of the person before you go on to read the second description.

Corlyn

Corlyn paused at the entrance to the room and glanced about. A well-cut black dress draped subtly about her slender form. Her long blonde hair gave her chiseled features the simple frame they required. She smiled an engaging smile as she accepted a cigarette from her escort. As he lit it for her she looked over the flame and into his eyes. Corlyn had that rare talent of making every male feel that he was the one man in the world.

She took his arm and they descended the steps into the room. She walked with an effortless grace and spoke with equal ease. They each took a cup of coffee and joined a group of friends near the fire. The flickering light danced across her face and lent an ethereal quality to her beauty. The good conversation, the crackling logs, and the stimulating coffee gave her a feeling of internal warmth. Her eyes danced with each leap of the flames.

Taken by itself this passage might seem just a description of an attractive girl. The favorable slanting by use of charged words has been done so skillfully that it is inconspicuous. Now we turn to the unfavorable slanted description of the "same" girl in the "same" actions:

Corlyn

Corlyn halted at the entrance to the room and looked around. A plain black dress hung on her thin frame. Her stringy bleached hair accentuated her harsh features. She smiled an inane smile as she took a cigarette from her escort. As he lit it for her she stared over the lighter and into his eyes. Corlyn had a habit of making every male feel that he was the last man on earth.
     She grasped his arm and they walked down the steps and into the room. Her pace was fast and ungainly, as was her speech. They each reached for some coffee and broke into a group of acquaintances near the fire. The flickering light played across her face and revealed every flaw. The loud talk, the fire, and the coffee she had gulped down made her feel hot. Her eyes grew more red with each leap of the flames.

When the reader compares these two descriptions, he can see how charged words influence the reader's attitude. One needs to read the two descriptions several times to appreciate all the subtle differences between them. Words, some rather heavily charged, others innocent-looking but lightly charged, work together to carry to the reader a judgment of a person and a situation. If the reader had seen only the first description of Corlyn, he might well have thought that he had formed his "own judgment on the basis of the facts." And the examples just given only begin to suggest the techniques that may be used in heavily charged language. For one thing, the two descriptions of Corlyn contain no really good example of the use of charged abstractions; for another, the writer was obliged by the assignment to use the same set of facts and so could not slant by selecting his material.

## Slanting and Charged Language

     ...When slanting of facts, or words, or emphasis, or any combination of the three *significantly* influences feelings toward, or judgments about, a subject, the language used is charged language...
     Of course communications vary in the amount of charge they carry and in their effect on different people; what is very favorably charged for one person may have little or no charge, or may even be adversely charged, for others. It is sometimes hard to distinguish between charged and uncharged expression. But it is safe to say that whenever we wish to convey any kind of inner knowledge—feelings, attitudes, judgments, values—we are obliged to convey that attitudinal meaning through the medium of charged language; and when we wish to under-

stand the inside knowledge of others, we have to interpret the charged language that they choose, or are obliged to use. Charged language, then, is the natural and necessary medium for the communication of charged or attitudinal meaning. At times we have difficulty in living with it, but we should have even greater difficulty in living without it.

Some of the difficulties in living with charged language are caused by its use in dishonest propaganda, in some editorials, in many political speeches, in most advertising, in certain kinds of effusive salesmanship, and in blatantly insincere, or exaggerated, or sentimental expressions of emotion. Other difficulties are caused by the misunderstandings and misinterpretations that charged language produces. A charged phrase misinterpreted in a love letter; a charged word spoken in haste or in anger; an acrimonious argument about religion or politics or athletics or fraternities; the frustrating uncertainty produced by the effort to understand the complex attitudinal meaning in a poem or play or a short story—these troubles, all growing out of the use of charged language, may give us the feeling that Robert Louis Stevenson expressed when he said, "The battle goes sore against us to the going down of the sun."

But however charged language is abused and whatever misunderstandings it may cause, we still have to live with it—and even by it. It shapes our attitudes and values even without our conscious knowledge; it gives purpose to, and guides, our actions; through it we establish and maintain relations with other people and by means of it we exert our greatest influence on them. Without charged language, life would be but half life. The relatively uncharged language of bare factual statement, though it serves its informative purpose well and is much less open to abuse and to misunderstanding, can describe only the bare land of factual knowledge; to communicate knowledge of the turbulencies and the calms and the deep currents of the sea of inner experience we must use charged language.

## Notes

1.  Of course, all three observers would probably report a good many facts in common-the height of the tree, for example, and the size of the trunk. The point we wish to make is that each observer would give us a different impression of the tree because of the different principle of selection that guided his observation.

2.  Notice that the "principle of selection" is at work as we take in knowledge, and that slanting occurs as *we express* our knowledge in words.

3.  When emphasis is present—and we can think of no instance in the use of language in which it is not—it necessarily influences the meaning by playing a part in the favorable, unfavorable, or balanced slant of the communicator. We are likely to emphasize by voice stress, even when we answer *yes* or *no* to simple questions.

4.    Consider the slanting achieved by punctuation in the following sentences: He called the Senator an honest man? *He* called the Senator an honest man! He said one more such "honest" senator would corrupt the state.

5.    *Verifiable facts* are facts that can be checked and agreed upon and proved to be true by people who wish to verify them. That a particular theme received a failing grade is a verifiable fact; one needs merely to see the theme with the grade on it. That the instructor should have failed the theme is not, strictly speaking, a verifiable fact, but a matter of opinion. That women on the average live longer than men is a verifiable fact; that they live better is a matter of opinion, a *value judgment*.

## For discussion

1.  Describe the reading abilities of the audience you think the Birks write for in this essay.

2.  The Birks use subheadings. Do you need subheadings, or do you consider subheadings an insult to your reading ability?

3.  Mark "the use of" in the Birks' sentences and subheadings. What do you think of that phrase?

4.  In their final paragraph, the Birks use the metaphor "the sea of inner experience." Is that a new metaphor for you? Is it effective?

5.  The essay suggests that it is impossible to construct a sentence without a built-in bias. What do you think about that idea?

6.  Do the Birks provide enough specific examples and other illustrations in each section to satisfy an educated adult reader?

## For writing

All writing suggestions for Chapter Four follow the discussion questions for the chapter's final essay. (See page 228.)

# Dictionaries

## Howard R. Webber

A DICTIONARY IS A BOOK in which the words of a language are arranged in alphabetical order. Dictionaries give many different kinds of information in many different ways.

Although people use a general-purpose dictionary primarily to find out the meaning of a word, a dictionary also tells you how to divide a word into syllables and how to pronounce it. It tells you about word histories, gives all of the different senses, or meanings, of a word, and tells you whether there is more than one way to spell it. A dictionary will also tell you whether the word may be used as more than one part of speech. For example, the word "walk" may be used as a verb or as a noun. Some dictionaries give examples of the correct use of a word in sentences. A dictionary will also tell you the spelling of different forms of words, such as plural forms.

Some dictionaries give information about famous people and places. They may also include other proper nouns (names of particular persons and places, always capitalized), abbreviations, illustrations, maps, diagrams, and special charts and tables. Most dictionaries contain a guide at the beginning of the book that explains how to use the particular dictionary.

Many people talk about "the dictionary" as if there were only one. There are in fact many different dictionaries of the English language—from small pocket dictionaries to very large ones that try to record the entire language. Some dictionaries deal only with special subjects, such as law, music, and science. There are two-language (bilingual) dictionaries, such as Spanish-English and French-English dictionaries. These dictionaries often have two parts. Each part translates the words of one language into the other language.

*From* The New Book of Knowledge, *1995 Edition. Copyright © 1995 by Grolier Incorporated. Reprinted by permission.*

## A Brief History of English Dictionaries

Dictionaries of the English language began to appear during the time of Queen Elizabeth I and Shakespeare, the end of the 16th century. The first great English dictionary was written by the English author Samuel Johnson and was published in 1755. It contained more than 40,000 words. Modern dictionaries contain more words, partly because there are more words in the language now. Many of the new words evolved from new technologies. Indeed, it has been estimated that 25–30 percent of the entries in current college-level dictionaries are scientific or technical. The basic organization of dictionaries, however, has remained the same.

Noah Webster, an American born in Connecticut, believed that the new United States needed its own schoolbooks and dictionaries that were different from their British counterparts. After many years of work, he published *An American Dictionary of the English Language* in 1828. It defined about 70,000 words.

Another New England lexicographer (dictionary author or editor), Joseph Worcester, published a rival dictionary in 1830. The "War of the Dictionaries" broke out in 1834, when a newspaper editorial suggested that Worcester had copied Webster. Long exchanges of letters were printed all over the country, and the battle between the two dictionaries continued to the end of the century. In 1860, Worcester published his *A Dictionary of the English Language,* containing more than 100,000 words. Webster's dictionaries, however, remained the more popular.

Beginning in 1857, a group of scholars in England began to put together the most thorough dictionary of the English language. Called *The Oxford English Dictionary*, its first volume was published in 1884. When the dictionary was completed in 1933, it filled 13 thick volumes. The *O.E.D.,* as it is called, gives the etymology (history and origin) of words, including numerous examples of their use in writing, and contains some 415,000 entries. Several supplements to this famous dictionary have since appeared.

Many American dictionaries have appeared since the time of Webster and Worcester. *The Century Dictionary and Cyclopedia,* which was published in 1889–1899, remained a landmark in the United States among dictionaries that give the etymology of words.

Although Noah Webster died in 1843, his name lives on in the titles of many other dictionaries published in the United States. In 1909 the first of the international dictionaries of English, containing words used in all the English-speaking countries, was published by the firm now known as Merriam–Webster, Inc. In 1961 the same company issued *Webster's Third New International Dictionary,* which has a vocabulary of over 450,000 words.

Most educated adults use a "college" dictionary containing about 150,000 entry words. Among the most important such dictionaries are: *The American*

*Heritage Dictionary, The Random House College Dictionary, Webster's New World Dictionary of the American Language, Webster's II New Riverside University Dictionary,* and *Webster's Ninth New Collegiate Dictionary.*

## Modern Technology and the Dictionary

Computers have been of great help to lexicographers. Computers are used to make sure that all the words used in definitions are also defined in the dictionary. Computers can count the number of times words appear in newspapers, magazines, and books and thus help dictionary editors decide what words belong in dictionaries at various levels. Lexicographers have long used examples from such sources to show particular meanings of known words or the meaning of a new word entering the language. In the past, examples had to be collected by hand and studied by editors, who then wrote the definitions. These examples can now be gathered by computers and stored on tapes, ready to be analyzed, though editors must still evaluate and define the words. Computerized dictionaries can serve as part of software that corrects spelling, suggests synonyms, and even spots errors of grammar in word processing.

## Children's Dictionaries

Until the 1930's, any adult dictionary edited to contain fewer words was thought suitable for children. About that time, Dr. Edward L. Thorndike, a psychologist, began scientifically studying the words children used most often and the words children would need to know to do their schoolwork. His studies were the basis of the *Thorndike–Century Junior Dictionary* published in 1935. Soon other dictionaries for young people began to appear. Word lists were based on careful studies of schoolbooks and other school materials. Among the notable children's dictionaries available today are *The American Heritage Children's Dictionary,* the *Macmillan Dictionary for Children,* and the *Scott, Foresman Beginning Dictionary.* Children's dictionaries contain many colorful illustrations.

**For discussion**

1. Describe the reading abilities of the audience for which you think Webber writes this essay. What age do you think his audience is?

2. Find examples of words Webber defines for his audience. The fact that he defines words in the text of the essay indicates that those words may be new for his audience. Is an in-text definition an insult to the audience for which Webber is writing? Is it an insult for you?

3. Do you find any vocabulary (diction) in this essay that stretches or challenges you?

4. Examine for structure the sentences in any paragraph other than paragraph one. Are the sentences simple structures, compound structures, complex structures, compound-complex structures? How many ideas are there in each sentence and how are the ideas in each sentence connected to each other?

5. What is the average number of words per sentence? What is the average number of sentences per paragraph?

6. Describe the organization of paragraph five ("A Brief History of English Dictionaries"). Is that an appropriately difficult/simple organization for Webber's audience?

7. The paragraph about the *O.E.D.* is typical size for this essay. How many pieces of specific information does it contain? Would that amount of detail satisfy you as a reader?

8. "Dictionaries" is a simple, straightforward title, and Webber's introductory paragraph is an easy definition. Do you think those are appropriate introductory devices for his audience? Is the title too general to interest a more mature reading audience?

# From Discourse to Dictionary: How Sexist Meanings Are Authorized

Paula A. Treichler

THE TERM *DICTIONARY* CAN DESIGNATE a concrete lexico-graphic object ("Turning to my Webster's, I find that *woman* is defined as an adult human female"); a more broadly institutionalized cultural authority ("As the dictionary makes clear, women are frequently viewed negatively in our culture"); or an abstract repository of linguistically coded entities available in the repertoire of individual speakers (For many English speakers the dictionary entry *woman* is coded human, adult, and female). All these meanings presuppose the conscious or unconscious construction of a set of "definitive" statements commonly thought to be founded on—deduced or extracted from—the study or observation of linguistic and material entities in the "real world." In turn, a dictionary definition places a word within a particular grammatical, cognitive, and material context, thus constraining (dictating) usage, conceptualization, and perception. It is the still, fixed outcome, in other words, of a set of interpretive practices that becomes, itself, interpreted. If discourse is the text from which a dictionary is constructed, a dictionary becomes the text that, in turn, constructs discourse. In this sense a dictionary is any kind of scholarly or authoritative text on words that claims to be—as most dictionaries do claim—on what is. This equation—provisional and problematic though it may be—is one way of understanding the process through which meanings—both sexist and nonsexist—are authorized.

In this essay I explore the relation between discourse and dictionaries in a specific context: the preparation of *A Feminist Dictionary* (by Kramarae and

Treichler). This project necessarily raised questions about how meanings are traditionally authorized, how feminists can intervene in this process, and how any authorization process can work for or against women's interests. In addition to illuminating specific linguistic practices and assumptions, the dictionary project more generally contributed toward an ongoing inquiry into feminist scholarship and the status of knowledge.

I first consider dictionaries as lexicographic objects, summarizing some of the ways traditional dictionaries have sanctioned sexist meanings. Then I briefly sketch the feminist dictionary project: its goals, assumptions, and alternative conceptualizations of *discourse* and *dictionary*. Finally, I note some of the issues involved in the production and authorization of meaning—issues that connect to more theoretical notions of a dictionary—and suggest approaches to examining them in greater depth.

## The Authorization of Sexist Meanings

Recent language and gender research indicates a number of ways that conscious or unconscious sexism may enter dictionaries (including historical, etymological, and concise "desktop" dictionaries).[1] The most obvious sexism in dictionaries—certainly the kind most criticized by feminist writers—is the inclusion of negative, stereotypical, and trivializing references to women. This is where much feminist work has concentrated. Ruth Todasco's *Feminist English Dictionary*, for example, subtitled *An Intelligent Women's Guide to Dirty Words*, was compiled from established English dictionaries—"museum pieces," in Todasco's words, "of an archaic culture"; in identifying "patriarchal epithets," it sought to demonstrate men's prejudiced myths about women and female sexuality and suggested the power of dictionaries to reinforce such means of expression. In "Gender-Marking in American English," Julia Penelope Stanley reports that in standard dictionaries words for women are much more frequent and much more negative than words for men. Feminists have also found androcentric or "male-centered" definitions of words for female sexuality. Thus *clitoris* is sometimes defined as "a failed or vestigial penis"; *Stedman's Medical Dictionary*, for example, describes it as a "homologue of the penis in the male except that it is not perforated by the urethra and does not possess a corpus spongiosum." An important point here is that these definitions are not simply "reflections" of an androcentric culture but ideological constructions of what that culture is to be. As Kate Millet argues in *Sexual Politics*, negative representations of women serve the interests of one group (men) at the expense of another (women). Though the sheer number of such derogatory terms may indeed reflect the mentality of "an archaic culture," their inclusion in a dictionary comes about in part because the editors themselves belong to that culture and make many choices that differentially affect how the culture is to be represented and authorized.

Various selection processes may work to introduce a male bias into the lexicon by valuing the public over the private sphere. Of the more than three thousand works listed in *Dictionaries of the World*, only a handful concern themselves with such traditionally female interests as sewing and fashion (e.g., *The Dictionary of Fashion*). A predominantly male lexicon—military battles, nautical terms, mining and metallurgy, rubber coating and refrigeration—is represented in all the others. Values clearly influence what goes into dictionaries, which dictionaries are published, and which are listed in bibliographies. It has traditionally been the public world of politics, policy, work, and commerce that has seemed to require authorization and community consensus on meaning—as opposed to private activities such as housekeeping and child care (but I discuss below how this situation is changing).

If the lexicon of a standard dictionary consists largely of words for activities, interests, and concerns associated primarily with men, the reason may be not only that men have had greater access to the world's resources but also that the documenters of the world have been largely male. Certainly male dictionary makers have not been reticent in expressing their opinions of women as language users: Samuel Johnson's notorious remark likening a woman preaching to a dog walking on its hind legs—the wonder is not how well she does it but that she does it at all—embodies a common judgment about women as public speakers and foreshadows James Murray's distrust of them as documenters of speech. In his desperation for help with the *Oxford English Dictionary*, Murray did enlist the services of women readers, many of whom derived satisfaction from contributing to this important scholarly project; though Murray was condescending toward them (particularly the "spinsters," into whose lives he believed the *OED* project infused purpose), he found their work efficient and accurate: they were, that is, satisfactory transmitters of the code.

Women's documented contributions to the study of language and the production of dictionaries have been the exception, not the rule. Elizabeth Elstob, author of the first Anglo–Saxon grammar, was one such exception. "I have but one thing more to add," she wrote in her 1715 book dedicated to the Princess of Wales, "that this present, worthless as it is, is the humble Tribute of a Female; the first, I imagine, of the kind that hath been offer'd to Your Royal Highness." Another exception was Janet Taylor, a student of mathematics and navigation who started a nautical academy for merchant service officers and in 1865 published *The Mariner's Friend: Or, Polyglot Indispensable and Technical Dictionary* of nautical and scientific terms in ten languages. A more recent example is Marghanita Laski, who worked on the *OED* supplement; an erudite journalist and book reviewer, Laski responded to the 1958 appeal for help published by Oxford University Press by volunteering to track down the life history of the term *alley cat*. In the end, she contributed more than 100,000 citations from contemporary authors and from particular subject areas, including fashion, food, social life, sewing, embroidery, gardening, and cookery. The existence of such women—and there are doubtless others—is significant, but it does not challenge or change the institutional nature of dictionary making and the authoritative procedures on which it depends. To rescue favorite words the Oxford staff thought were obsolete, Laski was not above including them in the work she herself published and then submitting these uses as citations (see Shenker 91–92). But few women are in a position to authorize their own words and definitions. More commonly women's influence over such activities is cited only when it is negative or aberrant. Thus Harold Whitehall, writing about Cooper's 1565 *Thesaurus*, made this comment:

> The history of dictionaries is larded with strange occurrences: we are not surprised, therefore, that the publication of Cooper's work was delayed five years because his wife, fearing that too much lexicography would kill her husband, burned the first manuscript of his magnum opus. (xxxii)

Nor were only English women chastised for subverting linguistic progress: the Cherokee Indian Sequoyah devoted ten years to creating a writing system for the Cherokee language. Ridiculed and rejected throughout this period, he nevertheless persisted, and by 1819 he had produced the 85 characters of Cherokee. At this point, according to John Howard Payne's contemporary account, "when all his friends had remonstrated in vain, his wife went in and flung his whole apparatus of papers and books into the fire, and thus he lost his first labor" (qtd. in Dykeman 21).

Though dictionary editors claim, sometimes militantly, that they collect words and definitions from diverse sources, their criteria and procedures for identification and preservation (both explicit and implicit) nearly always preclude gathering women's definitions. Definitions for many dictionaries, for example, are constructed from usages found in works by the "best authors"; though what this designation means has been challenged in recent years, it has usually meant "male authors." Admitting some women into this canon or even permitting them to participate in the canonization process reproduces a linguistic class system in which an authorized elite continues to separate, in Nancy Mitford's words, the U from the non-U (see Ross).

One criterion for the lexicalization of a "new word" (legitimation through inclusion in a dictionary) is the number of times it is found in print; given current cultural practices, men's words are far more likely to appear in mainstream publications (see, for example, Barnhart). In addition, few dictionary editors have regular access to print media where women's words would predominate (such as women's periodicals) or where nonstandardized meanings would predominate (such as feminist periodicals).

Dictionary editors typically talk about "backing winners and losers" in the incorporation of new words and meanings. Israel Shenker recounts an example involving *housewife* (34–36). Editors of leading English-language dictionaries were asked in the 1970s whether they would consider revising their definitions of the word in the light of objections by feminists and housewives themselves to the notion of a housewife as "someone who does not work for a living." Feminist writing, in contrast, would more typically define the housewife as the manager of a household—thus one who works inside rather than outside the home. In general, according to Shenker, the editors defended traditional definitions. Some editors made jokes. One said he would consider substituting the notion of a married woman "not gainfully employed." Robert W. Burchfield, the editor of the *Supplement to the OED*, told Shenker that, according to a national census, housewives themselves objected to the label *housewife*. "This wouldn't affect our definition," he said. We would simply have *housewife* in its traditional definition. But we will react positively to the women's liberation movement, and if they have an alternative, we'll consider it." (The final volume of the *Supplement*, published in 1986, does list the entry *wimmin*, defining it as a semiphonetic spelling of *women*, adopted by some feminists.) Though the lack of enthusiasm for a feminist definition of *housewife* as "a winner" is of interest, I mention it here chiefly to emphasize that words and definitions are competitive and that acceptance may be a function of special-interest lobbies.

Historical reconstructions of form and meaning may also display the bias of etymologists and lexicographers. One example occurs in the positing of cognates and glosses for attested and unattested forms of many words related to women, including *woman, wife, spinster,* and *widow*. Susan J. Wolfe and Julia Penelope Stanley scrutinized accounts of the hypothesized Indo-European kinship system in this regard and concluded that most etymologies tell us more about the etymologists' world view (and woman view) than about the Indo-Europeans' languages or their cultural context. "Every word tells its story," as the philologist Max Müller wrote in 1888 (x), but the crucial point seems to be whom it tells its story to. In *Grammar and Gender* Dennis Baron examines in detail the historical accounts of many loaded sex-related words, including *marriage*, which, he notes, has called forth the passions and prejudices of both usage critics and etymologists (45–49). Baron cites Richard Grant White's 1870 rejection of any sentence asserting that women marry men; both etymologically and practically, White maintained, women cannot serve as the subject of marry as an active verb but must remain grammatically and socially passive:

> Properly speaking, a man is not married to a woman, or married with her; nor are a man and a woman married with each other. The woman is married to the man. It is her name that is lost in his, not his in hers; she becomes a member of his family, not he of hers; it is her life that is merged, or supposed to be merged, in his, not his in hers; she follows his fortunes, and takes his station, not he hers. (46)

As Wolfe and Stanley note, along with Baron, this view of man as semantic agent and woman as passive object is also reflected in contemporary linguistics. Emile Benveniste explains that there is no term for marriage in Proto-Indo-

European, because "the situation of the man and that of the woman have nothing in common." According to Benveniste, this absence indicates a patrilineal social organization whose terms reflect a basic disparity between men and women: the man "leads" home the woman whom another man has "given" him—the woman enters into "the married state," she does not accomplish an act. The woman does not "marry"—she "is married" (195). (The *New York Times* and some other newspapers maintained this usage convention until quite recently.)[2] Again, Benveniste's interpretation may derive as much from his own cultural and professional conditioning as from the "facts" of the Indo-European lexicon. Wolfe and Stanley, Baron (*Grammar and Gender*), and Carol F. Justus discuss the relation between linguistic evidence and cultural reconstructions.

Not only are etymological data constructed or interpreted to support certain views of linguistic data, but an uneasy and somewhat ad lib relation between the linguistic and the nonlinguistic is often used to justify the status quo. Thus, on the one hand, the "intolerable" homophony of the third-person male and female pronouns in Old English has been invoked to account for the development of a palatalized female form (*she*), while in recent times linguistic convention is called on to show that the pseudogeneric pronoun *he* is not intolerably ambiguous (Wolfe; Baron 15–20).

Exemplary sentences—both excerpts from published writing (chiefly by male authors, as noted above) and examples concocted by the editors—are often male-biased. H. Lee Gershuny cites "She made his life a *hell* on earth," chosen by the *Random House Dictionary* to illustrate usage of the word *hell* ("Public"). Even in stereotypically "feminine" contexts like cooking, the "she" of the sample sentences fares poorly. The entry for *overdone* provided this sentence: "She gave us *overdone* steak." Though less common today, such sexism persists in some dictionaries.

More subtly, according to Meaghan Morris, a dictionary may also disguise women's power or even their presence. She faults the 1981 Australian *Macquarie Dictionary* (ed. Delbridge) for limited definitions that obscure women's linguistic and political achievements. It defines *sexism*, for example, as "the upholding or propagation of sexist attitudes," a *sexist attitude* as one that "stereotypes a person according to gender or sexual preference, etc.," and *feminism* as an "advocacy of equal rights and opportunities for women." Morris argues that women originally used *sexism* within a broad theory of patriarchy; to say that it means espousing certain "attitudes" that stereotype a "person" is essentially to obliterate its original political meaning. Equating *feminism* with its lowest common denominator ignores both current and historical distinctions among different feminist positions. "While it is true," writes Morris, "that the usages accepted by the *Macquarie* are standard liberal currency today, the point is that the concepts developed by feminists are not even marginalized into second place, but rather omitted entirely" ("Amazing" 89). Teresa deLauretis makes the same charge about the term *family violence*; though research indicates that incest, child abuse, and spouse battering are overwhelmingly committed by male assailants against female victims, the terms suggest that these are "family problems" rather than problems related at least in part to male supremacy ("Violence").

## The Discourse Dictionaries Record

My central argument should be clear from this review. When I speak of the dictionary's authority, I do not mean simply that it selectively "authorizes" (through lexicalization, dissemination, and so on) language usage that exists in a culture. Like other scholarship, it also constructs and creates usage. Dictionary editors claim simply to report usage. But usage itself is a complex notion: not only is it a function of social, cultural, and situational variables, it occurs within an intricate network of relationships and idiosyncratic histories. Further.., usage—and this is certainly true of women's usage—is itself constrained by social rules and conventions regarding who can speak, whose words will be more heavily weighted, who will listen, who will record, and so on. Thus, in addition to the gatekeeping mechanisms in the authorization process I have detailed, there are differing probabilities about whose discourse will constitute "usage."

A dictionary, then, is not an isolated institution that functions as the cultural authority for a given society. Rather, it is constructed within a given culture, and it may variously embody that culture's values and practices. There is considerable diversity here, of course. The term *dictionary*, most readily identified with the *Oxford English Dictionary* or with the familiar American desktop dictionary, is expected to display authority, comprehensiveness, legislative value, and scientific objectivity. But the term—which in its most generic sense means simply "word book"—designates not only the *Oxford English Dictionary, Webster's New Third International, The Random House Dictionary, The American Heritage Dictionary,* and other standard contributions to lexicography but also a range of different, often eccentric projects, including Gustave Flaubert's *Dictionary of Accepted Ideas*, Ambrose Bierce's *Devil's Dictionary*, and perhaps even Raymond Williams's *Keywords*.[3] Dictionaries vary in such features as organization (*Roget's Thesaurus*, for example, follows a semantic category arrangement instead of an alphabetical format), purpose (some dictionaries are essentially glossaries or explications of "hard words" or problematic terms), accessibility (the language in which the book is published affects this), influence (again, the status of the language of publication is critical), and methodology (for example, entries may be primarily qualitative, as in most desktop dictionaries, or quantitative, as in most linguistic atlases and dialect dictionaries). Finally, dictionaries are differently institutionalized. Some are individual and quirky, often short-term products of a single person. In contrast, the *Oxford English Dictionary* involved hundreds of contributors and took 70 years to produce; though money, space, and other arrangements had to be continually and often vituperatively renegotiated, the project came increasingly to be regarded as a unique national resource. *Webster's Third* was estimated to have required 757 "editor years" and to have cost more than $3.5 million (Gove). The first volume of *The Dictionary of American Regional English*, a project conceived in 1889, was published in 1985; it covers letters A through C in 903 pages. The project's resources have, in recent years, been considerable. As the chief editor, Frederick G. Cassidy, notes in his introduction, the sine qua non for the dictionary's success was full-time editorial direction and full-scale funding; the initial volume lists more than 150 staff members and acknowledges widespread support from foundations, government agencies, corporations, and private donors.

In the United States and Great Britain, considerable authority has been vested in many dictionary projects. Despite periodic attempts in these countries to establish governmental or academic bodies as Keepers of the Code, an anti-authoritarian tradition has generally prevailed, with dictionaries—beginning with Samuel Johnson's influential *Dictionary* of 1755—fulfilling this codifying function. Dictionary makers have taken this role seriously. When the final volume of the *OED* was published in 1928 (70 years after the Philological Society [of London] had initiated the project), the Oxford University Press declared the dictionary's superiority to all other English dictionaries, in accuracy and completeness....[It] is the supreme authority, and without a rival" (K.M.E. Murray 312). Like the *OED*, other English and American dictionaries have sought to document existing language forms; a tradition of lexicographic positivism lays claim to some degree of "scientific objectivity" in this regard, and a seamless methodology often obscures the inevitable editorial bias.

There is no doubt that many dictionaries strive for authority, comprehensiveness, and so on. The quest for an illusion of authority, indeed, seems to be an occupational disease of dictionary making:

> To me, making a dictionary has seemed much like building a sizable house singlehanded; and, having built it, wiring, plumbing, painting and furnishing it. Moreover, it takes about as long. But there can be no question that there is great satisfaction in the labour. When at last you survey the bundles of manuscript ready for the press you have the pardonable but, alas, fleeting illusion that now you know everything; that at last you are in the position to justify the ways of man to God. (Cuddon 1)

Yet interestingly—and disturbingly—even when dictionaries explicitly disavow claims of authority and prescriptive definitiveness, the ultimate outcome for women is the same: dictionaries have generally excluded any sense of women as speakers, as linguistic innovators, or as definers of words. Whatever the editors' aims, dictionaries have perpetuated the stereotypes and prejudices of writers, editors, and language commentators, who are almost exclusively males. At no point do they make women's words and women's experiences central. Thus, despite the unique scholarly achievements and undeniable wit of many of these dictionaries, they have been produced within a social context that is inhospitable to women.

## A Feminist Position

*A Feminist Dictionary*, a scholarly project reflecting many contributions and perspectives, represents a different position. As the introduction states, the dictionary is a word book with several purposes:

> to document words, definitions, and conceptualizations that illustrate women's linguistic contributions and the ways in which they have sought to describe, reflect upon, and theorize about the world; to identify issues of language theory, research, usages, and policy that bear on the relationship between women and language; to demonstrate ways in which women are seizing the language; to broaden knowledge of the feminist lexicon; and to stimulate research on women and language. The dictionary is intended for feminists, scholars, feminist scholars, and the general interested reader. Like many other dictionaries, it is a compendium of words arranged in alphabetical order together with definitions, quoted citations and illustrations, and other forms of commentary. (Kramarae and Treichler 1)

Although *A Feminist Dictionary* acknowledges the situation of women's language and its own production within a system of patriarchal and hierarchical social relations, its authors make several important assertions:

1. They recognize women as linguistically creative speakers—that is, as originators of spoken or written language forms. The identification, documentation, and analysis of women's words and definitions depart from traditional lexicographic practice. Let me return to an earlier example and compare the definitions for the word *woman* in a standard dictionary—the *OED*, say—with those in *A Feminist Dictionary*. Under its first definition of *woman* as "an adult female human being," the *OED* lists 12 usages. Virtually all of them represent views of women that we would now describe as somewhat stereotypical: they depict women in relation or contrast to men, as representative of various traditional (often negative) female qualities, or as sexual; the one exception, in which woman is used to mean "one's own woman," is taken from a text in which the woman speaking is a prostitute—one's own woman in a profession dedicated to the service of men. The whole range of meanings, then, depend [sic] on men—men's beliefs, comforts, needs, and economic support. In contrast, *A Feminist Dictionary*'s definitions encompass notions of women as autonomous individuals; as distinct from their portrayal by men and male institutions; as confined and imprisoned slaves; as outside the category human; as "the first sex," now reduced from a former more radiant state; and as the embodiment of hope for the

future. These usages are more than metaphoric: they are situated in texts that represent various feminist world views and give them concrete and sometimes literal meaning.

2. The dictionary also acknowledges the sociopolitical aspects of dictionary making. Criticizing current and past practices that privilege some forms of language over others, many entries question the ways words get into print, the reasons they go out of print, and the politics of bibliography and archival storage, of silence and speech, of what can be said and who can speak. The authors acknowledge the problems inherent in their own selection process and the inevitability of its privileging mechanisms. In the back of the book, they explicitly invite criticism, commentary, and contributions, giving their address and including several blank pages for readers' notes and definitions.

3. *A Feminist Dictionary* draws heavily on excerpted material from feminist publications, many of them virtually inaccessible to the general reader. Women's words become the chief resource for the construction of definitions; acknowledging the incomplete and inevitably partial outcome of this process, the authors suggest other ways that they might have obtained information about words and their meanings. Further, they often stop short of explicit interpretation and offer no "definitions," letting verbatim usages speak for themselves. The focus on women's definitions contrasts with the practice of most other dictionaries, as I noted above in discussing the word *housewife*. Another example of the feminist approach is the way that the National Advisory Committee on Sexual Harassment on campuses constructed its working definition of *sexual harassment* for a US Department of Education report. Responding to questionnaires completed by women students who detailed what the term meant to them, the committee broadened its initial definition to take the varieties of personal experience into account.

4. In relying primarily on feminist rather than mainstream sources, *A Feminist Dictionary* does not seek to capture "an internalized norm" for a given community of speakers. Thus, entries rarely specify "part of speech" (e.g., noun or verb) or linguistic or social status (e.g., standard, obsolete, rare, neologism, or folk linguistics). Labels like *coined, nontraditional*, and *nonstandard* have meaning only in reference to a "real" body of "authorized" words, and, as I have already noted, women have reason to doubt this authorization process. The dictionary also seeks to present rather than to resolve controversy. Definitions of the word *feminist* alone, to return to one of Morris's examples, differ broadly across the women's movement, encompassing the positions of radical feminists, liberal feminists, women of color, Marxists, cultural feminists, and so on. At the same time, the dictionary draws words and definitions from such utopian and science-fiction texts as Monique Wittig and Sande Zeig's *Lesbian People: Material for*

*a Dictionary*, Marge Piercy's *Woman on the Edge of Time*, and Suzette Haden Elgin's *Native Tongue*, thereby blurring the line between words that "are" and words that "might be."

5. The dictionary represents not just feminist usages but also traditions of feminist conceptualization. This policy raises the question of the relation between a book about words and a book about the world. As I noted above, some etymologists use the word *marriage* to reinforce a prescription for women's passivity. The *OED*, however, generally defines *marriage* as a union between two persons whom it implicitly defines as equal (the condition of being a husband or wife; the relation between married persons; spousehood; wedlock). Many of the feminist dictionary definitions of marriage challenge this notion of equality: "Leave matrimony alone, Girls," advised the nineteenth-century writer Fanny Fern. "It's the hardest way on earth of getting a living." Feminist writers have consistently put forward the idea of marriage as "woman's trade"; also important is the view (going back at least to the eighteenth century) that marriage is "legalized prostitution." Though at least one *OED* definition refers to marriage between "contracting parties" and though a number of the citations involve economic aspects of marriage, the notion of marriage as women's profession is entirely absent (*marriage bawd* and *marriage broker*, two terms hinting that marriage is an economic exchange, are characterized as "opprobrious").

6. Whereas several previous feminist dictionaries criticize the negative view of women embodied in traditional dictionaries, *A Feminist Dictionary* tends to emphasize women's definitions of themselves. In the dedication to one of her novels, Fanny Fern, who disavowed membership in the established male literary fraternity, pictured her book being read in a cozy family setting around the fire. Midway through the nineteenth century, using a metaphor particularly appropriate to the concerns of this essay, she told her women readers, "Should any dictionary on legs rap inopportunely at the door for admittance, send him away to the groaning shelves of some musty library, where 'literature' lies embalmed with its stony, fleshing joints, and ossified heart, in faultless preservation" (qtd. in Baym 33). *A Feminist Dictionary*, likewise, does not use male authority as its constant reference.

A feminist dictionary can be a significant scholarly and political intervention. Kramarae and Treichler's is proving controversial, and no doubt it should be, for the authors have never claimed that their motives are pure or their methods objective. Yet my argument in this essay is not that dictionaries are constructed in selected and biased ways that may ultimately be sexist or non-sexist. Rather, it is that there are important relations between dictionary making and theoretical questions involving lexical definitions and the delineation of concepts: the construction of a "real" dictionary invokes the abstract construction of a dictionary from discourse and the ongoing interplay between discourse and dictionary as we use language in our "real lives."[4]

Taking a term like *women*—perhaps the abiding point of inquiry and renewal for a feminist dictionary—we might entertain the following questions. Where do meanings come from? What does "a meaning" formally consist of? What is its linguistic and material history? Whose text does it circumvent or undermine? Does a meaning exist if no dictionary affirms it? What is the relation between the lexical entries of an individual speaker and those of the culture as a whole? Between meanings in "the culture as a whole" and it subcultural discourses? In what form do lexical disjunctions occur? What strategies come into play when meaning and countermeanings clash? What are the function and value of semantic intervention? Who may intervene? How does the weight of prior discourse constrain the production of future meaning? Whose discourse? Whose future? How does meaning constrain usage? When we consciously or unconsciously produce meaning, where do our data come from: introspection, eternal verities, lived experience, empirical research, cultural productions, theories of how the world works, dreams, other speakers, other texts? What authorizes a given usage at a given moment? Whose interpretations are authorized? What are the consequences—economic, symbolic, legal, medical, social, professional—of given meanings? What are the consequences if meanings are not fixed, are seemingly limitlessly inchoate? Does any given meaning construct or entail the potential existence of its opposite? Can one circumvent such binary oppositions? From what position does one propose and authorize new definitions without thereby reproducing the apparatus of authority and false universality? What can be the claim of "new" meanings within a system of social arrangements and material conditions that privileges "old" meanings? On what grounds can these questions be addressed?

## Notes

1.    Dictionaries are commonly classified as etymological, historical, foreign-language, new-word, hard-word, specialized, and concise. The concise dictionary is a particularly American creation, differing in kind from its English predecessors. It is more "democratic" in being typically a single volume, modestly priced (nowadays usually available in paperback), with functional, idiomatic definitions directed toward usage. Harold Whitehall's sketch of dictionary history attributes this format to the large immigrant population in the United States, to the system of widespread popular education, and "to the vast commercial opportunities implicit in both of these" (xxxiii).

2.    In June 1986, the State Supreme Court of Maine ruled that women as well as men can commit rape and that males as well as females can be rape victims. The *New York Times* headlined this story, "Woman May Be Rapist, Maine High Court Holds."

3.　　　For at least a century in Britain, the term *dictionary* signified one thing only: Samuel Johnson's *Dictionary* of 1755. According to Whitehall, a bill was once thrown out of the British Parliament because a key term was not "in the Dictionary" (xxxii). As James Murray told the story in a 1900 lecture, however, the minister requesting a definition of an agricultural *allotment*, not then known to English law, was told to "look in the Dictionary." When his questioning persisted, he was further instructed: "Johnson's Dictionary! Johnson's Dictionary!"; amid the laughter in the House, he at last subsided into silence. Indeed, notes Murray, *allotment* in this particular sense is *not* to be found in Johnson's Dictionary. "But the replies...are typical of a large number of persons, who habitually speak of 'the Dictionary,' just as they do of 'the Bible,' or 'the Prayer-book,' or 'the Psalms'; and who, if pressed as to the authorship of these works, would certainly say that 'the Psalms' were composed by David, and 'the Dictionary' by Dr. Johnson" (5-6).

　　　　The term *dictionary* derives from the Medieval Latin word *dictionarium,* a nominalization formed on the participial stem of *dicere*, 'to say.' Dennis Baron has suggested to me that *dictionary* might literally be best interpreted to mean a "thing of saids," though others render *dictionary* as a repository or housing for sayings, speaking, and words. The broad meaning "word book" appears in the *Random House Collegiate,* the *Encyclopedia Brittanica*, and elsewhere. In his 1900 lecture, Murray noted that

> it would have been impossible to predict in the year 1538, when Sir Thomas Elyot published his "Dictionary," that this name would supplant all the others, and even take the place of the older and better-descended word *Vocabulary*; much less that *Dictionary* should become so much a name to conjure with, as to be applied to works which are not word-books at all, but reference-books on all manner of subjects.... (18)

I cannot resist adding that it would doubtless have been impossible for Murray to predict that his own dictionary, fondy termed GOD (great Oxford dictionary) by some of its readers, would be fully computerized by 1989, all 16 volumes accessible on three compact disks (Clines). The acronym for the massive multimillion-dollar task of bringing the *OED* into the computer age is OEDIPUS, the last four letters standing for integration, proofing, and updating system; and to the dictionary itself, no longer GOD, the project staff have given the name *Oedipus Lex.*

4.　　　In a useful commentary on this problem, George Lakoff and Mark Johnson claim that the following assumptions underlie most discussions of meaning by linguists and philosophers:

> Truth is a matter of fitting words to the world.

> A theory of meaning for natural language is based on a theory of truth, independent of the way people understand and use language.

Meaning is objective and disembodied, independent of human understanding.

Sentences are abstract objects with inherent structures.

The meaning of a sentence can be obtained from the meanings of its parts and the structure of the sentence.

Communication is a matter of a speaker's transmitting a message with a fixed meaning to a hearer.

How a person understands a sentence, and what it means to *him*, is a function of the objective meaning of the sentence and what the person believes about the world and about the context in which the sentence is uttered. [The emphasized male "generic" him is in the original.] (196)

Lakoff and Johnson argue against this "objectivist" position. Their alternative seeks to link the meaning of a sentence to a conceptual structure that is in turn grounded in our subjective experience of, and interaction with, the world. Yet, like the tradition they challenge, they also assume the existence of a "natural" world that structures our conceptualizations and understandings. This position seriously underestimates the degree to which language is permeated by other language as well as by experience.

## Works Cited

Barnhart, Clarence L. *Second Barnhart Dictionary of New English*. New York: Harper, 1980.

Baron, Dennis E. *Grammar and Gender*. New Haven: Yale UP, 1986.

Baym, Nina. *Woman's Fiction: A Guide to Novels by and about Women in America 1820–1870*. Ithaca: Cornell UP, 1978.

Cuddon, J. A. *A Dictionary of Literary Terms*. Garden City: Doubleday, 1977.

deLauretis, Teresa. "The Violence of Rhetoric: Considerations on Representation of Gender," *Semiotica* 54 (1985): 11–31.

Dykeman, Wilma. "Honoring a Cherokee." *New York Times* 2 Aug. 1987, sec. 10: 21+.

Gershuny, H. Lee. "Public Doublespeak: The Dictionary." *College English* 36 (1975): 938–42.

Justus, Carol F. "Indo-Europeanization of Myth and Syntax in Anatolian Hittite: Dating of Texts as an Index." *Journal of Indo-European Studies* 11 (1983): 59–103.

Kramarae, Chris, ed. *The Voices and Words of Women and Men*. Oxford: Pergamon, 1986.

——, and Paula A. Triechler, with the assistance of Ann Russ. *A Feminist Dictionary*. London: Pandora–Routledge, 1985. New York: Methuen, 1986.

Millet, Kate. *Sexual Politics*. New York: Avon, 1971.

Morris, Meaghan. "Amazing Grace: Notes on Mary Daly's Poetics." *Intervention* 16 (1982): 70–92.

Müller, Max. *Biographies of Words and the Home of the Aryas*. London, 1888.

Murray, K. M. Elisabeth. *Caught in the Web of Words: James Murray and the Oxford English Dictionary*. Oxford: Oxford UP, 1977.

Nilsen, Alleen Pace, Haig Bosmajian, H. Lee Gershuny, and Julia P. Stanley, eds. *Sexism and Language*. Urbana: NCTE, 1977.

Ross, Alan S. C. "U and Non-U." *Noblesse Oblige*. Ed. Nancy Mitford. New York: Harper, 1956. 55–89.

Shenker, Israel. *Harmless Drudges: Wizards of Language—Ancient, Medieval, and Modern*. New York: Barnhart, 1979.

Stanley, Julia Penelope (see also Penelope, Julia). "Gender-Marking in American English." Nilsen et al., 43–47.

Todasco, Ruth, ed. *The Feminist English Dictionary: An Intelligent Woman's Guide to Dirty Words*. Chicago: Loop Center YWCA, 1973.

Wolfe, Susan J., and Julia Penelope Stanley. "Linguistic Problems with Patriarchal Reconstructions of Indo-European Culture: A Little More than Kin, a Little Less than Kind." Kramarae, *Voices* 227–37.

### For discussion

1. Describe the reading abilities of the audience for which you think Treichler has written this essay.

2. Is any of the vocabulary difficult for you? Why doesn't Treichler usually define words for her audience?

3. Analyze the sentence structures in any typical paragraph of this essay. How many ideas does the average sentence contain?

4. How many sentences does the average paragraph of this essay contain?

5. How many pieces of specific development does the average paragraph contain? Is that enough development to convince you? Is it enough to satisfy you? Is it enough to stretch you?

6. Find the paragraphs in Webber's essay that discuss the same ideas Treichler discusses, and contrast the amount or depth of discussion.

7. Treichler develops ideas that Webber doesn't even suggest. Are those ideas and their development appropriate for the audience for which Treichler writes?

# Making Changes: Can We Decontaminate Sexist Language?

## Deborah Cameron

IN THE LAST CHAPTER I LOOKED AT THE SEXISM which is expressed in linguists' analyses of language, arguing that although its effects are not insignificant, this sexism lies essentially in the metasystem used by linguists rather than in the language itself. This chapter, however, concerns the sexism that feminists have found more of an everyday problem, since it is, so to speak, in the language itself. Most of all, this chapter concerns the theory and the practice of feminist linguistic reform.

The sexism of languages (as usual I shall be dealing primarily with English, but languages vary in the type and degree of sexism they display) is a subject invented and researched by feminists. The ideological framework they have used is simple and explicit: briefly, they start with the hypothesis that the lexicon, grammatical structure, etc. of a given language will contain features that exclude, insult or trivialise women, and they set out to identify the features in question. Some researchers posit underlying mechanisms of language change to account for asymmetries; others concentrate, as I did in the previous chapter, on prescriptive processes; some are interested in language as a sociological research tool, relating the changing definitions and uses of words to the differing forms of women's subordination; while others see it as their task to suggest changes that will eliminate or modify offensive forms.

Nor has this kind of 'verbal hygiene' been ignored. Many people who would never have thought about the matter just a few years ago believe now in the existence of 'sexist' and 'non-sexist' language, and expressions designated 'non-sexist' are turning up more and more in the usage of the media (an informal look at one day's newspapers, for instance, yielded an item on whether to replace generic *he* with *he or she* or *they*, a reference to *angry young men and women* and the word *spokeswoman* in a news report). Such awareness and willingness to change could not have come about without pressure from the women's movement.

Of course, many institutions and individuals—perhaps most—continue to use sexist language, and to defend its use. Their argument in doing so, however, has had to change. Instead of denying that a male bias exists, they pretend to object to change on the grounds that one should not tamper with grammar, that non-sexist forms are aesthetically inferior or even, as a last resort, that any willed change in language automatically ushers in 1984: 'The feminist attack on social crimes may be as legitimate as it was inevitable. But the attack on words is only another social crime—one against the means and the hope of communication.'[1] Once again, we have this notion of 'the language' as a hallowed institution whose traditions may not be queried. 'Words' may be attacked independently of their users, and this will be disastrous because it will render communication impossible. This picture of language as something external, independent and disinterested stops us asking whose language it is, whose traditions will be under attack if the conventions are changed. In this chapter, questions like these must be asked. It is not good enough to shrug our shoulders and say that male bias in usage is purely grammatical, and that therefore it does not matter.

Obviously, it does matter to feminists. Most of us are now thoroughly aware of the ways in which English insults, excludes and trivialises us (universal male pronouns, misogynist insult words, patriarchal personal names, trivialising suffixes for women in professions (*authoress*), *girl* used in contexts where *boy* would be unacceptable, words like *blonde* standing for the whole woman; etc., etc. and there is no need to rehearse them all over again....

What does need to be discussed, though, is precisely *why* all this is so offensive. Is it just an unpleasant reminder that men see us either as scapegoats or as non-entities? Or is it positively harmful? Can we eliminate it through linguistic reform, and if so, should we?

Questions like these are especially interesting because feminists themselves do not agree on the answers. Although there may seem to be a consensus, the united front soon turns out to be an illusion: most feminists believe that sexist language is a bad thing, but they believe it for different reasons. A particularly important difference is between those who consider language 'symptomatic' and those who consider it 'causal.'

The 'symptomatic' camp believes that sexist language is a symptom, a piece of rudeness which may well be quite unintentional. To the extent that it is the product of carelessness, ignorance and laziness, it can be cured by the linguistic reformer. The reformer works by (*a*) drawing the speaker's attention to the offending form, and to the underlying prejudice of which it is a symptom, and (*b*) suggesting a non-sexist alternative which the speaker, now made aware, can substitute for it.

Casey Miller and Kate Swift, authors of a comprehensive guide to non-sexist English, represent admirably the attitudes of the 'symptomatic' tendency.[2] For them, sexist language is an outdated excrescence which everyone but a few reactionaries would dearly love to be rid of; mere force of habit is the only thing that props it up. Since Miller and Swift subtitled their earlier book (*Words and Women*)[3] *New Language in New Times,* it seems they take the optimistic view that we are now living in a post-feminist world, and that their job is to help language catch up with society. Miller and Swift are strong on common sense and the 'facts':

> The public counts on those who disseminate factual information...to be as certain that what they tell us is as accurate as research and the conscientious use of language can make it. Only recently have we become aware that conventional English usage...obscures the actions, the contributions and sometimes even the very presence of women. Turning our backs on that insight is an option, of course, but it is an option like teaching children the world is flat.[4]

In other words, sexist language is to be condemned because it distorts the truth: once aware of this startling fact, right-thinking people will immediately proceed to self-criticism and reform. Purged of its prejudices, our language can indeed in the mouth of a 'conscientious' user, disseminate 'accurate' information.

I have no wish to belittle the important work of Miller and Swift, especially the detail in which they have worked out non-sexist alternative usages so that the most unimaginative writer, if well-meaning, can eliminate gross bias without gross inelegance. However, the stance of those who advocate non-sexist writing for the reasons Miller and Swift do is a theoretical reformism which leaves an enormous amount to be desired. One of the aims of this chapter is to produce a critique of theoretical reformism and of the assumptions about language that lie behind it.

Recently, the reformism of the 'symptomatic' camp has been explicitly criticized by other feminists. Dale Spender, for example, is a well-known supporter of the idea that language *causes* women's oppression rather than being a symptom of it. It is through a language that trivialises, excludes and insults us that we come to know our subordinate place in the world.

The 'causal' tendency has also extended the boundaries of what counts as sexism in language. Miller and Swift have a well-defined set of targets for reform: generic masculine pronouns, sex-differentiated job descriptions, *girl* used of adult women and so on. Dale Spender would insist that all words are sexist, since their meanings are fixed by men and embody male misogyny.

The question of whether linguistic sexism is a cause or an effect of women's oppression, and the problem of defining its boundaries, ultimately links up with the debate on language and reality, who controls language and who is alienated from it. I shall be examining that debate in detail in the next two chapters. In this chapter, however, I shall confine myself to the sorts of linguistic phenomena that worry both reformists and radicals: usages that are always and obviously sexist, and which might conceivably be the targets of organized reform campaigns. I particularly want to look at the ways in which feminists are hitting back at sexism informally, through private 'reclamation' and the coining of new terms, and institutionally, through demands for reforms in lexicographical and journalistic practice, etc.

Where sexism in language is concerned, feminists tend to proceed in two ways. When a problem area is identified, they are concerned both to draw out the political and historical implications of linguistic facts, and to consider changes in their linguistic practice. These changes are often very inventive: words may be 'reclaimed' either by revaluing their connotations or reviving obsolete definitions, or they may undergo changes in spelling or morphology. Sometimes feminists wage war on a word, while at other times they introduce one. This subversive feminist metalinguistics, a product of the wish to understand and manipulate language, can be illustrated with a number of specific examples.

## Insults: Verbal Violence Against Women

Many commentators have noted that more words are available to insult women than men; and that generally speaking, taboo words tend to refer to women's bodies rather than men's. Thus for example *cunt* is a more strongly tabooed word than *prick*, and has more tabooed synonyms. Even words like *bugger* and *arsehole* whose reference is male are insulting because they connote homosexuality, which is not only taboo in itself but associated with femininity as well.

The asymmetry continues. There are terms for women collectively as sexual prey such as *ass, tail, crumpet, skirt* and *flash*. No such terms exist for men, nor do we have male analogues for *slag, tart, nympho* or *pricktease*.

Presumably this has something to do with the double standard and the heterosexual state of play in general. Women are thought not to have sexual desires, and if they either show that they *do* have such desires, or refuse to meet the needs of men, they will be censured. On the other hand they are vilified as prostitutes. Julia Stanley has observed that for English-speakers the prostitute is 'paradigmatic woman.' Male prostitutes have no comparable richness of terminology associated with them, for after all they are far from being paradigmatic men.

To say that the asymmetry of insult terms 'reflects reality,' however, would be banal. We need to consider whether general linguistic processes bring it about, and whether its effects on women are significant.

It has been argued by Muriel Schulz that the asymmetry we are considering comes about because of a systematic process of language change called 'semantic derogation.'[5] Terms like *tart* and *harlot* have developed from non-insulting unisex words (*tart* for instance was once an endearment like *honey* or *sweetie*). When they became associated with women rather than men, they acquired negative connotations and eventually came to mean *prostitute*.

This process of pejoration can be seen at work in a number of male/female pairs. Whereas the male terms connote power, status, freedom and independence, the female, which in many cases used to be parallel, now connotes triviality, dependence, negativity and sex.

For instance, *bachelor* (positive, independent, sexual libertine) is opposed to *spinster* (ugly, sexless and frustrated). When the positive aspects of being single came to be associated with women, the term *spinster* seemed so unsuitable that *bachelor girl* had to be coined.

Other examples of semantic non-equivalence are *governor* (powerful, ruler) and *governess* (poor woman looking after children); *master* (competent or powerful man) and *mistress* (sexual and economic dependent); *tramp* (homeless man) and *tramp* (prostitute woman).

The suggestion that politically motivated processes operate systematically in language change is an interesting one for sociolinguists, for it confirms their belief that language change is not a random but a socially significant occurrence which may be discussed in a 'scientific' way. Feminists, however, are likely to find it more interesting that we can reconstruct the history of patriarchy, at least to a small extent, through the history of words.

Yet the feminist analysis of insult terms would be missing something if it stopped there. The existence of so many insulting words for women, many of them meaning the same thing, has a significance over and above what it tells us about cultural beliefs. It is, in fact, itself a form of social control. We can make an analogy here with pornography (since the word *pornography* means 'pictures of prostitutes,' perhaps *pornoglossia* would be a good name for the language that reduces all women to men's sexual servants). Feminists have always seen pornography as a symbol of men's desire to objectify and humiliate women. It depicts the woman as an object to be abused, reduces her to body parts and dwells explicitly on rituals of punishment. But more recent analyses of pornographic images (for instance Andrea Dworkin's *Pornography: Men Possessing Women*)[6] stress that these images *are* violence against women, with effects similar to those of physical violence on women's self-image and attitude. To see degrading images and know men seek them out for pleasure, teaches us that we are despicable, expendable objects. It teaches us that men want to hurt us, and that we had better be afraid.

The same is true of sexual insults. They are verbal violence against women, expressing both our essential qualities in patriarchy (repositories of sexuality, prostitutes) and male woman–hatred, which makes women afraid. Since *cunt* and *slag* are bandied about even more often than the cock and the fist, this violence is no trivial matter, but a source of male power and a means whereby women are daily humiliated.

In several conferences and sessions on language, feminists have discussed this problem and asked how to cope with verbal violence. One solution which has been canvassed for some words is 'reclaiming'—that is, reinvesting a word with a more positive meaning. The word *dyke*, for instance, a disparaging term for Lesbian women, has been rehabilitated to some extent, and there have been suggestions that the same could be done for *cunt* because it denotes the most female and potent area of their bodies.

Two problems arise with the reclamation approach. First, there is a content problem, for although some words are suitable for celebration, since they refer to revalued conditions of life such as Lesbianism, female anatomy, spinsterhood and so on, many other words are not suitable. Reducing ourselves to body parts (e.g. by referring to women as *cunts*) could never be a compliment to our feminist selves. Nor should we glorify the sexual dependence of prostitution.

The second problem is one of *intent*. An important part of the meaning of an insult is the intention behind it, or more precisely, what the receiver takes the speaker's intention to have been. We all recognize that what men mean by *cunt* and *dyke* is violent and contemptuous. Just as black people may call themselves *nigger* in friendship (though many, of course, would never do so) without eliminating the racism of the word when white people use it, so we can reclaim certain words amongst ourselves without touching their status as insults in the mouths of men.

## Linguistic Herstory: Reclaiming and Rejecting

It is not only insults that feminists have subjected to close examination and found wanting. Their relationship with many words, and even spellings, demonstrates their consciousness of their meaning and history. Many feminist writers turn frequently to etymological dictionaries to find out when a word entered the language, whether it was coined or borrowed from another language, what it meant and how it has changed.

For instance, in the discussion of the word *cunt* which I mentioned above one woman said that for her, the word and its synonyms conjured up pornographic stories, and therefore she had always used *vagina*. However, she had recently discovered that *vagina* came from Latin, where it meant 'where you sheath your sword.' She found this so offensive that she had abandoned *vagina* as well. And apart from this, she felt she had learned from etymology something about the history of sexism which she did not know before.

In other cases, however, history is deliberately ignored. The word *history* is a good example: feminists often respeak/write it as *herstory*. This reflects the idea that *history* means his–story (so that *herstory* becomes the female equivalent). In fact it comes from Latin *historia* which has no connection with the

English word *his*. Similarly, *women* is often spelt by feminists *wimmin*, so that the *-men* element does not appear in it, even though this element is not actually pronounced.

Linguists find this kind of thing irritating (there is no doubt that any attempt to start a 'herstory' course at Harvard would once again cause havoc in the faculty of linguistics) because it is inconsistent—sometimes history is counted as relevant, sometimes not—and in any case they tend to dislike the un-Saussurean view that linguistic history is at all salient for speakers of current English. For feminists, however, the main consideration in using or not using forms like *herstory* ought to be political. *Herstory* is an excellent word in many contexts pointing out with wit and elegance that most history is precisely the story of men's lives; while *wimmin* might be universally applauded as a clever piece of spelling reform, had it not become associated with the unpopular 'extremism' of the women's movement.

The creative use of linguistic structure and linguistic history is a characteristic of much feminist writing. Mary Daly's classic *Gyn/Ecology* is a good example of the 'reclaim and rename' approach: as well as playing on words with great felicity, Daly tried to reclaim obsolete meanings of familiar words like *glamour*, *haggard* and *spinster*. She shows that women's power has been erased from definitions (for instance, the kind of glamour now associated with film stars is a far cry from the magical powers once denoted by the word *glamour*) and wonders why feminists cannot, by the same token, 'wrench back some wordpower' by conscious redefinition.[7] I shall consider this problem (for it is obvious to me that we cannot just redefine in the same way that those with institutional power have done) later in this chapter.

Apart from the 'content and intent' problems we have already touched on, there is a further problem with the work of Daly—many women find it elitist and unreadable. Constant wordplay and extensive terminological definition are not immediately accessible devices, and feminists need to consider very carefully to what extent they are politically productive. (Indeed, as we shall see in later chapters, this is a debate of some importance in current feminism.) Certainly they are not applicable in everyday speech, however well they work in writing.

## Gaps in Terminology: Saying is Believing

Feminists are hopeful that old words can be given new meanings. But equally, they are hopeful that we can make new words up to name the things that have so far remained unlabelled. For they remind us that if the first principle of sexist language is that female words must be negative, the second is that positive aspects of femaleness should remain unnamed.

In the introduction I referred to the idea of 'naming' to which Adrienne Rich and Dale Spender give so much emphasis. To these writers, it sometimes seems nothing exists until a specific label is hung upon it. I have already said that this strikes me as an extreme claim (and I shall be arguing later that it demonstrates a misunderstanding of the nature of language). Labels may give some sort of social validity to experiences, but the lack of labels does not render any experience ineffable. However, certain terminological lacunae are frequently discussed by feminists because they demonstrate that what naming has been done, has been done from a male viewpoint.

The paradigm example of this sort of discussion concerns terms for sex and sexuality. It is striking, for instance, that what to women is often the most satisfying part of heterosexual lovemaking is called *foreplay*. For the namer, obviously, this activity comes 'before' the real thing, i.e. penetration, and thus the namer must be a man. Indeed, the word *penetration* betrays male origins; women would have called it *enclosure*! As things stand, most words for the sexual act (itself a revealing term: since when was there only *one* sexual act?) make it into something men do to women: *fuck, poke, screw*. At school I was taught that the word *lover* was not appropriate for women, since it denoted activity, and for the passionate women in Racine's plays we were to use the term *mistress*.

The male slant in the lexicon of sex would be very difficult for anyone to deny, and feminists have made it clear that here, as in other areas, they are dissatisfied. Beyond the sociological analysis of language lies the tantalizing possibility of reform: but we must now look at a number of reasons why thoroughgoing institutional reform of the English lexicon is difficult for any progressive political movement to bring about.

## Spreading the Word: The Gatekeepers

A number of processes are common in the history of words. Words are lost: others are invented, either made from old words joined together in new ways (like *palimony* and *denationalize*), borrowed from foreign languages (like *crèche*) or created from the coiner's imagination. The meanings of words (by which I mean the senses listed in dictionaries) do not stay constant forever, but gradually change. One reason for this is that people do not learn most words from dictionaries but infer their meanings from hearing them used in particular contexts: we may all differ slightly in our beliefs about what words 'really mean.' If enough people infer from reading the word *prevaricate* that it means 'stall, play for time' (to take a recent example discussed in the newspapers), that meaning will challenge the one *prevaricate* is given in dictionaries. It will be no good telling speakers that *prevaricate* 'really means' 'lie' rather than 'stall,' because the meaning of words is ultimately a matter of the way the community uses them in talk. Unless they are compulsive users of dictionaries, this will be determined by contextual inference, and meaning will be inherently unstable.

However, it is not true that the process of semantic change operates magically, untouched by anything but the collective mind. Whether new meanings and new words catch on depends to some extent on what means exist to disseminate them. The mass media are powerful in this respect, and so is education (which is currently fighting a rearguard action against the falling together of pairs like *infer/imply* and *disinterested/uninterested*). The dictionary, too, though it cannot be an exhaustive record of what any word 'means,' has a certain role to play by legitimating some definitions over others.

The point is that conscious linguistic reform by feminists, or even 'natural' change deriving from women's changing experience and consciousness, is not simply left to take its chance with other social forces affecting language in a free-market competition for semantic supremacy. Any new terms feminists come up with, in order to be institutionalised in the official and public domains of language use, have to pass a number of 'gatekeepers'—the media, education, lexicography—who are very far from being neutral.

The media have sometimes been our allies in spreading new terms and thus new concepts—*sexism, sexual harassment, battered wives, male chauvinism*. They have shown no such enthusiasm for *unwaged, double loaded, heterosexism, male violence* or *patriarchy*, and it is significant that this second set of terms is less widely known than the first outside the women's movement. Moreover, the media have played a large part in pejorating some words that were meant to improve women's position, such as *Ms, person*, and even *feminist*.

Education is a considerable force in retarding the growth of non-sexist language. Prescriptive rules about generic *he* are enforced as 'grammatical' and many teaching materials still exemplify everything feminists would want to take issue with.

The dictionary is in many ways less influential, since for the majority of English speakers it is an irrelevance. Its sexism, however, is clear. It fails to invest feminist words and definitions with permanence, official sanction and authority, and it contains many negative and offensive definitions of females. Progressives of all stripes should be more aware than they are of the biases that affect the compiling of dictionaries.

It is frequently claimed that dictionaries, like linguistic enterprise in general, are descriptive rather than prescriptive. They merely record the way people use words, without fear or favour. This has sometimes served as an excuse for including very offensive definitions: those who protested at the inclusion of 'Jew' as a verb meaning 'cheat financially' on the grounds that such a definition promoted anti-semitism got short shrift from the disinterested lexicographers in pursuit of English usage. But how accurate is this picture of unbiased scholarship?

The most important bias of dictionaries is toward the written rather than the spoken word. Lexicographers do not begin the quest for current usage in the street or on the bus, but in libraries. Even then they begin their search with literature rather than say, comic books, graffiti or political pamphlets. The consequence is that the coinings of dictionaries are the coinings of those who write literature—middle-class men. The vitality of home and street vernacular is simply ignored. Common words like *skive* and *moonlight* are either absent from dictionaries, or else they are given a special marking as 'colloquial' or 'dialectal.'

The implication here is that the words of educated middle-class speakers are somehow not dialectal (though in fact, if Yorkshire miners speak 'a dialect' so do BBC newsreaders). What dictionaries assume is that while the less privileged will want (need?) to look up the words used by their betters, the reverse is unlikely to be true. No one needs to look up a word it would be beneath her dignity to use. Clearly, then, dictionaries reflect the prejudices of the ruling class.

This is also shown by the definitions they include (and those they do not). Dictionaries in any case foster the illusion that words have a limited number of meanings which can be listed out of context; but worse still, the ones they list tend to be ideologically loaded though they masquerade as objective. For whom, for example, does the word *woman* mean 'weak and lacking in vigour'? Which groups in society concur with the definition of *unfeminine* (as in 'unfeminine hair') as 'not characteristic of women'? What woman considers her clitoris as 'a rudimentary sexual organ in females, analogous to the penis'? (All these definitions came from ordinary dictionaries that are currently on sale, and so probably in current use by school children, scrabble players, etc.)

Dictionaries speak only for some people, and their authority is political, not grammatical. This does not mean they are valueless, of course, for arguably those who aspire to educated middle-class usage require a reference book. But they are not the objective and exhaustive record they claim to be. Until we have more control over metalinguistic processes and practices like education and lexicography, we will find it hard to disseminate innovations and changes that we think are desirable, or even see words defined in anything like the way we use them. Feminist reformers, in other words, are put at a disadvantage by the reactionary nature of prescriptive institutions.

## Gender Revisited: Making Women Visible

The best-known aspect of sexism in language is what feminist linguists call 'he/man language': the use of male pronouns as generic or unspecified terms, as in 'no one would do that if he could help it,' and the use of *man* and *mankind* to mean the whole human race. A great deal of effort has gone into making institutional changes in this area, since many feminists consider pronouns an important subliminal influence on people's perception of women as secondary or marginal.

Miller and Swift sum up what is wrong with the universal male: 'What standard English usage says about males is that they are the species. What it says about females is that they are a sub-species.'[8] Experiments in linguistics reveal that when faced with generic *man* women consciously exclude themselves from the reference. We equate *man* specifically with males. For many commentators this fact implies that language is more than just trivially offensive: it is able to persuade its speakers that women do not exist. This misleading impression is what reformists set out to correct by means of non-sexist language.

## The Myth of Non-Sexist Language

Non-sexist language is language which excludes neither women nor men. It involves recasting words and sentences so that all terminology is neutral. For instance, in a non-sexist formulation *mankind* becomes *humanity, craftsman* becomes *artisan,* spaceman becomes *astronaut, forefathers* become *ancestors* and *chairman* becomes *chairperson* or *chair. They* is employed as a singular indefinite pronoun ('no one would do that if they could help it') and generic pronouns are avoided where possible, either by recasting a sentence (e.g. 'pick up baby when he cries' could become 'always pick up a crying baby') or by pluralizing ('pick up babies when they cry').

This kind of language is less overtly offensive than the kind it replaces. Nevertheless there are plenty of reasons to suppose that it is ineffective in the sense that it does not really bring women into people's mental landscape at all. The reformists feel that words like *spaceman* have a special place in the lexicon of prejudice. Because *spaceman* incorporates the word *man*, whose meaning has narrowed (become more specialized) from meaning 'person' to meaning 'male person,' it strongly suggests a male referent. The implication of *spaceman* is that women cannot fly rockets, walk on the moon, etc. But once the linguistically marked male element *man* is removed, the argument runs, people will not think male anymore. The possibility will exist that women can fulfil the new role, non-sexistly designated *astronaut*.

But what if the word *astronaut*, despite having no overt markers of maleness, is used by most people as if it too were male-only? There is a large amount of evidence that this is in fact what happens with words that are not linguistically gender-marked. Consider, for example, the following extracts from newspapers:

> The lack of vitality is aggravated by the fact that there are so few able-bodied young adults about. They have all gone off to work or look for work, leaving behind the old, the disabled, the women and the children.
>
> *The Sunday Times*

> A coloured South African who was subjected to racial abuse by his neighbours went berserk with a machete and killed his next-door neighbour's wife, Birmingham Crown Court heard yesterday.
>
> *Guardian*

In these examples, two phrases without overt linguistic marking of gender are used as if they could only be applied to men: *able bodied young adult* and *next-door neighbour*. In the first case, the disabled, the old and the non-adult are clearly excluded by the meaning of the words which make up the phrase. But how are women excluded? In the second case, since apparently the murdered woman lived next door to the attacker, why was she not 'the next door neighbour' but just the 'next door neighbour's wife'?

Evidently many language-users, when saying or writing common terms that might in principle refer to either sex, simply do not think of them as referring to women. The words are neutral on the surface, but masculine underneath. Non-sexist language guidelines are a verbal Sex Discrimination Act, in that they legislate on the form of words without being able to alter the meaning. They're a purely cosmetic measure which enables us to see justice being done without really doing us justice.

From where the reformists stand, this must seem very odd. For as we have seen, Miller and Swift *et al.* regard non-sexist language as a necessary and long overdue corrective which will make our speech and writing more accurate: 'The point is not that we SHOULD recognize semantic change, but that in order to be precise, in order to be understood, we must.'[9] Why then should anyone be perverse enough to use words which are not inherently misleading, such as *neighbour* and *adult*, to falsify reality?

Sociologists of literature have pointed out that exactly this question can be asked about popular fiction, for instance the romantic novels bought by large numbers of women.[10] Although most readers would declare these novels realistic in mode, the heroines in fact have attributes not granted to their real-life counterparts. The nurse or secretary in a novel can always maintain a lifestyle superior to anything her real-life salary would allow: she also marries a higher-class, higher-income, more educated man at the end of the book. Is this a deliberate distortion? Is it a sinister plot to misrepresent the world and sustain female false-consciousness?

Feminist discussion on this point stresses the propaganda function of romantic novels, the part they are meant to play in sustaining sexist ideology and their real power to mislead. Hall, however, considers this view naive, simplistic and politically unsophisticated. Hall suggests that literature is not really about faithfully depicting actual states of affairs. Its referent is not the real world so much as the belief-system prevalent in particular parts of it. Far from misrepresenting the world, then, popular literature mirrors the ideological universe of its readers. If this is true of symbolic and representational media generally, it would be entirely beside the point to criticize language for being 'misleading' as to the state of affairs which obtains in the world. Language is not a limpid pool through which the truth may be glimpsed, but a way of representing, a vehicle for 'discourses' and 'ideology.'

Cultures not only tolerate but in many cases seem to demand a contradiction between what people can see for themselves and what they believe to be true, or right. For instance, the notion that women cannot do heavy work (which carries high rates of pay) ought not to cut any ice with women who regularly lift heavy children and stones of shopping, but it does. Women who clean up after incontinent elderly relations ought not to entertain the oft-repeated observation that some jobs are too unpleasant and dirty for women to do, but apparently they accept it. Everyone knows that many women nowadays either choose or are forced to support children on their own: yet women will still say they do not believe in equal pay, because men have families to support. It is not convincing to claim that because women believe incorrect and sexist propositions, they must have been misled about the facts.

Miller and Swift believe that language change is threatening because it 'signals widespread changes in social mores.'[11] In fact, few people notice language change, but reform, deliberate intervention for some stated purpose, brings out the colonel Blimp in many people. This is not necessarily because it 'signals widespread changes in social mores.' Observers in developing cultures report that language lags behind social change, often to the extent that expert 'language planners' are employed.[12] What institutional language reform really signals is an agreement on the part of those who have power to recognize a new 'discourse' or way of understanding things, which challenges the appearance of immutable truth previously enjoyed by the old one.

The outcry which so often attends the demand for linguistic reform comes from those who do not want to be shaken out of the old way of looking at things. If these people are numerous and powerful, strong conservative forces come into play and reform does not succeed.

The cause of such conservatism is only partly anti-feminism, fear of social and political upheaval. Resistance to language change is also related to the way in which people conceptualize language itself as a fixed point in the flux of experience, providing names (their essential correctness guaranteed by history) for phenomena that would otherwise elude our collective grasp. Thus the anthropological linguist Sapir could speak of 'that virtual identity...of word and thing which leads to the magic of spells.'[13] And the conservative philosopher Roger Scruton, talking about feminist proposals to reform language, insists, 'Each of us inherits in language the wisdom of many generations. To mutilate this repository of human experience is to mutilate our most fundamental perceptions.'[14]

## Positive Language

It should be clear by now that while I feel as excluded as any other woman by 'he/man' language, I cannot put my faith in the non-sexist alternatives which pay only lip-service (literally) to my presence in the world. What sort of changes would I like to make?

The strategy I believe is helpful is the one used in this book—every indefinite or generic referent is feminine. I and several other linguists use this practice all the time. When questioned by people who find it odd, we reply that we are practicing positive discrimination through positive language. If it comes naturally to men to say/write *he*, obviously it comes naturally to me to use *she*. In a non-patriarchal world, would we not tend to visualize someone rather like ourselves?

I have no illusions that positive language will change the world. More women will not take up science just because scientists are referred to as *she*. But what might be achieved is a raising of people's consciousness when they are confronted with their own and others' prejudices against saying *she*.

It is still true that women have difficulty in using positive language. (One woman said she could not use it in essays because her subject was theology: on being asked by another woman in the group whether she saw God as male or female, she replied, 'Neither: I see him as an absolute supreme Being!') It seems particularly odd to refer to engineers and astronauts as *she* when everyone knows that the vast majority of them are men; yet when similar untruths are perpetrated by *he* (for instance, when it is used to refer to teachers or hospital patients, most of whom are women) we do not notice.

From time to time, the possibility is mooted of inventing new, sex-indefinite pronouns for the English language (*E, tey* and *per* have all been suggested). It is interesting to consider what might happen to such a pronoun in common usage (if indeed it ever caught on).

As we have seen, 'neutral' words tend to make people assume a male referent. So perhaps the new pronoun would be masculinized, and a feminine variant coined. More likely, however, the new pronoun would go the way of the suffix—*person*, whose short history is an object lesson to all reformers. Words like *chairperson* and *sportsperson* were supposed to be sex-neutral replacements for *chairman* and *sportsman*, but in fact they are only ever used for women: Cecil Parkinson is Chairman of the Tory Party, but Joan Ruddock is Chairperson of CND.

It seems that a peculiar odour attaches to the suffix *-woman* even in the humblest of contexts, and *-person* is being used as a sort of euphemism: 'Of course full justice to a steamed pudding can only be done by a true trencherman. The term is used advisedly, for I have never encountered a feminine trencherperson whose curves could easily expand to accommodate a second helping' (*Sunday Times*). In this case, speakers have refused to accept a feminist reform, and indeed have used the letter against the spirit. We are left with a net loss, for if men are spokes*men* while we are spokes*persons*, the presence of women is not being drawn explicitly to anyone's attention. If reclaiming language works, and if it is thought desirable, the word *woman* should be at the top of the list for reclamation.

As many writers have shown, languages and their history are invaluable resources for feminists in their analysis of society. But reform on a wide scale is more problematic, and it is especially unhelpful when it proceeds from simplistic theories about the workings of language in general. As we have seen, supporters of 'non-sexist' language believe that language exists to represent reality as neutrally/objectively as possible. Therefore, in the interests of accuracy we should strive to include the female half of the human race by replacing male terms with neutral ones. But the 'reality' to which language relates is a sexist one, and in it there are no neutral terms. Words cannot be brought before some linguistic United Nations for definitive judgement; this one is sexist, that is neutral, the other is feminist. Words exist, the theories of linguists notwith-standing, only when they are used. Their meanings are created (within limits, certainly, but pretty elastic limits) by a speaker and hearer in each uniquely defined situation.

For feminists this may prove to be a bitter pill. It means that when we proclaim certain items positive, rehabilitated and so on, we can have no authority outside our own narrow circle, unless the means exist for us to influence the usage of others (and even this is only possible up to a point). In the mouths of sexists, language can always be sexist.

**Notes**

1.      Stephen Kanfer, 'Sispeak,' *Time,* 23 Oct. 1972.

2.      C. Miller and K. Swift, *The Handbook of Non-Sexist Writing* (Women's Press, 1980).

3.      C. Miller and K. Swift, *Words and Women: New Language in New Times* (Penguin, 1976).

4.      *Ibid.,* p. 8.

5.      Muriel Schulz, 'The Semantic Derogation of Women,' *Language and Sex: Difference and Dominance*, ed. B. Thorne and N. Henley (Newbury Hall, 1975).

6.      Andrea Dworkin, *Pornography: Men Possessing Women* (Women's Press, 1981).

7.      Mary Daly, *Gyn/Ecology: The Metaethics of Radical Feminism* (Women's Press, 1978).

8.      Miller and Swift, *Handbook,* p. 4.

9.      *Ibid.,* p. 8.

10.     Cf. John Hall, *The Sociology of Literature* (Longman, 1979).

11.     Miller and Swift, *Handbook,* p. 4.

12.     I am indebted to Peter Mühlhäusler for pointing this out to me.

13.     D. Mandelbaum (ed.), *Selected Writings of Edward Sapir* (University of California Press, 1949).

14.     Roger Scruton, 'How Newspeak Leaves Us Naked.' *The Times*, 2 Feb. 1983.

**For discussion**

1. Describe the reading abilities of the audience for which you think Cameron writes this essay.

2. Cameron chooses words for their connotations as well as for their denotations. What does she suggest with the connotations of "decontaminate" (title) and "pretend" (paragraph four), for example? What other words do you think are particularly strong in their connotations?

3. Is Cameron's introductory paragraph suitable for her audience? Why or why not?

4. Read the last sentence in paragraph two. What structure is that sentence? If you think it is an appropriate structure for Cameron's audience, explain why you think it is.

5. Examine and describe the organization of any specific section of the essay. What transitions does Cameron provide for her audience? Are those transitions suitable for an audience of experts?

6. Examine and describe the overall organization. Is it appropriate for Cameron's audience? Why or why not?

7. In paragraph five, Cameron writes, "there is no need to rehearse" examples of words that insult, trivialize, and exclude women. Has she made an appropriate choice for developing an idea, or should she provide a number of examples, even for a knowing audience?

8. Is the amount of development in the section entitled "Insults: Verbal Violence Against Women" sufficient for an audience of experts?

## For writing

1. Choose a word that has powerful connotations (either positive or negative) for you and explain how you learned those connotations. For your paper, assume an audience that reads as well as you do.

2. Contrast definitions from *A Feminist Dictionary* to definitions from a traditional dictionary to support a thesis about the power of defining or about the ways in which definitions shape our perceptions. Use definitions of the following words as at least a starting point: *feminist, sexism, rape, work, wife, history, politics, lesbian, lady, prostitute.* Assume that your audience has a feminist consciousness. Discuss that potential audience with your instructor and your classmates to be sure that you have examined your assumptions about a feminist audience or an audience with a feminist consciousness.

3. Contrast two pieces of exposition written for two audiences markedly different in reading ability. Build your contrast on at least four of these points: diction, sentence structure and length, amount of development, organization, introductory devices (title and first paragraph). Assume that your audience reads as well as you do and is as well informed about language as you are.

4. Examine several of your textbooks to determine whether the authors have made appropriate choices for a college audience. Beyond the linguistic and rhetorical choices (organization, diction, sentence structure and length, amount and kind of development), consider whether the author has in mind an audience of women, of men, of both women and men. Have authors stereotyped women and men in your college texts, assuming, for example, that women will be the audience for office-management and nursing texts and that men will be the audience for chemistry, computer-assisted drafting, and history texts? (What audience do you think I have had in mind in *Counterbalance*?) For your paper, assume an audience of textbook authors or publishers.

5. Analyze the linguistic and rhetorical choices of any essay in Chapter Three to determine whether the essay is appropriate for a college audience. Assume that your classmates are your reading audience.

# Chapter Five:

# It's a Maze

# It's a Maze

## Introduction

ALL THAT WE HAVE SEEN IN THIS BOOK TELLS US that language is a very complicated human construct. It defines the world into which we are born, telling us what we are and what the world is. Language makes it possible for us to communicate involved ideas and simple reactions, and it allows us a variety of choices in the way we use words and in the sentences and paragraphs we construct of words. Language is profoundly involved in our thought processes. It is at once a marvelous and a dangerous human product, because it can open our minds and it can close them.

As we learn words, we learn what is in the world as our language names the world. Usually, we learn words from other people rather than by reading dictionaries. So as we learn words, we learn not only how they sound, what they stand for, and where they fit in sentences; we learn words in contexts, including the speaker's tone of voice, which can indicate acceptance or approval or disapproval of the word's referent. Even when we read words, we see them in contexts that can indicate disapproval or approval. When we learn words in these ways, we are usually learning their connotations as well as their denotations. When we learn a word, often we learn at the same time whether to approve or disapprove, to like or to dislike what the word stands for. We learn to accept someone else's evaluation or judgment of what the words stand for. This fact about language learning creates a maze: as words allow us to know about and to think about what is in our world, they open paths for us; but words can also keep us from questioning and from thinking beyond our original learning, leading us only to blocked alleys in the maze. We need words to think, but words can keep us from thinking. The only way to avoid dead ends in this endless maze is to use more words and more thought.

One subtle path in the language maze is the vocabulary we learn for work, opening our minds to some thoughts and closing them to other thoughts. Among other words and phrases, our vocabulary for work includes "actress/actor," "authoress/author," "aviatrix/aviator," "woman doctor/doctor," "executrix/executor," "woman Supreme Court Justice/Supreme Court Justice," "farm wife/ farmer," "woman professor/professor," "woman rancher/rancher," "seamstress/ tailor," "stewardess/steward," "waitress/waiter." As we learn these words, we learn that there are many kinds of work in the world. We also learn that for most work, men are the "real" workers because they get the "real" titles, the unmarked titles—farmer, doctor, professor, poet. The words tell us that although women may farm or teach or write or fly, they do it in a small, diminished way, as a kitchenette is a diminished, less-than-"real" kitchen. We also learn that in some work men are out of place; the language clearly identifies a male nurse to indicate that nursing is "women's work." But English has no titles or affixes to suggest that males are diminutive nurses or less-than-"real" elementary school teachers or secretaries or nannies.

"Poetess," "farm wife," "aviatrix", and similar words can make us think that women—and men—should do only certain kinds of work. Those words can keep us from seeing that a farm wife usually knows how to do—and often participates in—all the work of the farm. She is a farmer. The words can keep us from seeing that a "poetess" writes poems as powerful, cogent, thought-provoking, and well crafted as poems written by a man. A word can keep us from seeing that Amelia Earhart, called an "aviatrix," was steps ahead of most men fliers of her time in skill and in daring.

When we learn the "women's work/men's work" vocabulary, we learn about work as English names work. On one hand, the words let us think about work; on the other hand, they constrict our thoughts about work if we accept those words that carry someone's approval or acceptance—not necessarily our own—as naming the only or the right work for women and men to do. The words can constrict us to inadequate and outdated definitions. If we think "rancher," "author," or "secretary," and automatically imagine man for the first two and woman for the third, we have let the language abandon us in an impasse. If we think that a woman *should not* be a rancher or an attorney and that a man *should not* be a nurse or a secretary, we have let words with someone else's definitions make our judgments for us. We have let words close our minds.

Words can close our minds in more dangerous ways as well. As a child, when I learned "doctor," I learned from my parents and from my community that medical doctors are to be respected and trusted because of the work they do and because of their education. The language itself and my family and the community defined "doctor" as "good person." Did you learn the same thing? I trusted and respected my family's doctor because I knew that I was supposed to. I was predisposed to think well of him, and I interpreted what he did as the actions and words of a good person because I knew that he was a "good person." And I was lucky. He *was* a good person as far as I know. But what if, like some other doctors, he had been a child molester, a rapist? Predisposed to believe that a doctor is a good person, would I have believed my own experience if he had molested me? Would anyone else have believed me? By definition, the doctor is the respectable, trustworthy authority. By definition, as a child, particularly a female child, I would have been suspect, untrusted, unbelievable. Would the labels "doctor" and "child" have blocked our ability (the community's ability, mine, my parents') to think clearly, to examine the evidence carefully? Would the words have blinded people?

Pejorative connotations can be as powerful and as dangerous in their thought-blocking effects as honorific connotations can be. As a child, I learned from my community and from my family that being homosexual was strange and unacceptable. I learned that lesson as much from the infrequency with which people said "queer" as from the way people said it. People did not talk much about homosexuals in my hearing when I was a child. So I learned that being homosexual is not acceptable (though I wasn't sure what it meant to be homosexual), that there aren't enough homosexual people even to talk about, and that children are not to learn of homosexual people even if there are some of those people around. What if the town's very best teacher had been homosexual? Would the label have blocked that very conservative community's ability to think clearly and to examine her teaching talents? Would the word have blinded us? Would the label have ruined her career?

When we have reason to question, or when we are mature enough, knowledgeable enough, confident enough to question what language has taught us, we can challenge and rethink what we know. I know now that a doctor is a woman or a man, capable of decent or despicable behavior. Now I must see some evidence before I decide whether I think a specific doctor is a "good person." I know now that homosexual people are a significant part of human populations and that there were homosexual people in my home town when I was growing up there. I now know that homosexual people are decent human beings or not, just as are heterosexual people.

Knowing that I learned words and attitudes, judgments, and prejudices simultaneously, I know that I must re-examine much of my knowledge. Some of what I learned not only did not match my own experiences, it kept me from having some experiences that would have taught me valuable lessons, information, and ideas. Some of what I learned includes attitudes and judgments that I do not want to keep or to perpetuate for others. I do not want to have my father's negative attitudes about African-American people or my mother's negative attitude about abortion. I do not want to have my home town's condemning judgments of lesbians and gay men or of Native Americans. On the other hand, having reconsidered them, I do want to keep my parents' respect for education and honesty and my community's respect for work. The only way I can re-examine and re-think is by using words. But words got me into the maze of knowing and believing and judging in the first place.

We need words if we are going to think in any depth about ideas, issues, people, questions, events, facts. But words can keep us from thinking clearly.

If we let words produce automatic reactions in us, either positive or negative, words can block thought. Some words that most powerfully block thought are the labels or stereotype names we attach to people and ideas. Two such labels that I learned in my childhood are "doctor" and "queer." What labels did you learn that constrict your ability to think clearly about people or ideas?

List the labels you have learned that put people down. Do you notice that the pejorative labels almost always name people outside the group that makes and attaches the labels and that the honorific labels almost always name people inside the group that makes the labels? The power of defining—one's self and other people—is of incalculable importance. Being defined by someone else usually puts us at a disadvantage, sometimes a disastrously destructive disadvantage because very often, those category names or stereotype labels intend to identify the least favorable fact about a person. Powerless people or groups usually do not have the advantage of defining themselves in positive ways to the larger community. People who have taken power for themselves usually announce their power by defining other people as inferior and expendable and by defining themselves as superior, right, and good.

We learn to stereotype people according to race, sex, occupation, ethnic origin, sexual orientation, religion, education, family, ability, and social affiliations, among other ways. And we learn, as we learn the names for those categories, to trust and to like or to distrust, fear, dislike, or feel sorry for people (and ideas) on the basis of one fact about them. Category names such as "Mormon," "Girl Scout," "Latina," "teacher," "doctor," "working class," "heterosexual," "disabled," "Ph.D.," "woman," and "Jewish" identify one fact about a person. Category names such as "liberal," "pro-choice," "feminist," "patriarchal," "scientific," "nationalistic," and "democratic" identify one fact about an idea. Those names cannot tell us everything we might want or need to know about a person or an idea. But too often we decide to like or dislike, trust or distrust, speak to or avoid, consider or reject a person or an idea because of a label. If we know that a person is Mormon, for example, we can decide, going on how we have learned to think about "Mormon," whether we like the person or not—without knowing anything more about her!

I don't know much about you if all I know is that you are a first-year student, or a Canadian, or a Muslim, or a motorcycle driver. But because stereotype labels are so potent, we often think that we have all the information we need about a person if we know that she is pro-choice or agnostic or a chemistry instructor, or if he is on welfare or is a fundamentalist Christian or is a florist.

Even if we identify a person by many identifiers, many names or descriptions, those labels with the strongest connotations will probably be the ones that we focus on, and we will ignore or forget the others. If I introduce you to my friend Kate, who is a Stanford University Ph.D., a writer, an aunt, an AIDS project volunteer, a tennis player, a university professor, a lesbian, a daughter, a feminist, a sister, and a Latina, what identifier sticks in your mind? What label stands out as the one you will use to think you know something important about my friend before you take time to know her? Is it that label that most differentiates Kate from you? Is it the most negative label? Is the most positive label the one you focus on?

These questions may be more difficult than they appear. Most of us like to think that we are too humane, too broad-minded, or too well educated to let labels affect us or our judgments. To answer the questions, we have to look past our labels for ourselves and be as honest as we can be. We have to think beyond our easy responses—"Oh, I don't have any prejudices," and "I don't have any problems with people who ___," and "I was raised to treat all people equally"— to examine our reactions.

In addition to closing our minds about other people, labels can close our minds about ourselves—if we let them. Think again about labels people might attach to you. Are you a woman? Are you a man? Are you an athlete? Are you a welfare recipient? Are you blond? Are you a feminist? Are you a single parent, or a good student, or an in-law? Because we all grow up in a linguistic environment that attaches labels to us, we are all defined in some ways by other people. And we may come to believe what the labels tell us about ourselves, whether the labels are honorific or pejorative.

We saw in Chapter One, for example, that language defines women as language users in pejorative ways: women "gossip," "chatter," "hesitate," "don't have anything important to say," "don't make authoritative statements." Some women learn to believe that evaluation of themselves, and they become what the label tells them they are "supposed" to be. Those women probably also believe that other women's language is also trivial and insignificant. This book, with its many essays by women, illustrates that women use language, as men do, for significant and seriously considered discourse about important issues.

If your teachers labeled you a "good student," you may have become a good student to meet their expectations; you may also have become a good student because they expected your performance to be above average and interpreted it as above average. Studies show that students behave and perform as their teachers expect them to. Is that because students who are told they are good students try harder and think better of themselves, or is it because they "really" are good, or is it because the teachers have the power to define and to create what is "good" and what isn't? In my first teaching job, I worked with a group of students who told me they were poor students. They believed the label because teachers had attached it to them in the first grade. But their work in my classes was not poor work. Had the school system created a group of poor students simply by labeling them and by repeating the label for years? Because those students believed the label, they didn't work very hard—they knew that no matter what they did, it would be judged as poor work—until they learned that a teacher saw their performance as good work.

We perpetuate stereotypes in both written and spoken language and in both subtle and blatant ways. Consider the stereotypes of women and of lawyers in the following excerpt from a handbook for lawyers:

> Women are contrary witnesses. They hate to say yes...A woman's desire to avoid the obvious answer will lead her into your real objective—contradicting the testimony of previous prosecution witnesses. Women, like children, are prone to exaggeration; they generally have poor memories as to previous fabrications and exaggerations. They also are stubborn. You will have difficulty trying to induce them to qualify their testimony. Rather, it might be easier to induce them to exaggerate and cause their testimony to appear incredible. An intelligent woman will very often be evasive. She will avoid making a direct answer to a damaging question. Keep after her until you get a direct answer—but always be the gentleman. (Bailey and Rothblatt, 1971)

Consider the stereotypes perpetuated in mother-in-law jokes, "dumb-blond" jokes, Jewish-American "princess" jokes, "old-maid" jokes. Perhaps those jokes seem innocent. But when we consider that they invite us to laugh *at* and to degrade another person and that most of us do not like to be the object of someone else's derisive laughter, we see in those jokes the barely concealed hostility for the stereotyped group.

We learn labels—usually for people unlike ourselves—as we learn all the language we know, from other people. We learn whether to think well or ill of people and ideas at the same time that we learn words, and we learn someone else's judgments and biases. Unless we question words and meanings, and unless we recognize stereotype labels as meanings other people have attached to words, we may let those labels close our minds to important and educational experiences and to people and ideas we might learn from and enjoy.

What do you think is the most important fact about you? If you are compelled to identify yourself by one label only, which label will you choose? Is your gender the most salient fact about you? Is your occupation or your social status? Is your skin color or your marital status or your family name your most important identifying label? Do you first identify yourself by your religious affiliation, or by your geographic location, or by the kind of car you drive? Most of us, asked to identify ourselves by one label only, would say no one identifier is sufficient to tell all that there is to tell about us. Are we willing to believe that no one identifier is sufficient to tell all that there is to tell about another person?

The essays in this chapter examine some of the questions of definitions and stereotypes that we have considered. As you read these essays, think about ways you have learned to stereotype people and about ways people may stereotype you. Think about how labels may close our minds. But don't be discouraged; the next chapter discusses ways to negotiate the maze.

# Works Cited

Bailey, F. Lee and Henry B. Rothblatt. *Successful Techniques for Criminal Trials.* Rochester, N.Y.: Lawyers Co-operative Publishing Co., 1971, p. 190. Quoted in Alette Olin Hill, *Mother Tongue, Father Time.* Bloomington: Indiana University Press, 1986.

# The Language of Indian Derision

## Haig A. Bosmajian

FEW WHITE AMERICANS OF THE PAST FEW CENTURIES were as understanding as Benjamin Franklin when he said of the Indians in 1784: "Savages we call them because their manners differ from ours, which we think the perfection of civility, they think the same of theirs....Our laborious manner of life, compared with theirs, they esteem slavish and base; and the learning on which we value ourselves, they regard as frivolous and useless."[1]

Still fewer whites ever recognized what Thomas Jefferson saw in the Indians: "I am safe in affirming that the proofs of genius given by the Indians of North America place them on a level with whites in the same uncultivated state. The North of Europe furnishes subjects enough for comparison with them, and for a proof of their equality, I have seen some thousands myself, and conversed much with them, and have found in them a masculine, sound understanding...I believe the Indian to be body and mind equal to the white man."[2]

Had these images, these definitions prevailed, the oppression of Indians would have been much more difficult to justify. It was much more defensible to rob them of their lands, to deny them ordinary human rights and privileges by defining them as the Pueblo Indians were by the New Mexico Supreme Court in 1869: "They were wandering savages, given to murder, robbery, and theft, living on the game of the mountains, the forest, and the plains, unaccustomed to the cultivation of the soil, and unwilling to follow the pursuits of civilized man. Providence made this world for the use of the man who had the energy and industry to pull off his coat, and roll up his sleeves, and go to work on the land, cut down the trees, grub up the brush and briars, and stay there on it and work it for the support of himself and family, and a kind and thoughtful Providence did not charge man a single cent for the whole world made for mankind and intended for their benefit. Did the Indians ever purchase the land, or pay anyone a single cent for it? Have they any deed or patent on it, or has it been devised to them by anyone as their exclusive inheritance?

"Land was intended and designed by Providence for the use of mankind, and the game that it produced was intended for those too lazy and indolent to cultivate the soil....The idea that a handful of wild, half-naked, thieving, plundering, murdering savages should be dignified with the sovereign attributes of nations, enter into solemn treaties, and claim a country five hundred miles wide by one thousand miles long as theirs in fee simple, because they hunted buffalo and antelope over it, might do for beautiful reading in Cooper's novels or Longfellow's *Hiawatha*, but is unsuited to the intelligence and justice of this age, or the natural rights of mankind."[3]

As Peter Farb declared in the December 16, 1971 issue of *The New York Review*: "Cannibalism, torture, scalping, mutilation, adultery, incest, sodomy, rape, filth, drunkenness—such a catalogue of accusations against a people is an indication not so much of their depravity as that their land is up for grabs."[4]

The land-grabbing, the "de-civilization," the dehumanization and redefinition of the "American Indian" began with the arrival of Columbus in the New World. The various and diverse peoples of the "Americas," even though the differences between them were as great as between Italians and Irish or Finns and Portuguese, were all dubbed "Indians," and then "American Indians." Having redefined the inhabitants, the invaders then proceeded to enslave, torture, and kill them, justifying this by labeling the Indians as "savages" and "barbarians."

Plundering and killing of the Indians in the West Indies outraged the Spanish Dominican missionary, Bartolome de las Casas, who provided the following account of the conquest of the Arawaks and Caribs in his *Brief Relation of the Destruction of the Indies*: "They [the Spaniards] came with their Horsemen well armed with Sword and Launce, making most cruel havocks and slaughters.... Overrunning Cities and Villages, where they spared no sex nor age; neither would their cruelty pity Women with childe, whose bellies they would rip up, taking the Infant to hew it in pieces...The children they would take by the feet and dash their innocent heads against the rocks, and when they were fallen into the water, with a strange and cruel derision they would call to them to swim.... They erected certain Gallowses...upon every one of which they would hang thirteen persons, blasphemously affirming that they did it in honor of our Redeemer and his Apostles, and then putting fire under them, they burnt the poor wretches alive. Those whom their pity did think to spare, they would send away with their hands cut off, and so hanging by the skin."[5]

After the arrival of the Spaniards "whole Arawak villages disappeared through slavery, disease, and warfare, as well as by flight into the mountains. As a result the native population of Haiti, for example, declined from an estimated 200,000 in 1492 to a mere 29,000 only twenty-two years later."[6]

The ideas of white supremacy which the Europeans brought with them affected the redefinition of the Indians. In his book *The Indian Heritage in America*, Alvin M. Josephy, Jr. observes that "in the early years of the sixteenth century educated whites, steeped in the theological teaching of Europe, argued learnedly about whether or not Indians were humans with souls, whether they were a previously subhuman species."[7] Uncivilized and satanic as the Indians may have been, according to the European invaders, they could be saved; but if they could not be saved then they would be destroyed.

As Roy H. Pearce has pointed out, "convinced thus of his divine right to Indian lands, the Puritan discovered in the Indians...evidence of a Satanic opposition to the very principle of divinity,"[8] although, somehow, the Indian "also was a man who had to be brought to the civilized responsibilities of Christian manhood, a wild man to be improved along with wild lands, a creature who had to be made into a Puritan if he was to be saved. Save him, and you saved one of Satan's victims. Destroy him, and you destroyed one of Satan's partisans."[9] Indians who resisted Puritan intrusions of their lands were "heathens" who could be justifiably killed if they refused to give up their lands to the white invaders: "When the Pequots resisted the migration of settlers into the Connecticut Valley in 1637, a party of Puritans surrounded the Pequot village and set fire to it.... Cotton Mather was grateful to the Lord that 'on this day we have sent six hundred heathen souls to hell.'"[10]

The Europeans, having defined themselves as culturally superior to the inhabitants they found in the New World, proceeded to their "manifest destiny" through massive killing of the "savages." The "sense of superiority over the Indians which was fostered by the religious ideology they carried to the new land," L.L. Knowles and K. Prewitt tell us in *Institutional Racism in America*, "found its expression in the self-proclaimed mission to civilize and Christianize—a mission which was to find its ultimate expression in ideas of a 'manifest destiny' and a 'white man's burden'"[11] But the Christianizing and "civilizing" process did not succeed and "thus began an extended process of genocide, giving rise to such aphorisms as 'The only good Indian is a dead Indian'....Since Indians were capable of reaching only the state of 'savage,' they should not be allowed to impede the forward (westward, to be exact) progress of white civilization. The Church quickly acquiesced in this redefinition of the situation."[12]

If the Indians were not defined as outright "savages" or "barbarians," they were labeled "natives," and as Arnold Toynbee has shrewdly observed in *A Study of History*, "when we Westerners call people 'Natives' we implicitly take the cultural colour out of our perceptions of them. We see them as trees walking, or as wild animals infesting the country in which we happen to come across them. In fact, we see them as part of the local flora and fauna, and not as men of like passions with ourselves; and, seeing them thus as something infra-human, we feel entitled to treat them as though they did not possess ordinary human rights."[13] Once the Indians were labeled "natives," their domestication or extermination became, ostensibly, permissible.

At the nation's Constitutional Convention in 1787 it had to be decided which inhabitants of the total population in the newly formed United States should be counted in determining how many representatives each state would have in Congress. The decision was that "representatives and direct taxes shall be apportioned among the several states...according to their respective numbers, which shall be determined by adding to the whole number of free persons, including those bound to service for a term of ten years, and excluding Indians not taxed, three fifths of all other persons." The enslaved black came out three fifths of a person and the Indian was treated as a nonentity.

When the Indians had been defined as "savages" with no future, the final result, as Pearce states, "was an image of the Indian out of society and out of history." Once the Indians were successfully defined as governmental non-entities, no more justification was needed to drive them off their lands and to force them into migration and eventual death. During the nineteenth century, even "civilized Indians" found themselves being systematically deprived of life and property. The Five Civilized Tribes (Choctaws, Chickasaws, Creeks, Cherokees, and Seminoles) took on many of the characteristics of the whites' civilization: "Many of them raised stock, tilled large farms, built European style homes, and even owned Negro slaves like their white neighbors. They dressed like white men, learned the whites' methods, skills and art, started small industries, and became Christians."[14]

They were still Indians, however, and in the 1820's and 1830's the United States Government forced the Five Civilized Tribes from their lands and homes and sent them "to new homes west of the Mississippi River to present-day Oklahoma, which was then thought to be uninhabitable by white men. Their emigrations were cruel and bitter trials."[15] Fifteen thousand Cherokees who had become "civilized" and "Christianized" and who resisted the whites' demands that they move west were systematically decimated by the United States Army: "Squads of soldiers descended upon isolated Cherokee farms and at bayonet point marched the families off to what today would be known as concentration camps. Torn from their homes with all the dispatch and efficiency the Nazis displayed under similar circumstances, the families had no time to prepare for the arduous trip ahead of them. No way existed for the Cherokee family to sell its property and possessions and the local Whites fell upon the lands, looting, burning, and finally taking possession."[16]

In a speech he delivered in 1846 Senator Thomas Hart Benton of Missouri spoke to the United States Senate about the inferiority of the Indians and the superiority of the white race. He gave the Indians a choice: become "civilized" or face extinction. Senator Benton expressed his preference for the white "civilization" over the Indians' "savagery": "the Red race has disappeared from the Atlantic Coast: the tribes that resisted civilization, met extinction. For my part,

I cannot murmur at which seems to be the effect of divine law....Civilization, or extinction, has been the fate of all people who have found themselves in the track of the advancing Whites, and civilization, always the preference of the Whites, has been pressed as an object, while extinction has followed as a consequence of resistance. The Black and Red Races have often felt their ameliorating influence." [17]

During debate on peace with the Indians, Senator Abraham Howard declared on July 17, 1867 that the Indian could not be "civilized" or "Christianized": "The Indians are a roving race. You will find it utterly impossible by any course of education or teaching or preaching, or by whatever means you may see fit to employ, to reconcile the wild Indians such as these tribes are to the business of agriculture or to the habits of civilized life. That experiment has been going on for the last two hundred years and more. It commenced with the very discovery of this country, and good men, philanthropists, Christians, missionaries of every denomination, have had the subject very much at heart, and have expended millions of dollars from the days that Elliot first commenced the attempt in Massachusetts down to the present time; and what is the present result of all these humane and philanthropic efforts to civilize and Christianize the Indian? Sir, the net result of the whole is hardly worth speaking about. From some fatality or other, no matter what, it is perfectly apparent that the North American Indians cannot be civilized, cannot be Christianized." [18]

Senator Howard went on to turn his attention to the necessity of the Indian to "yield before the advance of the white man": "He cannot throw himself across the path of progress. It is the very nature of things that barbarism, which is but another name for feebleness and dependence, must yield before the firm tread of the white man, carrying forward, as he always will, the flag and the institutions of civilization." [19]

Senator Howard's portrayal of the Indian as a "barbarian" who could never be "civilized" was attacked by Senator Edward Morrill in the Senate debate: "Sir, there are civilized Indians in this country. Does the Senator know that? There are many civilized Indians. In spite of the merciless and faithless policy of this Government there are civilized Indians, and there are many of them, and there are enough to repel this assumption of the honorable Senator and to vindicate their race to a place in the scale of humanity, and show that they are the children of a common father; that they belong to human kind, that they are susceptible to its emotions, that they may be influenced by the considerations which influence other human beings. The history of American civilization shows no such thing as the honorable Senator supposes, and I am sorry that the utterance has come from him." [20]

Later in the debate, Senator Morrill spoke of the spirit in which Indians were absorbed into white communities: "Is the spirit of the border eminently kind to the Indian? Not a bit of it. The sentiment is, 'he is a savage; he is a barbarian; a bounty on his head; is his presence compatible with our rights?' That is the spirit of the border. Nobody will deny that. And that spirit is to absorb him! I have already said what that means; it means extinction. Absorption is the Indian's scalp for a bounty."[21]

In response to Morrill's criticisms of the whites' treatment of the Indians, Senator Howard retorted: "Sir, it is not necessary for me to vindicate the character and policy of the Government of the United States against so serious an imputation as this; and I will content myself simply saying that, according to my reading of the history of our relations with the Indians, there are very few cases in which the United States have been in the wrong."[22] Having defined the Indians as he did, Senator Howard's attempts to justify the whites' treatment of the Indians was greatly simplified.

In 1879, with the addition of the Fourteenth Amendment to the Constitution, it was decided that "all persons born or naturalized in the United States, and subject to the jurisdiction thereof, are citizens of the United States and of the State wherein they reside."

But the Fourteenth Amendment was subsequently held not to apply to the Indians. The question came to the United States Supreme Court in 1884 in *Elk v. Wilkins*,[23] a case involving an Indian who had moved off the reservation, severed tribal ties and completely surrendered himself to the jurisdiction of the United States and of his resident state, where he attempted to register to vote and was refused. The Court decided against John Elk, contending that the Fourteenth Amendment had not made him a citizen. In its decision the Court affirmed that the Fourteenth Amendment applied to the freed slaves, "but Indians not taxed are still excluded from the count, for the reason that they are not citizens. Their absolute exclusion from the basis of representation, in which all other persons are now included, is wholly inconsistent with their being considered citizens."[24] The Court placed the "privilege" of defining citizenship rights of Indians in the hands of the national government; it was the government which was to decide whether the Indians had advanced far enough in the white civilization to warrant citizenship. Even the Indians who had left their tribes to take up the ways of the whites, who left their "barbaric" state to become "civilized," could in no way be defined as citizens.

In *Elk v. Wilkins* the Court cited Judge Deady of Oregon, who stated in *United States v. Osborne* that "an Indian cannot make himself a citizen of the United States without the consent and co-operation of the government. The fact that he has abandoned his nomadic life or tribal relations, and adopted the habits and manners of civilized people, may be a good reason why he should be made a citizen of the United States, but does not of itself make him one."[25] By some strange white logic, the blacks taken from their tribal homes in Africa to be placed in slavery in the United States came to be defined as citizens of this country, while the original inhabitants, the Indians, were to remain defined as inferior and uncivilized nomads in their own land.

In an effort to "civilize" the Indians, the Government established schools for the "savages," and one aspect of the education received by the children was an attempt to teach the Indians to pay homage to their oppressor. In 1901 the United States Superintendent of Indian Schools prepared "A Course of Study for Indian Schools" which was printed by the Government Printing Office and distributed to "Agents, Superintendents, and Teachers of Schools." It was the author's hope that this course of study would lead the Indians to "better morals, a more patriotic and Christian citizenship and ability for self support."[26] While most of the publication dealt with subjects such as agriculture, baking, basketry, gardening, and harness making, a chapter was devoted to the study of history. While recognizing the need for the teacher to relate to the Indians something about their heritage, the chapter also suggested that the teacher instruct the youths in the history of the United States; the course of study recommended that the Indians should know enough about United States history "to be good, patriotic citizens:"

"They should learn a few important dates, such as that of the discovery of America, settlement of Virginia, Declaration of Independence, etc.

"Describe historical events, as the discovery of America and the landing of the Pilgrims.

"See that the event turns on the person, showing examples of patriotism, valor, self-sacrifice, heroism....

"The names of our greatest men, such as Washington, Franklin, and Lincoln, should also be learned and something about the character and work of each."[27]

The chapter suggested that the teacher also adapt "stories appropriate to Thanksgiving, Christmas, New Year's Day, Arbor Day, etc. Enlarge upon national holidays; history of our flag; patriotism; loyalty to a cause; one's institution; one's country."[28]

The teacher was told that "patriotic songs must be taught in every school, and every child should be familiar with the words as well as the music of our inspiring national songs."[29] Further, "in every school the salute to the flag must be taught and where the climate will permit, this exercise must be engaged in out of doors, by the whole school, morning and evening; and where the climate is too severe, it can be done in the classroom daily and at the evening hour."[30] This practice of demanding that the oppressed honor and pay homage to the oppressor was itself part of the dehumanizing process.

By some strange reasoning, "the important date" of the settlement of Virginia was considered something which would contribute to the "patriotism" of the Indians, although in Virginia the white invaders had referred to the Indians as "beasts," "savages," "miscreants," and "barbarians." In Virginia in 1622, after the Indians had killed approximately three hundred fifty English invaders, the English took revenge by burning the crops of the Indians, putting the torch to their homes, and driving them from their villages. In 1623 Indians who approached the Virginians with the intent to sue for peace were shot. To teach Indian youths to see the white Virginia "colonists" as examples of "patriotism, valor, self-sacrifice, and heroism," to teach these students to regard the very people who had suppressed and killed their ancestors as exemplary was a travesty of education.

The travesty and humiliation were compounded by requiring the Indian children to learn the words of "our inspiring national songs." The significance to the Indian of one of these songs has been observed by Vine Deloria, Jr., in *Custer Died for Your Sins: An Indian Manifesto:* "One day at a conference we were singing 'My Country 'Tis of Thee' and we came across the part that goes: 'Land where our father died, Land of the Pilgrims' pride....'Some of us broke out laughing when we realized that our fathers undoubtedly died trying to keep those Pilgrims from stealing our land. In fact, many of our fathers died because the Pilgrims killed them as witches. We didn't feel much kinship with those Pilgrims, regardless of who they did in."[31]

Not only were Indian youths to be taught to show delight in the discovery of America and the settlement of Virginia and to learn the words of "our inspiring national songs," they were also to be taught the salute to the flag of the United States at a time when Indian citizenship was not guaranteed, when Indian suffrage was denied in various states, when "liberty and justice for all" simply did not apply to Indians. The children were in effect forced to salute the flag under which their conquerors and oppressors had marched. One might as well have forced the blacks in this country to salute the Confederate flag or the Jews in Germany to salute the Nazi swastika flag. If an oppressed group of people can be forced, without their actively rebelling, to pledge allegiance to the flag of their masters, the humiliation and subjugation are outwardly manifested for all to see.

One of the rituals some Indians were subjected to when they sought to become citizens required they give up their "Indian names" and take on "white ones." The ritual clearly compelled the Indian to deny his or her previous identity through the renaming and redefining process. For male Indians the procedure was as follows:

"For men: (Read name)—(White name). What was your Indian name? (Gives name).—(Indian name.) I hand you a bow and an arrow. Take this bow and shoot the arrows. (He shoots.)

—(Indian name.) You have shot your last arrow. That means that you are no longer to live the life of an Indian. You are from this day forward to live the life of the white man...."[32]

The male Indian then was asked to place his hands on a plow to symbolize the choice to "live the life of the white man—and the white man lives by work." Then he was given a purse: "(White name.) I give you a purse. This purse will always say to you that the money you gain from your labor must be wisely kept." Then an American flag was placed in his hands and he was told: "This is the only flag you have ever had or ever will have...." The ritual was similar for the female Indian, except that she had placed into her hands a work bag and a purse. In taking these items she had "chosen the life of the white woman—and the white woman loves her home."[33] A ritualistic effort requiring one to deny one's identity, to give up one's control over his or herself, could hardly have been more complete.

While the state and church as institutions have defined the Indian into subjugation, there has been in operation the use of a suppressive language by society at large which has perpetuated the dehumanization of the Indian. Commonly used words and phrases relegate the Indian to an inferior, infantile status: "The only good Indian is a dead Indian"; "Give it back to the Indians"; "drunken Indians"; "dumb Indians"; "Redskins"; "Indian giver." Writings and speeches include references to the "Indian Problem" in the same manner that references have been made by whites to "the Negro problem" and by the Nazis to "the Jewish problem." There was no "Jewish problem" in Germany until the Nazis linguistically created the myth; there was no "Negro problem" until white Americans created the myth; similarly, the "Indian problem" has been created in such a way that the oppressed, not the oppressor, evolve as "the problem."

As the list of negative "racial characteristics" of the "Indian race" grew over the years, the redefinition of the individual Indian became easier and easier. He or she was trapped by the racial definitions, stereotypes, and myths. No matter how intelligent, how "civilized" the Indian became, he or she was still an Indian. Even the one who managed to become a citizen (prior to 1924) could not discard his or her "Indian-ness" sufficiently to participate fully in white society. The law's language was used to reinforce the redefinition of the oppressed into nonpersons and this language of suppression, as law, became governmentally institutionalized, and in effect legitimatized. In 1831, the United States Supreme Court defined the Indians "in a state of pupilage. Their relation to the United States resembles that of a ward to his guardian."[34]

In 1832 the Alabama Supreme Court labeled the Indians "beasts," "savages," and "wildmen," definitions which in turn were used to "prove" that the Indians were not entitled to "rank in the family of independent nations," that the Indians' lands could be appropriated by the whites since "the right of the agriculturists was paramount to that of the hunter tribes."[35]

Alabama's high court asked: "Were the natives of this vast continent, at the period of the advent of the first Europeans, in the possession and enjoyment of those attributes of sovereignty, to entitle them to rank in the family of independent governments?"[36] The court answered its question by declaring in part: "The fairest quarter of the globe is roamed over by the wildman, who has no permanent abiding place, but moves from camp to camp, as the pursuit of game may lead him. He knows not the value of any of the comforts of civilized life. As well might a treaty, on terms of equality, be attempted with the beast of the same forest that he inhabits."[37]

In 1857, at the same time he was denying human rights to the black slaves in the United States, Chief Justice Taney of the United States Supreme Court declared in his *Dred Scott* opinion: "Congress might...have authorized the naturalization of Indians, because they were aliens and foreigners. But, in their then untutored and savage state, no one would have thought of admitting them as citizens in a civilized community....No one supposed then that any Indian would ask for, or was capable of enjoying, the privileges of an American citizen, and the word white was not used with any particular reference to them."[38]

One of the most blatant examples of the use of the racial characteristic argument is evident in an 1897 Minnesota Supreme Court decision dealing with the indictment of one Edward Wise for selling intoxicating liquors to an Indian who had severed all his relations with his tribe and had through the provision of the "Land in Severalty Act" of February 8, 1887, become a citizen of the United States. Wise was indicted for violating a statute which provided that "whosoever sells...any spirituous liquors or wines to any Indian in this state shall on conviction thereof be punished...."

In finding against Wise, the Minnesota Supreme Court emphasized the weakness of the "Indian race" and the fact that as a race Indians were not as "civilized" as the whites: "...in view of the nature and manifest purpose of this statute and the well-known conditions which induce its enactment, there is no warrant for limiting it by excluding from its operation sales of intoxicating liquors to any person of Indian blood, even although he may have become a citizen of the United States, by compliance with the act of congress. The statute is a police regulation. It was enacted in view of the well-known social condition, habits, and tendencies of Indians as a race. While there are doubtless notable individual exceptions to the rule, yet it is a well-known fact that Indians as a race are not as highly civilized as the whites; that they are less subject to moral restraint, more liable to acquire an inordinate appetite for intoxicating liquors, and also more liable to be dangerous to themselves and others when intoxicated."[39]

The Minnesota statute, said the court, applied to and included "all Indians as a race, without reference to their political status....The difference in condition between Indians as a race and the white race constituted a sufficient basis of classification."[40] Under the court's reasoning, the individual Indian could not control his or her identity. Like it or not, the individual Indian was defined by the court's language, by the "well-known fact" that "Indians as a race are not as highly civilized as whites," that Indians are "less subject to moral restraint." Like it or not, the individual Indian was identified in terms of "characteristics" of the "Indians as a race," whether he or she had those characteristics or not, whether he or she was a citizen of the United States or not.

Twenty years later Minnesota denied voting rights to Indians on the basis of their not being "civilized." In *In re Liquor Election in Beltrami County*,[41] the state's Supreme Court, denying voting rights to the Minnesota Indians involved in that 1917 case, noted their "uncivilized" status. The court's language was in keeping with the spirit of the Minnesota Constitution which stipulated that every male person of the age of twenty-one years and older belonging to one of the following three classes was entitled to vote if he had resided in the state and election district the specified time: (1) citizens of the United States who have been such for a period of three months next preceding any election; (2) persons of mixed Indian blood, who have adopted customs and habits of civilization; (3) persons of Indian blood who have adopted the language, customs and habits of civilization.

The inhumanity of the racist language in *In re Liquor Election in Beltrami County* was complemented by the sexism in the decision: "It is true that a mixed-blood Indian is a citizen if his father was....And no doubt more mixed bloods spring from a white father and an Indian or mixed-blood mother than from a white mother and an Indian or mixed-blood father. But it is also probably true that very many of the mixed bloods of a white father are not the issue of lawful wedlock. An illegitimate child takes the status of the mother....It is also well known that many of the white men who assumed relations with Indian women were not citizens. The citizenship of mixed and full bloods residing upon this reservation seems to us so extremely doubtful that we think contestant made a prima facie case of noncitizenship as to all of the 68 who voted...."[42]

Minnesota's Supreme Court then turned its attention to whether the Indians in question were qualified to vote under the second provision cited above. It decided that the mixed-bloods did not fall into the second category: "It is not to be denied that these mixed-bloods have adopted the habits and customs of civilization to a certain extent. With the assistance of the federal government and the schools maintained by it these Indians have advanced considerable on the road to civilization. They, however, still cling to some of the customs and habits of their race, and are governed in their relation with each other by their peculiar tribal rules and practices."[43]

Asserting that the framers of the Constitution did not intend to grant the right of suffrage to persons who were under no obligation to obey the laws enacted as a result of such grant, the court said: "No one should participate in the making of laws which he need not obey. As truly said by contestant: 'The tribal Indian contributes nothing to the state. His property is not subject to taxation, or to the process of its courts. He bears none of the burdens of civilization and performs none of the duties of the citizens.'"[44] The court concluded by stating that the right of suffrage in Minnesota was "held out as an inducement to the Indians to sever their tribal relations and adopt in all respects the habits and customs of civilization."[45]

How was an Indian to demonstrate that he or she had taken on "the habits and customs of civilization"? How was a person of mixed-blood to demonstrate that he or she was living "a civilized life"? In a case involving the segregated schools in Sitka, Alaska, the court dealt with a statute which said in part: "That the schools specified and provided for in this act shall be devoted to the education of white children and children of mixed blood who lead a civilized life. The education of the Eskimos and Indians in the district of Alaska shall remain under the direction and control of the Secretary of the Interior...." The court explained, "a clear distinction is here made between the school for the native— i.e., the Eskimo and the Indian, whether civilized or otherwise—and the school for the white child, or the child with the white man's blood in its veins, though it be mixed with that of another race. But of the child of mixed blood there is made the further requirement, to wit, that he shall live in a civilized life."[46]

In deciding that two of the children, ages seven and eight, had been legitimately prohibited from attending the whites' school, the court pointed to the "fact" that the children came from a family which was not "civilized": "Walton [stepfather of the youths] owns a house in the native village, lying on the outskirts of the town of Sitka. The children live there with their mother and stepfather. Their associates and playmates are presumably the native children who live in the Indian village. So far as these plaintiffs are concerned, there is nothing to indicate any difference between them and the other children of the Sitka native village, except the testimony of Walton and others as to Walton's business. Walton conducts a store on the edge of the town of Sitka, in which he manufacturers and sells Indian curios, and for which he pays the business license tax by the law of Alaska....He and his family have adopted the white man's style of dress. All who testified concerning Walton himself speak of him as an industrious, law-abiding, intelligent native. He seems, so far as business matters are concerned, to have endeavored to conduct his business according to civilized methods, even to the installation of an expensive cash register in his store. He speaks, reads, and writes the English language."[47]

But conducting business, manufacturing curios, paying the business license tax, adopting the whites' style of dress, being industrious, law-abiding, and intelligent "native," speaking, reading and writing English—characteristics and qualities many whites themselves did not possess—were not enough to make the Walton family "civilized."

The court went on to ask: "What is the manner of their life? What are their domestic habits? Who are their associates and intimates? These matters do not appear. True, the Waltons are members of the Presbyterian Church; but many natives, for whom the claim of civilization would not be made, are members of churches of the various denominations which are striving to better the conditions of this country....The burden of establishing that the plaintiffs live the civilized life is upon them, and I fail to find in the testimony evidence of a condition that inclines me to the opinion that the...children have that requisite."[48] Having thus defined the "native" family and children the court justified the segregation of the children and ordered them out of the whites' school.

In determining the "civilized" status of another family whose child was also prohibited from attending the white school the court took into consideration the following:

"It appears that his [plaintiff's] wife is a good housekeeper, so far as their means, and station in life will allow her to be; that the pots and kettles and frying pans are not left upon the floor, after the native fashion, but are hung up, and that curtains drape the windows of their house. This indicates progress; but does it satisfy the test? It is urged that Allard and his wife have been entertained by white men of culture and refinement; but that cannot be considered as a criterion of civilization...it is an evidence of the kindliness and of the interest and effort of the hosts in behalf of a people among and for whom they have labored long and assiduously, not an evidence of the civilization of the guests....Those who from choice make their homes among an uncivilized or semi-civilized people and find there their sole social enjoyments and personal pleasures and associations cannot, in my opinion, be classed with those who live a civilized life."[49] As in the Walton case, the court found the Allard children and family "uncivilized" and denied the children access to the Sitka school established for "the education of white children and children of mixed blood who lead a civilized life."

In 1944 five states prohibited intermarriages between Indians and whites: Arizona, Nevada, North Carolina, South Carolina, and Virginia. The Supreme Court of Arizona upheld a lower court holding that the marriage between a descendant of an Indian and a member of the Caucasian race was illegal and void. Arizona's miscegenation statute read: "The marriage of persons of Caucasian blood, or their descendants, with negroes, Hindus, Mongolians, members of the Malay race, or Indians, and their descendants, shall be null and void." In describing the two persons involved in the marriage considered in *State v. Pass,* the court stated:

"The evidence is undisputed that defendant's mother was the child of an English father and Piute Indian woman and that his father was a Mexican, so he was a descendant of three races, to wit, Caucasian, Indian and Mexican.

"Ruby Contreras Pass testified that her father was a Spaniard and her mother half French and half Mexican. And to the question, 'Do you have any Indian blood in you?' she answered, 'Not that I know of.' Thus she is a descendant of two races, to wit, Spanish and French."[50]

The absurdity of Arizona's miscegenation statute was not missed by the court even though it held the statute constitutional: "It makes a marriage of a person of Caucasian blood and his descendants to one of Indian blood and his descendants null and void. Under it a descendant of mixed blood such as defendant cannot marry a Caucasian or a part Caucasian, for the reason that he is part Indian. He cannot marry an Indian or a part Indian because he is part Caucasian. For the same reason a descendant of mixed Negro and Caucasian blood may not contract marriage with a Negro or a part Negro, etc. We think the language used by the lawmakers went far beyond what was intended. In trying to prevent the white race from interbreeding with Indians, Negroes, Mongolians, etc., it has made it unlawful for a person with 99% Indian blood and 1% Caucasian blood to marry an Indian, or a person with 99% Caucasian blood and 1% Indian blood to marry a Caucasian. We mention this and the absurd situations it creates believing and hoping that the legislature will correct it by naming the percentage of Indian and other tabooed blood that will invalidate a marriage. The miscegenation statutes of the different states do fix the degree or percentage of blood in a Negro, an Indian, etc. preventing marriage alliances with Caucasians."[51]

In 1944, two years after the above Arizona Supreme Court decision, the Circuit Court of Appeals, Tenth Circuit, decided in Oklahoma that the marriage of Stella Sands, "a full-blooded Creek Indian," to William Stevens who was of African descent was a "nullity" since under Oklahoma law as "a full-blooded Creek Indian" she was classified as white, and Oklahoma law prohibited marriages between whites and persons of African descent. In deciding the marriage a "nullity," the Circuit Court cited Article XXIII, Section 11, of the Oklahoma Constitution which provided that "wherever in the constitution and laws of the state the word or words 'colored' or 'colored race,' 'negro' or 'negro race,' are used it or they shall be construed to mean and apply to all persons of African descent, and that the term 'white race' shall include all other persons."[52] The effect of the inconsistencies of white legislators and judges was that a person was defined "white" in one state and not "white" in another.

Arizona, the state with the largest Indian population, until 1948 did not allow Indians the right to vote. Article 7 of the state's Constitution concerning the qualifications of voters placed the Indians in the same category as traitors and felons, the same category as persons not of sound mind and the insane. Article 7 provided in part: "No person under guardianship, *non compos mentis* or insane shall be qualified to vote in any election or shall any person convicted of treason or felony, be qualified to vote at any election unless restored to civil rights."

In 1928 the Arizona Supreme Court decided in *Porter v. Hall*[53] that Arizona Indians did not have the right to vote since they were within the specific provisions of Article 7 denying suffrage to "persons under guardianship." The court held that "so long as the federal government insists that, notwithstanding their citizenship, their responsibility under our law differs from that of the ordinary citizen, and that they are, or may be, regulated by that government, by virtue of its guardianship, in any manner different from that which may be sued in the regulation of white citizens, they are, within the meaning of our constitutional provision, 'persons under guardianship,' and not entitled to vote."[54]

In defining the Indians of Arizona as it did in *Porter v. Hall,*, the Arizona Supreme Court denied suffrage rights to the Indians even though four years earlier, on June 2, 1924, all non-citizen Indians born within the territorial limits of the United States were declared citizens thereof by an Act of Congress. After devoting a paragraph to defining "insanity" and *"non compos mentis, "* the court followed with a definition and discussion of "persons under guardianship," the category into which the Indians were placed:

"Broadly speaking, persons under guardianship may be defined as those, who, because of some peculiarity of status, defect of age, understanding, or self-control, are considered incapable of managing their own affairs, and who therefore have some other person lawfully invested with the power and charged with the duty of taking care of their persons or managing their property, or both. It will be seen from the foregoing definitions that there is one common quality found in each: The person falling within any one of the classes is to some extent and for some reason considered by the law as incapable of managing his own affairs as a normal person, and needing some special care from the state."[55]

In 1948, however, the *Porter* decision was overruled in the case of *Harrison v. Laveen,*[56] thus allowing Indians in Arizona the right to vote. In the 1948 decision, the Supreme Court of Arizona stated that the designation of "persons under guardianship" as it appeared in Article 7 did not apply to Indians. As to the argument that the Indians generally fell into that group of people "incapable of managing their own affairs," the court said in 1948 that "to ascribe to all Indians residing on reservations the quality of being 'incapable of handling their own affairs in an ordinary manner' would be a grave injustice, for amongst them are educated persons as fully capable of handling their affairs as their white neighbors."[57]

At long last, four and a half centuries after Columbus "discovered" America, almost all the descendants of the original occupants of this land were allowed by the descendants of the invaders to participate through the vote, in affecting some control (however small) over their destiny in their own land. Almost all of the "red natives" of the land finally were recognized legally as beings as fully capable of handling their affairs as "their white neighbors." Almost all.

As late as the middle of the 1950's Indians were still battling for the right to vote. In 1956, the Utah Supreme Court, in *Allen v. Merrell,*[58] denied the vote to reservation Indians in Utah, arguing, among other things, that low literacy and lack of civic involvement and responsibilities were Indian characteristics which disqualified them from having voting rights in Utah. The Utah court listed the Indians' "deficiencies":

"It is not subject to dispute that Indians living on reservations are extremely limited in their contact with state government and its units and for this reason also, have much less interest in or concern with it than do other citizens. It is a matter of common knowledge that all except a minimal percentage of reservation Indians live, not in communities, but in individual dwellings or hogans remotely isolated from others and from contact with the outside world. Though such a state is certainly not without its favorable aspects, they have practically no access to newspapers, telephones, radio or television; a very high percentage of them are illiterate; and they do not speak English but in their dealings with others and even in their tribal courts, use only their native Indian languages."[59]

But how to reconcile the fact that Utah had no literacy requirement for voters with the argument that, since the Indians were illiterate they could not be allowed to vote? The Utah Supreme Court added the following footnote to its "observation" about the high percentage of the Indians being illiterate: "Utah has no literacy requirement. This observation relates only to their present general character of life."[60] After pointing out the Indians' lack of civic involvement, the court stated that "it is thus plain to be seen that in a county where the Indian population would amount to a substantial proportion of the citizenry, or may even outnumber the other inhabitants, allowing them to vote might place substantial control of the county government and expenditures of its funds in a group of citizens who, as a class, had extremely limited interest in its function and very little responsibility in providing the financial support thereof."[61] In effect the same legal system which made it virtually impossible for Indians to practice "civic involvement" ruled that Indians could not vote because of their lack of "civic involvement." The same system which kept the Indians isolated ruled that Indians could not vote because they lived in communities and dwellings "isolated from others and from contact with the outside world."

The definitions and stereotypes of the Indians developed over the past three centuries found their way into the history books. The linguistic dehumanization of Indians in history texts and the effects of these portrayals on Indian children have been noted by Alvin Josephy, Jr., Mary Gloyne Byler and others.

Josephy, observing that "many historians termed them [Indians] dirty, lazy, brutish, unproductive, and on the level with wild beasts,"[62] has called attention to the effects of such definitions: "There are now some 750,000 Indians and Eskimos in the United States, and many of their children are attending schools and colleges where they are subjected to the use of insulting books. Their high dropout rates, self-hatred, a suicide rate far in excess of the national average, and their lack of motivation can be traced in great part to the feelings of disgrace and humiliation they suffer from their continual confrontation with stereotype thinking about them."[63]

In her study of the image of American Indians projected by non-Indian writers, Mary Gloyne Byler observes that "it has been well established by sociologists and psychologists that the effect on children of negative stereotypes and derogatory images is to engender and perpetuate undemocratic and unhealthy attitudes that will plague our society for years to come."[64]

Once one has been categorized through the language of oppression, one loses most of the power to determine one's future and control over one's identity and destiny. As a writer observes in *Our Brother's Keeper: The Indian in White America,* "ultimately, self-realization requires the power to shape one's future, to control one's destiny, to choose from a variety of alternatives. The Indian has no such power, no control and no choice."[65] Once the Indians had been successfully defined by the Europeans and their descendants as "heathens," "beasts," "savages," "barbarians," "wildmen," "uncivilized," "in a state of pupilage," their power to define themselves and their destinies passed from their own hands to the hands of their oppressors.

## Notes

1.   Cited in Jack Forbes (ed.), *The Indian in America's Past* (Englewood Cliffs, New Jersey: Prentice-Hall, 1964), p. 19.

2.   *Ibid.*

3.   *United States v. Lucero,* 1 N.M. 422 (1869).

4.   Peter Farb, "Indian Corn," *New York Review,* 17 (December 16, 1971), p. 36.

5.   Alvin M. Josephy, Jr., *The Indian Heritage of America* (New York: Bantam Books, 1969), p. 286.

6.   Peter Farb, *Man's Rise To Civilization As Shown By the Indians of North America From Primeval Times To the Coming of the Industrial State* (New York: E.P. Dutton and Company, 1968), p. xx.

7.   Josephy, p. 4.

8.   Roy H. Pearce, *The Savages of America* (Baltimore: The Johns Hopkins Press, 1965), p. 21.

9.   *Ibid.,* pp. 21–22.

10.   Farb, *Man's Rise to Civilization,* p. 247.

11.   Louis L. Knowles and Kenneth Prewitt, (eds.), *Institutional Racism in America* (Englewood Cliffs, New Jersey: Prentice-Hall, 1969), p. 7.

12.   *Ibid.*

13.   Arnold Toynbee, *A Study of History* (London: Oxford University Press, 1935), I, p. 152. For further discussion of the connotation of "natives," see Volume II of *A Study of History,* pp. 574–580.

14.   Josephy, p. 107.

15.   *Ibid,* p. 108.

16.   Farb, *Man's Rise to Civilization,* p. 253.

17.   U.S., *Congressional Globe,* 29th Cong., 1st Sess., 1846, 15, p. 918.

18.   U.S., *Congressional Globe,* 40th Cong., 1st Sess., 1867, 38, p. 684.

19.   *Ibid.*

20.   *Ibid.,* p. 685.

21.   *Ibid.,* p. 686.

22.   *Ibid.,* p. 712.

23. *Elk v. Wilkins*, 112 U.S. 94 (1884).

24. *Ibid.,* p. 102.

25. *Ibid.,* p. 109.

26. Estelle Reel, *Course of Study for the Indian Schools* (Washington, D.C.: Government Printing Office, 1901), p. 6.

27. *Ibid.,* p. 145.

28. *Ibid.,* p. 146.

29. *Ibid.,* p. 109.

30. *Ibid.,* p. 111.

31. Vine Deloria, Jr., *Custer Died for Your Sins: An Indian Manifesto* (New York: Avon Books, 1970), p.10.

32. Vine Deloria, Jr. (ed), *Of Utmost Good Faith* (San Francisco: Straight Arrow Books, 1971), p. 93.

33. *Ibid.*

34. *The Cherokee Nation v. The State of Georgia*, 30 U.S. 1, 16 (1831).

35. *Caldwell v. State of Alabama*, 1. Stew. & Potter (Ala.) 327, 335 (1832).

36. *Ibid.,* p. 333.

37. *Ibid.,* p. 334.

38. *Dred Scott v. Sanford*, 61 U.S. 1, 23 (1857).

39. *State v. Wise,* 72 N.W. 843, 844 (1897).

40. *Ibid.,* p. 844.

41. *In re Liquor Election in Beltrami County*, 163 N.W. 988 (1917).

42. *Ibid.* p. 989.

43. *Ibid.*

44. *Ibid.*

45. *Ibid.,* p. 990.

46. *Davis v. Sitka School Board,* 3 Alaska 481, 484 (1908).

47. *Ibid.,*p. 490–491.

48. *Ibid.* p. 491.

49. *Ibid.,* p. 494.

50. *State v. Pass*, 121 P. 2d 882 (1942).

51. *Ibid.,* p. 884.

52.     *Stevens v. United States,* 146 F.2d 120, 123 (1944).

53.     *Porter v. Hall,* 271, p. 411 (1928).

54.     *Ibid.,* p. 419.

55.     *Ibid.,* p. 416.

56.     *Harrison v. Laveen,* 196 P.2d 456 (1948).

57.     *Ibid.,* p. 463.

58.     *Allen v. Merrell,* 305 P. 2d 490 (1956).

59.     *Ibid.,* p. 494.

60.     *Ibid.*

61.     *Ibid.,* p. 495.

62.     Alvin M. Josephy, Jr., "Indians in History," *Atlantic Monthly,* 225 (June 1970), p. 68.

63.     *Ibid.,* p. 71.

64.     Mary Gloyne Byler, "The Image of American Indians Projected By Non-Indian Writers," *Library Journal,* 99 (February 15, 1974), p. 549.

65.     Edgar S. Cahn (ed.), *Our Brother's Keeper: The Indian in White America* (Washington, D.C.:  New Community Press, 1969), p. 123.

## For discussion

*Content*

1.  What new information does Bosmajian give you?

2.  According to Bosmajian, what are some of the most destructive results of attaching derisive labels to people?

3.  Bosmajian provides an abundance of clearly documented specific support. Why does he use so much evidence? Is it an appropriate amount of development for an educated adult audience?

4.  If you learned "Indian" as a derisive label, or if you have learned a negative stereotype about Native Americans, does this essay help you to see some of the origins of the stereotype? Does it help you to re-examine what you know?

5. Do you imagine that caucasian people have interpreted Native American behavior according to stereotyped expectations, no matter what Native American behavior actually was? For example, is it possible that caucasians encountered "savages" only because they expected to encounter "savages"? Could the behavior of caucasians have caused Native Americans to be "savage"? If caucasians had the notion that Native American men made Native American women do all the work, is it possible that those caucasians would not have interpreted Native American men's activities as work? Is it possible that observer bias, created by stereotypes, skewed the evidence?

6. If someone defines a group as dependent and then passes laws to make that group dependent, will those people become dependent?

7. What stereotypes do you know about Native American women and men? Are the stereotypes of Native American women different from the stereotypes of Native American men?

8. When you read this essay, do you specifically imagine Native American women? In the history Bosmajian reports, do you have a clear sense of what happened to Native American women? Why or why not?

*Style*

1. Discuss the essay's overall organization. How does Bosmajian clarify that organization? Does the order effectively emphasize Bosmajian's thesis?

2. Is Bosmajian's comparing caucasian settlers in America to Nazis an effective analogy?

3. Evaluate Bosmajian's title and introductory paragraph.

4. Evaluate his conclusion.

## For writing

All writing suggestions for Chapter Five follow the discussion questions for the chapter's final essay. (See page 282.)

# Heard Any
# Good Jews Lately?

## Thomas Friedmann

THE HORRORS OF MASS MURDER can be made bearable if the intended victim is made to appear an object that deserves extermination. The Nazis understood this. Thus, while their bureaucrats searched for the means by which the wholesale destruction of Europe's Jews could be carried out, their propagandists primed the populace to accept psychologically the annihilation of those Jews. In their manipulation of language to justify the "Final Solution," the Nazis resorted to terminology that had been utilized earlier to render Jews subhuman. Martin Luther, urging the expulsion of Jews, had written about them as "a plague and pestilence." In 1895, three and a half centuries after Luther, a deputy in the German *Reichstag* made clear that Luther's characterization had not been forgotten. He described Jews as "parasites" and "cholera germs." Hitler's propagandists preserved the tradition. They continued to disseminate the notion that Jews were a lower species of life, designating them "vermin," "lice," and "bacilli."

Then, in an act that might be considered almost poetic were it not so horrifying and grotesque, the Nazi administrative apparatus captured the spirit of the metaphor its propagandists had devised. It contacted the chemical industries of the *Reich*, specifically the firms that specialized in "combating vermin." Simply, it requested that these manufacturers of insecticides produce another delousing agent, one a bit stronger than the product used for household ticks and flies, but one that would be used for essentially the same purpose. The companies complied. Thus was *Zyklon B* created. The gas, used in a milder form for occasionally fumigating the disease-ridden barracks where the victims were penned, killed millions of men, women and children. Obscenely clinging to the metaphor they had accepted, the Nazis herded their Jewish victims into gas chambers of death that were disguised as "showers" and "disinfectant centers."

What the bureaucrats accomplished, the propagandists had made psychologically possible. How could anyone object when, with the whiff of invisible gas from the crackling blue crystals of *Zyklon B*, millions of Jews were exterminated? Is not extermination the deserved fate of all vermin?

But that was Nazi Germany, people tend to say. The mass murder of so many people was an aberration, an accident of history. That artificial, created language that made it possible for participants to accept the horror of the Holocaust would not have the power again. Surely, that manufactured imagery, that inhuman metaphor, no matter how traditional, can never again conceal that these are Jews that are being threatened, not subhuman creatures. Call them by their name—Jew—and you could never forget that they are people. Certainly the name is an affirmation. *Jew*, by way of Middle English *Giv*, Old French *juiu*, Latin *Judäeus* and Hebrew *Yehudi*, derives from Judah, the foremost of the Twelve Tribes of Israel. Its name means "praised," its emblem is the lion, it has borne a line of kings. Surely the name itself can withstand the ravages of prejudice!

But the King's English has not retained the proud heritage of the name. Eric Partridge, in *A Dictionary of Slang and Unconventional English*, lists *Jew* as a verb meaning "to drive a hard bargain," or "to overreach or cheat." In addition, *Jew* as prefix yields to *Jew-down*, meaning to haggle unfairly, *Jew-bail*, meaning "worthless bail," *Jew-balance*, a name for the hammerhead shark, *Jew-food*, mockingly ham, the food forbidden to Jews, *Jew's harp*, whose French origin has nothing to do with Jews but whose sound was picked up by English dramatists to mean Jew and hence an instrument of lesser value, and finally, two astounding phrases, *worth a Jew's eye* and *a Jüdische compliment* or *a Jew's compliment*. As with the slur *sheeny*, which is probably a perversion of the flattering *shaine* (Yiddish) or *schön* (German), meaning "beautiful," both of these apparent phrases of flattery are, in fact, derogatory. To receive *a Jew's compliment* is apparently to be blessed with the misfortune of having "a large penis but little money." The great worth of *a Jew's eye* exists because that was the organ removed when a Jew failed to pay his levy or tax. Another source suggests that it was the teeth that would be threatened with removal. Because Jews invariably paid up, the expression became popular, as in, "If a Jew is willing to pay that much for his teeth, imagine the worth of a Jew's eye."

*Jew* also figures in the acronym JAP, applied to certain young women. A JAP, Jewish American Princess, is meant to describe a pampered, snobbish, money-conscious female who is princess in her parents' household. *Jew* is also a pejorative when used in *Jewess*. Why is there no *Protestantess*? Feminists find it doubly offensive, since the *-ess* generally reduces the worth of the noun, as in *poetess*. And, when accounting is dubbed *Jewish engineering*, a cash register a *Jewish piano*, and a dollar bill the *Jewish flag*, the term *Jew* is unmistakably being used as an insult. One thinks of the Greeks for whom anyone not Greek was a foreigner and hence primitive and uncivilized, a barbarian. Imagine the Jew whose very name is a negative term. Naming himself, he excludes himself from mankind.

Only the use of *Indian* comes to mind in this context. As *Jew, Indian* is often found as a damning prefix in such compounds as *Indian-cholera, Indian giver*, and *Indian tobacco*, this last the name given to a poisonous North American plant. And while the negative use of *Indian* is at least partially mitigated by neutral uses (Indian pipe, Indian bread), no balance exists for *Jew*.

Given the derision attached to *Jew* itself, one can imagine the multiplied power of the slur in the slang versions of *Jew: Jew-boy, geese, kike, mockie,* and *sheeny. Sheeny*, incidentally, is thought by some sources to have come from "shiny," a comment on the brilliantined hair of many young British Jews. The coinage of *kike*, the most familiar of these slurs, is attributed by some writers, rather gleefully perhaps and without documentation, to *Jews*. According to Ernest Von Den Haag, German Jewish immigrants, the earlier arrivals to the United States, were the ones who formulated *kike*, to identify their Eastern-European brethren, whom they considered their inferiors. The term is thought to have been derived from *-ki* or *-ky,* the final syllable of many Polish and Russian names. More plausible seems Leo Rosten's suggestion that *kike* comes from "kikel," the Yiddish word for circle. This was the mark with which Jewish immigrants would sign their names when they could not write, preferring it to the commonly used X which they thought resembled a cross. Whatever the origin of the term, there is no question that it is a pejorative. At Queen Victoria's court Prime Minister Disraeli wryly defined the name. "A kike," he said, "is a Jewish gentleman who has just left the room."

In addition to these opprobations, American English has accepted a great many Yiddish words which are used as insults. A partial list would include: *gonif* (thief), *gunsel* (catamite), *dreck* (feces, junk), *kibbitzer* (irritating bystander), and a host of *sch* words: *schnook, schmuck, schlep, schlock, schmaltzy, schlemiel, schlamazel, schwantz, schnorrer*, and possibly *shyster* (by way of *schiess*—shit). While such easy adoption of foreign words might be considered a sign of the pluralistic nature of the English language and a source of its astonishing variety, the terms cannot help but remind users of their source. Were they not, after all, insults applied by Jews to other Jews in their own tongue?

A few words, finally, about Jewish jokes or more precisely, jokes about Jews. One of the more bizarre aspects of Nazi propaganda was its utilization of toys, games, and jokes. German children played with "Jews Get Out," a board game produced by Fabricus Co., and their elders had the opportunity to laugh at caricatures of Jews. A typical one shows a hooknosed Jew in the form of a snake, being crushed under the boot of a National Social German Workers' Party (Nazi) member. Other cartoons, particularly political appeals, contained messages about the acquisitive nature of Jews, and hence, their exploitation of

Germans. Below is an update indicating that jokes with a similar message have been reinvented in this country. Note that each of the jokes reproduced below is American, containing either an American locale or an American idiom. These are "Made in USA," not imported and translated.

| | |
|---|---|
| *Question*: | How was the Grand Canyon formed? |
| *Answer*: | A Jew lost a nickel in a crack. |
| *Question*: | Why do Jews have big noses? |
| *Answer*: | Air is free. |
| *Question*: | Why are few Jews in jail? |
| *Answer*: | Crime doesn't pay. |

The message in each case is clear. What is the basic nature of Jews? They are money-hungry creatures with no moral restraints who will go to great lengths for financial gain. Just jokes, right? Professor Harvey Mindess, who organized the International Conference on Humor at Antioch College, suggested that jokes are good, that laughter "lets out a little of the devil inside all of us." What about the great big devil jokes let in, allowing people to make subtle distinctions between "them" and "us," using laughter as the great divider? Jokes about Jews, about any ethnic group, communicate negative stereotypes that become just a little bit more credible with each telling.

A rather self-deprecating joke Israelis tell about themselves points out the increasingly secular nature of their country. The anecdote is about the immigrant Israeli mother who wanted her son to learn Yiddish so he would remember that he was Jewish. But the typical news commentator fails to see the distinction the joke makes. Israel is inevitably "the Jewish State," her neighbors "Arab countries." Why not "Moslem countries"? Why not the "Hebrew State"?

And it is similarly good for a laugh when the Mary Tyler Moore character in the film *Ordinary People* responds with a raised eyebrow and an unhappy face upon being informed that her son is not only seeing a psychiatrist but that this psychiatrist is named Berger. One of *those* people, of course. Even when they change their names, thanks to Archie Bunker their secret identities as Jews can be penetrated. It's all in the first name, Archie has explained. "They" may be named Smith or Jones, but one knows who they really are when their first names are Moe, and Iz, and Ben, unmistakably Jewish first names, right, Abe Lincoln? Oh yes, those Jewish lawyers, they're not always such smart Ginsbergs!

Personally, Archie, I have suffered from reverse discrimination. To this day, it is my first name that draws questions from Jew and Gentile alike. "Tom? What kind of a name is that for a Jewish boy?" And the little jokes go on with their work. Like maggots and earthworms they grind the ground in the quiet, preparing the soil for another little seed of prejudice.

**For discussion**

*Content*

1. Explain how the metaphor of Jew as parasite, in its many versions, could shape the attitudes of nearly an entire nation against Jews. If you know the stereotype for Jewish American Princess (JAP), how did you learn it and what is it? Why is that stereotype anti-Semitic? How does it separate you from Jewish women? If you are a Jewish woman, how does the stereotype separate you from other Jewish women?

2. Does Friedmann's discussion of stereotypes of Jews suggest any other racial or ethnic stereotypes? Have any other stereotypes been so destructive?

3. We may be shocked to learn that Nazi propaganda used toys and games derisive to Jews. But how many of us as children played games in which a racial or ethnic group is the victim or the enemy? In how many front yards have you seen little statues of African-American men in livery? Is there a difference between Nazi propaganda and caucasian American propaganda?

*Style*

1. What is the reference in Friedmann's title? Is it an effective title?

2. Examine Friedmann's diction choices in sentence one. Which words in that sentence are especially strong? Do they make an effective introduction?

3. What is the effect of sentence two?

4. Discuss the purpose and the effect of paragraph four.

5. Evaluate Friedmann's metaphor in the final paragraph.

# Death of Expression and the Shroud of Words

## Jim Rowe

WHO ARE YOU? WHAT, OR WHO, ARE YOU? Who are you? Have you ever looked in a mirror, any reflecting surface, and asked "who are you?" Yes. You have. I have. Without words, you've asked. You've asked "who are you?" of whatever or whomever you're looking at/into.

Think of words. Think of the words "who are you?" Think of yourself now. Are you words? Is that who you are? What you are? What are you? What is your answer? In words.

I'll tell you some things, and with the telling I'll give you some packages of words, terms, labels. I'll give you a present of words. First, though, I'll give you a question again: Who are you?

I am a gay man, young when I'm writing this in a fit of anxiety. I enact a kind of death of expression when I tell you that I am gay—because I imagine, rightly, I suspect, that I know what you think I mean, I know that which you think I mean, and I know that because, quite honestly, I grew up knowing what you meant. Death of expression because the door is shut, and I now wear the shroud of words.

You'll want the facts. Just the facts, man. The facts of my story are wound up in this critical point, though, I'll warn you: you must know primarily that silence figures into it significantly. This story starts with a telling of silence, and you will see that this is a story of many languages, and you will see that silence is a language too, and not the least of the languages represented here.

I grew up on ranches in Wyoming and Montana in my early years, and later in a small town in Wyoming. Very early, I became aware, I don't know how, of a great difference in how I felt and perceived the world and the way those around me felt and perceived the world. But what child, at age 5 or 6, has the words to describe differences of this sort and magnitude? And, even if I had the words, how could I have dared to articulate what was so forbidden that nobody even joked about it? This was my introduction to and budding awareness of the invisible language of difference—I realized a depth of emotion for men, for the ranch hands around me, that I did not see expressed anywhere, even if I felt its residue, a gentle color, in some of these men.

Children are very perceptive, often more so than their adult counterparts, because they haven't learned how to perceive "properly," or how to interpret the information they receive. Children read emotion instinctively. I felt instinctively that I was different, yet I participated in this world, never understanding this world as its native inhabitants understood it, but as one compelled to understand by necessity of survival. This invisible difference communicated itself to me, language invisible and silent, vocabulary emotive: inexpressible, as far as I knew or could know.

Now, later on, as I grew up, began school, interacted with other children and with adults, I began to learn *the* vocabulary for/of this difference from other children: words like "faggit," "queer," "homo," and "gay"—always used in emotionally pejorative contexts. The fact that nobody could explain these words, at least not these children, not at first, didn't stop anybody from using these words.

At first, I did not associate these words, or the emotions that they came cloaked in, with my invisible difference, but later in school, as body-image and bodies and sex (like "male and female") became important, the words carried more and more weight, until, finally, I understood that these words apparently described me, described the difference, and that the difference was "bad." I assumed these words, ingested them, and I grew heavy with their weight, their density. It was as though something inside of me had begun wearing leaden clothing—and this is important: because under the words, something told me that these words did not really fit, these words were not "me," these *words* were wrong, not that for which the words stood, that (thing) which the words buried.

Yet, the years embroidered meanings in heavy, lurid threads upon these words, meanings ever more complex, ever more terrible, until I cracked into pieces, and this familiar difference pulled me into the/a void by the awful weight, leaving a pretending, terrified husk. I walked in a perpetual dusk, a haze of loathing. I wore the words, and the words wore me.

Words are like clothing, in that we use them, put them on, how we accessorize them and how they make us appear. Words illustrate who we are, how we think, our class, our station—words clothe us. And sometimes we inherit words—ill-fitting hand-me-downs that we dislike, that we do not care for, but rarely do we question whether they fit in any sense/way. The vocabulary of invisibility depends on visible, imagistic speech to keep it locked away. All the words I learned, put on, wore, did, in a way and for a time, fit me. The vocabulary of invisibility became a depressing wardrobe for me—heavy, meaningful things that meant more to me because they ostensibly discussed and defined me but which meant little to the main users of the language because these words defined Them in terms of what They were not. These words described boundaries, limits or borders, past which "normal" ceased to be operative, "natural laws" that fell down or disintegrated, and people who were/could be described by these words were lawless. Not only that, but words explained things visually, or at any rate carried visual weight, conveyed some visual message. People "described" by the words would pick them up in descriptions of themselves—and the legacy would (will) continue. In fact, put the last two sentences in the present tense. Consider the points. What you get is an operational paradigm, a kinetic matrix of words and people interacting. This is the invisible language of difference, an invisible yet tangible energy, like magnetism: you cannot see it, but you clearly see its effects. You see that it has an effect.

I began to search for information about this difference, to do research into it, and what I found amazed me. I found the words "homosexual" and "homosexuality." Dictionaries used clinical, if derogatory, language about them—words like "illness," "perversion" and "abnormality" fit into definitions. I found a conflicting source: the *Life Science Books* referred to homosexuality as either a "stage" for some people or a "normal" way of life for others. But, in either case, it was "natural." In the end, I merely became more confused than ever, more self-loathing and fearful and withdrawn, though I would often refer to these sources as if I had missed something before. The majority of texts referred to homosexuality in negative and purely sexual terms, as an unnatural outgrowth in behavior of some trauma or psychological illness, as a refusal to mature to "normalcy": a perversity. Fiction seemed to ignore it entirely.

To complicate matters exceedingly, my family got deeply involved with a pentecostal christian sect when I was about 13, and we all moved to Florida. Possibly it was my own fixation on the subject, but this group seemed unusually interested in homosexuality—and either joked about it or railed against it violently. Ministry dogma on the subject was that homosexuals were diseased, void of any morals or moral fibre whatever, pedarasts, liars, and, most distressing to me, possessed by "devil spirits." This added unpleasant spiritual dimensions to an already wretched situation, and it added horror to the loathing. Homosexuals must be evil beasts indeed, I reasoned. Earlier information I had sought out on it, and that to which I had been exposed in school and so forth did not colour homosexuality with such a heavy hand. The terms, the vocabulary, expanded from the silent, invisible to-be-avoided to the luridly grotesque. Homosexuals had gone from unmentionable to despicable to evil in a few short years, and this caused such a breach in me as to leave me frantic with terror of discovery. Who was "I"? Was this "I"? Instead of answering questions, it encouraged deception, self-loathing, duplicitous behavior and a litany of lies in an otherwise honorable human being.

In somewhat calmer moments, though, I had a hard time imagining that I could be a child molester, transvestite, perverted, void of morals or principle, or be possessed by spirits of any kind. I knew, if I did not want to admit it to myself, that I regularly had crushes on guys, that I felt strangely light, giddy, foolish, and *right* in the presence of these fellows. My most perverted desire was to hold His hand, maybe kiss Him.

Then I would fall on my knees in a sweat, pray and pray that God would change me, make me normal, make me like women. Because it seemed that this all centred on the question of sex, that is, what sex one "preferred," whether one chose to have sex with a member of the same sex, what kind of sex one chose to have, and so forth, I addressed the issue from the standpoint of sex. I wanted to want sexual feelings for women, wanted to have sexual feelings for women. I tried everything from dating to prayer to pornography in an effort to change. It did nothing, and it was not for a lack of trying. And I think now that part of my problem was with the terms, the imposed vocabulary: one that I now see as unnaturally, or at least inordinately, preoccupied with sex. It literally went without saying that an emotional connection, like love or romance, between men was impossible. And, again, I had no vocabulary by which to articulate this notion, because the vocabulary provided me by the heterosexual world did not encompass any such thing, and I, as something of a product of a heterosexual world, yet not *of* the heterosexual world, had only a heterosexual, indeed, heterosexist vocabulary with which to work and express myself (and to be expressed). Intrinsically, I knew that my "sexuality" centered on the emotional rather than the sexual, but all I had was impressive images and no way to explain them to myself, let alone others.

In fact, you see, that which cracked my shell was a simple, adolescent romance. Initially, it led to guilt and wretchedness, but something also snapped back into place in me, and I began to pick at the threads of this suit of loathing. I began to reason through all of the words and images I had for/of myself, all of the things that I had ever heard, began to sift through the vocabulary and I began to hate it instead of myself. Anger drove me to question deeply what I formerly wouldn't dare to consider, and that reminds me that anger involves dignity. I may have buried that dignity with self-loathing, but it came when I needed it most, and dignity remains with me.

Questioning the "obvious" allowed me to expose the duplicity of the language, the inherent fear in the heterosexual vocabulary—the self-mistrust of the same. I began to seize my voice, even if I used it to talk only to myself. I grabbed it and refused to let go of it, refused to be intimidated into relinquishing it—and I have been trying to say this for years. Once I began questioning homosexuality, and, by extension, the foundations of heterosexual/heterosexist language, I began to take note of the millions of messages that stated and reinforced the heterosexual model, that punished any digression from this "norm." And here it is, the crux of the matter: when someone speaks for you, especially against your will, they steal not only your voice, but they steal your agency as well. When I first realized this, I came out. The process was slow and painful, but my life had been this anyway, and I thought "for gods' sake, Jim, speak up, or at least refuse to lie." That is what I did, and this began a process that I can best describe as "becoming-by-unfolding." I began to speak the invisible language of difference, learning it by unfolding in(to) it/by its unfolding in(to) me. I refused to become the sanctioned image of despised homosexuality because (A) it did nothing to describe me, and (B) to do so would only be betraying what I was/am all over again.

Let me present you with a composite picture of "the homosexual." This creature is usually a male, limp wristed, outrageous, bitchy, irritating, infantile, narcissistic, rude, mincing, "effeminate," lewd and shocking, or some creeping filth of an alcoholic, repulsive and cloaked in a dark raincoat, lurking in alleys or public toilets to prey on unwary youngsters. On the surface, the images and language (as well as the parodied actions) used to represent homosexuals add up to something diminutive and pathetic, but dig into the emotions behind them and you will find something dangerous, sinister, corruptive, corrosive and lethal. My own confusion began and ended in the juxtaposition of who I knew myself to be and the thing(s) that I did not want to become. So, by refusing to give admission or to admit to my "homosexuality," I avoided becoming a homosexual. I had no way of knowing any better. But coming out was an act of reclaiming myself, an act of discarding a useless wardrobe and mountains of baggage. I stripped and hurled myself into the abyss.

And this was (is) the Death of Expression. It begins with a question: "Who Are You?" And what you find may please or shock you—but, more important, does the language suit you? And how? How do you suit the language? How do you use the language, and how in fact, does it use you? The Death of Expression encompasses a zone, a landscape of conflicting questions (and answers), a cessation of whatever matrix you are thrall to. It is a casting off of the shroud of words. You drink of the river, and you forget for a while, and then you begin to remember, but the remembering is on your own terms, and it fits within the scope and realm of your agency.

This is a story about "who am I?" This is a story about the fear of being known, and the fear of knowing, discovery and dis-covering. This is a story about responsibility to language and to yourself, and the responsibility we all have to threaten ourselves with the Death of Expression. And, not least of all, the way that we can language ourselves back to life.

## For discussion

*Content*

1. What new information does Rowe give you about homosexuality?

2. What do you think of the fact that, even without understanding the words, people use pejorative labels such as "queer," "faggot," "homo"?

3. Define internalized oppression and internalized homophobia and discuss their effects on people. What effects did internalized homophobia have on the author?

4. Discuss the importance—to any group or individual—of self-definition.

*Style*

1. Are Rowe's opening questions an effective introduction? How or why?

2. Is Rowe's controlling metaphor, "shroud of words," new to you? Is it effective? Explain.

3. What effect does Rowe achieve by stating bluntly at the beginning of paragraph four, "I am a gay man"?

4. What effect does he achieve by putting the words "normal" and "natural" in quotation marks?

5. Rowe's final statement tells us that "we can language ourselves back to life." What do you think of his use of the word "language," a noun, as a verb? What do you think of my frequent use of the word "language" as an adjective (as in "language environment")?

# La Güera

## Cherríe Moraga

> It required something more than personal ex-
> perience to gain a philosophy or point of
> view from any specific event. It is the qual-
> ity of our response to the event and our ca-
> pacity to enter into the lives of others that
> help us to make their lives and experiences
> our own.
>
> Emma Goldman[1]

I AM THE VERY WELL-EDUCATED DAUGHTER of a woman who,
by the standards in this country, would be considered largely illiterate. My mother was born in Santa Paula, Southern California, at a time when much of the
central valley there was still farm land. Nearly thirty-five years later, in 1948,
she was the only daughter of six to marry an anglo, my father.

I remember all of my mother's stories, probably much better than she real-
izes. She is a fine storyteller, recalling every event of her life with the vividness
of the present, noting each detail right down to the cut and color of her dress.
I remember stories of her being pulled out of school at the ages of five, seven,
nine, and eleven to work in the fields, along with her brothers and sisters;
stories of her father drinking away whatever small profit she was able to make
for the family, of her going the long way home to avoid meeting him on the
street, staggering toward the same destination. I remember stories of my mother

lying about her age in order to get a job as a hat-check girl at Agua Caliente Racetrack in Tijuana. At fourteen, she was the main support of the family. I can still see her walking home alone at 3 a.m., only to turn all of her salary and tips over to her mother, who was pregnant again.

The stories continue through the war years and on: walnut-cracking factories, the Voit Rubber factory, and then the computer boom. I remember my mother doing piecework for the electronics plant in our neighborhood. In the late evening, she would sit in front of the T.V. set, wrapping copper wires into the backs of circuit boards, talking about "keeping up with the younger girls." By that time, she was already in her mid-fifties.

Meanwhile, I was college-prep in school. After classes, I would go with my mother to fill out job applications for her, or write checks for her at the supermarket. We would have the scenario all worked out ahead of time. My mother would sign the check before we'd get to the store. Then, as we'd approach the checkstand, she would say—within earshot of the cashier—"oh honey, you go 'head and make out the check," as if she couldn't be bothered with such an insignificant detail. No one asked any questions.

I was educated, and wore it with a keen sense of pride and satisfaction, my head propped up with the knowledge, from my mother, that my life would be easier than hers. I was educated; but more than this, I was "la güera": fair-skinned. Born with the features of my Chicana mother, but the skin of my Anglo father, I had it made.

No one ever quite told me this (that light was right), but I knew that being light was something valued in my family (who were all Chicano, with the exception of my father). In fact, everything about my upbringing (at least what occurred on a conscious level) attempted to bleach me of what color I did have. Although my mother was fluent in it, I was never taught much Spanish at home. I picked up what I did learn from school and from over-heard snatches of conversation among my relatives and mother. She often called other lower-income Mexicans "braceros," or "wet-backs," referring to herself and her family as "a different class of people." And yet, the real story was that my family, too, had been poor (some still are) and farmworkers. My mother can remember this in her blood as if it were yesterday. But this is something she would like to forget (and rightfully), for to her, on a basic economic level, being Chicana meant being "less." It was through my mother's desire to protect her children from poverty and illiteracy that we became "anglocized"; the more effectively we could pass in the white world, the better guaranteed our future.

From all of this, I experience, daily, a huge disparity between what I was born into and what I was to grow up to become. Because, (as Goldman suggests) these stories my mother told me crept under my "güera" skin. I had no choice but to enter into the life of my mother. *I had no choice.* I took her life into my heart, but managed to keep a lid on it as long as I feigned being the happy, upwardly mobile heterosexual.

When I finally lifted the lid to my lesbianism, a profound connection with my mother reawakened in me. It wasn't until I acknowledged and confronted my own lesbianism in the flesh, that my heartfelt identification with and empathy for my mother's oppression—due to being poor, uneducated, and Chicana—was realized. My lesbianism is the avenue through which I have learned the most about silence and oppression, and it continues to be the most tactile reminder to me that we are not free human beings.

You see, one follows the other. I had known for years that I was a lesbian, had felt it in my bones, had ached with the knowledge, gone crazed with the knowledge, wallowed in the silence of it. Silence is like starvation. Don't be fooled. It's nothing short of that, and felt most sharply when one has had a full belly most of her life. When we are not physically starving, we have the luxury to realize psychic and emotional starvation. It is from this starvation that other starvations can be recognized—if one is willing to take the risk of making the connection—if one is willing to be responsible to the result of the connection. For me, the connection is an inevitable one.

What I am saying is that the joys of looking like a white girl ain't so great since I realized I could be beaten on the street for being a dyke. If my sister's being beaten because she's Black, it's pretty much the same principle. We're both getting beaten any way you look at it. The connection is blatant; and in the case of my own family, the difference in the privileges attached to looking white instead of brown are merely a generation apart.

In this country, lesbianism is a poverty—as is being brown, as is being a woman, as is being just plain poor. The danger lies in ranking the oppressions. *The danger lies in failing to acknowledge the specificity of the oppression.* The danger lies in attempting to deal with oppression purely from a theoretical base. Without an emotional, heartfelt grappling with the source of our own oppression, without naming the enemy within ourselves and outside of us, no authentic, non-hierarchical connection among oppressed groups can take place.

When the going gets rough, will we abandon our so-called comrades in a flurry of racist/heterosexist/what-have-you panic? To whose camp, then, should the lesbian of color retreat? Her very presence violates the ranking and abstraction of oppression. Do we merely live hand to mouth? Do we merely struggle with the "ism" that's sitting on top of our own heads?

The answer is: yes, I think first we do; and we must do so thoroughly and deeply. But to fail to move out from there will only isolate us in our own oppression—will only insulate, rather than radicalize us.

To illustrate: a gay male friend of mine once confided to me that he continued to feel that, on some level, I didn't trust him because he was male; that he felt, really, if it ever came down to a "battle of the sexes," I might kill him. I admitted that I might very well. He wanted to understand the source of my distrust. I responded, "You're not a woman. Be a woman for a day. Imagine being a woman." He confessed that the thought terrified him because, to him, being a woman meant being raped by men. He had felt raped by men; he wanted to forget what that meant. What grew from that discussion was the realization that in order for him to create an authentic alliance with me, he must deal with the primary source of his own sense of oppression. He must, first, emotionally come to terms with what it feels like to be a victim. If he—or anyone—were to truly do this, it would be impossible to discount the oppression of others, except by again forgetting how we have been hurt.

And yet, oppressed groups are forgetting all the time. There are instances of this in the rising Black middle class, and certainly an obvious trend of such "unconsciousness" among white gay men. Because to remember may mean giving up whatever privileges we have managed to squeeze out of this society by virtue of our gender, race, class, or sexuality.

Within the women's movement, the connections among women of different backgrounds and sexual orientations have been fragile, at best. I think this phenomenon is indicative of our failure to seriously address ourselves to some very frightening questions: How have I internalized my own oppression? How have I oppressed? Instead, we have let rhetoric do the job of poetry. Even the word "oppression" has lost its power. We need a new language, better words that can more closely describe women's fear of and resistance to one another; words that will not always come out sounding like dogma.

What prompted me in the first place to work on an anthology by radical women of color was a deep sense that I had a valuable insight to contribute, by virtue of my birthright and background. And yet, I don't really understand first-hand what it feels like being shitted on for being brown. I understand much more about the joys of it—being Chicana and having family are synonymous for me. What I know about loving, singing, crying, telling stories, speaking with my heart and hands, even having a sense of my own soul comes from the love of my mother, aunts, cousins....

But at the age of twenty-seven, it is frightening to acknowledge that I have internalized a racism and classism, where the object of oppression is not only someone outside of my skin, but the someone inside my skin. In fact, to a large degree, the real battle with such oppression, for all of us, begins under the skin. I have had to confront the fact that much of what I value about being Chicana, about my family, has been subverted by anglo-culture and my own cooperation with it. This realization did not occur to me overnight. For example, it wasn't until long after my graduation from the private college I'd attended in Los Angeles, that I realized the major reason for my total alienation from and fear of my classmates was rooted in class and culture. CLICK.

Three years after graduation, in an apple-orchard in Sonoma, a friend of mine (who comes from an Italian Irish working-class family) says to me, "Cherríe, no wonder you felt like such a nut in school. Most of the people there were white and rich." It was true. All along I had felt the difference, but not until I had put the words "class" and "color" to the experience, did my feelings make any sense. For years, I had berated myself for not being as "free" as my classmates. I completely bought that they simply had more guts than I did—to rebel against their parents and run around the country hitch-hiking, reading books and studying "art." They had enough privilege to be atheists, for chrissake. There was no one around filling in the disparity for me between their parents, who were Hollywood filmmakers, and my parents, who wouldn't know the name of a filmmaker if their lives depended on it (and precisely because their lives didn't depend on it, they couldn't be bothered). But I knew nothing about "privilege" then. White was right. Period. I could pass. If I got educated enough, there would never be any telling.

Three years after that, another CLICK. In a letter to Barbara Smith, I wrote:

> I went to a concert where Ntosake Shange was reading. There, everything exploded for me. She was speaking a language that I knew—in the deepest parts of me—existed, and that I had ignored in my own feminist studies and even in my own writing. What Ntosake caught in me is the realization that in my development as a poet, I have, in many ways, denied the voice of my own brown mother—the brown in me. I have acclimated to the sound of a white language which, as my father represents it, does not speak to the emotions in my poems—emotions which stem from the love of my mother.

> The reading was agitating. Made me uncomfortable. Threw me into a week-long terror of how deeply I was affected. I felt that I had to start all over again. That I turned only to the perceptions of white middle-class women to speak for me and all women. I am shocked by my own ignorance.

Sitting in that auditorium chair was the first time I had realized to the core of me that for years I had disowned the language I knew best—ignored the words and rhythms that were the closest to me. The sounds of my mother and aunts gossiping—half in English, half in Spanish—while drinking cerveza in the kitchen. And the hands—I had cut off the hands in my poems. But not in conversation; still the hands could not be kept down. Still they insisted on moving.

The reading had forced me to remember that I knew things from my roots. But to remember puts me up against what I don't know. Shange's reading agitated me because she spoke with power about a world that is both alien and common to me: "the capacity to enter into the lives of others." But you can't just take the goods and run. I knew that then, sitting in the Oakland auditorium (as I know in my poetry), that the only thing worth writing about is what seems to be unknown and, therefore, fearful.

The "unknown" is often depicted in racist literature as the "darkness" within a person. Similarly, sexist writers will refer to fear in the form of the vagina, calling it "the orifice of death." In contrast, it is a pleasure to read works such as Maxine Hong Kingston's *Woman Warrior*, where fear and alienation are described as "the white ghosts." And yet, the bulk of literature in this country reinforces the myth that what is dark and female is evil. Consequently, each of us—whether dark, female, or both—has in some way *internalized* this oppressive imagery. What the oppressor often succeeds in doing is simply *externalizing* his fears, projecting them into the bodies of women, Asians, gays, disabled folks, whoever seems most "other."

> call me
> roach and presumptuous
> nightmare on your white pillow
> your itch to destroy
> the indestructible
> part of yourself
>
>                    Audre Lorde[2]

But it is not really difference the oppressor fears so much as similarity. He fears he will discover in himself the same aches, the same longings as those of the people he has shitted on. He fears the immobilization threatened by his own incipient guilt. He fears he will have to change his life once he has seen himself in the bodies of the people he has called different. He fears the hatred, anger, and vengeance of those he has hurt.

This is the oppressor's nightmare, but it is not exclusive to him. We women have a similar nightmare, for each of us in some way has been both oppressed and the oppressor. We are afraid to look at how we have failed each other. We are afraid to see how we have taken the values of our oppressor into our hearts and turned them against ourselves and one another. We are afraid to admit how deeply "the man's" words have been ingrained in us.

To assess the damage is a dangerous act. I think of how, even as a feminist lesbian, I have so wanted to ignore my own homophobia, my own hatred of myself for being queer. I have not wanted to admit that my deepest personal sense of myself has not quite "caught up" with my "woman-identified" politics. I have been afraid to criticize lesbian writers who choose to "skip over" these issues in the name of feminism. In 1979, we talk of "old gay" and "butch and femme" roles as if they were ancient history. We toss them aside as merely patriarchal notions. And yet, the truth of the matter is that I have sometimes taken society's fear and hatred of lesbians to bed with me. I have sometimes hated my lover for loving me. I have sometimes felt "not woman enough" for her. I have sometimes felt "not man enough." For a lesbian trying to survive in a heterosexist society, there is no way around these emotions. Similarly, in a white-dominated world, there is little getting around racism and our own internalization of it. It's always there, embodied in some one we least expect to rub up against.

When we do rub up against this person, *there* then is the challenge. *There* then is the opportunity to look at the nightmare within us. But we usually shrink from such a challenge.

Time and time again, I have observed that the usual response among white women's groups when the "racism issue" comes up is to deny the difference. I have heard comments like, "Well, we're open to *all* women; why don't they (women of color) come? You can only do so much..." But there is seldom any analysis of how the very nature and structure of the group itself may be founded on racist or classist assumptions. More importantly, so often the women seem to feel no loss, no lack, no absence when women of color are not involved; therefore, there is little desire to change the situation. This has hurt me deeply. I have come to believe that the only reason women of a privileged class will dare to look at how it is that they oppress, is when they've come to know the meaning of their own oppression. And understand that the oppression of others hurts them personally.

The other side of the story is that women of color and working-class women often shrink from challenging white middle-class women. It is much easier to rank oppressions and set up a hierarchy, rather than take responsibility for changing our own lives. We have failed to demand that white women, particularly those who claim to be speaking for all women, be accountable for their racism.

The dialogue has simply not gone deep enough.

I have many times questioned my right to even work on an anthology which is to be written "exclusively by Third World women." I have had to look critically at my claim to color, at a time when, among white feminist ranks, it is a "politically correct" (and sometimes peripherally advantageous) assertion to make. I must acknowledge the fact that, physically, I had a choice about making that claim, in contrast to women who have not had such a choice, and have been abused for their color. I must reckon with the fact that most of my life, by virtue of the very fact that I am white-looking, I identified with and aspired toward white values, and that I rode the wave of that Southern California privilege as far as conscience would let me.

Well, now I feel both bleached and beached. I feel angry about this—the years when I refused to recognize privilege, both when it worked against me, and when I worked it, ignorantly, at the expense of others. These are not settled issues. That is why this work feels so risky to me. It continues to be discovery. It has brought me into contact with women who invariably know a hell of a lot more than I do about racism, as experienced in the flesh, as revealed in the flesh of their writing.

I think: what is my responsibility to my roots—both white and brown, Spanish-speaking and English? I am a woman with a foot in both worlds; and I refuse the split. I feel the necessity for dialogue. Sometimes I feel it urgently.

But one voice is not enough, nor two, although this is where dialogue begins. It is essential that radical feminists confront their fear of and resistance to each other, because without this, there will be no bread on the table. Simply, we will not survive. If we could make this connection in our heart of hearts, that if we are serious about a revolution—better—if we seriously believe there should be joy in our lives (real joy, not just "good times"), then we need one another. We women need each other. Because my/your solitary, self-asserting "go-for-the-throat-of-fear" power is not enough. The real power, as you and I well know, is collective. I can't afford to be afraid of you, nor you of me. If it takes head-on collisions, let's do it: this polite timidity is killing us.

As Lorde suggests in the passage I cited earlier, it is in looking to the nightmare that the dream is found. There, the survivor emerges to insist on a future, a vision, yes, born out of what is dark and female. The feminist movement must be a movement of such survivors, a movement with a future.

September, 1979.

## Notes

1.     Alix Kates Shulman, "Was My Life Worth Living?" *Red Emma Speaks* (New York: Random House, 1972), p. 388.

2.     From "The Brown Menace or Poem to the Survival of Roaches," *The New York Head Shop and Museum* (Detroit: Broadside, 1974), p. 48.

## For discussion

*Content*

1.  What is dangerous about ranking oppressions?

2.  Have you ever been oppressed? If so, does the experience give you a better understanding of the oppression of others? Does it help you to avoid oppressing others?

3.  Moraga states, "We need a new language, better words that can more closely describe women's fear of and resistance to one another; words that will not always come out sounding like dogma" (paragraph 16). What are the old words for that fear and resistance? Suggest new words that would do a better job.

4. Explain what it means to internalize oppression (racism, homophobia, sexism, for example), and how internalizing oppression perpetuates stereotypes.

5. If you know someone who deliberately acts to shatter a stereotype (for example, a librarian who deliberately encourages people to talk out loud in a library, or a gay man who is deliberately not limp-wristed, or an athlete who deliberately discusses intellectual issues), do that person's actions destroy the stereotype for you? Or are you inclined to think that the person is just an exception to the stereotype ("Oh, Joyce is not like all the other sorority girls") and to keep the stereotype intact?

6. What stereotypes do you know for Hispanic women and for Hispanic men? Do you know different specific stereotypes for Hispanic women and for Hispanic men? How did you learn those stereotypes? Does Moraga's essay help you to rethink any of those stereotypes?

7. What stereotypes do you know for caucasian (or anglo, or white) women and for caucasian men? Do you know different specific stereotypes for caucasian women and for caucasian men? How did you learn those stereotypes? How do they influence your thinking?

8. Near the end of the essay in a single-sentence paragraph, Moraga says, "The dialogue has simply not gone deep enough." Explain how talking can help us dispel stereotypes and oppression. Explain how having learned to talk politely could hinder some women's participation in that dialogue.

*Style*

1. Sentence one of paragraph four creates a contrast between Moraga's life and her mother's. Is that an effective contrast, or should she have given more details about being a college-prep student?

2. Discuss the effectiveness of the structure of the last sentence in paragraph five.

3. What does Moraga mean by using "CLICK"? Is that word an effective choice?

# The "F" Word

## Catharine R. Stimpson

*FEMINISM* ENTERED THE ENGLISH LANGUAGE in 1895, *X ray* in 1896. Feminism was to film our behavior as sharply as X rays did our bones. However, nearly a century later, people say X rays without sputtering. Feminism is an X-rated word.

I understand some distrust of feminism. We have made wild claims in our day, insisting, for example, that all women are the same, despite differences of class, race, or age.

However, much of the X-rating is vicious, fearful, or irrational. At its most zany, the resistance to feminism lurches into phobia. Where a reasonable person sees walls, the claustrophobe sees walls collapsing. Where a reasonable person sees change, the feminaphobe, female or male, sees a world collapsing if women change.

The fear of feminism, in mild or phobic form, wells up, whether feminism seems puny or powerful. In many ways, it is both. We still lack influence in certain areas: podium, pulpit, TV studio, White House briefing room. But feminism offers three potent gifts: a moral vision of women, in all their diversity, and social justice; political and cultural organizations (like shelters for battered women) that translate the vision into action; and psychological processes that enable men and women to re-experience and re-form themselves.

Inevitably, as feminism has grown and become more diverse, as it has become feminisms, the forms of resistance to it have also altered. I now hear at least six voices that choke on the sentence: "I am a feminist."

*From* Ms. Magazine. *July/Aug. Copyright 1987. Reprinted by permission of the author.*

## Type A—The Neoconservative

Type A labels feminism a violation of the laws of God, man, and nature. The conservative man who dreads the loss of women's cheap labor is a familiar example; the conservative woman is not so well understood. She may have translated her fear of economic insecurity, and her ardent devotion to family as a source of security, into a fear of feminism. Or she may simply disregard the feminine role when it suits her purposes. ("I can work outside the home, but if all those other women do, too—watch out!")

## Type B—The Scapegoater

Every society creates boundaries. Every society also creates scapegoats, pushes them beyond the boundaries, and then punishes them for being out there. Women have often been malleable candidates for scapegoathood. Around 1486, two papal inquisitors named Heinrich and James labeled certain women witches. Witches raise hailstorms and tempests instead of children; killed the children they did have; sterilized men and beasts; and flew through the air to copulate with devils. Today, we still hear echoes of Heinrich and James—except now they're saying that feminists sleep with each other instead of warlocks.

## Type C—"I'm not a Feminist, I'm a Rugged Individualist"

Americans traditionally, if self-deceptively, think of themselves as individuals, not as ideologues. Ironically, feminism, which is ideological, urges each woman to think of herself as an individual as well as a citizen of a community. Women who really ought to consider themselves feminists can still do things like ask their sons to wash the dishes without being called "libbers"—they simply call themselves individualists.

## Type D—"I want Mommy"

Most of us want to be special, showered with care, bathed in nurture—no matter how fiercely we might repress these longings. Symbolically, the "good mother" provides these blissful services. Feminists may disagree about a biological mother's natural right to her baby, but we agree on many of the points: that fathers can mother; that parents deserve real rewards; that men and women need new child-care systems; and that women other than Mother Teresa can refuse to bear children. Many people misinterpret these positions and think of feminism as the ax murderer of the Good Mother.

## Type E—The Languid Heiress

In 1937, the first woman to get tenure on the graduate faculties of Columbia University, Marjorie Hope Nicolson, decided that the professional women of her generation occupied a unique position. Born in the last decade of the 19th century, they were old enough to "escape the self-consciousness and belligerence" of the feminist pioneers and young enough to escape the constrictions society placed on white women after the fight for suffrage was over. Some postfeminists are a 1980s equivalent. Born in the years between *The Second Sex* (1953) and *Sexual Politics* (1970), they are the beneficiaries of the will of the active feminists of the 1960s and 1970s. They are now living on a trust fund from history. Like many children with inherited money, they heedlessly spend the income and refuse to add to the principal.

## Type F—The Feminist Mystique

Feminism, like other movements for social justice, is demanding. Erasing the images of Betty Crocker or Aunt Jemima and generating new models is much harder than whipping up a waffle. Even feminists fear feminism. We underestimated how difficult it would be to wipe out the psychological residue of the feminine mystique. Many of us still carry within ourselves a conflict about what gender and change mean. We say, "I am a feminist," but we often whisper, with irritation, guilt, and ennui, "I wish I did not have to be."

If all women's lives continue to change as they have been changing, many people will be able to say "feminist" as casually as they now say "wife" or "kid" or "snack." The feminist analyses of injustice—of domestic violence or of women's incomes—are too compelling to ignore. The feminist remedies—social support for child care, for example—are too appealing. Ultimately the X-raters and feminaphobes will lose their power.

Until then, those of us who call ourselves feminists might revise our strategy. First of all, let's just take to calling it the F word. It might deflect a little of that hostility back to where it came from. And it will help us to remember how long it has taken all of us to learn to say "feminist" without stammering. Next, we need even more audacity, more humor, when we speak of feminism. We are strong enough to know that self-satire does not signify self-contempt. Finally, we must be aware that the sentence, "I am a feminist," translates into many social languages, each with its own rhythm, idioms, and nuance. The more we say it, the more reasonable it will become—and then it will be G rated.

**For discussion**

*Content*

1. What new information does Stimpson give you about feminism or about feminists?

2. Stimpson writes that feminism offers three gifts to society. Name them and explain each in your words.

3. Why, according to this essay, are some people hostile toward feminism? What does Stimpson think feminists should do to lessen hostility?

4. "Feminism" is powerful in its denotations and in its connotations. List as many denotations and connotations of the word as you and your classmates can find.

*Style*

1. What effect does Stimpson's title have?

2. Is Stimpson's analogy of "feminism" and "x ray" an effective beginning? If so, why?

3. Are the subheadings as useful to you as topic sentences would be in the place of subheadings?

4. Paragraph three has two parallel complex sentences. What effect does Stimpson gain with these structures?

5. Analyze the essay's overall organization. Why do you think the organization is effective (or not effective)?

**For writing**

1. Identify a stereotype that you have. Write a paper in which you examine how you learned that stereotype and the ways it affects your thought, behavior, and language.

2. If you identify yourself as a feminist, define the term as you understand it. Write a paper in which you persuade your audience not to fear feminism.

3. In "What It Is I Think I'm Doing Anyhow," Toni Cade Bambara writes, "The old folks say, 'It's not how little we know that hurts so, but that so much of what we know ain't so'" (*The Writer on Her Work*. Ed. Janet Sternburg [New York: W.W. Norton and Company, Inc., 1980], 155). Write a paper in which you explore how a group or an individual is hurt by what "ain't so," by a stereotype label.

# Chapter Six:

# Keep Moving

# Keep Moving

## Introduction

CHAPTER FIVE USED THE ANALOGY OF LANGUAGE as an inescapable maze. We need words if we are going to think in any depth, and words can keep us from thinking in any depth. Words can trap us in dead ends, but words are also the way to paths that allow us to keep moving. This chapter will focus on how we can use words to negotiate the maze.

To learn more than a label tells me about a person or an idea, and to grow beyond the shallow and narrow definition a label provides, I must use language. To free myself, I must think, listen, read, and sometimes write and speak. And all these activities require words. If I want to protect myself from the too-easy notion that all doctors are good or that homosexuals are so tiny a minority as to be insignificant, I must have more information than a label and its connotations give me. I can get that information by reading, by talking to people who have a different view, by thinking about all the evidence I can find, and perhaps by writing and speaking about what I have learned in my research.

As we have already seen, if we want to get out of the closed paths such words as "heroine" and "woman rancher" create, we can think about the effects of those titles. We can also read what others have written about them. One advantage of written language is that it can be fairly permanent; we can read the words of people from other times and places. In 1911, in *The Vote*, J. Beanland wrote:

The discrimination between the sexes in all that is worth having or being is so unfairly partisan as almost to give the impression that the distribution of our English affixes is the outcome of a misogynist's spleen. For a woman, equally with a man, may be an imbecile, a convict, a liar, a thief, or a fool, without any terminological inexactitude. But when we come to the other side of the shield, she may not be a hero, a benefactor, an administrator, a prophet or a poet, because these things are masculine prerogatives.... everything denoting prominence or superiority must carefully distinguish between the real thing and its mere imitation.

Reading Beanland's analysis allows me to reconsider other words and to open my mind to further thought. I have never heard a woman labelled "thiefette," "cowardess," "molesterine," "battererette", or "drunkardess." But does that mean, as Beanland suggests, that women and men get equal attention from the titles for dishonorable or unworthy behavior, or does it mean that those titles— "coward," "liar," "drunk," "murderer," "abuser"—call up images of men? If the latter is true, shall we argue that language is unfair to men, or shall we argue that by insisting on "-ess" and "-ette" endings for words that denote women, men have dug a linguistic hole for themselves?

Using language to think, read, talk, and listen, I can work my way out of the particular dead-end alley of using silly diminutive affixes for words. Once I can see my way out of that narrow thinking, I can change my linguistic habits and free myself for clearer, deeper thinking.

But freeing myself from one path doesn't free me from all. I must be alert constantly because I live in a language that has many dead-end paths. I cannot and would not want to free myself from a linguistic inheritance or a linguistic environment, but it is important for me to remember that languages reflect the prejudices of the cultures that create those languages. English has a variety of built-in biases, reflecting the culture's attitudes about women and men, race, class, political systems, and sexual orientation, for example. Unless I want to wander unwittingly into any of those biases, I must constantly use language to learn and to think. Finding clear ways to negotiate the maze requires effort and vigilance and sometimes discomfort and risk.

Some of the paths that can stop us in the middle of a maze are comfortable and some are subtle. An apparently innocent linguistic habit English speakers inherited before the 1970s was the one that identified women as either "Mrs." or "Miss" and men as "Mr." Before they married, women were "Miss"; they were "Mrs." after they married. Men were "Mr." all their lives. A woman who started her life as Miss Janet Blue became Mrs. James White when she married, and Janet Blue disappeared. But a man who started his life as Mr. James White was Mr. James White all his life whether he married or not. Lucy Stone objected to that linguistic social ritual in the 1800s and refused to change her name when she married Henry Blackwell. She risked social disapproval, and she lost her right to vote in a local election because she refused to register as Mrs. Henry Blackwell. The district collected taxes from Lucy Stone, and Lucy Stone should be the voter, Stone reasoned. Again in the early 1970s, women objected to "Miss" and "Mrs.," arguing that women lose their identities when they change their names (once or many times, depending on how often they marry) and that women are disadvantaged by having their names announce their marital situation and therefore their sexual availability. To avoid the asymmetry in women's and men's titles, women created "Ms." as a parallel to "Mr." Those women risked social disapproval and faced derision. Many people were comfortable with "Miss" and "Mrs." and did not want to change. They argued that there is no need for change, that it is foolish for women to tamper with language, that it is useful to know if a woman is sexually available.

Again, if I want to free my mind for clearer thinking, I can examine my old habit of referring to women who are married to men as "Mrs." and to women who are not married to men as "Miss." I can read about the history of "Mrs." and I can read and think about the implications of women's abandoning their personal identities. I can find out for whom and why it is useful to know whether a woman is available. By using language to read, listen, and think, I can learn about language changes and new words added to language as people need them. I can consider the effects on my own thinking of calling women "Ms." and men "Mr." and of my complete inattention to a woman's marital situation if I call her "Ms."

Another subtle and apparently innocent thought-blocking path is the contemporary social habit of calling by their first names adults we don't know well or who are in positions of authority. Does first-naming indicate friendliness, as so many people think it does? Is it appropriate for me to establish a friendly relationship with my doctor in her office? I am not there for a social call, and I won't feel better physically if she and I appear to be friends. Would our first-naming each other indicate a lack of respect and undue familiarity? Do people first-name women more than they first-name men, and if they do, does that suggest that women, like children, should be subordinate? We use language to ask these questions and to think about this linguistic habit.

We can also read about this issue and talk about it with people to find out what they think. We can listen to learn what effects peoples' choices have on others. For example, in your college classes do instructors call students by first names? Do they call only women students by their first names? How do instructors expect students to address them? What difference does it make to you whether you are addressed by your first name or by "Ms. XXX" or "Mr. XXX"? How does addressing your instructor as "Ms. XXX" or "Mr. XXX" or "Doctor XXX" instead of as "Carolyn" or "Jimmie" or "Bonnie" affect your attitude about your work in a class? Having learned by reading, listening, thinking, and talking about this linguistic habit, we can make choices of address effective for audience, purpose, and situation. We do not have to first-name everyone if doing so confuses or blocks our thoughts or if it makes an uncomfortable or inappropriate situation.

Having thought and read and talked and listened, we may decide to invite readers to consider our ideas as ways to negotiate the maze of language. We write to clarify ideas and information for ourselves and for others, and we may write to redefine and rename ourselves and others. If you have been stereotyped as a "dumb blond," as a "dumb jock," as a "dyke" or a "faggot," as a "wagon burner," as a "spic," as a "liberal," or as any of the other stereotypes people use to put each other down, you may choose to re-define a label so that it is not a put-down. Your writing may help others learn to think more clearly and openly. If you use language precisely, you may even help yourself and others avoid stereotypes. If, instead of choosing "bra burners," you choose the more precise "feminists," you can create for yourself and others a more thought-provoking image. If you choose "woman-identified woman" rather than "lezzie," you allow yourself and others to avoid a mind-blocking stereotype; you use words precisely to encourage people to re-think a stereotype. If you use "Native American" or "American Indian," your choice encourages thought; "squaw" and "redskin" encourage only emotional response. People created "Black is beautiful," "Homophobia is a social disease," "Hatred is not a family value," and "Gay and proud," to change the society's views about labels, about the people those labels defined, and about ideas. You may want to use language to persuade readers to reconsider their ideas and biases.

Whether we are trying to learn ways out of too-limited thinking that comes from our learning to identify people and ideas by labels or we are trying to learn ways out of ineffective linguistic habits, language is our path out. Reading, writing, listening, talking, and thinking allow us to question what we know and to learn perspectives different from those with which we've become comfortable. The risk is that we may learn unsettling new information or ideas that we then must evaluate. But when we have seen the evidence, we may choose to keep old knowledge if it still seems true or sensible. And we can choose to change our ideas, our behavior, even our language, if new information and thought seem true and sensible.

The essays that follow invite us to reconsider old definitions and ideas. As you read each essay, consider whether it helps you to see from a new perspective and whether the new information and ideas help you to find open paths in the linguistic maze. Consider whether the essayists use language effectively enough to persuade you to rethink what you know.

In this chapter, general questions about linguistic choices and about learning precede the essays, and suggestions for writing and for a library paper follow the chapter's final essay. (See page 331.) I did not make specific content discussion questions for each essay in this chapter because you are now able to discuss independently each essay's content and to see relationships among essays.

**Works Cited**

Beanland, J. "The Sex War in Language." *The Vote* 18 Feb. 1911: 207. Rpt. in *Language, Gender, and Professional Writing*. Eds. Francine Frank and Paula Treichler. New York: The Modern Language Association of America, 1989.

**For discussion**

Each writer in Chapter Six tries to persuade readers to rethink a label, an idea, or an issue. Each writer shows us a way to negotiate the maze. To understand each writer's strategies for solving a problem caused by a too-narrow definition or by a linguistic habit that hobbles people, analyze each writer's language choices:

1. Are the writer's title and introduction effective?

2. Does the writer provide enough evidence to persuade you of her or his thesis? What kind of evidence is it? Is it well-chosen? Does it help you to think your way out of a dead-end?

3. What organization does the writer use? Does s/he provide clear transitions? If s/he uses subheadings, are they effective? Does the organization of evidence help support the thesis?

4. Are the writer's diction choices precise and accurate for denotation and for connotation? Do the diction choices help us avoid stereotypes?

5. Does the writer control sentence structures for meaning, variety, and emphasis?

6. Does the writer use language economically?

7. Does the writer use active and passive voice effectively?

8. Does the writer use euphemisms effectively, if at all?

9. Does the writer create new metaphors? Are they effective?

10. Is the writer's conclusion strong? What makes it so, or not?

11. Do you find other strategies than those we've considered in this book? If so, what are they? Are they effective?


The preceding set of questions is specific to the linguistic choices writers make; the set of questions below is specific to you as a reader and as a writer.

1. What stereotypes have you had to rethink as you read the essays? What specific information have you learned? What new ideas has any writer given you that help you to think more clearly?

2. As you read the essays in this chapter, what ideas did you encounter that would encourage you to write a re-definition of a label that "fits" you or that "fits" someone else? What writing strategies would be especially useful to you?

3. In what specific ways do you think you have grown as a reader in this course?

4. In what specific ways do you think you have grown as a writer in this course?

5. How have you grown as a thinker?

6. Out of what dead-end paths has your reading (and thinking, talking, listening, and writing) in the course helped you to learn your way?

# Black Children, Black Speech

## Dorothy Z. Seymour

"C'MON, MAN, LES GIT GOIN,'" called the boy to his companion. "Dat bell ringin'. It say, 'Git in rat now!'" He dashed into the school yard.

"Aw, f'get you," replied the other. "Whe' Richuh? Whe' da' muvvah? He be goin' to schoo'."

"He in de' now, man!" was the answer as they went through the door.

In the classroom they made for their desks and opened their books. The name of the story they tried to read was "Come." It went:

*Come, Bill come*
*Come with me.*
*Come and see this.*
*See what is here.*

The first boy poked the second. "Wha' da' wor'?"
"Da' wor' *is*, you dope."
"*Is*? Ain't no wor' *is*. You jivin' me? Wha' da' wor' mean?"
"Ah dunno. Jus' *is*."

To a speaker of Standard English, this exchange is only vaguely comprehensible. But it's normal speech for thousands of American children. In addition it demonstrates one of our biggest educational problems: children whose speech style is so different from the writing style of their books that they have difficulty learning to read. These children speak Black English, a dialect characteristic of many inner-city Negroes. Their books are, of course, written in Standard English. To complicate matters, the speech they use is also socially stigmatized. Middle-class whites and Negroes alike scorn it as low-class poor people's talk.

Teachers sometimes make the situation worse with their attitudes toward Black English. Typically, they view the children's speech as "bad English" characterized by "lazy pronunciation," "poor grammar," and "short, jagged words." One result of this attitude is poor mental health on the part of the pupils. A child is quick to grasp the feeling that while school speech is "good," his own speech is "bad," and that by extension he himself is somehow inadequate and without value. Some children react to this feeling by withdrawing; they stop talking entirely. Others develop the attitude of "F'get you, honky." In either case, the psychological results are devastating and lead straight to the dropout route.

It is hard for most teachers and middle-class Negro parents to accept the idea that Black English is not just "sloppy talk" but a dialect with a form and structure of its own. Even some eminent black educators think of it as "bad English grammar" with "slurred consonants" (Professor Nick Aaron Ford of Morgan State College in Baltimore) and "ghettoese" (Dr. Kenneth B. Clark, the prominent educational psychologist).

Parents of Negro school children generally agree. Two researchers of Columbia University report that the adults they worked with in Harlem almost unanimously preferred that their children be taught Standard English in school.

But there is another point of view, one held in common by black militants and some white liberals. They urge that middle-class Negroes stop thinking of the inner-city dialect as something to be ashamed of and repudiated. Black author Claude Brown, for example, pushes this view.

Some modern linguists take a similar stance. They begin with the premise that no dialect is intrinsically "bad" or "good," and that a nonstandard speech style is not defective speech but different speech. More important, they have been able to show that Black English is far from being a careless way of speaking the Standard; instead, it is a rather rigidly-constructed set of speech patterns, with the same sort of specialization in sounds, structure, and vocabulary as any other dialect.

## The Sounds of Black English

Middle-class listeners who hear black inner-city speakers say "dis" and "tin" for "this" and "thin" assume that the black speakers are just being careless. Not at all; these differences are characteristic aspects of the dialect. The original cause of such substitutions is generally a carryover from one's original language or that of his immigrant parents. The interference from that carryover probably caused the substitution of /d/ for the voiced *th* sound in *this*, and /t/ for the unvoiced *th* sound in *thin*. (Linguists represent language sounds by putting letters within slashes or brackets.) Most speakers of English don't realize the two *th* sounds of English are lacking in many other languages and are difficult for most foreigners trying to learn English. Germans who study English, for example, are surprised and confused about these sounds because the only Germans who use them are the ones who lisp. These two sounds are almost nonexistent in the West African languages which most black immigrants brought with them to America.

Similar substitutions used in Black English are /f/, a sound similar to the unvoiced *th*, in medial word-position, as in *birfday* for *birthday*, and in final word-position, as in *roof* for *Ruth* as well as /v/ for the voiced *th* in medial position, as in *bruvver* for *brother*. These sound substitutions are also typical of Gullah, the language of black speakers in the Carolina Sea Island. Some of them are also heard in Caribbean Creole.

Another characteristic of the sounds of Black English is the lack of /l/ at the end of words, sometimes replaced by the sound /w/. This makes words like *tool* sound like *too*. If /l/ occurs in the middle of a Standard English word, in Black English it may be omitted entirely: "I can hep you." This difference is probably caused by the instability and sometimes interchangeability of /l/ and /r/ in West African languages.

One difference that is startling to middle-class speakers is the fact that Black English words appear to leave off some consonant sounds at the end of words. Like Italian, Japanese and West African words, they are more likely to end in vowel sounds. Standard English *boot* is pronounced *boo* in Black English. *What* is *wha*. *Sure* is *sho*. *Your* is *yo*. This kind of difference can make for confusion in the classroom. Dr. Kenneth Goodman, a psycholinguist, tells of a black child whose white teacher asked him to use *so* in a sentence—not "sew a dress" but "the other *so*." The sentence the child used was "I got a *so* on my leg."

A related feature of Black English is the tendency in many cases not to use sequences of more than one final consonant sound. For example, *just* is pronounced *jus'*, *past* is *pass*, *mend* sounds like *men* and *hold* like *hole*. *Six* and *box* are pronounced *sick* and *bock*. Why should this be? Perhaps because West African languages, like Japanese, have almost no clusters of consonants in their speech. The Japanese, when importing a foreign word, handle a similar problem by inserting vowel sounds between every consonant, making *baseball* sound like *besuboru*. West Africans probably made a simpler change, merely cutting a series of two consonant sounds down to one. Speakers of Gullah, one linguist found, have made the same kind of adaptation of Standard English.

Teachers of black children seldom understand the reason for these differences in final sounds. They are apt to think that careless speech is the cause. Actually, black speakers aren't "leaving off" any sounds; how can you leave off something you never had in the first place?

Differences in vowel sounds are also characteristic of the nonstandard language. Dr. Goodman reports that a black child asked his teacher how to spell rat. "R-a-t," she replied. But the boy responded "No ma'am, I don't mean rat mouse, I mean rat now." In Black English, *right* sounds like *rat*. A likely reason is that in West African languages, there are very few vowel sounds of the type heard in the word *right*. This type is common in English. It is called a glided or dipthongized vowel sound. A glided vowel sound is actually a close combination of two vowels; in the word *right* the two parts of the sound "eye" are actually "ah-ee." West African languages have no such long, two-part, changing vowel sounds; their vowels are generally shorter and more stable. This may be why in Black English, *time* sounds like *Tom*, *oil* like *all*, and *my* like *ma*.

## Language Structure

Black English differs from Standard English not only in its sounds but also in its structure. The way the words are put together does not always fit the description in English grammar books. The method of expressing time, or tense, for example, differs in significant ways.

The verb *to be* is an important one in Standard English. It's used as an auxiliary verb to indicate different tenses. But Black English speakers use it quite differently. Sometimes an inner-city Negro says "He coming"; other times he says "He be coming." These two sentences mean different things. To understand why, let's look at the tenses of West African languages; they correspond with those of Black English.

Many West African languages have a tense which is called the habitual. This tense is used to express action which is always occurring and it is formed with a verb that is translated as *be*. "He be coming" means something like "He's always coming," "He usually comes," or "He's been coming."

In Standard English there is no regular grammatical construction for such a tense. Black English speakers, in order to form the habitual tense in English, use the word *be* as an auxiliary: *He be doing it. My Momma be working. He be running.* The habitual tense is not the same as the present tense, which is constructed in Black English without any form of the verb *to be: He do it. My Momma working. He running.* (This means the action is occurring right now.)

There are other tense differences between Black English and Standard English. For example, the nonstandard speech does not use changes in grammar to indicate the past tense. A white person will ask, "What did your brother say?" and the black person will answer, "He say he coming." (The verb *say* is not changed to *said*). "How did you get here?" "I walk." This style of talking about the past is paralleled in the Yoruba, Fante, Hausa, and Ewe languages of West Africa.

Expression of plurality is another difference. The way a black child will talk of "them boy" or "two dog" makes some white listeners think Negroes don't know how to turn a singular word into a plural word. As a matter of fact, it isn't necessary to use an *s* to express plurality. In Chinese and Japanese, singular and plural are not generally distinguished by such inflections; plurality is conveyed in other ways. For example, in Chinese it's correct to say "there are three book on the table." This sentence already has two signals of the plural, *three* and *are*; why require a third? This same logic is the basis of plurals in most West African languages, where nouns are often identical in the plural and the singular. For example, in Ibo, one correctly says *those man*, and in both Ewe and Yoruba one says *they house*. American speakers of Gullah retain this style; it is correct in Gullah to say *five dog*.

Gender is another aspect of language structure where differences can be found. Speakers of Standard English are often confused to find that the non-standard vernacular often uses just one gender of pronoun, the masculine, and refers to women as well as men as he or him. "He a nice girl," even "Him a nice girl" are common. This usage probably stems from West African origins, too, as does the use of multiple negatives, such as "Nobody don't know it."

Vocabulary is the third aspect of a person's native speech that could affect his learning of a new language. The strikingly different vocabulary often used in Negro Nonstandard English is probably the most obvious aspect of it to a casual white observer. But its vocabulary differences don't obscure its meaning the way different sounds and different structure often do.

Recently there has been much interest in the African origins of words like *goober* (peanut), *cooter* (turtle), and *tote* (carry), as well as others that are less certainly African, such as *to dig* (possibly from the Wolof *degan*, "to understand"). Such expressions seem colorful rather than low-class to many whites; they become assimilated faster than their black originators do. English professors now use *dig* in their scholarly articles, and current advertising has enthusiastically adopted *rap*.

Is it really possible for old differences in sound, structure, and vocabulary to persist from the West African languages of slave days into present-day inner city Black English? Easily. Nothing else really explains such regularity of language habits, most of which persist among black people in various parts of the Western Hemisphere. For a long time scholars believed that certain speech forms used by Negroes were merely leftovers from archaic English preserved in the speech of early English settlers in America and copied by their slaves. But this theory has been greatly weakened, largely as the result of the work of a black linguist, Dr. Lorenzo Dow Turner of the University of Chicago. Dr. Turner studied the speech of Gullah Negroes in the Sea Islands off the Carolina coast and found so many traces of West African languages that he thoroughly discredited the archaic-English theory.

When anyone learns a new language, it's usual to try speaking the new language with the sounds and structure of the old. If a person's first language does not happen to have a particular sound needed in the language he is learning, he will tend to substitute a similar or related sound from his native language and use it to speak the new one. When Frenchman Charles Boyer said "Zees ees my heart," and when Latin American Carmen Miranda sang "Souse America way," they were simply using sounds of their native languages in trying to pronounce sounds of English. West Africans must have done the same thing when they first attempted English words. The tendency to retain the structure of the native language is a strong one, too. That's why a German learning English is likely to put his verb at the end: "May I a glass beer have?" The vocabulary of one's original language may also furnish some holdovers. Jewish immigrants did not stop using the word *bagel* when they came to America; nor did Germans stop saying *sauerkraut*.

Social and geographical isolation reinforces the tendencies to retain old language habits. When one group is considered inferior, the other group avoids it. For many years it was illegal to give any sort of instruction to Negroes, and for slaves to try to speak like their masters would have been unthinkable. Conflict of value systems doubtless retards changes, too. As Frantz Fanon observed in *Black Skin, White Masks*, those who take on white speech habits are suspect in the ghetto, because others believe they are trying to "act white." Dr. Kenneth Johnson, a black linguist, put it this way: "As long as disadvantaged black children live in segregated communities and most of their relationships are confined to those within their own subculture, they will not replace their functional nonstandard dialect with the nonfunctional standard dialect."

Linguist have made it clear that language systems that are different are not necessarily deficient. A judgment of deficiency can be made only in comparison with another language system. Let's turn the tables on Standard English for a moment and look at it from the West African point of view. From this angle, Standard English: (1) is lacking in certain language sounds, (2) has a couple of unnecessary language sounds for which others may serve as good substitutes, (3) doubles and drawls some of its vowel sounds in sequences that are unusual and difficult to imitate, (4) lacks a method of forming an important tense, (5) requires an unnecessary number of ways to indicate tense, plurality and gender, and (6) doesn't mark negatives sufficiently for the result to be a good strong negative statement.

Now whose language is deficient?

How would the adoption of this point of view help us? Say we accepted the evidence that Black English is not just a sloppy Standard but an organized language style which probably has developed many of its features on the basis of its West African heritage. What would we gain?

The psychological climate of the classroom might improve if teachers understood why many black students speak as they do. But we still have not reached a solution of the main problem. Does the discovery that Black English has pattern and structure mean that it should not be tampered with? Should children who speak Black English be excused from learning the Standard in school? Should they perhaps be given books in Black English to learn from?

Any such accommodation would surely result in a hardening of the new separatism being urged by some black militants. It would probably be applauded by such people as Roy Innis, Director of C.O.R.E., who is currently recommending dual autonomous education systems for white and black. And it might facilitate learning to read, since some experiments have indicated that materials written in Black English syntax aid problem readers from the inner city.

But determined resistance to the introduction of such printed materials into schools can be expected. To those who view inner-city speech as bad English, the appearance in print of sentences like "My mama, he work" can be as shocking and repellent as a four-letter word. Middle-class Negro parents would probably mobilize against the move. Any stratagem that does not take into account such practicalities of the matter is probably doomed to failure. And besides, where would such a permissive policy on language get these children in the larger society, and in the long run? If they want to enter an integrated America they must be able to deal with it on its own terms. Even Professor Toni Cade of Rutgers, who doesn't want "ghetto accents" tampered with, advocates mastery of Standard English because, as she puts it, "if you want to get ahead in this country, you must master the language of the ruling class." This has always been true, wherever there has been a minority group.

The problem then appears to be one of giving these children the ability to speak (and read) Standard English without denigrating the vernacular and those who use it, or even affecting the ability to use it. The only way to do this is to officially espouse bidialectism. The result would be the ability to use either dialect equally well—as Dr. Martin Luther King did—depending on the time, place, and circumstances. Pupils would have to learn enough about Standard English to use it when necessary, and teachers would have to learn enough about the inner-city dialect to understand and accept it for what it is—not just a "careless" version of Standard English but a different form of English that's appropriate in certain times and places.

Can we accomplish this? If we can't, the result will be continued alienation of a large section of the population, continued dropout trouble with consequent loss of earning power and economic contribution to the nation, but most of all, loss of faith in America as a place where a minority people can at times continue to use those habits that remind them of their link with each other and with their past.

# The Transformation of Silence into Language and Action

## Audre Lorde

I HAVE COME TO BELIEVE OVER AND OVER AGAIN that what is most important to me must be spoken, made verbal and shared, even at the risk of having it bruised or misunderstood. That the speaking profits me, beyond any other effect. I am standing here as a Black lesbian poet, and the meaning of all that waits upon the fact that I am still alive, and might not have been. Less than two months ago I was told by two doctors, one female and one male, that I would have to have breast surgery, and that there was a 60 to 80 percent chance that the tumor was malignant. Between that telling and the actual surgery, there was a three-week period of the agony of an involuntary reorganization of my entire life. The surgery was completed, and the growth was benign.

But within those three weeks, I was forced to look upon myself and my living with a harsh and urgent clarity that has left me still shaken but much stronger. This is a situation faced by many women, by some of you here today. Some of what I experienced during that time has helped elucidate for me much of what I feel concerning the transformation of silence into language and action.

In becoming forcibly and essentially aware of my mortality, and of what I wished and wanted for my life, however short it might be, priorities and omissions became strongly etched in a merciless light, and what I most regretted were my silences. Of what had I ever been afraid? To question or to speak as I believed could have meant pain, or death. But we all hurt in so many different ways, all the time, and pain will either change or end. Death, on the other hand, is the final silence. And that might be coming quickly, now, without regard for whether I had ever spoken what needed to be said, or had only betrayed myself into small silences, while I planned someday to speak, or waited for someone else's words. And I began to recognize a source of power within myself that comes from the knowledge that while it is most desirable not to be afraid, learning to put fear into a perspective gave me great strength.

I was going to die, if not sooner then later, whether or not I had ever spoken myself. My silences had not protected me. Your silence will not protect you. But for every real word spoken, for every attempt I have ever made to speak those truths for which I am still seeking, I had made contact with other women while we examined the words to fit a world in which we all believed, bridging our differences. And it was the concern and caring of all those women which gave me strength and enabled me to scrutinize the essentials of my living.

The women who sustained me through that period were Black and white, old and young, lesbian, bisexual, and heterosexual, and we all shared a war against the tyrannies of silence. They all gave me a strength and concern without which I could not have survived intact. Within those weeks of acute fear came the knowledge—within the war we are all waging with the forces of death, subtle and otherwise, conscious or not—I am not only a casualty, I am also a warrior.

What are the words you do not yet have? What do you need to say? What are the tyrannies you swallow day by day and attempt to make your own, until you will sicken and die of them, still in silence? Perhaps for some of you here today, I am the face of one of your fears. Because I am woman, because I am Black, because I am lesbian, because I am myself—a Black woman warrior poet doing my work—come to ask you, are you doing yours?

And of course I'm afraid, because the transformation of silence into language and action is an act of self-revelation, and that always seems fraught with danger. But my daughter, when I told her of our topic and my difficulty with it, said, "Tell them about how you're never really a whole person if you remain silent, because there's always that one little piece inside you that wants to be spoken out, and if you keep ignoring it, it gets madder and madder and hotter and hotter, and if you don't speak it out one day it will just up and punch you in the mouth from the inside."

In the cause of silence, each of us draws the face of her own fear—fear of contempt, of censure, or some judgment, or recognition, of challenge, of annihilation. But most of all, I think, we fear the visibility without which we cannot truly live. Within this country where racial difference creates a constant, if unspoken, distortion of vision, Black women have on one hand always been highly visible, and so, on the other hand, have been rendered invisible through the depersonalization of racism. Even within the women's movement, we have had to fight, and still do, for that very visibility which also renders us most vulnerable, our Blackness. For to survive in the mouth of this dragon we call america, we have had to learn this first and most vital lesson—that we were never meant to survive. Not as human beings. And neither were most of you here today, Black or not. And that visibility which makes us most vulnerable is that which also is the source of our greatest strength. Because the machine will try to grind you into dust anyway, whether or not we speak. We can sit in our corners mute forever while our sisters and our selves are wasted, while our children are distorted and destroyed, while our earth is poisoned; we can sit in our safe corners mute as bottles, and we will still be no less afraid.

In my house this year we are celebrating the feast of Kwanza, the African-american festival of harvest which begins the day after Christmas and lasts for seven days. There are seven principles of Kwanza, one for each day. The first principle is Umoja, which means unity, the decision to strive for and maintain unity in self and community. The principle for yesterday, the second day, was Kujichagulia—self-determination—the decision to define ourselves, name ourselves, and speak for ourselves, instead of being defined and spoken for by others. Today is the third day of Kwanza, and the principle for today is Ujima—collective work and responsibility—the decision to build and maintain ourselves and our communities together and to recognize and solve our problems together.

Each of us is here now because in one way or another we share a commitment to language and to the power of language, and to the reclaiming of that language which has been made to work against us. In the transformation of silence into language and action, it is vitally necessary for each one of us to establish or examine her function in that transformation and to recognize her role as vital within that transformation.

For those of us who write, it is necessary to scrutinize not only the truth of what we speak, but the truth of that language by which we speak it. For others, it is to share and spread also those words that are meaningful to us. But primarily for us all, it is necessary to teach by living and speaking those truths which we believe and know beyond understanding. Because in this way alone we can survive, by taking part in a process of life that is creative and continuing, that is growth.

And it is never without fear—of visibility, of the harsh light of scrutiny and perhaps judgement, of pain, of death. But we have lived through all of those already, in silence, except death. And I remind myself all the time now that if I were to have been born mute, or had maintained an oath of silence my whole life long for safety, I would still have suffered, and I would still die. It is very good for establishing perspective.

And where the words of women are crying to be heard, we must each of us recognize our responsibility to seek those words out, to read them and share them and examine them in their pertinence to our lives. That we not hide behind the mockeries of separations that have been imposed upon us and which so often we accept as our own. For instance, "I can't possibly teach Black women's writing—their experience is so different from mine." Yet how many years have you spent teaching Plato and Shakespeare and Proust? Or another, "She's a white woman and what could she possibly have to say to me?" Or, "She's a lesbian, what would my husband say, or my chairman?" Or again, "This woman writes of her sons and I have no children." And all the other endless ways in which we rob ourselves of ourselves and each other.

We can learn to work and speak when we are afraid in the same way we have learned to work and speak when we are tired. For we have been socialized to respect fear more than our own needs for language and definition, and while we wait in silence for that final luxury of fearlessness, the weight of that silence will choke us.

The fact that we are here and that I speak these words is an attempt to break that silence and bridge some of those differences between us, for it is not difference which immobilizes us, but silence. And there are so many silences to be broken.

# Beyond Wifehood

## Una Stannard

### No Less Perfect than Man

"WOMAN IS a most arrogant and intractable animal; and she would be worse if she came to realize that she is no less perfect and no less fit to wear breeches than man." That was why, explained the sixteenth-century Italian anatomist Borgarucci, nature "placed the female testicles internally." For if woman knew she was endowed with "what is necessary for our procreation," her "continual desire to dominate" would be unbridled; therefore, a wise nature "arranged things so that every time she thinks of her supposed lack, she may be humbled and shamed." Similarly, another sixteenth-century anatomist, de Valverde, in a book on the structure of the human body, said he would have preferred to omit the chapter on the female testicles "that women might not become all the more arrogant by knowing that they also, like men, have testicles, and that they...too put something of their own into it [the child]."

What these anatomists thought women put "of their own" into the child was far inferior to what men contributed, but they did not like to think women contributed anything at all. After de Graaf discovered the ovarian follicles, one scientist insisted they were of no more functional value than men's nipples. Men wanted to go on believing woman conceived the way Catholics imagined Mary had, as the result, as it were, of an electric discharge from a superman's dynamo, woman herself containing no life-generating power. Men were terrified that if women should prove to be equally important in the creation of new life, they would cease to feel "humbled and shamed," would think themselves just as important as men and would become just as arrogant. No wonder it was not until

1827 that von Baer discovered the ovum.

It may well be that a man was finally able to see the ovum, the largest cell in the human body and visible to the naked eye, because men had been forced to see women in a different way. Starting in the late eighteenth century, women began to reason that the female sex must have been created no less perfect than the male sex, and women became more arrogant, loudly asserting woman's equality with man. Constrained to look upon women in a new aggressive light, scientists may at last have been able to see the ovum playing an active part in procreation. Be that as it may, the scientific discovery that women were equally necessary in the generation of new life went hand in hand with women's self-discovery that they were "no less perfect and no less fit to wear breeches than" men.

For hundreds of years men and women had believed that God or nature had created the female sex defective, that women could not generate physical life in their wombs, that they could barely generate mental life in their heads, and that they were as weak in body as in mind. Men and women therefore believed women were created to serve the perfect sex, to function as the womb for men's babies, a belief that succeeded in turning women into cripples, creatures with over-developed wombs and breasts, with tiny heads and rudimentary arms and legs that needed the support of man's strong mind and body in order to survive. The aim of the feminist movement, at its simplest and most fundamental, was to give woman back her head and strong limbs and to detach her body and womb from man so she need not cling like a swollen leech to a husband.

During the nineteenth and twentieth centuries feminists have been demonstrating that women are complete human beings who can stand on their own feet. Women proved that the head on their shoulders was not a dummy, establishing in virtually all fields woman's intellectual equality with man. Women also forced men to accept the fact that women are bifurcated creatures, that they too have those instruments of strength and assertion alleged to be distinctively male, which was why when feminists in the early 1850s put on Bloomers they shocked the world, a shock still reverberating in 1969 when Representative Charlotte Reid's wearing a pantsuit into the House made the front pages of newspapers throughout the country. Reid would not have shocked her colleagues if she had worn the then fashionable miniskirt, which exposed women's legs almost to the crotch. For women were eventually permitted to reveal their legs when they displayed them as decorative sexual props as unlike men's as possible, which was why women's legs had to be shaved of hair, covered with sheer fabrics and were admired for being slim. Not until the late 1960s did a few women dare to stop artificially feminizing their legs by leaving them as hairy as nature made them, by covering them with trousers most of the time and by not fearing to develop the muscles in their calves and thighs by exercise. Female athletes in the 1970s finally got over their fear of having "masculine" biceps and, like men, began to use weights to develop their muscles. Such athletes and the college women who now participate in almost as many sports as men are the heirs of the bold young women in the 1890s who dared take up bicycle riding and the other nineteenth-century sportswomen who began the process of demonstrating that women were not fragile flowers but could be almost as strong as men.

At the same time as women were strengthening their bodies and, by demonstrating their intellectual competence, proving they need not be helpless creatures dependent upon some man, they were also detaching themselves from husbands. Not only did it become much easier for wives to permanently separate themselves from husbands by divorce, but within marriage wives succeeded to a large extent in being treated as separate entities, as persons who could act independently by buying property on their own and by suing and being sued on their own. The process of political separation also began, its aim being to treat women as citizens in their own right, not as potentially or actually merged in the husbands who represented them in the public forum. In other words, women in certain states and for certain purposes won the right to vote, a right fully won in the twentieth century, when women also succeeded in making their wombs their own. In the 1920s women in large numbers began to learn how by various contraceptive devices they themselves could limit the number of babies they had, and in the 1960s and 70s the contraceptive pill made pregnancy a matter of choice determined by the woman alone. And should contraception fail, 1970s court decisions have given the wife the right to have an abortion. The United States Supreme Court held in 1973 that because of a person's right to privacy the decision to have an abortion rested solely with the woman and her physician (Roe v. Wade and Doe v. Bolton, 401 United States Reports 113, 179), a decision interpreted as meaning a wife may have an abortion or be sterilized without her husband's consent. The Oklahoma Court of Appeals, for example, decided in 1974 that a wife had the right to be sterilized in spite of her husband's objections, the judges asserting that "the right of a person...to control his own body is paramount" (Murray v. Vandevander, 522 Pacific Reporter 2d 302). Missouri and other states did pass laws making the husband's consent necessary for an abortion, but in another decision rendered in 1976 the Supreme Court declared such laws unconstitutional (Planned Parenthood of Central Missouri v. Danforth, 96 Supreme Court Reports 2831).

No court would have or could have decided a wife had the right to have an abortion over her husband's objections if men were still believed to be the sole progenitors and women the wombs in which men's seed was brought to fruition. No court would have or could have decided a wife had paramount control over her own body if it had not been discovered that women contributed as much as men to the generation of new life, that women were the procreative equals of men.

## Liberation Names

When women were believed to be merely the conduit pipes through which men reproduced, it made sense that children were given the surname of their only begetter. Recognition of woman's procreative equality with men will mean, therefore, that the custom of giving children the father's surname will break down and, in fact, the tradition of handing down only male names to posterity has already begun to be seriously challenged and defied.

Even in the late nineteenth century one can find occasional rebellions against the male naming tradition among feminists and women outside conventional society. In the 1880s the feminist Alice Chenoweth Smart, instead of merely divesting herself of her husband's surname and using again the name her father conferred on her mother, chose a new, non-hereditary name for herself—Helen Hamilton Gardener. In 1887 the actress Ellen Terry had the surname of her two natural children by Edwin Godwin changed to Craig, a name chosen because on a trip to Scotland she had been struck by the beautiful name of a rock called Ailsa Craig. During the first sixty years of the twentieth century dissatisfaction with the male naming tradition began to increase. In Charlotte Perkins Gilman's 1911 novel *Moving the Mountain* the members of a Utopian community in which men and women were equal gave male children the father's surname and females the mother's, but then the community began to feel that naming system was unsatisfactory: "There's a strong movement on foot to drop hereditary names altogether." Gilman, as usual, was ahead of her times. During the next several decades a few women, like Margaret Bourke-White in the 1920s, Flanders Dunbar in the 1940s, or Dr. Judianne Densen-Gerber in the 1950s, made their mother's maiden surname part of their own name. Rare women, like Dr. May Wilson and Dr. Edith Summerskill, gave their children their own surname, and a handful, like Dr. Marie Stopes, Elsie Hill and Flanders Dunbar, gave their children the combined surname of both parents. But not until the late 1960s did there begin to occur a strong movement to break away from the solid dynasty of male names.

At the March 1970 convention of the National Organization for Women, the resolution advocating that married women keep their own names also suggested that a husband and wife might choose "a neutral second name to be used also by the children" or that the children "use both the wife's and husband's name." During the next few years, in addition to the thousands of women who decided to retain or resume their own name after marriage, a few hundred chose to give themselves or their children a non-traditional name, either a hyphenated or combined surname that recognized woman's contribution to heredity, a mother's surname or first name converted to a surname, or a totally non-hereditary name.

In a 1971 pamphlet a Washington woman informed her parents "Why I Added Legally My Mother's Maiden Name to My Father's Surname." The former Joy Conrad had become Conrad-Rice, adding her mother's maiden name to her father's in order "to declare more accurately my genetic composition."

Conrad-Rice's desire to have her surname reflect her ancestry on her mother's as well as her father's side was shared by many couples who gave their children hyphenated surnames. For example, in 1973 Diana Altman and Richard Siegal of Massachusetts named their daughter Claudia Altman-Siegal and in 1974 Janice Abarbanel and Marshall Wolff of Connecticut named their son Benjamin Abarbanel-Wolff. An Arizona Appeals Court in 1975 had to deal with what the court thought was the first reported case "where the mother has attempted to add her maiden name to the given surname" of her children. A divorced woman, Nancy Eliot Laks, had wanted to change the name of her three children from Laks to Eliot-Laks as "an appropriate recognition of the interests of both parents in a child's name" (Laks v. Laks, 540 Pacific Reporter 2d 1277). Since her ex-husband objected, the court refused her request, but so long as a father did not object, there was no legal obstacle to giving a child a hyphenated surname. There was, rather, the pyramiding obstacle. For should Claudia Altman-Siegal marry Benjamin Abarbanel-Wolff, would their children bear the surname Altman-Siegal-Abarbanel-Wolff? And in the next generation would a husband and wife who each had four surnames give their children eight surnames? Conrad-Rice felt that such a naming system was the only accurate one and that some of the surnames could be abbreviated for most purposes. Other women felt that husband and wife could choose two surnames from the pair each had or that, instead of a hyphenating system, female children could be given the mother's surname and male ones the father's, a naming system advocated by Lucia Lane in her 1974 pamphlet *Equal Names for Equal Sexes*. A few couples obviated the problem by combining their surnames into a single name. Thus in 1975 the former Johanna Boswell and James Hagelin of California had their names legally changed to Boslin.

Other feminists broke with the solid dynasty of male names by changing their surname to their mother's maiden name. A bill introduced into the California legislature in 1971 would have given any person over the age of twenty-one the right to change his or her name to the mother's maiden one. A Massachusetts woman, who in 1973 could not get her own surname recorded as the surname of her child on its birth certificate, demanded that the Attorney General research the law and in January 1974 he issued the opinion that under Massachusetts law a child need not bear its father's surname, that it was only a custom, a custom he felt was likely to change now women were recognized as legal entities and many wives were keeping their own identity after marriage.

Other women, feeling their mother's maiden name was just another male name handed down to posterity, adopted as a surname their mother's first name to which they added the suffix "child" or (much less often) "daughter." Pinny Lauerman in 1971 petitioned an Arizona court to have her surname changed to Debrachild, Debra being her mother's given name. Similarly, the former Kathie Amatniek, a New York radical feminist, changed her surname to Sarachild.

Other women and men broke with tradition by adopting for themselves and/

or their children a name that had no connection with their mother's or their father's. In 1971 the former Mrs. Ron Szymalak of New York, whose maiden name had been Nola Claire Dorries, dropped both her husband's and father's name and had her name legally changed to Nola Claire. In 1972 Susan Sadoff-Lorenzi and Henry Lorenzi of Washington D.C., upon the birth of a child, adopted Sojourner as a family surname, a name chosen to honor Sojourner Truth, the nineteenth-century black woman who preached against slavery and for women's rights, a name that also appealed to them because of the meaning of sojourn—a brief resting place in "the long journey which is life for us all." In 1973 before Ann Gelb and Arnell Pope of San Francisco married, they had their surnames legally changed to Sebastian, a name chosen from Sebastian Dangerfield in J.P. Donleavy's *The Ginger Man,* a character whose confusion and indecisiveness they empathized with. Starting about 1969 a fair number of feminists decided to change their surname or whole name to one symbolic of woman's struggle for equality, among them Ann Forfreedom, Varda One, Ann Pride, Una Stannard, Dair Struggle, Laura X, names Varda One dubbed "liberation names."

A few women and couples decided to give their children a surname different from their own or their spouse's. When the rock star Grace Slick had a daughter in 1971 she said she was not going to give her the name of her husband Jerry Slick or of the child's father Paul Kantner. As she told a *Newsweek* reporter, "Some one else is already using these names." When the actress Jane Fonda and Tom Hayden had a son in 1973 they chose to give him the name Troy O'Donovan Garity.

Fola La Follette in her 1914 speech on a woman's right to keep her name had suggested that parents might "pick the last name for the child the same way they select the first name," and in the future parents might think it as absurd to give each of their children the same surname as we would now think it absurd to give each child the same first name. If each child in a family were given its own surname, that naming system, though it would drive genealogists wild, would not be at odds with the new facts of heredity. A child does get its genes from both parents, but it is no simple amalgam of their traits since it gets only half of each parent's genes, genes, moreover, that are variously recessive and dominant and may give it traits not manifest in the parents but in grandparents or earlier ancestors, all of which variables insure that no person (except for identical twins) is like any other. Since, therefore, every child is unique, it would be biologically accurate to give each child a unique name.

Whatever naming system prevails in the future, the era when children were given only the father's surname is ending because the era when women were believed to be the wombs in which their husbands' progeny was nurtured is also ending....

# AIDS: The Linguistic Battlefield

## Michael Callen

AIDS IS THE MOMENT-TO-MOMENT MANAGEMENT of uncertainty. It's like standing in the middle of the New York Stock Exchange at midday, buzzers and lights flashing, everyone yelling, a million opinions. AIDS is about loss of control—of one's bowels, one's bladder, one's life. And so there is often a ferocious drive by those of us with AIDS to exert at least *some* control over it. When I was diagnosed in 1982, I decided that I'd have to pay close attention to the language of AIDS—to keep my wits about me in order to see beyond the obfuscating medical mumbo-jumbo meant to dazzle me into a deadly passivity.

AIDS is a sprawling topic. War is being waged on many fronts. From the beginning of this epidemic, there have been a number of important battles over how we speak about AIDS which have had subtle but profound effects on how we think about—and respond to—AIDS. These linguistic battles have also affected how those of us diagnosed as having AIDS experience our own illness.

In the early seventies, the gay liberation movement won a smashing victory when it forced the American Psychiatric Association to declassify homosexuality as an illness. But with the creation of a new disease call G.R.I.D., or gay-related immune deficiency, as AIDS was first termed, in an instant, those of us whose primary sexual and affectional attraction is to members of our own sex once again became medicalized and pathologized—only now we were considered literally, as opposed to merely morally, contagious.

Soon, gay-related immune deficiency was discovered in nongay people and a new name for this disease had to be found. All factions were poised for a political battle over the new name. Instinctively, those empowered to create and police the definition of AIDS (and those who would be profoundly affected by it) were aware that the new name would affect how the epidemic would be handled by the federal government and the "general" (meaning, generally, the non-homosexual, non-IV-drug-using, rest-of-you) public.

In the end, a neutral sounding, almost cheerful name was chosen: A.I.D.S. Words can resonate with other words and take on subtle, sympathetic vibrations. AIDS: as in "health and beauty aids" or, to retain some of the sexual connotations of the disease, "marital aids." Or AIDS: as in "aid to the Contras." Or, "now is the time for all good men to come to the aid of their country." "AIDS" sounded like something...well, helpful.

My highly trained eye can now spot the letters A-I-D on a page of newsprint at lightning speed. It's amazing how often those three letters appear in headlines: afrAID, mislAID, medicAID, pAID—even bridesmAIDS. Every time I would hear a newscaster say "The president's aide reported today...," I'd be momentarily disoriented by the linkage of "president" and "AIDS."

It's interesting to speculate, by the way, what the public response to AIDS might have been had the name proposed by a group from Boston prevailed: *herpes virus reactivation syndrome.* Prior to AIDS, the American public—general or otherwise—had been barraged by *Time* magazine cover stories about another fearsome, sexually transmitted epidemic: herpes. If those with the power to name the current plague had linked its name to the herpes epidemic, getting the American public to take AIDS seriously might not have been quite so difficult. One important consequence (some would say cause) of the profound immune disturbance we now call AIDS is that latent herpes viruses are re-activated, leading to a vicious cycle of immune suppression. Had the name *herpes virus reactivation syndrome,* or HVRS, been selected instead of AIDS, it might not have taken so long to convince Americans to support research into a disease which, by name at least, everyone was theoretically at risk for. But perhaps because HVRS, as an acronym, does not roll tripplingly off the tongue, the more neutral sounding AIDS was chosen.

## What the "L" is Going on Here?

The most momentous semantic battle yet fought in the AIDS war concerned the naming of the so-called AIDS virus. The stakes were high; two nations—France and the United States—were at war over who first identified (and therefore had the right to name) the retrovirus presumed to cause AIDS. Hanging in the balance was a Nobel prize and millions of dollars in patent royalties.

U.S. researcher Dr. Robert Gallo had originally proposed that HTLV-I (human T-cell leukemia virus) was the cause of AIDS. Meanwhile, scientists at the Pasteur Institute isolated a novel retrovirus, which they named LAV, to stand for "Lymphadenopathy Associated Virus." The U.S. scoffed at French claims, arrogantly asserting that HTLV-I or HTLV-II must be the cause of AIDS. When it became obvious that neither HTLV-I or II could possibly be the cause, if for no other reason than because Japan (where HTLV-I and II are endemic) was not in the midst of an AIDS epidemic, the U.S. had to find some way to steal both LAV itself as well as the credit for having discovered it first, while covering over the embarrassing fact that they had proposed the wrong virus as "the cause" of AIDS.[1]

What to do? In an election year (1984), it was simply unthinkable that the French could so outshine U.S. medical research. The United States hit upon a brilliant solution. Gallo simply renamed LAV "HTLV-III" and Secretary of Health and Human Services Margaret Heckler staged a preemptive press strike. She declared that another achievement had been added to the long list of U.S. medical breakthroughs: "the probable cause of AIDS has been found—HTLV -III, a variant of a known, human cancer virus...."

The ploy was certainly ballsy. And looking back, amazingly successful.

But what was going on here? The L in HTLV-I and II stands for leukemia, since it is proposed that HTLV-I and II account for a particular form of leukemia. Unfortunately for the perpetrators of this massive fraud, it just so happens that leukemia is one of the few diseases which is *not* a complication of AIDS. So, in order to retain the symmetry of nomenclature, Gallo quietly proposed that the L in HTLV-III and HTLV-IV now stand for *lymphotropic* instead of *leukemia*.

It is now widely acknowledged that HIV is not a member of the HTLV family at all. It is a lentivirus. But the consequences of Gallo's bold attempt at semantic damage control are still with us. The *Index Medicus* listing for AIDS still refers to HTLV-III, not HIV. The legal dispute was eventually settled by the state department; the presidents of the U.S. and France signed an agreement whereby their nations would share credit and royalties, a settlement potentially worth billions. But what was the cost in human lives lost from research delays caused by the willfull misclassification of HIV?...

## Who Has the Power to Name?

The question of who has the power to name is an ongoing turf battle between people with AIDS and those who insist on defining us as victims. I was at the founding of the people with AIDS self-empowerment movement in Denver, Colorado, in 1983. When the California contingent insisted that we make part of our manifesto the demand that we be referred to as "people with AIDS" (or the inevitable acronym "PWAs") instead of "AIDS victims," I must confess that I rolled my eyes heavenward. How California, I thought.

But time has proven them right. Americans, whose ability to think has been desiccated by decades of television and its ten-second sound-bite mentality, think in one-word descriptors. Someone on the TV screen must be labeled: a feminist, a communist, a homosexual, an AIDS victim. The difference between the descriptors *person with AIDS* and *AIDS victim* seems subtle until one watches oneself on reruns on TV. To see oneself on screen and have the words *AIDS victim* magically flash underneath has a very different feel about it than when the description *person with AIDS* appears. Its very cumbersomeness is startling and makes the viewer ask: "Person? Why person? Of course he's a person...." In that moment, we achieve a small but important victory. Viewers are forced to be conscious, if only for a moment, that we *are* people first.

The founding statement of the PWA self-empowerment movement (known as the "Denver Principles") is quite eloquent on this point:

> We condemn attempts to label us as "victims," which implies defeat; and we are only occasionally "patients," which implies passivity, helplessness and dependence upon the care of others. We are "people with AIDS."[2]

This statement was further refined in the founding Mission Statement of the National Association of People with AIDS (NAPWA):

> We are people with AIDS and people with AIDS-Related Complex (ARC) who can speak for ourselves to advocate for our own causes and concerns. We are your sons and daughters, your brothers and sisters, your family, friends and lovers. As people now living with AIDS and ARC, we have a unique and essential contribution to make to the dialogue surrounding AIDS and we will actively participate with full and equal credibility to help shape the perception and reality surrounding this disease.
>
> We do not see ourselves as victims. We will not be victimized. We have the right to be treated with respect, dignity, compassion and understanding. We have the right to lead fulfilling, productive lives—to live and die with dignity and compassion.

In a gratuitous aside in his best-selling AIDS epic, *And the Band Played On*, Randy Shilts attacked the right of people with AIDS to choose how they wish to be referred to. Completely twisting the empowering impulse of people with AIDS to wrest some control of our lives, Shilts accused us of attempting to minimize the tragedy of AIDS:

> AIDSpeak, a new language forged by public health officials, anxious gay politicians, and the burgeoning ranks of "AIDS activists." The linguistic roots of AIDSpeak sprouted not so much from the truth as from what was politically facile and psychologically reassuring. Semantics was the major denominator of AIDSpeak jargon, because the language went to great lengths never to offend.
>
> A new lexicon was evolving. Under the rules of AIDSpeak, for exam-

ple, AIDS victims could not be called victims. Instead, they were to be called People with AIDS, or PWAs, as if contracting this uniquely brutal disease was not a victimizing experience. "Promiscuous" became "sexually active," because gay politicians declared "promiscuous" to be "judgemental," a major cuss word in AIDSpeak. The most-used circumlocution in AIDSpeak was "bodily fluids," an expression that avoided troublesome words like "semen."

...Thus, the verbiage tended toward the intransitive. AIDSpeak was rarely empowered to motivate action; rather, it was most articulately pronounced when justifying inertia. Nobody meant any harm by this; quite to the contrary, AIDSpeak was the tongue designed to make everyone content. AIDSpeak was the language of good intentions in the AIDS epidemic; AIDSpeak was a language of death.[3]

Shilts notwithstanding, there is now a movement to further emphasize hope. In some quarters PLWAs and PLWArcs have entered the language: Persons *Living* with AIDS and Persons *Living* with ARC, respectively. There is also a new movement to organize all individuals suffering from conditions related to immune deficiency. Acronym conscious, its leaders say they are "PISD" (pronounced "pissed"), which stands for "Persons with Immune System Disorders"...

## An Epidemic of Acronyms

There is a separate, specialist language of the AIDS subculture which must be mastered if one wishes to be considered AIDS literate. And this language contains a great deal of shorthand. To the uninitiated, hearing a conversation among urban gay men is like stumbling into a medical convention and being dazzled and dazed by an explosion of acronyms. Here are just a few one must recognize to be included among the AIDS cognoscenti: AB+; Ab-; ACTG/ATEU; ARC; ASFV; AZT; CBC; $CD_4+$; CD8+; CDC; CMV; ddA; ddC; ddI; DFMO; DHEA; DHPG; DNCB; DTC; EBV; ELISA; EPO; FDA; GM-CSF; HBLV; HBV; HIV; HIV-1; HIV-2; HSV-1; HSV-2; HTLV-I, II, III, and IV; IL-1 and IL-2; IND; IVDAs or IVDUs; KS; LAS; LAV; MAI; NIAID; NIH; NK; O/I; PCR; PCP; $T_4$; TB; TNF; and WBC.

We're in the midst of an epidemic of acronyms. Whatever else AIDS may be, it is itself an acronym. When first introduced, AIDS used to be clearly identified as an acronym because it always appeared with dots: A.I.D.S. Then, consistent with the American tendency towards elision, reduction, and (over) simplification, AIDS rapidly dropped the periods and became a thing in and of itself. In Britain, except for the curious initial capital A, AIDS has lost all sense of ever having been an acronym; it is generally referred to as "Aids." (One never sees *syphilis* or *gonorrhea* with an initial capital.)

The acronym epidemic threatens to get out of hand. We even have acronyms within acronyms, as in AIDS-Related Complex—which stands for Acquired Immune Deficiency Syndrome-Related Complex. It verges on an infinite regress. ARC-related symptoms actually translates: Acquired Immune Deficiency Syndrome Related Complex related symptoms. Another redundancy in common usage is *HIV virus,* which translates into "Human Immunodeficiency Virus Virus." I propose that we insist on referring to "the human immuno-deficiency virus" or "the HI virus."

Is there anyone who can talk about AIDS and emerge from the battle unscathed? Probably not. We all want to control AIDS somehow, and at times language seems to be our only weapon. But we must not try to master AIDS by crushing its complexities, mysteries, and terrors into convenient labels that roll trippingly and with false authority off the tongue. We must always speak fully and carefully about AIDS, even if that often requires a mouthful—cumbersome constructions full of words strung together by hyphens—to say precisely what we mean. The stakes are simply too high to do otherwise.

**Notes**

1.  The saga of the competition between U.S. and French AIDS researchers reads like a bad espionage novel. Gallo requested, and the French twice supplied, cultures of LAV. At the time, Gallo claimed that he was not able to grow LAV from these samples. A recent BBC documentary, however, produced evidence of altered documents, suggesting that in fact U.S. researchers had grown LAV from the French cultures. Embarrassingly for Gallo, when he first published on "HTLV-III," he mistakenly provided an electron micrograph photo of "LAV" taken for the French. More damning still, when a DNA-fingerprinting was done on Gallo's HTLV-III and the French's LAV, they were found to be essentially identical.

2.  "The Denver Principles," quoted in *Surviving and Thriving with AIDS: Collected Wisdom,* vol. 2, ed. Michael Callen (New York, 1988).

3.  Randy Shilts, *And the Band Played On: The Politics of AIDS* (New York, 1987), pp. 314–15.

# Sex, Class and Race Intersections/Visions of Women of Color

## Carol Lee Sanchez

*"As I understand it," said the American Indian [to one of the Puritan Fathers], "you propose to civilize me."*

*"Exactly."*

*"You want to get me out of the habit of idleness and teach me to work."*

*"That is the idea."*

*"And then lead me to simplify my methods and invent things to make my work lighter."*

*"Yes."*

*"And after that I'll become ambitious to get rich so that I won't have to work at all."*

*"Naturally."*

*"Well what's the use of taking such a roundabout way of getting just where I started from? I don't have to work now."*

*(American Jokelore)*

TO IDENTIFY INDIAN IS TO IDENTIFY with an invisible or vanished people; it is to identify with a set of basic assumptions and beliefs held by *all* who are not Indian about the indigenous peoples of the Americas. Even among the Spanish-speaking Mestizos or mezclados, there is a strong preference to "disappear" their Indian blood, to disassociate from their Indian beginnings.

To be Indian is to be considered "colorful," spiritual, connected to the earth, simplistic, and disappointing if not dressed in buckskin and feathers; shocking if a city-dweller and even more shocking if an educator or other type of professional. That's the positive side.

On the negative side, to be Indian is to be thought of as primitive, alcoholic, ignorant (as in "Dumb Indian"), better off dead (as in "the only good Indian is a dead Indian" or "I didn't know there was any of you folks still left"), unskilled, non-competitive, immoral, pagan or heathen, untrustworthy (as in "Indian-giver") and frightening. To be Indian is to be the primary model that is used to promote racism in this country.

How can that happen, you ask? Bad press. One hundred and fifty years of the most consistently vicious press imaginable. Newspapers, dime novels, textbooks and fifty years of visual media have portrayed and continue to portray Indians as savage, blood-thirsty, immoral, inhuman people. When there's a touch of social consciousness attached, you will find the once "blood-thirsty," "white-killer savage" portrayed as a pitiful drunk, a loser, an outcast or a mix-blood not welcomed by, or trusted by, either race. For fifty years, children in this country have been raised to kill Indians mentally, subconsciously through the visual media, until it is an automatic reflex. That shocks you? Then I have made my point.

Let me quote from Helen Hunt Jackson's book, *A Century of Dishonor*, from the introduction written by Bishop H. B. Whipple of Minnesota, who charged that:

> the American people have accepted as truth the teachings that the Indians were a degraded, brutal race of savages, who it was the will of God should perish at the approach of civilization. If they do not say with our Puritan fathers that these are the Hittites who are to be driven out before the saints of the Lord, they do accept the teaching that manifest destiny will drive the Indians from the earth. The inexorable has no tears or pity at the cries of anguish of the doomed race.

This race still struggles to stay alive. Tribe by Tribe, pockets of Indian people here and there. One million two hundred thousand people who identify as Indians—raised and socialized as Indian—as of the 1980 census, yet Cowboys and Indians is still played every day by children all over America of every creed, color, and nationality. Well—it's harmless isn't it? Just kids playing kill Indians. It's all history. But it's still happening every day, and costumes are sold and the cheap western is still rolling out of Hollywood, the old shoot-'em-up westerns playing on afternoon kid shows, late night T.V. Would you allow your children to play Nazis and Jews? Blacks and KKKs? Complete with costume? Yes! It is a horrifying thought, but in thinking about it you can see how easy it is to dismiss an entire race of people as barbaric and savage, and how almost impossible it is, after this has been inculcated in you, to relate to an Indian or a group of Indians today. For example, how many famous Indians do you know offhand? Certainly the great warrior chiefs come to mind first, and of course the three most famous Indian "Princesses"—Pocahantas, Sacajawea and La Malinche. Did you get past ten? Can you name at least five Indian women you know personally or have heard about? That's just counting on one hand, folks.

As Indians, we have endured. We are still here. We have survived everything that European "civilization" has imposed on us. There are approximately 130 different Indian languages still spoken in North America of the some 300 spoken at contact; 180 different Tribes incorporated and recognized by the Federal Government of the approximately 280 that once existed, with an additional 15 to 25 unrecognized Tribes that are lumped together on a reservation with other Tribes. We still have Women's Societies and there are at least 30 active women-centered Mother–Rite Cultures existing and practicing their everyday life in that manner, on this continent.

We have been displaced, relocated, removed, terminated, educated, acculturated and in our hearts and minds we will always "go back to the blanket" as long as we are still connected to our families, our Tribes and our land.

The Indian Way is a different way. It is a respectful way. The basic teachings in every Tribe that exists today as a Tribe in the western hemisphere are based on respect for all the things our Mother gave us. If we neglect her or anger her, she will make our lives very difficult and we always know that we have a hardship on ourselves and on our children. We are raised to be cautious and concerned for the *future* of our people, and that is how we raise our children—because *they* are *our* future. Your "civilization" has made all of us very sick and has made our mother earth sick and out of balance. Your kind of thinking and education has brought the whole world to the brink of total disaster, whereas the thinking and education among my people forbids the practice of almost everything Euro-Americans, in particular, value.

Those of you who are socialists and marxists have an ideology, but where in this country do you live communally on a common land base from generation to generation? Indians, who have a way of life instead of an ideology, do live on communal lands and don't accumulate anything—for the sake of accumulation.

Radicals look at reservation Indians and get very upset about their poverty conditions. But poverty to us is not the same thing as poverty is to you. Our poverty is that we can't be who we are. We can't hunt or fish or grow our food because our basic resources and the right to use them in traditional ways are denied us. In order to live well, we must be able to provide for ourselves in such a way that we can continue living as we always have. We still don't believe in being slaves to the "domineering" culture systems. Consequently, we are accused of many things based on those standards and values that make no sense to us.

You want us to act like you, to be like you so that we will be more accept-able, more likeable. You should try to be more like us regarding communal co-existence; respect and care for all living things and for the earth, the waters, and the atmosphere; respect for human dignity and the right to be who they are.

During the 1930s, '40s and '50s, relocation programs caused many Indians to become lost in the big cities of the United States and there were many casual-ties from alcoholism, vagrancy and petty crime. Most Indians were/are jailed for assault and battery in barroom brawls because the spiritual and psychological violation of Indian people trying to live in the dominant [domineering] culture generally forces us to numb ourselves as frequently as possible. That is difficult, if not impossible, for you to understand. White science studies dead things and creates poisonous substances to kill and maim the creatures as well as the hu-mans. You call that progress. Indians call it insanity. Our science studies living things; how they interact and how they maintain a balanced existence. Your science disregards—even denies—the spirit world; ours believes in it and re-mains connected to it. We fast, pray to our ancestors, call on them when we dance and it rains—at Laguna, at Acoma, at Hopi—still, today. We fight among ourselves, we have border disputes, we struggle to exist in a modern context with our lands full of timber, uranium, coal, oil, gasoline, precious metals and semi-precious stones; full—because we are taught to take only what we need and not because we are too ignorant to know what to do with all these resources. We are caught in the bind between private corporations and the government—"our guardian"—because they/you want all those resources. "Indians certainly don't need them"—and your people will do *anything* to get their hands on our miner-al-rich lands. They will legislate, stir up internal conflicts, cause inter-Tribal conflicts, dangle huge amounts of monies as compensation for perpetual con-tracts and promise lifetime economic security. If we object, or sue to protect our lands, these suits will be held in litigation for fifteen to twenty years with "white" interests benefiting in the interim. Some of us give up and sell out, but there are many of us learning to hold out and many many more of us going back to the old ways of thinking, because we see that our ancestors were right and that the old ways were better ways. So, more Indians are going "back to the blanket," back to "Indian time," with less stress, fewer dominant [domineering] culture activities and occupations. Modern Indians are recreating Indian ways once again. All this leads to my vision as an Indian woman. It is my hope:

1. that you—all you non-Indians—study and learn about our systems of thought and internal social and scientific practices, leaving your Patriarchal Anthropology and History textbooks, academic training and methodologies at home or in the closet on a dusty shelf.

2. that your faculties, conference organizers, community organizers stop giving lip service to including a "Native American" for this or that with the

appended phrase: "if we only knew one!" Go find one. There are hundreds of resource lists or Indian-run agencies, hundreds of Indian women in organizations all over the country—active and available with valuable contributions to make.

3. that you will strongly discourage or STOP the publication of any and all articles *about* Indians *written by non-Indians,* and publish work written by Indians about ourselves—whether you agree with us, approve of us or not.

4. that you will *stop colonizing us* and reinterpreting our experience.

5. that you will *listen* to us and *learn* from us. We carry ancient traditions that are thousands of years old. We are modern and wear clothes like yours and handle all the trappings of your "civilization" as well as ours; maintain your christianity as well as our ancient religions, and we are still connected to our ancestors, and our land base. You are the foreigners as long as you continue to believe in the progress that destroys our Mother.

You are not taught to respect our perfected cultures or our scientific achievements which have just recently been re-evaluated by your social scientists and "deemed worthy" of respect. Again, let me re-state that 150 years of bad press will certainly make it extremely difficult for most white people to accept these "primitive" achievements without immediately attempting to connect them to aliens from outer space, Egyptians, Vikings, Asians and whatever sophisticated "others" you have been educated to acknowledge as those who showed the "New World" peoples "The Way." Interestingly, the only continents that were ever "discovered" (historically) where people already lived are North and South America. Who discovered Europe? Who discovered Africa? Who discovered Asia? Trade routes, yes—continents, no. Manifest Destiny will continue to reign as long as we teach our children that Columbus "discovered" America. Even this "fact" is untrue. He actually discovered an island in the Caribbean and failed to discover Cathay!

When we consistently make ourselves aware of these "historical facts" that are presented by the Conqueror—the White Man—only then can all of us benefit from cultural traditions that are ten to thirty thousand years old. It is time for us to share the best of all our traditions and cultures, all over the world; and it is our duty and responsibility as the women of the world to make this positive contribution in any and every way we can, or we will ultimately become losers, as the Native Race of this hemisphere lost some four hundred years ago.

# What's in a Name?

## Gloria Naylor

LANGUAGE IS THE SUBJECT. It is the written form with which I've managed to keep the wolf away from the door and, in diaries, to keep my sanity. In spite of this, I consider the written word inferior to the spoken, and much of the frustration experienced by novelists is the awareness that whatever we manage to capture in even the most transcendent passages falls far short of the richness of life. Dialogue achieves its power in the dynamics of a fleeting moment of sight, sound, smell and touch.

I'm not going to enter the debate here about whether it is language that shapes reality or vice versa. That battle is doomed to be waged whenever we seek intermittent reprieve from the chicken and egg dispute. I will simply take the position that the spoken word, like the written word, amounts to a non-sensical arrangement of sounds or letters without a consensus that assigns "meaning." And building from the meanings of what we hear, we order reality. Words themselves are innocuous; it is the consensus that gives them true power.

I remember the first time I heard the word nigger. In my third-grade class, our math tests were being passed down the rows, and as I handed the papers to a little boy in back of me, I remarked that once again he had received a much lower mark than I did. He snatched his test from me and spit out that word. Had he called me a nymphomaniac or a necrophiliac, I couldn't have been more puzzled. I didn't know what a nigger was, but I knew that whatever it meant, it was something he shouldn't have called me. This was verified when I raised my hand, and in a loud voice repeated what he had said and watched the teacher scold him for using a "bad" word. I was later to go home and ask the inevitable

*From* The New York Times, *Feb. 20, 1986. Copyright © 1986 by Gloria Naylor. Reprinted by permission of the author.*

question that every black parent must face—"Mommy, what does 'nigger' mean?"

And what exactly did it mean? Thinking back, I realize that this could not have been the first time the word was used in my presence. I was part of a large extended family that had migrated from the rural South after World War II and formed a close-knit network that gravitated around my maternal grandparents. Their ground floor apartment in one of the buildings they owned in Harlem was a weekend mecca for my immediate family, along with countless aunts, uncles and cousins who brought along assorted friends. It was a bustling and open house with assorted neighbors and tenants popping in and out to exchange bits of gossip, pick up an old quarrel or referee the ongoing checkers game in which my grandmother cheated shamelessly. They were all there to let down their hair and put up their feet after a week of labor in the factories, laundries and ship-yards of New York.

Amid the clamor, which could reach deafening proportions—two or three conversations going on simultaneously, punctuated by the sound of a baby's crying somewhere in the back rooms or out on the street—there was still a rigid set of rules about what was said and how. Older children were sent out of the living room when it was time to get into the juicy details about "you-know-who" up on the third floor who had gone and gotten herself "p-r-e-g-n-a-n-t!" But my parents, knowing that I could spell well beyond my years, always demanded that I follow the others out to play. Beyond sexual misconduct and death, everything else was considered harmless for our young ears. And so among the anecdotes of the triumphs and disappointments in the various workings of their lives, the word nigger was used in my presence, but it was set within contexts and inflections that caused it to register in my mind as something else.

In the singular, the word was always applied to a man who had distinguished himself in some situation that brought their approval for his strength, intelligence or drive:

"Did Johnny *really* do that?"

"I'm telling you, that nigger pulled in $6,000 of overtime last year. Said he got enough for a down payment on a house."

When used with a possessive adjective by a woman—"my nigger"—it became a term of endearment for husband or boyfriend. But it could be more than just a term applied to a man. In their mouths it became the pure essence of manhood—a disembodied force that channeled their past history of struggle and present survival against the odds into a victorious statement of being: "Yeah, that old foreman found out quick enough—you don't mess with a nigger."

In the plural, it became a description of some group within the community that had overstepped the bounds of decency as my family defined it: Parents who neglected their children, a drunken couple who fought in public, people who simply refused to look for work, those with excessively dirty mouths or unkempt households were all "trifling niggers." This particular circle could forgive hard times, unemployment, the occasional bout of depression—they had gone through all of that themselves—but the unforgivable sin was a lack of self-respect.

A woman could never be a "nigger" in the singular, with its connotation of confirming worth. The noun girl was its closest equivalent in that sense, but only when used in direct address and regardless of the gender doing the addressing. "Girl" was a token of respect for a woman. The one-syllable word was drawn out to sound like three in recognition of the extra ounce of wit, nerve or daring that the woman had shown in the situation under discussion.

"G-i-r-l, stop. You mean you said that to his face?"

But if the word was used in a third-person reference or shortened so that it almost snapped out of the mouth, it always involved some element of communal disapproval. And age became an important factor in these exchanges. It was only between individuals of the same generation, or from an older person to a younger (but never the other way around), that "girl" would be considered a compliment.

I don't agree with the argument that use of the word nigger at this social stratum of the black community was an internalization of racism. The dynamics were the exact opposite: the people in my grandmother's living room took a word that whites used to signify worthlessness or degradation and rendered it impotent. Gathering there together, they transformed "nigger" to signify the varied and complex human beings they knew themselves to be. If the word was to disappear totally from the mouths of even the most liberal of white society, no one in that room was naïve enough to believe it would disappear from white minds. Meeting the word head-on, they proved it had absolutely nothing to do with the way they were determined to live their lives.

So there must have been dozens of times that the word "nigger" was spoken in front of me before I reached the third grade. But I didn't "hear" it until it was said by a small pair of lips that had already learned it could be a way to humiliate me. That was the word I went home and asked my mother about. And since she knew that I had to grow up in America, she took me in her lap and explained.

# When the Words Open into Some Not Yet Open Space

## Minnie Bruce Pratt

LAST FRIDAY I CLEANED OUT MISS BROWN'S APARTMENT, full of old newspapers, roaches, leaking canned goods, empty tubes of zinc oxide for bed sores, greeting cards from the women she'd once clerked with at Lansburg's. I saved some of the cards, her brush and comb, underwear, a few dresses; she can't keep much in a two-foot wide closet in the nursing home. I found letters that she'd written last spring when she'd been so worried about money: the same sentence, written over and over, instructions to Social Security on how to send her money to her home address, not to the bank, she was ninety-two, couldn't go out anymore to the bank, couldn't get her money unless they'd send it to her home address, 518 Ninth St., #203, she was ninety-two, not strong enough to go out, wouldn't be able to get her money unless they sent it to her home, not the bank, not strong enough to go out, she was ninety-two ....Pages and pages of the same letter, stuck in old phone books, in a dictionary, in her kitchen cabinet in piles of folded wax paper, between paper plates with quarters and pennies in case of an emergency. Pages of pleading messages, never mailed, but written over and over, a prayer, a magic incantation, the words willing that some action be taken, that help appear: the words calling up action.

Back in town at the end of last spring, after a long absence, I heard from Mr. Cox that Miss Brown was distraught. I went to her and settled how she could get her money. The written word had not brought me; but she had fixed her need inexorably in her fading mind by writing over and over, by repeating to herself and then to others what was necessary, until something was done.

Now her piles of old newspapers, clippings of celebrities and atrocities, remind me of my own boxes of yellowed papers, cut from the newspaper of any town where I've lived, and saved as notes for some future poem or essay. I finger her desperate letters to the authorities and think of the book of poems that I've just finished, the poems where I tell over and over the story of my life, my love for another woman, the loss of my two boys to their father: anger, injustice, grief, almost unendurable pain, isolation, joy, reconciliation, defiant laughter, poem after poem. But was my writing the same as hers? A shout to someone to do something; a reminder to myself of what I needed to remember, words to center me in a hostile and chaotic universe; a clinging to what I needed in order to go on with my life on the edge, on the margin of power. I shudder with recognition at the repeated phrases, at her grip on the centrality of her own need, her life.

After a poetry reading at a small new women's bookstore, a woman approaches and says to me, "I feel that if I said what you just said, lightning would strike me." I had just read some poems that were explicitly sexual and lesbian; I'd talked about my children, my lover, my mother; I'd said the word *lesbian* several times. Her reaction to this wasn't uncommon: sometimes after I read my work, women are silent or shrink back from me as if there is some scorched smoking circle of dirt around me, as if I'd been struck, for my sin, with lightning by god; as if I might be struck down, for my rebellion, by some unseen power.

During this reading, as I spoke I had a flash, a jump of my heart, that I was saying the word *lesbian* too many times. After all, it was a new bookstore; perhaps this first reading would give it a reputation as "too lesbian" and women would be afraid to come. And the program for which I was in town as resident writer was a community program; maybe it would damage them somehow that I and my poems were being so unmistakably clear. A flash of doubt, though I didn't change anything I was saying or reading, a flashback on other moments when I opened up my mouth and *lesbian* came out in one form or another; and I feared the blow. As if my word might vaporize my children, my mother, the person offering me a job I needed, might obliterate me and my lover in a public place. The power of my own word turned against me.

After the reading, I talk to another woman who comes up to thank me. I speak of my fear of saying too much, of being "too lesbian." She is surprised that I still worry about this, surprised that I would hesitate. She thinks of me as "brave," as "strong," as "beyond" that fear. I don't think of myself as brave or strong. The only way to understand that I exist from one day to the next, one year to the next, is to write down my life, and in the end, send this out to others. The poems sent or read aloud: like someone writing an obscure sacred document. Is this power? It does not feel like power, but necessity.

Yet there are moments when the words open into some not yet open space. Then I feel I am stepping into power. And perhaps it is then, hearing those words, that others think, "This is the moment she will be struck down."

When I was thirteen I began keeping a journal in spiral-bound flimsy notebooks. But I never promised myself that I would be a writer. Instead I said: *I'll learn to fly a plane, I'll travel around the world.* Escape, escape. I quit writing in my journals when I left home for college, though I wrote a few poems during my first two years at the university.

Finally, I married the man who was the editor of a literary magazine, a poet. (I joke bitterly sometimes that I wanted to be a poet and married one instead, the same way my girl cousin who wanted to be a veterinarian married one.) Not long after we married, at a party at our house in the middle of a smoldering cloud of cigarette smoke and a fog of alcohol, our philosophy professor pointed at me and declared: "You'll go to grad school; you can have an academic career." Laying his hand on my husband's arm, he said: "You will be the poet."

I stopped writing poetry after I married at twenty, had a child at twenty-one, and another child eighteen months later. For a long time after I married and bore my two sons, I heard nothing inside me, nothing at all, as if a door had closed on some inner voice, a heavy wooden door, thick, impenetrable. Perhaps I had closed it myself.

Ten years later, I began a new poem, one about my husband trying to kill me in various ways—with a homemade bomb, by handing me over to men who shot me, by turning me over to the police. A poem with images of him rising from pond water, a dead man "glowing yellow-green/bloated with invitation." A poem about my running away from him with the children, across the South "on Greyhounds, in strangers' cars."[1]

A poem in which I leave out the reason I fear him: I have fallen in love with another woman, am mad for her, mad about her, and he knows. I drink power from her body and mine, sexual power that opens and unfolds into another future, an ecstatic vista, unseen, unknown, taken on faith. I'm afraid he will pursue me down that mysterious way, coming after the power I take away from him; my sex, my secret, my words, my need, my key to the door he has not yet entered himself.

A few weeks after the beginning of my first love affair with a woman, I attended with her a conference where, one night, Robin Morgan read. I admired her work as ambitious, I envied her rolling lines, her weightiness; yet now I can't remember a single word she spoke. But I have carried with me since then the words of the other poet who read that night, Audre Lorde. She was the first writer, and the first poet, I heard speak publicly as a lesbian. That night she began with the revelatory words of her love poem to another woman: "Speak earth and bless me with what is richest."[2] Words praising her life, my life, spoken out loud before thousands of other women.

I was blessed, as a lesbian poet, that I could turn to Lorde's writing for hope in the flesh; and to Judy Grahn's poems for her answer to those who would try lesbians with a bitter judgment, condemn us to suffering and death. I was blessed to begin my life as a writer when women who loved other women were creating a world of politics and culture from their lives. I think I began to live as a lesbian and work as a poet only because other lesbians asserted that there *was* an *us* to listen, to talk to. Slowly, I began to write poetry and to think of myself, not yet as a poet, but, in Grahn's words, as "a woman who believes her own word."[3] These two women, close to me in age, but seemingly separated from me, one by class, one by race, gave me the clearest answers to the question, "What would happen if one woman told the truth about her life?/The world would split open."[4]

When I turned for guidance to the woman who had asked this question in her own poetry, a woman of my mother's generation, Muriel Rukeyser, I learned that she also was a lover of women. I looked in her work for this love. But in the few possible poems the pronoun was *you*; there was no *she*; and the most explicitly lesbian poem (about nonprocreative sex) was "the Conjugation of the Paramecium," which described a slow "inexplicable" exchange of "some bits of nucleus" between two of these simple one-celled animals. She did assign "renewal/strength another joy" to this process, but this was hardly the grandeur with which she expanded on the life of Kathe Kollwitz, wife, mother, artist, who was the inspiration for her lines on truth and the splitting of the world. I could find in Rukeyser's poetry no similar nakedness of truth about a lesbian life. I felt a huge anger, a condemning anger, the anger of betrayal: why had she not told her *own* life clearly?

I felt the same anger when I turned to the words of Lillian Smith, who was, like me, white and Southern-born, also of the generation before me, whose work I had leaned on, who knew how each person had within her "a poet and a demagogue," one creating, the other attempting to destroy. And I learned that Smith had loved Paula Snelling for forty years, and had lived with her, and was her lover for at least some of this time, but that she could not bear the word *lesbian*, and with despisal had denied her own name.

In her essay, "The Role of the Poet in a World of Demagogues," Smith speaks of "the beats and the smokers of pot and the kids in high school who are now drug addicts and the young homosexuals flaunting their deviations and the young heterosexuals flaunting theirs. So few thinking in terms of the *quality* of relationships...."[5] But what of the quality of her relationship with Paula, denied for all those years?

Smith said in this same essay: "It is the omissions, *the absence of context,* that so dangerously distorts things." Did she think she would be struck down, blown up, if she spoke of her love for another woman? Did she think she would lose everything she loved, beyond what she lost by speaking out against segregation in the South? I say angrily to myself and to her, dead now twenty years:

*What about the omission of "the deep truths" of your life with Paula? What about this distortion?* Angrily, because I needed her life as a way of understanding how to live my own.

I am angry because now I have to do, as a lesbian, the work she did not do—the splitting of the self open, over and over, the telling of the story, the risk of condemnation, the risk of loss. But I know that Lillian, and Muriel, did not have an *us*, and that I can write of my lesbian life only because a circle of women has been created to speak into.

As I work at my desk, under my window, two floors down, the next-door church is having Sunday morning service, and the day vibrates with gospel song, handclaps, the beat of drum and tambourine, crying out to God. At home on Sunday mornings when I was little, I could hear through the silence our church bell clanging, flat, brassy, calling us to come hear the voice of God in his Word. Three times a week I sat and listened to those beautiful and terrifying words, spoken by men who firmly believed in leading me down their way.

I had no place to go, three times a week, to hear a lesbian voice. How have we ever found each other? For a long time we sought each other only through the wordless look: searching for the other woman who was also looking, *really looking at you,* and seeing you, the woman who was the other lesbian. For a long time there were no public words for us, no definition for *lesbian* in the dictionary that described our life, no books in the library that named us other than "sick," "unnatural," "kin to thieves, murderers, and liars," and those books usually kept behind locked doors where perverted books belonged.

How did we find each other? We made a political movement and a culture; we taught ourselves to speak, to write, to sing; we heard each other and we found each other. Travelling one winter after I had left my husband, I went to a solstice ritual in Atlanta, held in a house the lesbian-feminist alliance had opened there, and I met Mab, a lesbian, a writer, also heading home to Alabama. I gave her a ride, and a friendship began that led to a decision: we couldn't wait for the world to name us writers, we must create ourselves. Mab asked me to work on the editorial collective of *Feminary*, literary journal for lesbians in the South, based in North Carolina; a publication rooted in a local women's liberation newsletter. We each self-published our first chapbooks of poetry. With other lesbians, we went on to organize a yearly writing conference for lesbians in the South, WomanWrites, also collectively run, with the firm rule that no "stars" were to be paid and brought in to teach us how to write: we would teach each other.[6]

And that is how I learned to be a lesbian poet: other lesbians taught me how. I learned by driving through the South in my VW bug to do the poetry readings that lesbians organized at a conference against domestic violence in Little Rock; at a women's health club in Fayetteville, Arkansas; at an abortion clinic in New Orleans; at a gay Metropolitan Community Church in Jackson, Mississippi; at someone's home in Gainesville, Florida; at a women's salon in a Quaker meeting house in St. Petersburg; at a women's bookstore in Birmingham; at a Women's Studies program in Tuscaloosa. I learned in writing groups with other lesbians; I learned from the comments and encouragement of lesbian editors and publishers.

They gave me the hope to keep on writing, the faith that there is another energy, another being, alert, looking for me, looking back. The faith that the words will find someone, not as a prayer to a god, but as the vibration of a sound that calls sound from another.

In the warm steam of us cooking supper together, I sat talking to other women, gathered by Susan and Betty, from all across the South: lesbians, poets, talking at once. I said loudly that I had vowed always to put something in my writing so people would know I was a lesbian. At the corner of the table one of us leaned forward to speak out of the bitter experience of years, "No matter what you say, they'll always deny it."

Years later, Joan and I, holding hands, were catcalled and harassed by a bunch of young white men, the usual ridicule and shouts and the car speeding by. From a friend, some weeks after, I heard that a print artist was looking for poems inspired by specific locations in D.C. I wrote a poem about that night as if to a passerby, "To Be Posted on 21st Street Between Eye and Pennsylvania."[7] I wrote about being a lesbian; about being hated because of how I love; about trying to open my life into places not yet open to me. The man rejected my poem, because it was "too long for the printing format," and also, he said, "Is it *really* a poem? It's so *direct*."

Unless I write explicitly of how I am a lesbian, I will be denied my identity, my reality. When I do write explicitly, I am denied art.

I could choose an aesthetic of indirection, like a flash of lightning, white, on blank white paper, a subtle illumination of nothing that can be named. Instead I keep trying to write poems that hold, in some way, the idea of *lesbian*.

In a literature seminar this past winter, a student asks, "Why do you *need* to describe yourself as a *lesbian poet* on the back cover of your book?" Sometimes I feel like I'm writing a letter, the page covered with scrawled words like a prayer, the same letter over and over, without knowing who will read or understand it.

But I have been answered. Sometimes the listener raises her hand to still my words because they clash with her life. Sometimes her hand and her voice send her own words back to me:

> In the very beginning Donna and Lucy in our living
> room: making me recite poems out loud to them,
> over and over, shaping my meaning, tone,
> phrasing, so I could go to my first public
> reading as a lesbian, "So you won't disgrace us."

The woman who wrote from prison to say:
"I have sincerely enjoyed your poems—
In your writings, you have expressed
so many of the walled-up feelings that
women have had in their hearts, and
many of your poems brought tears to
my eyes.—You said so many things
That we carry locked up inside from
generation to generation passed on
from mother to daughter, from a
grandmother! Sisterly, I remain, Helene."

At a conference on battered women,
the lesbian who walked out while I was reading,
who later told me she couldn't bear the splitting
images of violence which offered her no relief from
her work every day.

The woman who wrote to say that as a
lesbian she'd been unable to look at her past, the
forced sex with men which she had always named
"not-rape," until reading some of my poems
she began to remember, and remember.

The young sorority women, reminding
me of myself twenty years before, who
chatted loudly as I read of the rape of
a woman lover; who were silenced by the cold
fury of my look; who walked out in the middle
of the next poem when I spoke, with a sacred
meaning, the word *cunt*.

The women friends who told me they kept my poems
by their bed and made love after reading them;
The dyke who said she read the love poems in
her bathtub; the university colleague, a lesbian,
who said uneasily that she felt like a voyeur
listening to me read erotic poems.

The woman who came up after a reading and said,
"I don't usually like poetry; it seems too
distant; nothing to do with me; but I like your
poetry."

The woman reviewer who, after finding me lacking
in comparison to Milton, said my work wasn't
poetry: I should simply stop writing.

The friend, a writer and a lesbian, who heard me
read some of the poems about my children; who
gave me nothing afterwards but a hug and a burning
look; who told me later she went home and started
a new short story; who said, "I kept thinking of
all the *work* in the poems."

My mother, sitting at the kitchen table,
who said of my work, "I can't be proud of you;
I want to be, but I can't." My acceptance of
that statement, as both rejection and love,
with my reply: "I know that; but I'm proud
of what I do." Admitting this moment as a
flash of truth between us, painful, intense;
my mother's honesty travelling with me
into my work.

The first time I read my poetry publicly
and as a lesbian, the woman who said to me,
"Write more. I want to know what happens next."

ACKNOWLEDGEMENTS

I thank Betsy Warland for her suggestions about how to edit early drafts of this essay.
I thank Mab Segrest, Cris South, and women I worked with on the *Feminary* collective
for my education as a lesbian poet. My grateful thanks to lesbians who have organized
and attended WomanWrites over the last fifteen years.

## Notes

1.  The Nightmare poem was "But Cato Said: Attach No Importance to Dreams,"
    in my chapbook, *The Sound of One Fork* (Durham, North Carolina: Night
    Heron Press, 1981).

2.  "Speak earth..." is from "Love Poem," in Audre Lorde's *The New York Head
    Shop and Museum* (Detroit: Broadside Press, 1974). Her other books of poetry
    include *From a Land Where Other People Live* (Detroit: Broadside Press,
    1973); *Coal* (New York: W.W. Norton, 1976); *The Black Unicorn* (New York:
    W.W. Norton, 1978); *Our Dead Behind Us* (New York: W.W. Norton, 1986).
    Some of her essays and speeches are collected in *Sister Outsider* (Freedom,

Calif.: The Crossing Press, 1984).

3.   Judy Grahn's classic poem "She Who," included in *The Work of a Common Woman: The Collected Poetry of Judy Grahn, 1964–1977* (New York: St. Martin's Press, 1978).

4.   From "The Conjugation of the Paramecium," in Muriel Rukeyser's *Collected Poems* (New York: McGraw–Hill Book Co., 1978).

5.   Lillian Smith's essay appears in a collection of her prose, edited by Michelle Cliff, *The Winner Names the Age* (New York: W.W. Norton, 1978).

6.   Information about WomanWrites, held yearly for Southern lesbian writers, can be obtained from the Atlanta Lesbian Feminist Alliance (ALFA), P.O. Box 5502, Atlanta, GA 30307, U.S.A.

7.   "To Be Posted..." appeared in *Sinister Wisdom* 35 (Summer/Fall 1988). The address for *Sinister Wisdom: A Journal for the Lesbian Imagination in the Arts and Politics* is P.O. Box 3252, Berkeley, CA 94703, U.S.A.

**For writing**

1. Interview several women to learn what they think about being first-named by people they don't know.

2. Interview several women to learn what they think about "Miss" and "Mrs." as ways of identifying their sexual availability. What do they think about "Ms." as a way of ignoring a woman's marital situation? Whose business is it if a woman is spouse-free?

3. Read and listen carefully to find "ess," "ette," "ix," and "ine" endings on nouns used to designate women. Analyze the effects of those endings.

4. Chapter Six discusses some dead-end paths in the language maze, but not all of them. Write about one that Chapter Six does not discuss.

5. Write a paper in which you respond to any of the essayists in Chapter Six.

*Suggestions for library paper*

1. Read several articles by or about a stereotyped group of people. Write a paper in which you explain what you have discovered about that group: did the label constrict your thoughts? Did you learn that the label is misleading? How do you perceive the group now that you have learned more? How has language helped you to think more clearly?

2. To free yourself from a dead-end path, read several articles about an issue of current debate, one that you already know about and have opinions about. To give yourself a different perspective, find articles that disagree with your opinion. Write a paper in which you state your original ideas about the issue, summarize the new ideas about it, and explain what change of mind your reading has caused or why you have not changed your ideas.

3. Rethink a scientific theory or scientific interpretation of data. Use Brian Easlea (Chapter Three) and Emily Martin (Chapter Five) as models of scientists rethinking what they know, but go beyond Easlea's and Martin's essays to learn what other scientists have written about the theory you choose to re-examine. Write a paper about the cultural assumptions and stereotypes that influence scientific thought and about how language liberated you to rethink a theory.

4. Research any language issue or question that interests you. Write a paper in which you explain your interest in the issue, what you have learned in your research, and what conclusions you draw from your reading and thinking.

# Chapter Seven:

# Pleasure and Power

# Pleasure and Power

## Introduction

THROUGHOUT THIS BOOK we have examined language as a human construct that tells us who we are and how we are to behave, that allows us many choices, and that allows us to think but that can constrict our thoughts. We have discussed language as an inheritance and as an environment in which we learn to function, rather than as a set of rules we are to follow.

But we have not discussed language as power or as pleasure. It is time, now, to look briefly at language from those perspectives, to see language as a means of empowering and of pleasuring people who know how to use it—as thinkers, as readers, and as writers. I will consider power not as power over but as power to, not as control or domination of others but as control of one's own thoughts, actions, and choices. Language can give us power to think clearly, act ethically, and choose wisely. It can empower us to rethink what we know and to make well-informed, well-considered decisions. Language can empower people to help others rethink and choose wisely. And language can give people pleasure, particularly the pleasure of knowledge and of discovery.

Charlotte Bunch writes, in *Passionate Politics*:

Reading and writing are valuable in and of themselves, and women should have access to their pleasures. Beyond that, they are vital to change for several reasons. First, they provide a means of conveying ideas and information that may not be readily available in the popular media....Second, reading and writing help develop an individual's imagination and ability to think....Third, an individual's access through reading to a variety of interpretations of reality increases that person's capacity to think for herself, to go against the norms of the culture, and to conceive of alternatives for society.... (250)

Reading, writing, and thinking, as we have seen, and as Bunch reiterates, are inseparable. All three depend on language. If we know our choices with language and if we are aware of the choices other writers and speakers make, we are empowered to see and to interpret the world more clearly.

And language can give pleasure. As we think and read and write, language allows us to discover new information and new ways of seeing the world. It gives us the pleasure of clarifying our ideas and of communicating our thoughts to other people. It gives us the pleasure of knowing what other people think and of seeing the world through their eyes.

People who understand their choices with language and who use language carefully can have the power to participate effectively in the discussion of ideas and in the pleasure that comes from participating. The essays in this chapter are part of that large discussion. These essays consider a variety of issues. As you read them, consider not only the ideas and information, but also yourself as a reading audience and as a writer who will participate in the open discussion of ideas and will use language effectively. How will you empower yourself and others? What pleasures will you have as a participant and what pleasures might you give your listening or reading audiences?

**Works Cited**

Bunch, Charlotte. *Passionate Politics: Feminist Theory in Action.* New York: St. Martin's Press, 1987.

# Talking Back

## bell hooks

IN THE WORLD OF THE SOUTHERN BLACK COMMUNITY I grew up in, "back talk" and "talking back" meant speaking as an equal to an authority figure. It meant daring to disagree and sometimes it just meant having an opinion. In the "old school," children were meant to be seen and not heard. My great-grandparents, grandparents, and parents were all from the old school. To make yourself heard if you were a child was to invite punishment, the back-hand lick, the slap across the face that would catch you unaware, or the feel of switches stinging your arms and legs.

To speak then when one was not spoken to was a courageous act—an act of risk and daring. And yet it was hard not to speak in warm rooms where heated discussions began at the crack of dawn, women's voices filling the air, giving orders, making threats, fussing. Black men may have excelled in the art of poetic preaching in the male-dominated church, but in the church of the home, where the everyday rules of how to live and how to act were established, it was black women who preached. There, black women spoke in a language so rich, so poetic, that it felt to me like being shut off from life, smothered to death if one were not allowed to participate.

It was in that world of woman talk (the men were often silent, often absent) that was born in me the craving to speak, to have a voice, and not just any voice but one that could be identified as belonging to me. To make my voice, I had to speak, to hear myself talk—and talk I did—darting in and out of grown folks' conversations and dialogues, answering questions that were not directed at me, endlessly asking questions, making speeches. Needless to say, the punishments for these acts of speech seemed endless. They were intended to silence me—the child—and more particularly the girl child. Had I been a boy, they might have encouraged me to speak believing that I might someday be called to preach. There was no "calling" for talking girls, no legitimized rewarded speech. The punishments I received for "talking back" were intended to suppress all possibility that I would create my own speech. That speech was to be suppressed so that the "right speech of womanhood" would emerge.

Within feminist circles, silence is often seen as the sexist "right speech of womanhood"—the sign of woman's submission to patriarchal authority. This emphasis on woman's silence may be an accurate remembering of what has taken place in the households of women from WASP backgrounds in the United States, but in black communities (and diverse ethnic communities), women have not been silent. Their voices can be heard. Certainly for black women, our struggle has not been to emerge from silence into speech but to change the nature and direction of our speech, to make a speech that compels listeners, one that is heard.

Our speech, "the right speech of womanhood," was often the soliloquy, the talking into thin air, the talking to ears that do not hear you—the talk that is simply not listened to. Unlike the black male preacher whose speech was to be heard, who was to be listened to, whose words were to be remembered, the voices of black women—giving orders, making threats, fussing—could be tuned out, could become a kind of background music, audible but not acknowledged as significant speech. Dialogue—the sharing of speech and recognition—took place not between mother and child or mother and male authority figure but among black women. I can remember watching fascinated as our mother talked with her mother, sisters, and women friends. The intimacy and intensity of their speech—the satisfaction they received from talking to one another, the pleasure, the joy. It was in this world of woman speech, loud talk, angry words, women with tongues quick and sharp, tender sweet tongues, touching our world with their words, that I made speech my birthright—and the right to voice, to authorship, a privilege I would not be denied. It was in that world and because of it that I came to dream of writing, to write.

Writing was a way to capture speech, to hold onto it, keep it close. And so I wrote down bits and pieces of conversations, confessing in cheap diaries that soon fell apart from too much handling, expressing the intensity of my sorrow, the anguish of speech—for I was always saying the wrong thing, asking the wrong questions, I could not confine my speech to the necessary corners and concerns of life. I hid these writings under my bed, in pillow stuffings, among faded underwear. When my sisters found and read them, they ridiculed and mocked me—poking fun. I felt violated, ashamed, as if the secret parts of my self had been exposed, brought into the open, and hung like newly clean laundry, out in the air for everyone to see. The fear of exposure, the fear that one's deepest emotions and innermost thoughts will be dismissed as mere nonsense, felt by so many young girls keeping diaries, holding and hiding speech, seems to me now one of the barriers that women have always needed and still need to destroy so that we are no longer pushed into secrecy or silence.

Despite my feelings of violation, of exposure, I continued to speak and write, choosing my hiding places well, learning to destroy work when no safe place could be found. I was never taught absolute silence, I was taught that it was important to speak but to talk a talk that was in itself a silence. Taught to speak and yet beware of the betrayal of too much heard speech, I experienced intense confusion and deep anxiety in my efforts to speak and write. Reciting poems at Sunday afternoon church service might be rewarded. Writing a poem (when one's time could be "better" spent sweeping, ironing, learning to cook) was luxurious activity, indulged in at the expense of others. Questioning authority, raising issues that were not deemed appropriate subjects brought pain, punishments—like telling mama I wanted to die before her because I could not live without her—that was crazy talk, crazy speech, the kind that would lead you to end up in a mental institution. "Little girl," I would be told, "if you don't stop all this crazy talk and crazy acting you are going to end up right out there at Western State."

Madness, not just physical abuse, was the punishment for too much talk if you were female. Yet even as this fear of madness haunted me, hanging over my writing like a monstrous shadow, I could not stop the words, making thought, writing speech. For this terrible madness which I feared, which I was sure was the destiny of daring women born to intense speech (after all, the authorities emphasized this point daily), was not as threatening as imposed silence, as suppressed speech.

Safety and sanity were to be sacrificed if I was to experience defiant speech. Though I risked them both, deep-seated fears and anxieties characterized my childhood days. I would speak but I would not ride a bike, play hardball, or hold the gray kitten. Writing about the ways we are traumatized in our growing up years, psychoanalyst Alice Miller makes the point in *For Your Own Good* that it is not clear why childhood wounds become for some folk an opportunity to grow, to move forward rather than backward in the process of self-realization. Certainly, when I reflect on the trials of my growing-up years, the many punishments, I can see now that in resistance I learned to be vigilant in the nourishment of my spirit, to be tough, to courageously protect that spirit from forces that would break it.

While punishing me, my parents often spoke about the necessity of breaking my spirit. Now when I ponder the silences, the voices that are not heard, the voices of those wounded and/or oppressed individuals who do not speak or write, I contemplate the acts of persecution, torture—the terrorism that breaks spirits, that makes creativity impossible. I write these words to bear witness to the primacy of resistance struggle in any situation of domination (even within family life); to the strength and power that emerges from sustained resistance and the profound conviction that these forces can be healing, can protect us from dehumanization and despair.

These early trials, wherein I learned to stand my ground, to keep my spirit intact, came vividly to mind after I published *Ain't I A Woman* and the book was sharply and harshly criticized. While I had expected a climate of critical dialogue, I was not expecting a critical avalanche that had the power in its intensity to crush the spirit, to push one into silence. Since that time, I have heard stories about black women, about women of color, who write and publish (even when the work is quite successful) having nervous breakdowns, being made mad because they cannot bear the harsh responses of family, friends, and unknown critics, or becoming silent, unproductive. Surely, the absence of a humane critical response has tremendous impact on the writer from any oppressed, colonized group who endeavors to speak. For us, true speaking is not solely an expression of creative power; it is an act of resistance, a political gesture that challenges politics of domination that would render us nameless and voiceless. As such, it is a courageous act—as such, it represents a threat. To those who wield oppressive power, that which is threatening must necessarily be wiped out, annihilated, silenced.

Recently, efforts by black women writers to call attention to our work serve to highlight both our presence and absence. Whenever I peruse women's bookstores, I am struck not by the rapidly growing body of feminist writing by black women, but by the paucity of available published material. Those of us who write and are published remain few in number. The context of silence is varied and multi-dimensional. Most obvious are the ways racism, sexism, and class exploitation act to suppress and silence. Less obvious are the inner struggles, the efforts made to gain the necessary confidence to write, to re-write, to fully develop craft and skill—and the extent to which such efforts fail.

Although I have wanted writing to be my life-work since childhood, it has been difficult for me to claim "writer" as part of that which identifies and shapes my everyday reality. Even after publishing books, I would often speak of wanting to be a writer as though these works did not exist. And though I would be told, "you are a writer," I was not yet ready to fully affirm this truth. Part of myself was still held captive by domineering forces of history, of familial life that had charted a map of silence, of right speech. I had not completely let go of the fear of saying the wrong thing, of being punished. Somewhere in the deep recesses of my mind, I believed I could avoid both responsibility and punishment if I did not declare myself a writer.

One of the many reasons I chose to write using the pseudonym bell hooks, a family name (mother to Sarah Oldham, grandmother to Rosa Bell Oldham, great-grandmother to me), was to construct a writer-identity that would challenge and subdue all impulses leading me away from speech into silence. I was a young girl buying bubble gum at the corner store when I first really heard the full name bell hooks. I had just "talked back" to a grown person. Even now I can recall the surprised look, the mocking tones that informed me I must be kin to bell hooks—a sharp-tongued woman, a woman who spoke her mind, a woman who was not afraid to talk back. I claimed this legacy of defiance, of will, of courage, affirming my link to female ancestors who were bold and daring in their speech. Unlike my bold and daring mother and grandmother, who were not supportive of talking back, even though they were assertive and powerful in their speech, bell hooks as I discovered, claimed, and invented her was my ally, my support.

That initial act of talking back outside the home was empowering. It was the first of many acts of defiant speech that would make it possible for me to emerge as an independent thinker and writer. In retrospect, "talking back" became for me a rite of initiation, testing my courage, strengthening my commitment, preparing me for the days ahead—the days when writing, rejection notices, periods of silence, publication, ongoing development seem impossible but necessary.

Moving from silence into speech is for the oppressed, the colonized, the exploited, and those who stand and struggle side by side a gesture of defiance that heals, that makes new life and new growth possible. It is that act of speech, of "talking back," that is no mere gesture of empty words, that is the expression of our movement from object to subject—the liberated voice.

# Listening for Women's Voices: Revisioning Courses in American Public Address

## Kristin S. Vonnegut

> When patriotism is discountenanced and pub-
> lick virtue becomes the ridicule of the sycophant—
> when every man of liberality, firmness, and penetra-
> tion, who cannot lick the hand stretched out to op-
> press, is deemed an enemy of the State—then is the
> gulph of despotism set open, and the grades to sla-
> very, though rapid, are scarce perceptible—then
> genius drags heavily its iron chain...the mind be-
> comes enervated, and the national character sinks into
> a kind of apathy with only energy sufficient to curse
> the breast that gave it milk.
>
> A Columbian Patriot[1]

AS IS TYPICAL OF EIGHTEENTH-CENTURY TEXTS, "Colum-
bian Patriot" was a pseudonym. To identify the "Columbian Patriot" I might
turn to traditional references from the period, such as Ford's (1888) collection
of pamphlets on the ratification of the U.S. Constitution. Yet, Ford erroneously
states that Elbridge Gerry wrote the pamphlet, *Observations on the New Constitution and on the Federal and State Conventions*, in 1788. Only by searching for
more detailed information on the "Columbian Patriot," would I learn that the
pseudonym belonged to Mercy Otis Warren. Further research would reveal that
Warren's *Observations* (1788/1986) is considered one of the most important ex-

*From* Communication Education, *Vol. 41, Jan. 1992. Copyright © by the Speech
Communication Association. 1992. Reprinted by permission of the publisher.*

positions of Antifederalist doctrine attendant to the American constitutional debates of the late eighteenth century (Kaminski & Saladino, 1986).

The confusion over the authorship of *Observations* illustrates three important issues related to women in American public address. First, it proves that there were American women rhetors before 1830—the approximate year that most scholars agree American women began to speak publicly. Warren's work also suggests the difficulty entailed in uncovering early American women's writing. Finally, it underscores the importance of including women's rhetoric in the American public address classroom. In the case of her *Observations*, Warren is relevant because she provides an influential example of Antifederalist rhetoric—a viewpoint often neglected by scholars. More significant, Warren's other works, including numerous plays and poems, and similar writing by other women, are notable because they open to the rhetorician a more complete picture of American public address.

Although public address scholars have not acknowledged them, women rhetors existed before 1830. Studying their rhetoric, as well as that of other marginalized groups, helps to expand and refine our understanding of the uses of rhetoric. As Hart (1986) argued:

> If one assumes, for example, that public rhetoric is a ubiquitous feature of collective life at all levels of society, and if one further assumes that theory is best that accounts for the greatest number of behavioral instances, then one would also assume that scholars should attend to the local rather than the national, to the ingenuous rather than the contrived, to the homely rather than the heralded. (p. 293)

Hart was commenting on the trend in American public address toward studying "newsworthy" subjects, but his thoughts underscore the point that any theory is only as comprehensive as its author's selection of texts.

While Warren's pamphlet (1788/1986) clearly demonstrates the problems inherent in attempting to include texts by female rhetors in American public address course materials, it does not reveal the extent of the problem nor address its causes or solutions. In this essay I discuss these three points. I have chosen to answer the question of women's absence from the American public address classroom, and the limited theoretical framework it implies, by analyzing its most difficult aspect: early American women's rhetoric. Proving that early American female rhetors existed and that their works are available should enable instructors to incorporate women's rhetoric, and the rhetoric of other marginalized or "muted" groups, in their American public address courses.

Women and other muted groups should be studied because it is the instructor's duty to help students of rhetoric to identify and discuss social truths as they emerge and are defined, debated, and revised in discourse. Kramarae (1981) explains the concept of *muted groups* as follows:

> The language of a particular culture does not serve all its speakers equally. ...Women (and members of other subordinate groups) are not as free or as able as men are to say what they wish, when and where they wish, because the words and the norms for their use have been formulated by the dominant group, men. So women cannot as easily or as directly articulate their experiences as men can. Women's perceptions differ from those of men because women's subordination means they experience life differently. However, the words and norms for speaking are not generated from or fitted to women's experiences. Women are thus "muted." (p. 1)

Because women and other muted groups have difficulty expressing their experiences in the language of the dominant culture, "they are likely to find ways to express themselves outside the system" (p. 12). Thus, studying the varied forms in which early American women expressed their views illustrates the diversity of our rhetorical tradition and contributes to the development of a more comprehensive theory that encompasses the different media through which cultural values emerge.

Some scholars have called for the development of theories that incorporate diverse modes of expression, especially those of women. In an early article, Kramer (1974) argued for more and better scholarship discussing the differences between men and women speakers. Campbell (1973, 1986, 1989c) has noted women's distinctive style in a variety of situations, including the rhetoric of the Women's Liberation Movement and of early African-American women, as well as in all women's struggles to discover unique strategies to overcome gender specific barriers to speaking. Pearson's (1975) study of Abigail Adams' use of the letter form is among the few works that addresses a particular rhetorical form women used. Other scholars who have remarked on the need for scholarship that addresses the unique communication of women include Foss and Foss (1983), Jenefsky (1987), and Campbell (1985).

## The Absence of Women's Voices

Despite the work of the authors mentioned above, the voices of women and other muted groups are almost entirely absent from the American public address classroom. For instance, at one major midwestern university, justly praised for its training of public address scholars, three semesters are devoted to American public address, and a fourth course is offered occasionally. Students read more than 100 texts; of those, only six are by women. At another prestigious institution, two classes in American public address are offered, and although women rhetors are discussed, no texts by women are analyzed. The contents of the three most recently published public address anthologies (Andrews & Zarefsky, 1988; Lucaites, 1989; Reid, 1988) demonstrate that these courses are typical.

Rhetoricians have ignored women in their critical work as well as in the classroom. In the most important collection of critical studies in public address,

*A History and Criticism of American Public Address*, only two of the 48 essays are about women. The first essay supplies short biographical sketches of numerous woman's rights speakers (Yoakam, 1943); the second is a lengthier study of one woman's rights activist, Susan B. Anthony (Twichell, 1955). The implication is that women contributed to American public address only for a few decades in the nineteenth century. Recently, however, some scholars have shown an increasing interest in women's contributions to rhetoric. For instance, Brock, Scott, and Chesebro's third edition of *Methods of Rhetorical Criticism* (1989) includes essays by feminist critics. In the previous two editions, feminist approaches to criticism were ignored.

Although scholars have made progress toward a more inclusive rhetorical theory, they continue to disregard the rhetoric of women during the founding of the nation. Very few scholars have noted women's contributions to early American rhetoric, although many books review the historical high-points of that period. Of four books interpreting the rhetoric and propaganda of the Revolution, only two mention any women (Mercy Otis Warren is the only woman mentioned and only two of her plays and her history of the Revolution are cited). A similar situation exists with regard to the scholarly articles written about the colonial and early republic years in America. Only two articles on women's rhetoric of the early period have appeared in communication journals (Hynes, 1975; Pearson, 1975).

The paucity of works by women in American public address classrooms is due, in part, to the lack of readily available texts. Of five anthologies of the rhetoric of the American Revolution and the Constitution, only two include work by women. One (Ford, 1888) includes Warren's pamphlet, but attributes it to Elbridge Gerry; another (Kaminski & Saladino, 1986) reproduces Warren's pamphlet and letters by Abigail Adams and Warren.

## Why Women's Voices are Absent

The common fallacy that female rhetors did not exist before 1830 has led students of public address to ignore early women's rhetoric. Because it was considered improper for women to speak in public before 1830, rhetoricians assume that women never expressed their opinions prior to that time. No scholar would claim that, because it was considered wrong to defame the King of England, men did not express their dislike for King George, yet many continue to believe that all women were effectively silenced.

As Warren's work (1788/1986) suggests, early American women expressed their opinions in public forums. Most avoided the platform, but some ventured to write for newspapers and magazines, and at least one authored a pamphlet. Admittedly, it is difficult to find "traditional" rhetorical texts by women, but some are available. In addition to Warren's tract, the *Columbian Magazine* contains an essay written by "A Lady" (1791) entitled "On the Supposed Superiority of the Masculine Understanding." Other examples are cited in the course of this essay.

In addition to more traditional rhetorical forms, women expressed their ideas in other modes. Plays, poetry, books, and diaries by women were published before 1830. For example, Warren (1774/1896, 1775/1918) and Esther De Berdt Reed (1780/1976) published works on the Revolution, Anne Dudley Bradstreet (1650/1932) wrote about women's misfortunes, and Mary Rowlandson (1682/1930) wrote about Indian captivity and religion—works that provide a rich and untapped resource for students and teachers of American public address. Unfortunately, because these forms do not fit traditional conceptions of rhetoric, these works often are dismissed as inappropriate for study.

Traditional theories have narrowed our view of the domain of our discipline and of its purposes excluding almost all rhetoric produced by those outside the dominant groups in society. This narrowing is exacerbated by an emphasis on the effects criterion, a limited definition of "public," and an elitist conception of the artistic criterion, which together have left public address scholars without appropriate tools to appreciate and understand the speeches of women and other muted groups.

For Aristotle (1954), the audience consisted of free white male citizens; similarly, for subsequent theorists, the audience is defined as consisting of white, male, political, social, and economic elites—audiences hostile to the views of women and other marginalized groups. Consequently, the application of Aristotelian theories demands forms of audience adaptation that are difficult for individuals who are not white, male, and economically advantaged.

Elizabeth Cady Stanton's first speech to the New York Legislature (1854/1989) is an excellent example of this situation. A woman speaking to men in the mid-nineteenth century was highly unconventional, thus, Stanton's audience perceived her as laughable or damnable rather than credible. This is exemplified by the comments of Mr. Burnett, a legislator from Essex County: "It is well known that the object of these unsexed women is to overthrow the most sacred of our institutions...and establish on its ruins what will be in fact and in principles but a species of legalized adultery" (cited in Grim, 1937, p. 175).

While Aristotle's emphasis on audience effects dooms most women's rhetoric to failure, his description of the rhetorical genres works to silence woman's voice absolutely. Each of his three genres—deliberative, forensic, and epideictic—is defined in terms of discourse produced in legislatures, law courts, and public rituals, scenes from which most women were barred through much of history, thereby eliminating them as part of rhetorical history.

The truth of this assertion seems evident when we consider that, according to Aristotle (1954), the deliberative orator should concern "himself" with ways and means, war and peace, national defense, imports and exports, and legislation. Before the mid-twentieth century, few women and non-white men were allowed to voice their views on such subjects; thus, centuries of women's thought has received little scholarly consideration.

The impact of narrow definitions of rhetoric based on the Aristotelian genres is illustrated by Susan B. Anthony's 1872-1873 address, "Is it a Crime for a U.S. Citizen to Vote?" (1874/1989). Although all U.S. women were barred from courtrooms either as pleaders or as witnesses in order to defend themselves against being punished for the "crime" of voting, Anthony delivered forensic addresses by fulfilling all the requirements of that genre, except their location in a courtroom. Although there is considerable evidence to indicate how persuasive her speeches of self-defense were (Campbell 1989a), because she did not speak in a courtroom as an officially designated lawyer, and because she was convicted and fined, her speeches fail to meet the requirements of traditional theory narrowly applied. Such a perspective ignores her rhetorical genius in creating a forensic rhetorical situation where none had previously existed.

Artistic criteria for judging style is a third aspect of traditional theories that circumvents women's voices. According to Aristotle (1954), the style of a speech should be clear, correct, and appropriate. Unfortunately, Aristotle defined these requirements in terms of the usage of an educated elite. The incorrect grammar of an uneducated man or the unusual diction of a slave woman would not meet the criteria of the educated elite, thus, these individuals would be discriminated against. Two women whose rhetoric represents these styles are Mary Harris "Mother" Jones, the Irish labor agitator (1912/1983; Tonn, 1987) and Sojourner Truth, the former slave and advocate for abolition and woman's rights (1878/1989; Campbell, 1989a).

Although much of Aristotle's theory might be applied in illuminating ways if it were recast to include all segments of society, the elite, male-centered interpretation has persisted into the twentieth century with few changes. Despite Black's (1978) path-breaking book that rejected neo-Aristotelian criteria for judgment, scholars still use a narrow interpretation of Aristotle's theory as an important component in the pedagogy and criticism of American public address. For instance, in the introduction to his recent anthology, Reid (1988) argues for the use of Aristotelian criteria to judge speeches. Solomon's (1988) critique of Emma Goldman's rhetoric suffers from the limited view of the effects criterion. Solomon argues that Goldman's intemperate radical ideology caused her to fail as a rhetor because her audience found her to be offensive and rejected her anarchist beliefs. Although Goldman converted few people to anarchism she aroused their attention and cleared the way for less radical speakers to change American society.

Some scholars, however, have argued for theories that highlight the special rhetorical strategies of rhetors from marginalized groups. In her essay, "The Rhetoric of Women's Liberation" (1973), Campbell asserts that women's liberation rhetoric might be seen as "anti-rhetorical" because it violates many of the traditional ideals of rhetoric that worked to exclude or silence women; therefore, existing theories of rhetoric are not equipped to discuss that rhetoric. Windt (1972) illustrates the need for more inclusive rhetorical theories in his analysis of Yippie rhetoric. By comparing Yippie rhetoric to that of the Greek Cynics who saw traditional modes of persuasion as immoral, Windt supplies an illuminating critique of the unorthodox strategies employed by Yippies.

Traditional theory is not flawed simply because it excludes muted groups; it limits critics as well. By narrowing the scope of rhetoric so that only certain standard texts are regarded as worthy of analysis, scholars are required to participate in academic one-upmanship. Kolodny (1980/1985) describes the process in a discussion of women's role in the literary canon:

> The fact of canonization puts any work beyond questions of establishing its merit, and instead, invites students to offer only increasingly more ingenious readings and interpretations, the purpose of which is to validate the greatness already imputed by canonization. (p. 150)

Although critical work is still needed to illuminate texts that are part of the traditional canon, scholars must acknowledge that the kind of criticism this encourages retains the blinders of the past and limits critical insight into the way people communicate. Studying the texts of muted groups forces consideration of rhetorical efforts from a variety of perspectives and may lead us to a more holistic theory of rhetoric.

Yet, women's exclusion from rhetorical studies follows only partially from strict reliance on traditional theories. Other areas of study, especially history, have contributed to the domination of male public discourse in classical and contemporary discussions of rhetoric.

Rhetoricians have relied on historians to punctuate the past by identifying the important periods of human existence. When their periodization is analyzed, it is apparent that historians have described important periods in men's existence, not human history: "Since history has traditionally made man as its subjects and measure, its periodization has little to do with changes in women's lives" (Cott & Pleck, 1979, p. 18). Because women's concerns were not considered in defining epochs and eras, women's voices have been ignored. Rhetoricians have relied on male-identified periodization; thus, many American public address courses are organized in terms of units on the rhetoric of the Revolution, the Constitution, the golden age of oratory, and so on.

In addition to delineating the time periods for study, historians have identified the individuals of importance in particular time frames. Not surprisingly, the majority of these individuals are elite white males in positions of political, military, and economic power. If history is the study of important political events, then it follows that the people who made that history were important political figures.

Rhetoricians have relied heavily on history as the study of "great men." A majority of critical studies has analyzed the rhetoric of male political leaders, and the majority of the figures studied in the American public-address classroom are those same male political leaders. When women speakers are included, representations of the socio-economic elite usually supersede ordinary women. Certainly, students must be exposed to the rhetoric of elites who helped to frame the understanding of social truths. However, the contributions of ordinary individuals are equally important to understanding those truths, particularly as they express dissenting views.

The traditional theories of history and rhetoric are wrought with interpretive misconceptions regarding women's rhetoric. They have obscured the voices of women and other muted groups. To hear women's voices and to refine scholars' and teachers' conceptions of rhetoric, they must alter their methods of studying and teaching American public address.

## Listening for Women's Voices

Teachers must initiate the process of change by acknowledging that women rhetors existed before 1830. According to historian Ulrich (1990), "Serious research in early American women's history is still far from easy....Yet the information is there for those who have the imagination and energy to find it" (p. 210). The same is true of early American women's rhetoric. Because anthologies tend to omit that rhetoric, the teacher should turn to other sources. Histories of the period offer clues to other texts, especially histories that emphasize women, making it possible to identify potential primary source material. Furthermore, works by Kerber (1980) and Norton (1985) offer specific references to the writings of many women.

In addition to supplying women's texts for analysis, teachers must help students to reconceptualize theories of rhetoric to allow for a fuller appreciation of a variety of texts. To compensate for the bias implicit in an emphasis on audience response, the teacher must take a broader approach to that criterion. Students should be encouraged to consider the different ways in which rhetors have attempted to identify with their audience without summarily dismissing rhetoric that is confrontational, protesting, or makes no overt effort at identification. The student must learn to consider the size and character of the obstacles created by the rhetorical situation in order to assess what kind or amount of persuasion was within the rhetor's potential. Furthermore, the teacher should encourage students to discover and factor into their evaluation who the rhetor identified as the target audience.

Instructors can draw on the work of critics such as Lake (1983) to provide instances of analyses that transcend basic effects criteria. For example, in his discussion of the Red Power movement, Lake describes contemporary Native American rhetoric as self-addressed. He then explains why the consummatory strategies that were perceived as inappropriate for the white majority of Americans were well adapted to the intended audience.

Works of social history, a theory of history that includes ordinary individuals, also furnish the teacher with resources to justify changes in the American public address curriculum. Social historians have helped to eliminate the interpretive sources. Traditional historians mined the speeches, essays, and private papers of great men—and a few great women—to understand the important issues of each era. In his historiographic review of social history, Stearns (1983) notes that "few if any groups are really inarticulate" (p. 15). Accordingly, social historians have turned to sources, such as wills, letters, diaries, census data, court testimony, tombstones, and organizational publications to provide a broader view of life than that revealed by earlier historians who studied "great men." If rhetoricians incorporate the perspective offered by social history, they can begin to identify rhetors from muted groups who contributed to our social reality in subtle but important ways. For example, some scholars have begun to identify distinctive forms of women's rhetoric in women's correspondence, diaries, and conversations (Kramarae, 1981), and early American women's needle-point (Lopez, 1990).

A final step in revising traditional theories of rhetoric is to reconsider the use of an elitist artistic criterion to judge rhetorical texts. This criterion often discriminates against those without access to education; it must be reevaluated. One way of transcending this bias is to introduce students to Frye's (1957) definition of "high style." Frye rejects the notion that a style developed in the upper classes is superior to that developed in the lower classes. He argues that

> genuine high style is ordinary style, or even low style, in an exceptional situation which gives it exceptional authority....High style in ordinary speech is heard whenever a speaker is honestly struggling to express what his society, as a society, is trying to be and do. (p. 45)

Frye's definition allows individuals from any class or group to be considered exemplary rhetors with valuable insights, regardless of their level of education.

The efforts of social historians to replace traditional periodization also can help the teacher of American public address justify similar changes in her or his classroom. By enabling students to view history and rhetoric through a wide angle lens, teachers may introduce the study of groups, movements, and ideas that were excluded from a history whose narrower focus highlighted wars and great men.

Social history also can help the teacher train the student to hear the voices of ordinary individuals as well as those of elites. According to Stearns (1983), the primary consequence of social history is a shift in historical priorities. Many scholars now believe that "the great and famous cause less than we used to think, while ordinary people cause more" (p. 6). By altering historical priorities and emphasizing the ordinary individual's level of importance to cultural development, the social historian has pointed to theory-building possibilities inherent in the study of muted groups' rhetoric.

While these new perspectives enable scholars to develop and refine rhetorical theories and support the efforts of instructors to introduce more works by women into their courses, teachers may require specific suggestions for ways to reorganize the American public address curriculum. The first essential adjustment of the curriculum requires altering the traditional organization of courses based on important periods in male history to allow for the integration of a multitude of events as well as significant ideas. Ideally, American public address would be taught over two semesters or three quarters, including work from the colonial period, the first century of the republic, and contemporary public address. This format would not split major political transformations into discrete sections based on a study of rhetorical types, nor would it divide social movements into separate courses based on traditional periods of study.

The second essential adjustment requires analyzing a variety of rhetorical forms. Instructors may structure units to include the following: the persuasive use of private forms—letters and diaries as rhetoric; the persuasive use of artistic forms—poems, novels, songs, and plays as rhetoric; and the persuasive use of public prose forms—sermons, speeches, pamphlets, and debates as rhetoric.

Throughout this essay I have illustrated the importance of broadening the theoretical landscape with regard to reclaiming early American women's rhetoric. Consistent with that emphasis, in what follows I discuss briefly how instructors might organize the initial course in colonial American public address.

This course might begin with a discussion of how so-called private forms may be used for persuasive purposes. As Sloman (1978) explains, episodic forms, such as letters and diaries, permitted women who feared public rejection to voice their opinions. In her discussion of English literature, Sloman argues that "not all women seem to have aimed at the novel, especially in earlier periods; publication imposed the need to be respectable and to fulfill conventional expectations" (p. 26). Thus, women turned to letters and diaries to express their opinions.

Because rhetoric is concerned with what is public, the teacher must choose works that reached an audience, and such texts do exist. For example, students could read letters of Abigail Adams, available in an edited selection by Butterfield, Friedlander, and Kline (1975). The best known and most circulated (an epistle to her husband which asks him to "remember the ladies" [1776/1975, p. 121] during the drafting of the *Declaration of Independence*) might be studied in contrast to the popular political rhetoric of the day. As many scholars have noted, Jefferson's *Declaration of Independence* and related works praised a type of liberty and independence possible only for wealthy white men. Students also might read Warren's (1787/1968) letters to Ann Gerry to understand the strategies she used to discover Elbridge Gerry's impressions of the constitutional convention of 1787.[2]

In addition, students could read Mary Rowlandson's (1682/1930) published account of her kidnapping by Indians, one of a number of works of this type. Rowlandson's extensive use of biblical analogies to describe the tortures she endured offers insight into women's strategies for establishing authority and for interpreting harrowing frontier experiences. An excellent supplementary reading for such a text is an essay by Kolodny (1981) in which she provides a feminist interpretation of captivity narratives. Another representative writing, the "Journal, 1778" of Mary Gould Almy (1778/1880), might be discussed as well. Each of these works illustrates how early American women struggled to bridge the gap between the private and public aspects of society through their rhetoric.

A course unit on the persuasive use of artistic forms could explore a wide range of women's poetry as well as their plays, novels, and songs. Ulrich (1990) explains that, "colonial 'poetesses' wrote about public affairs as well as private events," and some had their poems published (p. 204). Students might analyze Bradstreet's work (1650/1932) to identify early methods of asserting woman's rights. Phillis Wheatley's poems (1773/1985) could shed light on the African-American woman's perspective of America. Warren's poem (1774/1896) urging women to boycott British goods is illustrative of women's efforts in support of the colonial resistance.

Warren also wrote numerous plays. For example, "The Group" (1775/1918) was circulated widely in newspapers and as a pamphlet, although it was never performed in the Colonies. That play and others helped establish her as one of the most noteworthy satirists of the American Revolution (Granger, 1960). These works and other literature by women might furnish students with a greater appreciation for the rhetorical strategies invoked by non-traditional writers.

The third unit of the initial course, persuasive uses of public prose forms, could include a variety of texts by women. For instance, students could analyze the 1638 trial of Anne Hutchinson (1894/1968) to ascertain how a woman defended herself in the court room—a domain outside of a woman's sphere—as well as to acquire a broader perspective of the Antinomian Controversy that shook Puritan New England in the 1630s. Reed's *Sentiments of an American Woman* (1780/1976) is also significant. The story of an organization of Philadelphia women who collected funds for Washington's troops and published the influential *Sentiments* is essential to students' understanding of women's political involvement in, and influence over, the Revolutionary War effort. Warren's *Observations* (1788/1986) could be studied to illuminate the antifederalist position in the ratification of the Constitution. Deborah Sampson Ganett fought as a soldier in the Revolution. Her lecture, a narrative of her experiences (1802/1984), supplies a different view of the War as well as insight into the strategies one woman used to defend and apologize for behavior considered inappropriate. The address of Miss Mason (1787/1887) to the graduates' parents and the faculty of an early female seminary in Philadelphia, a clever and startling vindication of woman's eloquence, stands in importance as perhaps the first public address by an American woman. Finally, Scotswoman Frances Wright's (1829/ 1984) stirring lectures explored the radical implications of natural rights philosophy.

A selection of these works should supplement and serve as a counterpoint to familiar materials in the American public address classroom. In this revised and expanded course of study, instructors expose students to a variety of texts both from traditionally recognized sources and from sources and forms not usually considered part of the canon. The works suggested here might be juxtaposed with more famous texts. For instance, the letters of Warren and Adams might be read with John Dickinson's letters from a Pennsylvania farmer (1767-1768/1967). Hutchinson's trial (1638/1968) might be discussed in conjunction with the constitutional ratification debates. By contrasting views developed from such divergent grounds, students should begin to understand how different groups use different rhetorical forms to achieve self-expression and larger social goals. They also might be able to analyze key issues from different viewpoints.

Possible major assignments in each course include:

1. Choose a text considered a rhetorical masterpiece and evaluate it from the perspective of a member of a muted group. What implications does this have for an analysis of audience adaptation? For instance, how might an African-American woman react to Jefferson's *Declaration of Independence*?

2. Identify and analyze one rhetorical document that has not been studied in this course, a critical article, or a thesis or dissertation. Is the author representative of a muted group? What special strategies does he or she use in order to be persuasive? How might those strategies reflect constraints placed upon the rhetor as a member of that muted group? For instance, what strategies does Deborah Sampson Gannet use in her narrative (1802/ 1984)? Do they reflect constraints placed upon her because she was a woman or because she was a soldier?

3. Critically compare two different rhetorical forms addressing the same issue. Identify and discuss the relevance of the variations in structure, strategies, arguments, persona, and evidence used. For instance, what are the similarities and differences between Warren's "The Group" (1775/1918) and Thomas Paine's *Common Sense* (1776/1967)?

In developing a more inclusive curriculum on the early period of American public address, teachers should turn to histories of the period to enrich their understanding of the time. Works by Ulrich (1980, 1990) on the lives of colonial women, Norton (1985), Kerber (1980), and Hoffman and Albert (1989) on women of the Revolution, as well as the traditional books by Bailyn (1967) and

Wood (1969), are particularly helpful. Additionally, Mathews' *American Diaries in Manuscript 1580-1954* (1974) may facilitate the search for texts.

For courses covering the later periods, the first century of the Republic and contemporary American public address, texts are more readily available. Campbell (1989a, 1989b) has published an award-winning two-volume work on early American feminist rhetors. Kennedy and O'Shields (1983) and Anderson (1984) also have produced anthologies of women speakers.[3] Manning (1980, 1988) has compiled two indexes to the speeches of American women. Historical works by Cott (1977, 1987), Fox-Genovese (1988), Evans (1989), Flexner (1959), and Lerner (1977), supply pertinent background information for the second course of study and lead the scholar to a large variety of sources for the study of women's rhetoric.

The texts, assignments, and background reading outlined above should enable public address teachers and their students to reconsider the traditional rhetorical strictures that exclude marginalized groups and help them to evolve a more inclusive theory of rhetoric. The end result should prove fruitful for pedagogy, criticism, and theory. If all American public address instructors strive to remove the artificial restraints of traditional rhetorical and historical theory, perhaps the chorus of American voices will once again be full, melodious, and truly expressive of our national experience.

## Notes

1.    Charles Warren (1930-1932) correctly attributed this work, *Observations on the New Constitution and on the Federal and State Conventions by a Columbian Patriot*, originally published in 1788, to Mercy Otis Warren (1788/1986).

2.    Campbell and Jerry (1988) have addressed the difficulties women speakers face in attempting to overcome the public/private dichotomy that worked to keep them away from the platform—a distinctly public, therefore masculine, sphere.

3.    Anderson (1984) includes "The Examination of Mrs. Anne Hutchinson" in this anthology, but it is not a complete text.

## References

A Lady. (1791). On the supposed superiority of the masculine understanding. *Columbian Magazine*.

Adams, A. (1975). Letter to John Adams, March 31, 1776. In L.H. Butterfield, M. Friedlander, & M. Kline (Eds.), *The book of Abigail and John: selected letters of the Adams family, 1762-1784* (pp. 120-121). Cambridge, MA: Harvard University Press. (Original work written 1776.)

Almy, M.G. (1880). Journal, 1778. *Newport Historical Magazine*, 1, 17-36. (Original work written 1778.)

Anderson, J. (Ed.). (1984). *Outspoken women: Speeches by American women reformers, 1635–1935*. Dubuque, IA: Kendall/Hunt.

Andrews, J., & Zarefsky, D. (Eds.). (1989). *American voices: Significant speeches in American history*. New York: Longman.

Anthony, S.B. (1989). Is it a crime for a U.S. citizen to vote? In K.K. Campbell (Ed.), *Man cannot speak for her: key texts of the early feminists* (Vol. 2, pp. 279–316). New York: Greenwood Press. (Original work published 1874.)

Aristotle. (1954). Rhetoric. In F. Solmsen (Ed.) & R. Rhys (Trans.), *The rhetoric and the poetics of Aristotle* (pp. 19–219). New York: Random House.

Bailyn, B. (1967). *Ideological origins of the American Revolution*. Cambridge, MA: Harvard University Press.

Berger, C. (1961). *Broadsides and bayonets: the propaganda war of the American Revolution*. Philadelphia: University of Pennsylvania Press.

Black, E. (1978). *Rhetorical criticism: A study in method* (2nd ed.). Madison: University of Wisconsin Press.

Bradstreet, A.D. (1932). The prologue. In J.H. Ellis (Ed.), *The works of Anne Bradstreet: In prose and verse* (pp. 100–102). New York: Peter Smith. (Original work published 1650.)

Brock, B., Scott, R., & Chesebro, J. (1989). *Methods of rhetorical criticism: A twentieth-century perspective* (3rd ed.). Detroit, MI: Wayne State University Press.

Butterfield, L.H., Friedlander, M., & Kline, M. (Eds.). (1975). *The book of Abigail and John: Selected letters of the Adams family, 1762–1784*. Cambridge, MA: Harvard University Press.

Campbell, K. K. (1973). The rhetoric of women's liberation: An oxymoron. *Quarterly Journal of Speech, 59*, 74–86.

Campbell, K. K. (1985). The communication classroom: A chilly climate for women. *ACA Bulletin, 51*, 68–72.

Campbell, K.K. (1986). Style and content in the rhetoric of early Afro-American feminists. *Quarterly Journal of Speech, 72*, 434–445.

Campbell, K.K. (1989a). *Man cannot speak for her: A critical study of the early feminists* (Vol. 1). New York: Greenwood Press.

Campbell, K. K. (1989b). *Man cannot speak for her: Key texts of the early feminists* (Vol. 2). New York: Greenwood Press.

Campbell, K.K. (1989c). The sound of women's voices. *Quarterly Journal of Speech, 75*, 212–220.

Campbell, K.K., & Jerry, E.C. (1988). Woman and speaker: A conflict in roles. In B. Brehm (Ed.), *Seeing female: Social roles and personal lives* (pp. 123–133). New York: Greenwood Press.

Cott, N. (1977). *The bonds of womanhood: Woman's sphere in New England, 1780–1835*. New Haven, CT: Yale University Press.

Cott, N. (1987). *The grounding of modern feminism*. New Haven, CT: Yale University Press.

Cott, N., & Pleck, E. (Eds.). (1979). *A heritage of her own*. New York: Simon & Schuster.

Dickinson, J. (1967). Letters from a farmer in Pennsylvania to the inhabitants of the British Colonies. In M. Jensen (Ed.), *Tracts of the American Revolution: 1763–1776* (pp. 127–163). Indianapolis, IN: Bobbs Merrill. (Original work published 1768.)

Evans, S. (1989). *Born for liberty: A history of women in America*. New York: Free Press.

Flexner, E. (1959). *Century of struggle: The woman's rights movement in the United States*. Cambridge, MA: Harvard University Press.

Ford, P. L. (Ed.). (1888). *Pamphlets on the Constitution of the United States*. Brooklyn.

Foss, K., & Foss, S. (1983). The status of research on women and communication. *Communication Quarterly*, 31, 195–203.

Fox-Genovese, E. (1988). *Within the plantation household: black and white women of the old South*. Chapel Hill: University of North Carolina Press.

Frye, N. (1957). *The well tempered critic*. Bloomington: Indiana University Press.

Gannett, D.S. (1984). An address on life as a female revolutionary soldier. In J. Anderson (Ed.). *Outspoken women: Speeches by American women reformers 1635–1935* (pp. 135–142). Dubuque, IA: Kendall/Hunt. (Original work published 1802.)

Granger, B. (1960). *Political satire in the American Revolution*. Ithaca, NY: Cornell University Press.

Grim, H.E. (1937). *Susan B. Anthony: Exponent of freedom*. Unpublished doctoral dissertation, University of Wisconsin, Madison.

Hart, R. (1986). Contemporary scholarship in public address: A research editorial. *Western Journal of Speech Communication*, 50, 283–295.

Hoffman, R., & Albert, P. (Eds.). (1989). *Women in the age of the American revolution*. Charlottesville: University Press of Virginia.

Hutchinson, A. (1968). A report of the trial of Mrs. Anne Hutchinson before the Church in Boston. In D. Hall (Ed.), *The Antinomian Controversy, 1636–1638: A documentary history* (pp. 349–388). Middletown, CT: Wesleyan University Press. (Original work published 1894.)

Hynes, S.S. (1975). Dramatic propaganda: Mercy Otis Warren's 'The Defeat.' 1773. *Today's Speech*, 23(3). 21–27.

Jenefsky, C. (1987, November). *Some notes on giving birth to a feminist rhetorical criticism*. Paper presented at the meeting of the Speech Communication Association, Boston, MA.

Jones, M. H. (1983). Speech at a public meeting at the baseball park, Montgomery, West Virginia. In P. H. Foner (Ed.). *Mother Jones speaks: Collected speeches and writings* (pp. 73–87). New York: Monad Press. (Original work published 1912.)

Kaminski, J., & Saladino, G. (Eds.). (1986). *The documentary history of the ratification of the Constitution* (Vol. 16). Madison: State Historical Society of Wisconsin.

Kennedy, P.S., & O'Shields, G.H. (Eds.). (1983). *We shall be heard: women speakers in America, 1828–present*. Dubuque, IA: Kendall/Hunt.

Kerber, L. (1980). *Women of the Revolution: Intellect and ideology in revolutionary America*. Chapel Hill: University of North Carolina Press.

Kolodny, A. (1981). Turning the lens on 'the Panther Captivity': A feminist exercise in practical criticism. *Critical Inquiry*, 8, 329–345.

Kolodny, A. (1985). Dancing through the minefield: Some observations on the theory, practice, and politics of feminist literary criticism. In E. Showalter (Ed.), *The new feminist criticism: Essays on women, literature, and theory* (pp. 46–62). New York: Pantheon Books. (Original work published 1980.)

Kramarae, C. (1981). *Women and men speaking: Frameworks for analysis*. Rowley, MA: Newbury House.

Kramer, C. (1974). Women's Speech: Separate but Unequal? *Quarterly Journal of Speech,* 60. 14–24.

Lake, R. (1983). Enacting Red Power: The consummatory function in Native American protest rhetoric. *Quarterly Journal of Speech,* 69, 127–142.

Lerner, G. (1977). *The female experience: An American documentary.* Indianapolis, IN: Bobbs Merrill.

Lopez, C. (1990, November). *"Sacred to the memory of the illustrious Washington":* Women's visual tributes to our first president. Paper presented at the meeting of the Speech Communication Association, Chicago, IL.

Lucaites, J.L. (Ed.). (1989). *Great speakers and speeches.* Dubuque, IA: Wm. C. Brown.

Manning, B. (1980). *Index to American women speakers, 1828–1978.* Meutchen, NJ: Scarecrow Press.

Manning, B. (1988). *We shall be heard: An index to speeches by women, 1978–1985.* Meutchen, NJ: Scarecrow Press.

Mason, M. (1887). First salutatory oration. *The Woman's Journal,* 17, 1. (Original work presented 1787.)

Mathews, W. (1974). *American diaries in manuscript 1580–1954.* Athens: University of Georgia Press.

Norton, M.B. (1985). *Liberty's daughters: The revolutionary experience of American women, 1750–1800.* Boston: Little, Brown.

Paine, T. (1967). Common sense. In M. Jensen (Ed.), *Tracts of the American Revolution: 1763–1776* (pp. 400–446). Indianapolis, IN: Bobbs Merrill. (Original work published 1776.)

Pearson, J. (1975). Conflicting demands in correspondence: Abigail Adams on women's rights. *Today's Speech,* 23(3), 29–33.

Reed, E. DeBerdt. (1976). The sentiments of an American woman. In L.G. DePauw & C. Hunt (Eds.). *Remember the ladies: Women in America, 1750–1815* (p. 93). New York: Viking Press, 1976. (Original work published 1780.)

Reid, R.F. (1988). *Three centuries of American rhetorical discourse: An anthology and a review.* Prospects Heights, IL: Waveland Press.

Rowlandson, M. (1930). *The narrative of the captivity and restoration of Mrs. Mary Rowlandson.* Boston: Houghton Mifflin. (Original work published 1682.)

Sloman, J. (1978). The fragmentary genres: Women writers and non-canonical forms. *Canadian Newsletter of Research on Women,* 7(2), 26–29.

Solomon, M. (1988). Ideology as rhetorical constraint: The anarchist agitation of 'Red Emma' Goldman. *Quarterly Journal of Speech,* 74, 184–200.

Stanton, E.C. (1989). Address to the legislature of New York. In K.K. Campbell (Ed.), *Man cannot speak for her: Key texts of the early feminists* (vol. 2, pp. 145–166). New York: Greenwood Press. (Original work published 1854.)

Stearns, P. (1983). The new social history. In J. Gardner & G.R. Adams (Eds.), *Ordinary people and everyday life: Perspectives of the new social history* (pp. 3–21). Nashville, TN: The American Association for State and Local History.

Tonn, M.B. (1987). The rhetorical personae of Mary Harris 'Mother' Jones: Industrial labor's maternal prophet. Unpublished doctoral dissertation, University of Kansas, Lawrence.

Truth, S. (1989). Speech at the Woman's Rights Convention, Akron Ohio, 1851. In K.K. Campbell (Ed.). *Man cannot speak for her: Key texts of the early feminists* (Vol. 2, pp. 99–103). New York: Greenwood Press. (Original work published 1878.)

Twichell, D.Y. (1955). Susan B. Anthony. In M.K. Hochmuth (Ed.), *A history and criticism of American public address* (pp. 97–132). New York: Longman, Green.

Ulrich, L.T. (1980). *Good vives: Image and reality in the lives of women in Northern New England, 1650–1750.* New York: Oxford University Press.

Ulrich, L.T. (1990). Of pens and needles: Sources in early American women's history. *Journal of American History,* 77, 200–207.

Warren, C. (1930–1932). Elbridge Gerry, James Warren, Mercy Warren and the ratification of the federal constitution in Massachusetts. *Massachusetts Historical Society Proceedings,* 64, 143–164.

Warren, M.O. (1896). The squabble of the sea nymphs: Or the sacrifice of the tuscararoes. In A. Brown (Biographer), *Mercy Warren* (pp. 202–204). New York: Scribner's. (Original work published 1774.)

Warren, M.O. (1918). The group. In M.J. Moses (Ed.), *Representative plays by American dramatists* (Vol. 1, pp. 220–232). New York: E.P. Dutton. (Original work published 1775.)

Warren, M.O. (1968). *Mercy Warren Papers.* Boston: Massachusetts Historical Society.

Warren, M.O. (1986). Observations on the new constitution and on the federal and state conventions by a Columbian patriot. In J.P. Kaminski & G.J. Saladino (Eds.), *The documentary history of the ratification of the Constitution* (Vol. 16, pp. 272–291). Madison University of Wisconsin Press. (Original work published 1788.)

Wheatley, P. (1985). On being brought from Africa to America. In S. Gilbert & S. Gubar (Eds.), *The Norton Anthology of Literature by Women: The Tradition in English* (p. 133). New York: W.W. Norton. (Original work published 1773.)

Windt, T. (1972). The diatribe: Last resort for protest. *Quarterly Journal of Speech,* 58, 1–14.

Wood, G. (1969). *The creation of the American republic, 1776–1787.* Chapel Hill: University of North Carolina Press.

Wright, Frances. (1984). Of free inquiry. In J. Anderson (Ed.), *Outspoken women: speeches by American women reformers: 1635–1935* (pp. 252–258). Dubuque, IA: Kendall/Hunt. (Original work published 1829.)

Yoakam, D. (1943). Woman's introduction to the American platform. In W.N. Brigance (Ed.), *A history and criticism of American public address* (pp. 153–192). New York: McGraw–Hill.

# Thirteen Ways of Looking at a Poem: Poetry as Play

## Margaret Demorest

"All life is a stage and a game: either learn
to play it, laying by seriousness, or bear its
pain."—Palladis

POETRY, AS MAE SWENSON KNOWS, is as useless as a dress
made of paper or as snow in New York. "What good is it? Who wants it?"
Ironically, the nuisance snow which falls on skyscrapers and city streets is recognized in country fields as the essential stuff of life. In a world where want-ads
clamor for engineers, computer operators, and accountants, it is easy to assume
that usefulness is the only value. Yet the word "value" is not confined to application in the practical and concrete world, but belongs also with the intangible
and unmeasurable qualities of an inner world. The ethical definition of "value"
is unrelated to material or monetary worth, but presents value as "that which is
worthy of esteem for its own sake; that which has intrinsic worth." It is this definition which applies to poetry and which leads the thoughtful person to as many
different perspectives as the thirteen ways Wallace Stevens found when he viewed a blackbird.

What is the appeal of poetry? Authorities think poetry may have been part
of the earliest language, its rhythms useful in chants, its moods suitable for sup-
plications, incantations, curses. We ourselves are rhythmic creatures, with regular heartbeats and physical responses to the cycles of the moon. No wonder poetry is part of our long heritage.

Sometimes the analysis of the parts and whole that make a poem results in
a reader's loss of the pleasure which is a fundamental reason for that study. Po-

etry, by its nature, opposes logic and analysis, slipping away from definition. In spite of age-old attempts on the part of poets to define their art, poetry remains undefinable; for, unlike the one-dimensional world of science, every form of literature must deal with two dimensions: its origin lies in the concrete world of real events, but its purpose is to create an abstract world which in some measure is a replication of the concrete one.

The versatile tool—language—belongs to both worlds. A word lies half-way between, for language is concrete in that it is audible when spoken and visible when written; and yet, through our own agreement, language becomes abstract as we use it to symbolize an object from the outer world or an emotion or concept from the inner one.

Poetry is the most concentrated form of literature. That is because it has the most difficult task and must utilize every resource of language. Though poetry, like fiction and drama, recreates situations from the external world, yet, more than any other form, poetry is intent upon the opposite world: that of the abstract, invisible, interior world of feelings and insight experienced in that external world. No matter how realistic, poetry necessarily evolves from the private and lonely and unutterable world of the individual's emotions.

I like to think of a poem as the attempted expression of an experience for which no word exists; and so the poet is being forced to invent a new "word"—a long, nearly hyphenated word made up of many parts. The particular sounds and images and meanings of numerous words—arranged in a specific order—combine to become equivalent to the inexpressible source. The new, lengthy, nearly-hyphenated "word" is the poem. This invented word may work through indirect expression (figures of speech, rhythm, mood music), yet it is the clearest, most concise, and most accurate way of saying what cannot otherwise be said.

When the beginning reader of poetry first glimpses the meaning of a complex passage, that reader sometimes asks, "If that's what the poem means, why didn't the poet come right out and say it straight?" The reply has to be, "The poet did 'say it straight.' The words that are used, arranged in this order, have become the way—the only way—the elusive meaning can be captured." A poem is not only "the best words in the best order." For the writer's purpose it is "the only words in the only order."

There is one uncustomary approach to poetry which, though perhaps not easier than other methods, may be richer, more interesting, more effective. This is through comparison of poetry to a metaphorical framework which provides unity and order to the way in which we analyze a poem. The vehicle in this metaphorical framework shares the characteristics of poetry, and is, like a poem, both multi-faceted and unified.

That framework is based upon the specific characteristics of "play" as defined by the historian Johan Huizinga in *Homo Ludens* (Man, the player). This book is a provocative examination of human existence. Huizinga sees a human being as the creature who has the ability and the need to handle abstractions, to create order, and to search for meaning. Those abilities are combined in the term "play" as he defines it. All culture—from stop-lights to peace treaties—is therefore included in his concept of play.

Before we can apply Huizinga's "play" to the analysis of poetry, we must understand the meaning of the term. Each phrase in his definition is important. He says of play:

> It is a voluntary activity which proceeds within certain limits of time and space, in a visible order, according to rules freely accepted, and outside the sphere of necessity or material utility. The play-mood is one of rapture and enthusiasm, and is sacred or festive in accordance with the occasion. A feeling of exaltation and tension accompanies the action; mirth and relaxation follow.

Play, he says, is "the opposite of seriousness." It is "pretending," and "freedom" and "order." Things there look different than they do in "ordinary life." Customary actions are suspended for this "magic circle"—an "intermezzo, an *interlude* in our daily lives." Through its action some tension is resolved, but the aim of play is "in itself." The "inner structure" makes it repeatable. He acknowledges a "close connection between mystery and play." Because a positive feature of play is order, Huizinga writes: "Into an imperfect world and into the confusion of life it brings a temporary, a limited perfection."

Huizinga tells us that we meet play under two basic aspects "a contest *for* something or a representation *of* something." It is under the second of these aspects—"a representation *of* something"—that we find poetry. Huizinga says that poetry "proceeds within the play-ground of the mind, in a world of its own which the mind creates for it." He points out that when the French poet Paul Valery called poetry "a playing with words and language," the statement is not metaphor: "it is the precise and literal truth."

Clearly, Huizinga views play not as a casual, nonsensical, and haphazard entertainment, but as an orderly, meaningful, and unified action which results in pleasure. Within an abstract framework the player creates a world where he is in charge of some tension, a symbolic replica of a single facet of the real world.

Thus play is related to ritual which, through re-creation of a significant and symbolic moment of the past, reaffirms the meaning represented by that moment. The ritual of communion in a church repeats the actions of Christ and his disciples at the Last Supper and reasserts the speaker's religious conviction. The public recitation of the Pledge of Allegiance to the flag is a statement of belief in the principles represented by that flag. Ritual links a group of human beings with the past, demonstrating their continuing belief in a value they hold in common.

And play is related to fantasy, which, through pre-creation of a wished-for condition, forecasts that value, linking the individual human being with a desired and unique future. Daydreaming is a form of play. To imagine being valedictorian or head of the company or even an alien from outer space explores "what-might-have-been"—sometimes "what-might-still-be." Like actual dreaming, fantasy can be a route to wish-fulfillment, even if the wish is only for excitement.

Freud discussed the pleasurable results of "play," stressing its capacity for re-enacting and symbolizing a single incident from real life. One of his examples is of a game invented by a baby whose mother went to work each day, leaving him with a sitter. The child did not understand why sometimes his mother appeared when he cried and other times no amount of crying would bring her. In his crib he played with a ball attached to a string. When he held the string and threw the ball over the edge of the crib, the ball disappeared. Each time he pulled on the string and the ball reappeared, he laughed. In this game Freud interprets the ball as symbolizing the mother's absence and re-appearance. The child's control of that action brought pleasure.

A friend told a similar story of a simple game of childhood which she and her sister invented to make long walks on the ranch more interesting. They found some object like an old tin can and then took turns hitting it with a stick. Wherever the tin can went, they went. Their game illustrates certain principles stated in Huizinga's definition of play: their action occurred within limits of time and place; it had rules which they established and willingly followed; and though it involved freedom, it also had a certain order. Their game had no practical purpose, yet it made the time pass more pleasantly. In a sense, that game—with its give and take, its limited control of uncertainty, and its voluntary interdependence—represents life.

The "magic circle" which Huizinga relates to play is reminiscent of the words of Coleridge concerning our approach to literature and its requirement of the "willing suspension of disbelief." Yet in literature there is also reason for belief. Aristotle pointed out that poetry (by which he meant all literature) is "truer" than history. A universal truth captured metaphorically by the writer is deeper and more enduring than the single and temporary persons, places, events, and numbers recorded by the historian. In the sixteenth century Sir Philip Sidney claimed that the poet is the person who never lies. The make-believe world, no matter how imaginative, always portrays a single truth from the world of reality—a truth as the poet conceives it.

That play is unlike "ordinary life" means it is unlike the world of work, with its required and necessary routines. Participation in that work-world holds two benefits: for society it brings a product that is needed and is therefore useful; for the worker it brings visible accomplishment that results in monetary reward and self-respect.

Unlike work, the action of play does not end with a utilitarian object beneficial to society or the player. Clearly, an amateur ball game or a chess game does not have for its object the production of food, lodging, or saleable objects. This is true also of the arts. Though commercial gain may be a by-product for the professional, the efforts of the dedicated painter, musician, dancer, sculptor, writer are engaged in primarily for their own sake.

A basketball game is played because it can be exhilarating for both the players and the audience. Competing teams have one objective: to make the higher number of baskets. Tension exists only because results are uncertain: the verdict can go either way. Opponents must be well matched, not necessarily with the same talents (height, weight, experience), but with equivalent abilities. If one team has shorter, slighter, newer members, it must have tenacity and courage equivalent to the skills of larger and more experienced opponents.

All games take place within limits of time and place, and they are made orderly by rules which are "freely accepted" but "absolutely binding." A football field is the physical location on which that contest occurs; each separate play, each quarter, is timed; and there are rules. At a football game these rules are not always "freely accepted" by everyone but nevertheless are "absolutely binding."

Ironically the "real" game of football (or of any game) is its abstract framework—the concept of that particular game. This framework is repeatable, and, though no two specific games are alike in performance, the concept of that framework will be employed again and again.

Rules govern procedures, formulate objectives, and limit time to bring a game to a clearly defined outcome. They protect the unity of the framework and bring justice. Except for rules, chaos would result. Victory for the deserving team would not be assured. Only the well-refereed game allows freedom which challenges and rewards the ability and ingenuity of the group or of an individual. In a chess game no move can be made which could not have been foreseen; perhaps the player is surprised by the opponent's action, but that opponent cannot act in any way which could not have been anticipated. Rules bring this protection, keeping out unrelated forces. Only in play is there contest which results in freedom, justice, and visible meaning.

Play is the opposite of the erratic, uncontrollable, disunified, unjust, and seemingly meaningless events of a world the existentialist terms "absurd." If life has meaning (and possibly it does), that meaning is only intermittently glimpsed by our fallible eyes. In real life a stranger behind the wheel of an automobile may be drunk for "reasons" which have nothing to do with other drivers on that road. By running a stoplight, the drunken stranger can intercept the path of the world's best driver and kill that person—unintentionally, unjustly. The tangling of unrelated forces brings absurdity.

Unlike art, with its principle of unity with variety, the real world is filled with variety but lacks unity. Disjunctive paths—like those of the two drivers—

clash, interrupting plans, disturbing lives. An overall view of any single "thread" of meaning is broken by unrelated forces. Perception of unity or coherence is impossible. Events of the real world—no matter how saddening—do not qualify for Aristotle's analysis of tragedy, with its structure of "beginning, middle, and end."

Play, with its limits of time and place, has "beginning, middle, and end." Finality brings decision regarding the winning. Because incidents in real life have no specific termination point, events there behave like chameleons: the unendingness of time allows them to change color. What seems good luck at one moment may prove later to have been the turning event that brought downfall; or apparent bad luck may eventually be recognized as the necessary stimulus that prompted a wiser choice. For that reason the word for "crises" in the Chinese language is identical with the word for "opportunity."

Only in the abstraction of play can time be arrested or meaning be made apparent and forced to hold still. It is from the isolation of a single experience and the preservation of its unity that art is able to defy flux and resist absurdity. Art critics have not overstressed the importance of unity. In all play, the purpose of the rules is to keep out unrelated forces, thereby maintaining order and preserving unity. The unified nature of the action that takes place within an abstract framework (protected by rules) is the essence of play.

In *Homo Ludens* Huizinga explores definitions of play in other languages. He relates "play" to the Chinese word "wan," which applies particularly to children's games and to frivolity. But he explains that the word also means "to finger, to feel, to examine, to sniff at, to twiddle little ornaments, and, finally, to enjoy the moonlight." It occurred to me that moonlight itself can be fingered and "played with" as well as enjoyed.

Moonlight, a cessation of clear, harsh day, is associated with mystery and illusive glimpses. The moon seems to have its own light, yet that light is reflected light, deriving from the sun which illuminates the everyday world. If, in the moonlight, we "handle" that muted radiance, there is no substance we are touching. We are playing with shadows made of darkness and reflected light. **To play is to handle moonlight.**

This is the first of the thirteen ways of looking at a poem. When you read or write a poem you are handling moonlight. In the same way in which moonlight derives from sunlight, the fragile poem derives from the real world but this new one is consciously of make-believe. Abandoned is everyday reality. Something unusual, something festive has replaced it, and the poet has created and entered a magic circle.

(The poems illustrating the thirteen ways of looking at a poem were written by students in my classes in freshman English at Casper College.)

Evolution

I wish I were a plant,
With a rough purple velvet flower
Plants don't care about:
            who
                 what
                      why
                           where.
Their uncaring is natural because they
            don't
                 need
                      a
                           brain.
Which puts them by far highest on the
            ladder of intelligence.
I'd consider it an HONOR to be a
            vegetable.
If they'd put a tulip up for president,
            I'd
                 vote
                      yes.
                           (Mark Weaver)

The source of a poem is from the inner world. Some emotion—some unresolved tension—is faced when the writer brings it into balance by expression. The poet selects, with sincerity and freshness, details which communicate feeling.

The second way of viewing a poem is as **A Cry.**

Loneliness

There it is...
Somewhere between where you swallow and where a sob starts.
There it is...
A hand that holds to that which swells and pulses inside you,
    An intimate, body-temperatured hand
            that stifles without strangling,
            that mangles without pain.
    Sometimes, when the crying starts, it loosens a little
            So the tears can squeeze through.
But it soon grasps hard again and once more, with crushing caress,
            There it is...
    Somewhere between where you swallow and where a sob starts.
                                (Evelyn Brummond)

The words of poetry are concrete, reminding the reader of personal experiences. Words which appeal to the five senses unite the inner and outer worlds, making the writing vivid, fresh, and real. The third of the ways of looking at a poem is as **A Sensation.**

Touching a Sunset

Place your right hand over the sunset. This way, with the fingers loose but straight, flat against the sky with the thumb along the bottom, resting on the horizon. Now, your hand placed thus, begin to feel heat where your thumb rests. The end of your little finger dips in warm thickness. Through the heel of your hand, cool streaks move rapidly outward. On the top edge, refreshing the skin, cool water lies. In your palm you hold a glorious burst of final warmness. Your other fingers, led by the middle one, wade through warm and then cool waters. Feel these and take your hand away. Isn't that what a sunset feels like?

(Aaron Wayne)

In order to communicate some abstract intangible perception from an inner world, the poet uses comparisons with tangibles known also to the reader. As in a dialectic, the unlikes merge, creating a synthesis which is new. In using figurative language (like metaphor, simile), the poet is translating from the inner personal realm of experience which is voiceless. The fourth way of looking at a poem is as **A Translation.**

Wind River

White froth-foam
leaping angrily into
pools of clear
stillness widening
into broad forest-mirrors
then tumbling over
boulders once again:
my mind.
(Barbara Van Maren)

Unity with variety—the essence of art—pleases. A poem repeats patterns of rhythm and yet at some point skillfully departs from the dominant pattern. Rhythms of iambic, trochaic, anapestic, dactylic are among the most common choices of the poet, though free verse, controlled and varied, is also satisfying. The fifth way of looking at a poem is as **A Drumbeat.**

Winter Thoughts

Snow flakes
and
Snow flakes
and
Soft hair
and
Laughter
and
Snow flakes
and
Snow flakes
and
Warm fire
and
Popcorn
and
Snow flakes
and
Snow flakes
and
Strong hands
and
Snow flakes
and
You.
(Pat Robinson)

Another form of repetition lies in repeated sounds. Tonal qualities of consonant and vowel—with their pitch and length—produce a kind of music. Rhyme, alliteration, and assonance plus rhythm are the tools of language used to transform words into music. The sixth way of looking at a poem is as **A Song**.

Pomegranite

A reddy rind of pomme of granite
bearing seeds
sweet
vita
vite vite!
Bite forbit break rind
and spilling from it rosy juicy dripping
staining

(the leaves)
Oh! in the Garden of Eden.
(Sally Sutton)

The words—as well as the ideas—of poetry can be organized into patterns: sonnets are lyrics of emotion; ballads are plotted action; limericks are humorous vignettes; "found" poems, "shaped" poems, haikus, sestinas, and villanelles are games for adventurous players. Like the rules of play, which bring order and preserve unity, the patterns employed by the poet are freely chosen and their restrictions willingly observed. Like the framework which is the "real" football game, the framework of a structured poem is repeatable, though each version placed within that framework will be unique. The seventh way of looking at a poem is as **A Building**.

(The following poem is a sonnet written by a sophomore who based it upon a free verse poem he had written as a freshman.)

The Demoniac

I thirsted for the mystery of sin.
I stood as Satan must have stood upon
The brink of Chaos, trapped by fear within
The bounds of Hell, not daring steps beyond.
In momentary weakness I, possessed
By demons, leapt into that deep abyss.
In fellowship with darkness not the Blessed
I gloried in my shame and sinfulness.
Embraced by devils, treacherously choked,
In pain I screamed, in helplessness I moaned,
"Deliver me from this," and I awoke
Fresh from the depths of Hell in bed alone.
And men came saying, "Poet, sing. In pain
Your cries escape like music. Sing again!"
(Rodney Gene Mahaffey)

A poem, like all play, takes place within limits of time and space. A strong poem wastes no detail, no word. The concentrated language could be compared to the way in which a prism seems to hold crystallized all the colors of sunlight. Perfect expression makes poetic language more memorable than ordinary prose. The eighth way of looking at a poem is as **A Prism.**

(This example of the haiku observes the requirements: a three-line description of a single moment from nature divided into contrasting parts, with five syllables on the first line, seven on the second, and five again on the third.)

Hawk cries chillingly,
sudden thrashing leaves...silence;
red sun hides its face.
(David Demorest)

Ordinary objects or experiences from everyday life, when transformed by the elements of poetry, acquire charm. The following poem—clearly derived from "real life"—illustrates the freedom possible within controlled conditions of the rhymed quatrain. This illustrates the ninth way of looking at a poem—that it is **A Mirror with a Candle Beside It.**

Finishd

Mah techer sea, "Now write a piem!"
Bud Ah coon't thank of whut wud riem.
Ah speeded most near all mah tiem
Trine to wride that thar dern piem.

Ah figered all the ferent thains
That Ah cud wride. Ah used mah brains.
Bud ever thain I shot, it saims,
Just woon't riem. Mah pour brains!

Ah thank an thank. The tiem past;
The day o' wrecknan hit at last.
Ah tired it in, as ya av gast;
Ah hope ya lack mah piem.
(Josephine Fagan)

Beauty and mystery create another world where we escape in dreams. Sometimes a poem comes from the subliminal world. The tenth way of looking at a poem is as **A Magic Lantern**.

Star Hounds Are Coming

Owl sentry upon the oak,
Star hounds are coming,
Star hounds are coming.
Spotted spider in a silver web,
Wrap me in your shadow cloak.
I am freer now,
Dappled fawn.
My lover is the star hound.
(Mary Woodall)

Allusions, which make it possible to include a long well-known story in a single word, increase the poet's ability to concentrate language, limiting time and space. The same benefit comes from the use of symbols and words with multi-level meanings. The reader is challenged by a complex, unfolding unity. We could compare this complexity to a Joshua plant. It seems at first glance to be one thing, but, given water, becomes something very different: its tightly-curled wiry fist of brown tendrils spreads until it has unfolded one part after another to become a complex living plant. The eleventh way of looking at a poem is as **A Joshua Plant**.

### Sagittarius

She offered honey cakes and jasmine tea,
Tales of bold Arachne;
With Oberon, the faery king,
She light-foot danced in magic ring;
At Chiron's school she learned to laugh,
And knew the boy Achilles' wrath;
With Orpheus she played the lyre
She watched the Titan bestow fire;
She learned of love from Guenevere,
Of lust, from Tiresias, the seer;
She knew full well Francesca's fate,
And cautiously locked her inmost gate.
She offered saffron tears and silver days,
Knowledge of the Naiad's ways.
But Charon, waiting at the door,
Wasn't pleased. He wanted more.

(Jill Arnott)

Riddles have always been a part of play. The double vision involved in ambiguity, irony, and paradox belongs with the same puzzling realm. Sometimes through the writing of a poem those problems emerge in a different light. The twelfth way of looking at a poem is as **A Sphinx**.

### Some Other Child

She heard a child crying.
Rushing outside in anguish over
   her own child,
      she was relieved.
It was some other child.

(Cathe Strader)

Sometimes a poem holds new perspectives that lead both the writer and the reader to greater understanding of self and of others. For the poet who has been following the "thread" that is the poem there is often more than pleasure, for through that exploration the writer may come upon some meaning that had been evasive. The tension which prompted the writing has been made to hold still, has been examined, and has been resolved. The reader, in understanding the poem, profits by sharing in that fresh knowledge and—by meeting in words the person who wrote—may also recognize a likeness to that writer. From that experience comes renewed awareness of the likeness of all human beings. Poetry brings an affirmation of human ties. The thirteenth way of looking at a poem is as **An Encounter**.

On Reading C. S. Pierce

A jolting lurch and fear settle somewhere
Deep below my heart as a dark brooding.
Half-conscious suspicion, long avoided
Like some vastly superior friend
I long to mark the depths of, yet fear
To show my lesser conversation,
Now joins with pure white light, my splinter light
Melded into greater. Before me
Lies the universe illumined,
And I learn the one truth I can ever know
With certainty. I may not say God
Has all the answers. For by virtue of
The limits of our conceiving, when
We conceive of God we only see
The upper limits of self.
The infallibility we often seek—
The knowing, the certainty to ease life—
Is not there. Nor does truth lie in numbers:
That all of us hold a thing to be true,
Means only that we have reached agreement.

(Lois Sargent)

Each characteristic of the definition of play fits poetry. A poem is a game engaged in for its own sake. The ordinary world is suspended in favor of one of make-believe. Within the playground of the mind, the poet creates an abstract, controllable world which reflects some one aspect of the real world. In playing this game, the poet utilizes every aspect of language—meaning, sound, rhythm, mood, associations, juxtaposition, and even the visible arrangement on the page. The same quality which produces tension in a game—the contest between equivalent forces—is at work in a poem. The single "action" takes place in limits of time and space, the rules preserving unity are willingly observed, and from the completed poem comes new understanding and pleasure.

My hope is that this study of poetry and play will bring to the student new understanding and pleasure.

# Mother Calls Herself a Housewife, But She Buys Bulls

## Katherine Jensen

I HAVE OFTEN BEEN STRUCK BY THE GREAT GAP between my unofficial existence as a woman made in rural America and my official training based on an urban perspective in sociology and women's studies. From my first days at college with housemates reared in New Jersey, Chicago, and Philadelphia, I knew that my life had been different. My classmates seemed not only urban, but urbane, better schooled, more sophisticated politically; these differences were not just ones of class. It was not until much later that I understood how much technical competence I had, as a rural woman born and bred, that was not only alien but terrifying to them, even though those skills seemed irrelevant to the mental exercises asked of me at the time.

True, most women in North American society are not rural women, even if many of us have a rural heritage. And many women who now "become" rural women may not share, or even really aspire to the contemporary rural subculture of the western United States that I want to analyze. It is a culture in which rural women's relation to economic production demands that they gain a higher level of skills and more diverse technological competence than is usually expected of urban women (and most urban men). I would argue that their competence and economic function give rural women greater authority and status within the family than they might have as urban wage-earners. Thus rural women are important not only as American cultural myth, but also as an important measure of changing contemporary reality.

The issues I want to deal with here are technical competence and control over technology. Feminist anthropologists have begun not only to question the idea that technology generally has come from the male domain, but to prove that it has not. Many early inventions not specifically attributed to women obviously belong in the larger history of rural women. Certainly horticultural techniques, food preservation, and clothing construction have been women's inventions and responsibilities in many different cultures for most of human history.[1] This technological skill extends to rural women today.

## Men's Work is Women's Work

A number of recent works—mostly oral history projects on rural women—have documented, though usually not analyzed, the roles and duties of rural women.[2] Over and over these histories reflect the apparent contradiction between a cultural norm and the social reality of women's work. Most women will say that while there is a general definition of "women's work" and "men's work" on farms and ranches, women regularly do "men's work," but men much less often engage in female responsibilities. The official division of labor follows the norms of the larger society in assigning women domestic, indoor labor, while men engage in the instrumental functions which reside primarily outdoors. The social reality, however, reflects greater complexity in work responsibilities:

> In the spring, before the lambing you have to shear. And that was hard work, especially for me. There were about 12 to 15 shearers and they brought with them about three wranglers and a wool tromper, and so with our herders and us, we hardly ever had less than 20 to cook for and that's what I did. Sometimes Bob would come in and say, "Stop your work in the house and go get your horse and help the herder bring in the sheep." The sheep went to a sweat shed to stay warm for the shearers because that way they shear better. You always kept your sweat shed full of sheep, especially if it looked like it was going to storm. You just can't shear sheep that are wet, and if the herder couldn't get the sheep in, I had to go and help him, and I'd be late with my evening meal. Bob'd get excited during shearing, because it is a precision-like deal, and it has to go right.[3]

> You wasn't in bed at five in the morning. And when we trailed cattle, you'd get up at two-thirty in the morning. I helped trail the cattle. We trailed from our place over to the Laramie Plains. We started in trailing right after the drought, well, you might say, in about 1933 and we trailed until in the '50s. We trailed cattle in the spring and fall. And you'd cook over a camp-fire and you get meals for the men as well as you help ride, too. But, if they needed me out in the hay field or on the horse, I was there. Wherever I was needed I would be there.[4]

There is a qualitative difference between these descriptions and those of the dual-career, urban, female wage-earner who must also do housework; this work is much more of a piece, partly because of the homestead-bounded enterprise.

Even household work is more clearly related to economic productivity than is usually the case in urban settings. A number of anthropologists have posited that women's relationship to exchange economy is fairly directly reflected by status within their families.[5] Several examples of traditional farm women's work with important economic value illustrate the point.

A woman who homesteaded in Wyoming with her husband in 1918 and lived there until 1958 described her daily chores:

> Well, (you) always get the meals, and of course you scrub the floor. You always done the washing and ironing and took care of the chickens and your turkeys and gathered the eggs. (You) took care of the milk and had to wash the separator and you churned, of course. You had to churn. Everybody churned, of course.

For most of U.S. history, women have sold eggs and butter or bartered them for other goods and services. This exchange value certainly exceeded "pin money," as demonstrated by a former schoolteacher who earned money from poultry after her marriage:

> I had a big incubator and I would hatch about 5,000 chickens every year and I kept a flock of about 300 hens and pretty much made a living for us for quite awhile, until we could get our farm paid for.

At the very least, women gathered, cleaned, packaged, and delivered the eggs to stores or individual buyers in town. The steady cash income they received was often very important to the family productive unit, which might otherwise have had to rely on annual or semiannual sales of agricultural products or livestock. But it was also cash to which women had access and over which they had control. Thus the technology of egg production and distribution was especially important to women and clearly under their control. This particular economic function has been largely eliminated in the last decade by large corporate egg factories of several million hens, making local egg production uneconomical. But for literally centuries, on both farms and ranches, poultry was a part of the rural economy which belonged to women.

Contemporary rural women still do work which may have a more direct economic import than appears on the surface. One example is the function of the noon meal, appropriately called "dinner" by all the rural people I know. Dinner is prepared by women, along with girls and young children of both sexes, as one might expect. It is the most important meal of the day; if the woman must be away from the household at noon or for part of the morning, it will most likely be prepared ahead of time and left waiting. Technological advances such as freezers, oven timers, and microwave ovens make that easier now than in the past.

Dinner is not simply a symbolic ritual of dominant men who come home to consume it; dinner is most literally a business lunch in which women directly participate. As an important respite in a long work day, dinner entails a full meal and perhaps a short midday nap afterward. It also typically includes reading the mail (mostly bills) and yesterday's just-arrived newspapers, hearing the news, weather, and market reports on the radio (all important factors in farm economics), and making several phone calls. Men and "men's work" are the focus of the meal, but women are included in the information, conversation, and usually the decision-making process. The movie image of a tableful of "hands" is often inaccurate. Meals produced for threshers and branders were important *annual* events, but hardly typical of daily routine. Indeed, the wife may be the only other adult present to hear about progress on the day's work: what machinery has broken down, the condition of the hay or grain, the health of the livestock.[6] In any case, she will be part of communication among workers who likely have been engaged in separate locations and activities during the morning.

That leads to a second important element of rural women's responsibility: going to town. Women very often go to town, because the men do not "have time." In fact, many women are skillful in finding reasons to have to go to town themselves. Most trips are multifunctional, related not only to domestic consumption (buying groceries) and social roles (going to meetings), but also to production demands (getting parts for machinery, doing bank business, buying feed or veterinary supplies, or taking a sick animal to the veterinarian). Rural women often go to social engagements in pick-up trucks or heavily-loaded station wagons.

The birthing and nurturing of young animals is another productive task in which women traditionally have been engaged. While pervasive Victorian ideas about female propriety and "the separation of the spheres" may have kept some women isolated from work such as breeding, branding, and castrating livestock, these sanctions by no means affected all women. Technological change actually has increased their participation: more women are likely to have run squeeze chutes than have ever roped calves, or have prepared equipment for artificial insemination than have managed bulls.

The birthing process (here calving and lambing) is one area in which there has rarely been much doubt about the appropriateness of women's participation; changes in farm economics and technology may actually have intensified that role. Corporate agriculture has made far fewer inroads in the "animal husbandry" area than in livestock feeding and feed grain production. Husbandry seems less amenable to large scale units, partly because it requires both intensive committed labor and sophisticated skills; it is ideal for a family enterprise. But technological change has meant a controlled breeding process in which more calves are born in fewer days, born larger, and born with more difficulty to younger mothers. Economic change means that survival rates must be higher for both the mothers, which are a major investment, and for the offspring, which keep production rates high.

Just as Eleanor Stewart helped "pull a calf" in the film *Heartland*, and the ranch wife in Theresa Jordan's book, *Cowgirls*, delivered a calf alone in the dead of night, many women continue to do this work in shifts alternating with their husbands.[7] Perhaps since birthing is a female process, and because women have most often gotten up in the night with small children, they are most likely to be the ones to make the late-night-to-early-morning rounds and vigils in the calving yards. Their knowledge of antiseptic techniques and birthing engineering can make hundreds or thousands of dollars difference with each difficult delivery.

Although large-scale poultry and egg production has had a negative effect on women's productive role on the farm, while new breeding techniques have increased their productive contribution, other technological changes have altered rural women's lives in mixed ways. The question is whether these changes help women participate more equally with their male partners, or whether they displace women from productive work because high technology is so frequently thought to belong to men. Paradoxically, technology seems to cut both ways.

## Modern Times

Virtually all of the women interviewed in the Wyoming Heritage and Contemporary Values Project mentioned the importance of the telephone to put them in touch with family members, neighbors, and friends who might be several or hundreds of miles distant. The telephone ended the near-total isolation of rural women from each other, eliminating the reports so often found in pioneer diaries of months spent without ever hearing another woman's voice. The telephone also lessened the likelihood that other family members, including husbands, might be out of communication with each other for days at a time in dangerous weather and dangerous terrain. More recently, shortwave radio and citizen band radios (CBs) have made communication possible even with people working in pastures or fields. In Wyoming, commercial radio stations still use regularly scheduled public service broadcasts to send personal messages for meeting arrangements between rural families. There is little doubt that the "isolation of the housewife" found its extreme in the sparsely populated rural west and that telephone contact has become an essential and often highly ritualized improvement.

Rural electrification provided more diffuse, though not necessarily more profound, changes. It often came later than dial telephones, finally replacing wind generators and carbide lighting:

We had a 32-volt plant, they called it. And, if the wind blew enough, which in Wyoming usually has a way of happening, I could use my iron. We always had lights. You couldn't use your...I don't think we had toasters...I think we just had the iron and I could use it if the voltage was up real good. And that's why we didn't have any other appliances, like you'd have with electricity, because it would pull down too much. Most of the time, couldn't even use the iron. I'd have to use a gas iron and the iron on the stove. And then when, it was about during the early '50s we got elec-tricity out here. But we battled for it for a good many years before we got it.

Significant changes in household technology, including convection ovens, automatic washing machines, refrigerators, and freezers have had profound effects on the lives of rural women and men. While standards of housekeeping have escalated for rural as well as urban householders, women potentially have more freedom to engage in different forms of productive labor.

Sociologists differ whether this is the case. Corlann Bush, argues, for example, that the introduction of household technology eliminated women's traditional work as critical to the economic function of the family at the same time that new agricultural technology enhanced the importance of men's activities. Thereby men's roles became more crucial and women's roles less crucial on the family farm, at least in the Palouse River region of eastern Washington and northern Idaho.[8] Some of this differential may have been more marked in large-scale farming than it was in ranching.

Bush makes a strong and convincing argument that cash income, the availability of fresh produce and inexpensive clothing, plus good roads and fast vehicles, have removed the economic necessity for a farm woman to do anything but shop. The farm woman's contributions, she contends, have become invisible and her function has shifted from production to consumption. However, this argument rests on the assumption not only of the separation of gender roles, but also on viewing traditional work in traditional ways. Bush acknowledges that women often drive huge grain trucks both in the fields and to the elevators in town during combining (grain harvesting) season, but she takes literally the frequently-used term "helping out" to mean that work to be exceptional, rather than integral to the female role.

Farm technology, like other technological advances, has to a large extent eliminated the muscular advantage men have had in engaging in productive physical labor. Women, girls, and boys can all drive tractors, trucks, or self-propelled machinery. That fact does not preclude the existence of a status hierarchy of machine operators, often based on the relative cost of the implement matched to the age (older is better) and sex (males are more competent) of the driver. When, as a 17-year-old daughter, I was allowed to drive the most expensive new piece of haying equipment, I felt clearly to be a trusted member of the family enterprise. But I think I also understood that my brothers ran the somewhat less expensive baler because it was more complex and more likely to break down.

Evidence from Third World developing countries demonstrates that as more complicated machinery is introduced, men are more likely to be its exclusive proprietors. In part this tendency can be explained by recognizing that mechanized agriculture is somewhat less labor intensive, making the labor of both women and children less necessary.[9] So, at the same time they are more able, females are needed less in the fields and pastures. Or, in reverse causality, machinery might be purchased to compensate for lost labor. My siblings and I noted that when all the children left home to go away to school, more equipment was purchased to handle the work we had done with our backs and arms. It also became apparent that when our mother spent less time parenting, she participated in new ways in the exchange economics and technology entailed in livestock purchasing, breeding programs, and fieldwork. (She still retained much of the bookkeeping responsibility she had always shared with my father.)

Seena Kohl shows that in Saskatchewan farm families, as in most of rural North America, women's educational level surpasses that of men in any cohort. Because of that difference women not only take care of the books and breeding records, but also write important letters to businesses and government agencies. She asserts that control of information is a source of power, particularly when the information is directly connected to the economic productivity of an enterprise. The capital investment needed for technological farming and the cash flow resulting from large-scale operation both require extensive bookkeeping and business skills, for which women have more formal training. Moreover, household technology has freed women from continuous cooking, cleaning, food production, and preservation burdens, making it *possible* for them to function in this new or expanded economic capacity. But the participation is by no means automatic. Even if the technology is benign, the institutions which promote new technology are hardly nonsexist.

Perhaps the greatest test of women's continued authority in farm families will lie in their competence with computer technology. As capital investment requirements increase and margins of profit tighten, precise data on such variables as optimal feed grain prices and nutritional levels, feeding rations and weaning times, crop fertilization schedules, machine time utilization, storage loss, and breeding stock productivity must all inevitably be computerized. Many farmers and ranchers have for years sent production records to state universities for computer analysis. But as production costs rise in relation to wholesale prices, more variables must be closely monitored. Family farms and ranches will need their own software and data storage in order to survive. If women have been part of both the decision-making and the record-keeping functions in the past, they may now be in a particularly good position to step into this important technological change. That will depend on a recognition and continuation of the family, including women, as a unit of production.

## Growing Up Rural

Even though it appears to me that the soundest explanation for women's place in rural families is their economic role rather than the socialization process, I want to return briefly to the theme of growing up rural. I believe that the socialization rural girls receive allows them to approach technology differently from the way many urban girls perceive it. The literature on child socialization generally suggests that the experiences of girls are more circumscribed; girls are protected from many experiences that boys have because girls grow up in more highly supervised and structured, usually indoor, environments.[10] In the country, even given the normative distinctions between "women's work" and "men's work," girls have responsibility for complicated technology that has an economically productive purpose.

An example from the early twentieth century describes expectations for children similar to my own experience:

> We leased (another ranch) so we could put up hay there and also we had our own place... I mowed every bit of hay on all those places. I had a bronc and Harv hooked up the bronc with a mare we had. He made five or six rounds, and then turned them over to me. Our daughter...did all the raking and (our son) had the sweep. (My husband) used to stack and the neighbors were all so worried for fear they'd have to help us out. But we beat them by three days. I didn't lose any time mowing, I can tell you. They would change my sickles or sharpen my sickles and I'd be off. (A man from town) cooked for us...Boy, he was a help because I didn't have to cook at noon. But he went home at night, and I had to cook and had all those cows to milk. Of course (my daughter) helped me milk, but we had maybe 16, 18, or 20 cows to milk by hand. I think it took me about ten minutes to a cow. The hardest thing to do was to carry it all in, and separate it, because we had a hand crank separator, and I'd have to stop and fill up the old bowl and go to her again—cranking.[11]

The point is not simply that girls are outdoors—as well as indoors—but that their chores, like their brothers', are directly connected to exchange productivity, rather than being artificial creations to "teach responsibility." In part, this means that girls as well as boys learn to hear when an engine or machine is malfunctioning, or to tell if a horse is lame, and to diagnose and repair the problem when possible. And they know the economic implications of failures in mechanical or physiological judgement. I would guess that most rural children still do not get "wages" in the form of an allowance in proportion to urban children. My siblings and I had the sense that during a "good year" we would share in the profits and that in a "bad one" we would do without, regardless of our personal merit, but still with the understanding that we could contribute or subtract in significant financial ways by our technological competence. We haven't forgotten those internalized lessons.

If that early experience makes females less technology-anxious, more confident of economic potential and responsibility, more assertive about power in family relationships, then there is something important to be studied further. Are there ways to maintain those socialization patterns in the face of less distinctively rural lifestyles and more corporate business styles? Are there ways of socializing our urban-reared daughters and sons with more egalitarian assumptions about technical competence and productive worth? My children are professors' kids, not ranchers' kids. I'd like to know.

## Notes

1.    Sally Slocum, "Woman the Gatherer: Male Bias in Anthropology," in *Toward an Anthropology of Women*, ed. Rayna Reiter (New York: Monthly Review Press, 1975).

2.    Joan Jensen, *Women Working on the Land* (Old Westbury, NY: Feminist Press, 1981); Sherry Thomas, *We Didn't Have Much, but We Sure Had Plenty* (New York: Anchor/Doubleday, 1981); Linda Rasmussen, Candace Savage, Lorna Rasmussen, and Anne Wheeler, *A Harvest Yet to Reap* (Toronto: Women's Press, 1976).

3.    Carol Rankin, "Spoken Words of Wyoming Ranch Women," a slide/tape presentation from a project sponsored by the Wyoming Council for the Humanities, 1979.

4.    This and following first-person quotes are from interviews for the Wyoming Heritage and Contemporary Values Project, an oral history project sponsored by the Wyoming Council for the Humanities and staffed by Bernice Harris, Melanie Gustafson, Pat Hale, and the author, 1979–1980.

5.    Peggy Sanday, "Female Status in the Public Domain," in *Woman, Culture and Society*, eds. Michelle Rosaldo and Louise Lamphere (Palo Alto, CA: Stanford University, 1974).

6.    Seena Kohl, "Women's Participation in the North American Family Farm," *Women's Studies International Quarterly* 1 (1977): 47–54.

7.    Theresa Jordan, *Cowgirls* (New York: Doubleday, 1982).

8.    Corlann Gee Bush, *The Barn Is His; The House Is Mine: The Impact of Technology on Sex Roles on the Family Farm* (New York: Sage, 1982).

9.    Special issue on "Development and the Sexual Division of Labor," *Signs* 7 (Winter 1981).

10.   Lenore Weitzman, "Sex Role Socialization," in *Women: A Feminist Perspective*, ed. Jo Freeman (Palo Alto, CA: Mayfield, 1979).

11.     Rankin, Op. Cit.